ALE, BEER,
AND BREWSTERS
IN ENGLAND

ALE, BEER, AND BREWSTERS IN ENGLAND

Women's Work in a Changing World, 1300–1600

JUDITH M. BENNETT

Oxford University Press
New York Oxford

Oxford University Press

Oxford   New York
Athens Auckland Bangkok Bogotá Buenos Aires Calcutta
Cape Town Chennai Dar es Salaam Delhi Florence Hong Kong Istanbul
Karachi   Kuala Lumpur Madrid Melbourne Mexico City Mumbai
Nairobi Paris São Paulo Singapore Taipei Tokyo Toronto Warsaw

and associated companies in
Berlin Ibadan

First published in 1996 by Oxford University Press, Inc.
198 Madison Avenue, New York, New York 10016

First issued as an Oxford University Press paperback, 1999

Oxford is a registered trademark of Oxford University Press

Library of Congress Cataloging-in-Publication Data
Bennett, Judith M.
Ale, beer, and brewsters in England : women's work in a changing
world, 1300–1600 / Judith M. Bennett.
p. cm.
Includes bibliographical references and index.
ISBN 0-19-507390-8
ISBN 0-19-512650-5 (pbk.)
1. Women brewery workers—England—History. I. Title.
HD6073.L62G723 1996
331.4′86342′0942—dc20   96-1271

1 3 5 7 9 8 6 4 2

Printed in the United States of America
on acid-free paper

※ FOR CYNTHIA ※

ACKNOWLEDGMENTS

This study of ale, beer, and brewsters has led me along so many unexpected paths that it is a sad task to bring it, at long last, to a close. But it is a happy task to acknowledge my gratitude to the many people who have facilitated this work.

Research of this sort is impossible without adequate funding, and I would like to begin by thanking those who provided financial assistance. At critical points in the development of this project, fellowships from the following institutions allowed me to focus exclusively on my research: the John Simon Guggenheim Memorial Foundation, the National Humanities Center (through funds provided by the Andrew W. Mellon Foundation), the Institute for Arts and Humanities at the University of North Carolina at Chapel Hill, and the Kenan Faculty Fellowship Program, also at UNC-CH. During the summers, my research was facilitated by grants from the American Philosophical Society, the National Endowment for the Humanities, and, again, the Institute for Arts and Humanities at UNC-CH. Miscellaneous research expenses were partly offset by the Small Grants Program at UNC-CH.

Thanks, in part, to this generous funding, I was able to pursue research in numerous English archives—not only the British Library and Public Record Office but also many county, civic, and private depositories. In all of them, I relied heavily on the assistance of ever-cordial archivists and their staff. I thank them all, particularly Christopher Whittick of the East Sussex Record Office, whose enthusiastic help at every stage of this project has made an enormous difference. Would that all historians could always rely on archivists as helpful and as knowledgable as Christopher Whittick. I am also very grateful to the librarians and staff of the Institute of Historical Research at the University of London. I have made much use of their invaluable collection of materials in local history, as well as their services for borrowing dissertations and theses.

I am happy to acknowledge Rosalie Radcliffe, who assisted me in preparing the bibliography and in other secretarial tasks associated with the production of this book.

Given the geographical and chronological breadth of this study, I could not have completed it without advice and information from many colleagues. I have tried to acknowledge specific instances of assistance in the footnotes, but some colleagues offered so much help that I would like to recognize them more generally:Caroline Barron, Christopher Baswell, Richard Britnell, E. Jane Burns, Martha Carlin, Anne DeWindt, Edwin DeWindt, Amy Froide, James Galloway, Jeremy Goldberg, Helena Graham, Barbara Hanawalt, Vanessa Harding, Cynthia Herrup, Derek Keene, Jane Laughton, Mavis Mate, Margaret Murphy, Lyndal Roper, Richard Smith, Richard Unger, Tim Wales, and the late Margaret Whittick. My colleagues in the North Carolina Research Group on Medieval and Early Modern Women commented on several chapters, and I have particularly benefited from the comments of Helen Solterer, Monica Green, and Judith Ferster, as well as the perceptive advice of Rachel Weil, who as an out-of-town visitor attended one meeting of the group. I would especially like to thank Maryanne Kowaleski (who generously provided information about her research on brewing in Exeter) and David Postles (who sent a steady stream of useful references my way). I am also very grateful to Elizabeth Heineman, who as a research assistant in the earliest phases of this project cheerfully executed many mundane tasks, and Sandy Bardsley, who has just as cheerfully assisted me at the end (especially with the index).

At the very moment that the fall semester began in 1994, I asked eight readers to review a full draft of this book: Barbara Harris, Cynthia Herrup, Nancy Hewitt, Ruth Karras, Maryanne Kowaleski, Christopher Whittick, Margaret Whittick, and Shirley Wilton. Without a murmur of protest, they settled down to the task, offering careful and thorough readings. I have not always revised as they suggested, but their criticisms have made this a much better book than it would otherwise have been. I am much in their debt, but of course any remaining errors are my responsibility alone.

I would like to acknowledge permissions granted to reuse materials originally written for other venues. Portions of chapter 5 appeared in a festschrift in honor of J. Ambrose Raftis: *The Salt of Common Life: Individuality and Choice in the Medieval Town, Countryside, and Church*, Edwin B. DeWindt, ed. (Kalamazoo, Mich., 1995). Chapter 7 expands on "Misogyny, Popular Culture and Women's Work," *History Workshop Journal* 31 (1991), pp. 166–188.

Throughout the years of working on this study, I have been sustained by some extraordinary friendships. Maryanne Kowaleski is my most honest and dearest friend. Susan Levine and Leon Fink have offered me much good food and good conversation, as well as the opportunity to know their children, Anna and Simon. James Epstein, Jan Ewald, Vanessa Harding, Barbara Harris, and Nancy Hewitt have been always available, always encouraging, always fun. With Christopher Whittick and Margaret Whittick, I have learned to love East Sussex in new ways; perhaps someday I'll learn to love opera, too. Annie and Izzie have asked very little of me and given me very much.

One of the pleasures of the years I have spent in the companionship of Cynthia Herrup is that our relationship has never conformed to what I had once thought intimacy entailed. Given the many pleasant surprises of our life together, it seems oddly conventional to acknowledge it with a book dedication. But I am more pleased than I can say to do just that, and to do it with both gratitude and happiness.

JMB

August 1995
Durham, North Carolina

CONTENTS

SEVEN

These Things Must Be if We Sell Ale:
Alewives in English Culture and Society

EIGHT

Women's Work in a Changing World

APPENDIX

Interpreting Presentments under the Assize of Ale

LIST OF ABBREVIATIONS

BL	British Library
CCR	*Calendar of Close Rolls*
CLB	*Calendar of Letter Books of the City of London*
CLRO	City of London Record Office
CPMR	*Calendar of Plea and Memoranda Rolls of the City of London*
CPR	*Calendar of Patent Rolls*
CSPD	*Calendar of State Papers Domestic*
EETS	Early English Text Society
ESRO	East Sussex Record Office
GL	Guildhall Library
L&P	*Letters and Papers, Foreign and Domestic, Henry VIII*
Norwich Leets	Leets held in Norwich, 1288–1391 (see the appendix for further details)
NRO	Norfolk Record Office
NtnRO	Northamptonshire Record Office
Oxford Assizes	Records of the enforcement of the assize of ale in Oxford, 1309–1351 (see the appendix for further details)
OUA	Oxford University Archives, Bodleian Library
PRO	Public Record Office
Rolls Series	Chronicles and Memorials of Great Britain and Ireland during the middle ages published under the direction of the Master of the Rolls
SRO	Southampton Record Office
STC	A. W. Pollard and G. R. Redgrave, *Short-title Catalogue of Books Printed in England, Scotland and Ireland and of English Books Printed Abroad, 1475–1640* (London, 1976–1991)
Statutes	*Statutes of the Realm*

VCH	Victoria History of the Counties of England
Wing	Donald G. Wing, Short-title Catalogue of Books Printed in England, Scotland, Ireland, Wales and British America and of English Books Printed in Other Countries, 1641–1700 (New York, 1972–1988)
YAS	Yorkshire Archaeological Society
YCA	York City Archives

In addition, the notes contain many shorthand references to materials collected in a survey of presentments made under the assize of ale. These references have been indicated by the word "Sample" followed by an abbreviated archival citation. Please consult the appendix for further details about these abbreviated citations.

A BRIEF NOTE ON
CONVENTIONS AND TERMS

I wish to clarify a few matters that might confuse some readers. Until 1971, the English monetary system was based on a shilling (s.) of 12 pence (d.) and a pound (£) of 20 shillings. The penny was broken into 2 halfpennies, or 4 farthings. I have retained this system here. For comparative purposes, it might help to remember that an adult male laborer might earn 1½d. a day in 1300, 3d. in 1400, 4d. in 1500, and 8d. in 1600. Wages for women were generally one-half to three-quarters the wages of men.

Ale and beer were measured in gallons (roughly 4½ liters—that is, today's imperial gallon, not the smaller U.S. gallon). A gallon was itself divided into 8 pints, 4 quarts, or 2 pottles. Brewed drink was also measured in barrels, each containing usually 32 gallons of ale or 36 gallons of beer. A barrel was divided into 4 firkins, or 2 kilderkins. Grain and malt were measured in quarters (roughly 290 liters), each quarter containing 8 bushels.

The calendar used in England until 1752 treated the feast of the Annunciation (25 March) as the beginning of the year, counting 1 January through 24 March as part of the preceding year. I have converted such dates to modern style. In identifying places, I have retained the old counties, as used before the reorganization of 1974. Spelling and punctuation are now much more standardized than was the case before 1600, and in the interest of improving the readability of passages quoted from original texts, I have not hesitated to modernize spelling and insert punctuation. I have, however, found it useful to retain some compound words—such as *singlewoman, alebrewer* and *beerbrewer*—that were common in fifteenth- and sixteenth-century English but have fallen out of use since then. Unless otherwise noted, all translations are my own.

ALE, BEER,
AND BREWSTERS
IN ENGLAND

BREWSTERS

Early in February each year, magistrates in many English towns come together in what are informally known as "brewster sessions." In these meetings, they supervise the trade in alcoholic beverages — not only ales and beers, but also wines, spirits, and other intoxicating liquors. They renew licenses for selling such drink, permit transfers of licenses between holders, grant new licenses, and even bestow occasional permissions for special occasions. In most jurisdictions, for example in the brewster sessions of Lewes, magistrates customarily hear a report from the licensing inspector. Within living memory, large numbers of licensees would come to hear this report and responses to it, ending the day with a celebratory dinner in a local public house.[1]

Except for brewster sessions, the word *brewster* has virtually disappeared from contemporary English. With *brewster* has disappeared a history that this book seeks to recover, a history of women in brewing. *Brewster* once had a clear and unequivocal meaning: a female brewer. In the fourteenth century, when women did most of the brewing in most places, their presence was signified in the various languages of the time: *braciatrices* and *pandoxatrices* in Latin texts, *braceresses* in Anglo-Norman, and *brewsters* in the English that was being used with more and more frequency. In *Piers Plowman*, William Langland created Betoun the Brewster, and well into the next century, *brewsters* often served as a female counterpart to *brewers* in the newly dominant English language of the day. By 1500, however, the neat gender distinction of *brewster* and *brewer* was fading away. In a trend common in English and other languages, the male *brewer* increasingly served for both sexes, but, rather surprisingly, *brewster* sometimes did the same, particularly in northern England. Over time, however, *brewer* won out as a term for both sexes, and *brewster* survived only in limited uses: as a surname, as a word known to some historians and literary scholars, and of course as a descriptive term still used in the ever-conservative traditions of English law.[2]

In losing *brewster*, we have lost sight of a critical part of history. Women once brewed and sold most of the ale drunk in England, and since ale was, as we shall see, drunk in vast quantities, women had to produce and market it in vast quantities as well. Today, most aspects of the brewing trade—production in breweries, distribution to retail outlets, ownership and management of pubs, and even selling behind the bar—rest largely in the hands of men. Women's work has now become men's work. When did this happen? Why? With what effect?

I came to these questions not by considering abstract issues of historical change and causation but instead by stumbling across the evidence. Like a protagonist in a mystery novel, I chanced on clues that demanded my further attention, on evidence I could not ignore. I found this evidence in the archives of medieval manors and towns, archives that quite literally abound with information about *brewers* (a term I will use, in its modern sense, to refer to both sexes, reserving *brewsters* for females only). Until the sixteenth century and even later in some areas, commercial brewers were supervised under an assize of ale—that is, a set of regulations specifying the quality, prices, and measures to be observed by brewers—whose enforcement rested with local courts. As a general rule, local officers, picturesquely and quite accurately called aletasters, monitored sales of ale, and eventually beer as well. When a brewer had a batch of ale ready for sale, she or he was supposed to summon the aletaster, who then tasted the ale to determine its quality, its marketability, and finally its fair price. Of course, brewers avoided supervision in a variety of ways, especially by refusing to summon the aletaster, by altering prices or quality, or by using deceptive measures. As a result, an aletaster's job was never ending; he (or very rarely, she) not only had to test ale when called by a particular brewer but also had to remain ever vigilant against the fraudulent machinations of *all* brewers.

Because aletasters had to keep such close watch over brewers, their presentments provide a virtual catalog of persons in the trade. Aletasters presented brewers on a regular basis (usually either twice a year at views of frankpledge or every three weeks at ordinary court sessions), and they commonly listed *all* persons involved in the trade—not only those who had cheated in some manner but also those who had brewed and sold honestly. Aletasters at Preston-on-Wye (Herefordshire), for example, reported all brewers, noting how often they had brewed and whether they had sold honestly (*tenuit assisa*).[3] Erring brewers were subject to either amercement or physical punishment (according to the gravity and frequency of their offenses), but even honest brewers often had to pay a small fine. In short, the assize, as policed by aletasters, functioned as a de facto system of licensing; all brewers were regulated, and as a rule, all brewers were reported in presentments made before local courts.

I am certainly not the first historian to have noticed the presentments of aletasters, but until recently, most historians have noted little more than their "monotonous regularity."[4] I began by seeing these lists in a different way, noticing that they included many women. When some aletasters stood before their local courts, they named many women, identifying them as the daughters, wives, or widows of local men. Indeed, in many jurisdictions, women appeared before their local courts as brewsters more often than in any other capacity—

more often than as landholders or artisans, as aggrieved victims or guilty thieves, as rural serfs owing services or urban citizens exercising privileges. Here, I thought, was an exceptional source for studying the history of women.

As we shall see, this exceptional source is, like any clue in a good mystery, difficult to understand and challenging to interpret. It is also only where my search began, and as I developed questions about why, when, and with what effect women stopped brewing for profit, I found more evidence in other sources—administrative records of attempts to regulate brewers through order, compromise, and threat; accounts that list sums paid by brewers; tax records reporting the wealth of brewers; royal papers about the involvement of various monarchs in the trade; gild records that detail brewers' attempts to organize themselves as a trade; and literary and artistic remains that depict brewers and popular opinions about them. To be sure, the evidence was incomplete (not surprisingly, for example, I found neither diaries nor accounts left by brewsters), but many types of evidence from many places and times contributed to my quest to understand the once-dominant place of women in English brewing.

As I was collecting and considering all this evidence, my emerging interpretation was shaped not only by what I found in archives and libraries but also by my ongoing work—in English history, in feminist history, and perhaps most of all in the classroom. In all of these guises, I have had to grapple with the provocative work of Alan Macfarlane who argued in 1978 that English society in 1200 was fundamentally similar to English society in 1700. To Macfarlane, England in 1200 was already a capitalist, market-oriented society made up of sturdy individualists, an England structurally similar in all essentials to the England of 1700. Although Macfarlane's argument has been justly criticized by many historians, it has had one very positive effect: it has forced us to look critically at the seemingly clear division—traditionally dated to 1485 or, more neatly, 1500—between medieval and modern England.[5]

Macfarlane's argument, tendentious as it was, did not spring fully armed from his head alone. Instead, it was based on more careful critiques by medieval historians of the traditional history of an England dramatically recast in the sixteenth century, a suddenly modern England utterly different from the medieval England of the past. As the work of Richard Smith and L. R. Poos has most recently demonstrated, English society was not transformed by the end of one dynastic struggle at Bosworth field in August 1485. The death of Richard III was momentous indeed, but it cannot compare in social and economic effect to the deaths of perhaps 2 million men, women, and children in the first outbreak of plague in 1348–49. I share the impatience of many historians of medieval England with the ways in which the traditional "master narrative" has sharply divided the fourteenth and fifteenth centuries from the sixteenth and seventeenth centuries. In determining the chronological limits of this study of English brewing—and the dates stated in the book's title are deliberately modest, for my evidence ranges back into the thirteenth century and forward into the seventeenth—I set out to traverse the great divide between medieval and modern England, to see whether the traditional chronology could be sustained. The history of brewing suggests, as we shall see, that the traditional chronology does not work: in brewing, as in other facets of social and economic history, 1350 is a truer watershed than 1500.

At the same time that I was questioning the historical traditions that had hitherto confined my scholarly interests to England before 1500, my work in women's history was reinforcing some of Macfarlane's suggestions. In this regard, I owe much to my students, who asked questions that I could not answer. The most momentous of these questions arose in a women's history class one lively morning in the autumn of 1987. I was talking about the work of women in late medieval Europe, offering the students examples of how women were often paid 1d. a day rather than the 1½d. or 2d. earned by men. As I was comfortably dispensing received knowledge and historical fact, a student at the back of the room raised her hand and asked a question that made me very uncomfortable. "How is that any different from today?" she asked. "How is that any different from the 68 cents that women now earn for every dollar earned by men?" The question carried clear polemical force, and as I like to recall, I diffused it by crisply historicizing the wages of medieval women. I talked about how relatively unimportant wage earning was to most medieval people, and I emphasized how wages were then frequently supplemented by food and other gratuities. In other words, I cobbled together a respectable answer and moved the focus on to other—and for me, more comfortable—topics. But I knew that I had finessed the question rather than answered it, and it is a question that has bothered me ever since. "How is that any different?" I have asked myself again and again. And I have had to answer in all too many cases, "Well, not very much."

Troubled, then, by this encounter in the classroom, I began to ponder some of the continuities in women's history that now lie at the heart of this study of ale, beer, and brewsters. I approached the subject from two directions. On the one hand, I began to focus on continuities in women's work during the seven centuries that divide the central middle ages from our own time. Surveying the extant literature and taking the broadest possible perspective, I found compelling continuities across the centuries—in the types of work undertaken by women, in the status accorded to women's work, and in the ability of women to support themselves independently. In other words, I found that a more honest answer to that haunting question, "How is that any different?" would have more fully acknowledged the presence of important structural continuities in women's work. In 1300, in 1600, and unless things change dramatically in the next few years, in 2000, most "women's work" can be characterized as low skilled, low status, and poorly remunerated. This remarkable fact needs to be not only recognized but also explained.[6]

On the other hand, I also began to look self-critically at myself as a historian of women. Why had I felt the need to defuse the polemical force of my student's question? Did not feminist politics belong in my classrooms as well as in my writings? Not surprisingly, this self-critique broadened into a critique of the relatively new field of women's history. What I feared in myself, I found elsewhere—an increasingly depoliticized women's history that muted righteous anger, preferred safe topics, and most of all avoided any discussion of that bugbear *patriarchy*. I have since argued, in a polemical piece of my own, that the project of historicizing patriarchy should take a prominent place on the agenda of women's history. To my mind, the sorts of continuities that I was finding in the history of women's work demand explanation. If women's work is characterized by low skill, low status, and poor remuneration in both rural and urban communities; in market economies, as well as in capitalistic economies; and in pre-industrial, industrial, and now even postindustrial societies, what forces have maintained this remarkable continuity?[7]

I then began to look at my research on brewsters in new ways. I had originally conceived of the project as a story of change, a story of how women were forced out of an industry as it became profitable and prestigious. In this rendition, my work on brewsters would have contributed primarily to a tradition in women's history that dates back to the pioneering work of Alice Clark. In *The Working Life of Women in the Seventeenth Century* (first published in 1919), Clark argued that the advent of what she called "industrial capitalism" profoundly limited and devalued women's work.[8] Before the rise of capitalism and industrialism, women enjoyed what the medievalist Eileen Power called a "rough-and-ready equality" with men; afterward, everything went downhill.[9] Brewing seemed to fit this pattern nicely, for before brewing expanded, capitalized, and centralized, women brewed; afterward, they increasingly did not.

Yet I began to see my information about brewsters and brewers in a different way. I began to see it not as a story of transformation in women's lives but instead as a story of remarkable stability for women despite considerable socioeconomic change. In this version of the history of brewing, the substantial transformation occurred not in women's opportunities for good employment but in brewing itself. Although in 1300 women had brewed for profit more frequently than they would in 1600, the status of their work did not really change. In 1300, brewsters were able to work because the trade was accessible to them; as low-status, low-skilled, poorly remunerated work, it attracted little male participation and it suited the domestic responsibilities of many women. In 1600, women still worked in areas of brewing that remained low status, low skilled, and poorly paid or that could be accommodated to family needs: they hawked ale in the streets, they sold ale from their homes, and they carried ale on their backs from brewhouses to clients. But as the actual production of ale and beer—that is, brewing per se—became so much more profitable and prestigious, it passed into male hands. In other words, there was a transformation (in the structures of the brewing industry); there was even a change in women's work (many more brewsters worked in 1300 than in 1600); but there was no transformation in the overall status of working women (most women in 1300 and 1600 worked in low-skilled, low-status, and poorly remunerated tasks).

Both of these stories about brewing—one emphasizing the change entailed in the cessation of brewing by women and the other emphasizing continuities in the low status of women's work—are important, and both are found in this book. But it is the latter story, the story of continuities, that now lies at the heart of this project. By reconceptualizing the history of brewing as a history of substantial continuity in women's work, I have been able to consider new interpretative possibilities. I have been able to investigate what happened to women as their economic choices were altered but not improved. When women could no longer rely on small-scale and often intermittent brewing to supplement their other sources of income, what did they do? I have also tried to trace how different women were affected by and responded to changing circumstances. Why were not-married women—particularly singlewomen but also widows—squeezed out of the brewing trade earlier than married women? And most important, I have attempted to explain women's experience of *histoire immobile*—to explain why women's status has often remained so low despite dramatic transformations in human life and experience. I have tried, in other words, to give patriarchy a history by showing how, in one trade, the broad relationship between male advantage and female disadvantage remained unchanged in a changing world.

As a teacher, I owe much to my students, for without them, the fundamental insight of this book—that women's work stood still in a changing economic world—might have eluded me. I have crafted this book with them always in mind, trying to provide the sort of honesty, clarity, and political engagement that they have demanded from me in the classroom. Luckily, the subject itself—ale and beer—is dear to the hearts of many students. This is certainly not a book about drinking customs and drinking songs, nor is it a book directed primarily at an audience of undergraduates, but I have attempted to present my findings in ways that will sustain the interest of as wide an audience as possible. I hope that students who read this book will find its arguments convincing, but I hope even more that they will take from it a fuller appreciation of the excitement, the diversity, and the challenges of the historian's craft.

This is, then, a book about structural continuities enduring in the midst of enormous historical change. The large questions raised by refocusing history on issues of continuity are the subject of the concluding chapter; we shall end, in other words, by considering how history can be written differently if we more closely observe continuities and more aggressively seek to explain them. But between that conclusion and this introduction, the book investigates a specific subject: the work of women in the English brewing trade between the thirteenth and seventeenth centuries. Exploring how enormous change in this one industry resulted in virtually no substantive change for women, it seeks to explain, in one instance, the stasis in women's condition that I now take to be a fundamental problem of women's history. I do not think that this one example can tell a universal story, but I do hope that it will demonstrate persuasively some of the forces that have worked, at some times and in some situations, to maintain the power of men over women.

From its medieval home-based origins to its precocious commercial development after the Black Death, brewing was always a vital English enterprise.[10] Brewing was especially important because its products—ale and (later) beer—were essential parts of the English diet. Since most people rarely drank water, milk, or wine, they relied on ale and beer for their basic liquid refreshment. Even the nobility, who could afford wine and drank it in considerable quantities, included brewed beverages as a regular part of their daily diet. To be sure, English people drank ale and beer, as we do today, for pleasure, conviviality, and inebriation. Yet they also drank ale and beer much more mundanely—in the morning, as well as in the evening; as simple liquid refreshment; and for its salubrity, not just its intoxicating effects.

Brewing was also important in a political sense. From a very early date, manorial lords and ladies, municipal mayors, and royal officers sought two things from the brewing trade. First, they tried to regulate brewers in the hope of assuring a steady supply of good ale. Like bread, ale was crucial to social order, and those responsible for order sought to ensure its ready availability. Second, they attempted to profit from the trade, levying a variety of fees and taxes on both the production and sale of brewed drink. Through these exactions, many polities came to rely heavily on income generated by the regulation of brewers. These complementary imperatives helped to generate the exceptionally thorough supervision of the trade by aletasters.

From the carefully preserved records of this supervision, one fact emerges very clearly: between 1300 and 1600, the brewing industry was transformed. In 1300, brewing was a small-scale, local industry pursued by women who worked from their homes. Compared to other industries (such as cloth working or goldsmithing or even the closely related baking), it was unorganized and underdeveloped. By 1600, brewing in many cities, towns, and villages was so large scale and so centralized that it was assuming a leading role—managerially, technically, and commercially—among other contemporary industries.[11] It was also largely controlled by men. All of these changes occurred slowly and unevenly, but they were inexorable. In 1600, although small brewers could still be found, especially in the north and west, the large commercialized breweries of London represented the future of the trade.

The transformation of brewing over these centuries sprang from many sources. It was partly a technical matter. When brewers in England began to use hops (an early fifteenth-century innovation that first took firm hold in towns of the southeast), they were able to produce a new beverage—called beer to distinguish it from unhopped ale—that was clearer, cheaper, and more easily preserved and transported. This simple change in the technology of brewing helps to explain not only the relative underdevelopment of English brewing (brewing on the continent began to professionalize and centralize much earlier) but also the dramatic expansion of the industry in the fifteenth and sixteenth centuries; with hops, brewers could produce more cheaply and market more effectively. Yet technology alone does not explain the transformation of brewing. In part, market forces accelerated the process. Late medieval brewers profited from urbanization, rising per capita standards of living, changing dietary habits, and even the growth of the alehouse as a social center. In part, trade organization contributed to the professionalization of brewers. Once brewers could organize themselves into gilds, they were able to bargain more effectively for good prices and good terms with those empowered to regulate their trade, especially mayors, aldermen, and other local authorities. And in part, regulation itself contributed to changes in the brewing industry. Anxious to ensure a steady supply of ale and beer, local and royal officers often encouraged the development of a restricted trade controlled by a small number of highly reliable brewers.

The problem addressed in this book arises from this transformation of brewing: what happened to brewsters as their industry was transformed? In a very important sense, the answer is predictable. As Joan Thirsk has recently noted in an overview of women's work in early modern England, "If a venture prospers, women fade from the scene."[12] Brewing—in which women worked with less and less frequency as the trade grew more profitable and more prestigious—is just one example of this general rule. But this answer begs the question, for in order to understand what happened to brewsters, we must understand why it happened. Why did women, who so numerically dominated the trade in 1300, cease to brew for profit as the trade expanded? Women were, after all, well-positioned to take advantage of the changes in brewing that accelerated so dramatically after the Black Death. They did not do so, and this book seeks to explain why not.

Chapter 2 sets the scene, exploring brewing in the decades that preceded the devastation wrought by the Black Death of 1348–49. In the late thirteenth and early fourteenth centuries, brewing was a widespread and relatively unspecialized trade. Brewers were everywhere. Most households had the capacity to brew ale, and most not only brewed ale but also occasionally offered it for sale to others. In these households, women took primary responsibility for brewing, both for domestic consumption by husbands, children, and servants and for commercial sale. Although many women were involved in commercial brewing, all did not rely with equal weight on its income, and this chapter therefore introduces crucial distinctions among commercial brewers: *occasional brewers* (who sold ale only rarely), *by-industrial brewers* (for whom brewing generated important supplementary income), and *professional brewers* (for whom brewing offered the primary income of the household). Before 1350, although many women brewed occasionally and by-industrially, few brewed professionally (neither did many men). Nevertheless, brewing was good work for women, offering them more profit and prestige than most other occupations available to them.

Although most brewsters in the period before the Black Death were married, a significant minority lived as singlewomen or widows. Chapter 3 traces how the commercial changes that began in the late fourteenth century slowly squeezed not-married brewsters out of the trade. After 1350, the market for ale expanded rapidly. Fewer people lived in England than before the Black Death, but because of an improved diet they drank more ale. The market for ale also grew more complex, with more people either drinking in alehouses or buying their ale from alesellers, who marketed what others had brewed. As the ale market expanded and divided into producers and retailers, brewing grew more industrialized and professionalized; brewers invested more in their operations, produced more ale in each brewing, and worked more regularly. For not-married women, who often brewed on an occasional basis only, these developments boded ill; they could not compete effectively with the professional brewers, who played such an increasingly dominant role in the trade. In 1300, perhaps one in every five brewsters had been not married, but by 1500, few singlewomen or widows (save for widows of male professional brewers) brewed for profit.

Chapter 4 turns to wives, using the extraordinary records kept by a clerk of the Brewers' gild in early fifteenth-century London to investigate how wives and husbands were renegotiating their respective positions in the trade. Wives still worked in brewing in London circa 1420, but their work was increasingly hidden behind the public personae of their husbands. In other words, although wives retained a place in brewing longer than not-married brewsters, their place was increasingly a private and unacknowledged one. This chapter also considers the implications of gild formation for women. As the brewing trade grew more profitable and more prestigious over the course of the later middle ages, brewers began—much later than many other tradespeople—to form themselves into gilds. In London, the mystery of brewers achieved formal recognition in the early fifteenth century, and brewers in many other cities had formed similar associations by the sixteenth century. In general, the formation of brewers' gilds undermined the work of women in the trade; most gilds either excluded women altogether or accepted them as only quasi members.

The major technical innovation of late medieval brewing was, of course, the introduction of hops. Because hopped beer offered so many advantages over unhopped ale, beerbrewers produced more than alebrewers, marketed their product more widely, and accrued larger profits. With remarkably few exceptions, beerbrewing was a male trade, and chapter 5 asks why the new technique of brewing with hops was so rarely used by women. As we shall see, the explanation is complex, involving the migration and settlement of foreigners in England, the demands of military provisioning, and the commercial requirements of successful beerbrewing.

Brewing was always subject to government supervision, even when it was a widespread and unprofessionalized trade before the Black Death, but the nature of that supervision changed over time. Chapter 6 considers how the regulation of brewing affected women and men in the trade. The assize of ale, which so shaped medieval regulation of brewers, remained in force in some sixteenth-century jurisdictions. Yet it was also often supplemented and sometimes replaced by new regulatory schemes, particularly schemes to license brewers and ale-sellers. Whatever its form, the force of regulation fell more heavily on women than on men. Opening with a survey of the general effects of regulation on women, this chapter concludes with the example of one town, Oxford, where the trade was regulated with particular severity from a very early date and where brewing quickly became a trade of men.

These chapters suggest, then, that the slow eclipse of brewsters was a complex matter, affecting singlewomen and widows earlier than married women and springing from commercial, technological, organizational, and regulatory factors. Chapter 7 adds a final ingredient: ideology. It seeks to discover, from a variety of literary texts and artistic remains, what English people thought about brewsters and how their ideas might have affected the ability of women to compete with men in the trade. From Betoun the Brewster in the fourteenth century to Mother Bunch in the seventeenth century, cultural representations of brewsters were deeply ambivalent; brewsters offered their customers good fun and good drink, but they also tempted people into sin, cheated their customers in devious ways, brewed unhealthy and disgusting drink, and ran disorderly establishments. It seems that public anxieties about the drink trade—its resistance to effective regulation, its encouragement of vice, its manipulation of the public—were displaced from *all* brewers onto *female* brewers alone.

All history is dependent on evidence, by the artifacts that those who came before us have left behind. If we could live for a few weeks in an English town of the late fifteenth century, we might observe how women were discouraged from commercial brewing by other factors not discussed here. Perhaps violence against women worked to keep women subservient to men, in brewing as in other matters. Perhaps reproductive issues—age of marriage, access to birth control and abortion, rates of child mortality—encouraged and discouraged female brewing. Perhaps sexual practices and ideas inhibited brewsters from plying their trade—as, for example, in the problems that not-married women seem to have encountered in keeping male servants in their households. These possibilities (and many others) are intriguing but largely unknowable, given the evidence at our disposal.[13] It is my hope that what *can* be demonstrated in this book—that a complex web of commercial, technological, organizational, regulatory, and ideological factors discouraged female brewing—will suffice to make an essential point about the historical persistence of patriarchy.

My students often seem to conceive of what they sometimes call "The Patriarchy" as a committee of men who plot and scheme to keep women in their subordinate places. Such simplistic notions have, I think, discouraged many historians from studying the historical forces of patriarchy and from grappling with the theoretical problems presented by long-term continuities in women's history. I am not sure that we will ever adequately define or describe "patriarchy," but—like "capitalism"—it is still worthy of historical investigation. By placing "capitalism" on the historical agenda, we have asked new questions about the past—questions about markets, monetary supply, production, ideology, consumption, and the like. We will probably always argue about the answers to questions such as that posed recently by Christopher Dyer: "Were there any capitalists in fifteenth-century England?"[14] But through seeking such answers, we have learned a lot more about the societies and economies of the European past. By placing "patriarchy" on the historical agenda, we will similarly open up new parts of the past, parts that can speak to us about the nature, sustenance, and endurance of powers derived from notions of difference in general and sexual difference in particular. It is to this subject—the project of historicizing patriarchy—that the final chapter turns.[15]

Much of the pleasure of this book comes from the evidence: the archival, literary, and artistic sources that tell us about brewsters and brewers in past times. The stories they tell are, of course, partial and incomplete. But these stories are often lively and amusing, and they are always challenging for us, removed by hundreds of years from the circumstances of their creation, to interpret. Even the long, repetitive presentments made by aletasters offer their occasional comic relief or human drama: a sarcastic couplet about the reliability of brewers scrawled in the margin, a story about an aletaster who fearfully refused to taste ale in the house of an angry neighbor, a brewster who taunted the ale-taster that she would not be ruled by him, or reports about ale brewed so badly that it made people ill. And even long, repetitive presentments of brewers—just names, after all, of those who brewed—provide surprisingly difficult clues that require cautious interpretation.

In using such sources, this book forges a careful path between history-as-amusing-anecdote and history-as-social-science. In each chapter, I have used whatever methods seemed best to answer my questions from the sources available. Readers will find an eclectic mixture: broad generalization and close case study; quantification and poetry; family reconstitution and literary analysis; hard fact and theoretical speculation. I have usually incorporated matters of method—what the sources are and how they have been used—into the relevant chapters. In one case, however, methodological considerations have demanded treatment in a separate appendix. Presentments by aletasters provide essential evidence for this study, but they are very difficult to analyze. Do they tell us about all brewers or just erring brewers? Do they actually name the person who brewed or do they substitute others (particularly husbands) for some brewsters? Do they provide reliable information about marital status? My answers to these questions have been particularly important to the arguments of chapters 2 and 3, but these answers were not easily achieved and are not easily explained. Rather than bog down interpretive chapters in methodological discussions, I have discussed these issues in an appendix. Specialists and other interested readers—and since I have used aletasters' presentments in new ways, I hope that many readers will be interested in these methodological issues—should begin their reading with this appendix.

CHAPTER TWO

WHEN WOMEN
BREWED

When Denise Marlere died in February 1401, she left behind a thriving brewing business in the town of Bridgwater. She bequeathed the bulk of her business to her servant Rose: half of a tenement, all her brewing vessels with a furnace, three sacks full of malt, a cup, a brass pot, a pan, a goblet bound with silver, a chafing dish, two silver spoons, and some other carefully specified goods. She also left brewing utensils to other heirs, giving a leaden vat each to her parish church, her parish priest, and two local monasteries, and leaving to her daughter, Isabel, two more leaden vats, a brass 3 gallon pot, a pan, a mortar and pestle, and the proceeds of one brewing. A widow, Denise Marlere enjoyed a very comfortable standard of living, thanks in large part to her commercial brewing. Although brewing utensils and supplies made up the bulk of her estate, she also bequeathed 80 pounds of white wool (suggesting that she might have supported herself by spinning as well as brewing), several chests and other household goods, coverlets and other clothing, and considerable amounts of cash. For Denise Marlere, brewing for profit seems to have been very profitable indeed.

Denise Marlere represents the apogee of commercial brewing by women in medieval England. She brewed for more than 20 years, she managed a successful business, and she invested heavily in her equipment and supplies. Yet, although Denise Marlere's work was impressive and important, it was limited in critical ways. By the late fourteenth century, some brewers were supplying markets beyond their immediate neighborhoods (sending their ale to nearby villages or even abroad), but as far as we know, Denise Marlere sold ale only in the town of Bridgwater itself. By the late fourteenth century, some brewers were working in brewhouses, but Denise Marlere seems to have pursued her trade from within her home. And by the late fourteenth century, brewing was the primary occupation of some households, but for Denise Marlere, as long as her husband,

Nicholas, lived, her brewing only supplemented his work as a butcher. Yet, despite these limitations, commercial brewing offered Denise Marlere an excellent option: a by-industry through which she added, as both a wife and a widow, to her household income.[1]

This chapter examines the circumstances under which women like Denise Marlere sought to profit from brewing ale in their villages and towns. We will begin by considering the brewing industry—how ale was consumed, produced, and marketed in the late thirteenth and early fourteenth centuries. We will then turn to brewers themselves: first, considering how the early fourteenth century was a time when women brewed almost to the exclusion of men and, second, identifying other characteristics of those who sought to profit from brewing in both town and country. We will end by assessing the importance of commercial brewing in the lives of Englishwomen before the plague. At a time when women had few good economic options, brewing was often an excellent choice for them. Yet, when women brewed, commercial brewing was a relatively low-status, low-skilled, poorly remunerated trade. Like Denise Marlere, some brewsters did well . . . *for women.*

Denise Marlere, whose work as a brewster spanned the last decades of the fourteenth century, represents not only the apogee of brewing by medieval Englishwomen but also the slow pace of the changes that began after the Black Death. This chapter focuses on brewsters in the classic period before 1350 when the market for drink had not yet changed in ways that discouraged women's work. Yet the changes that came after the Black Death were so slow and uneven that many women continued to brew much as women had in the past (and in some places, women continued to do so well beyond the fifteenth century). In 1400, Denise Marlere still profited from brewing as her mother or grandmother might have done, and in 1500 or even 1600, women in other places still sold ale in much the same ways their ancestors had in the fourteenth century.[2] Yet in many parts of England—particularly in cities but also in villages in the south and east—the circumstances of brewsters changed slowly but surely after 1350. The experiences of women in brewing before 1350 provide, therefore, our "ground zero" from which we can then trace the pace, nature, and meaning of subsequent developments.

As is so often the case in historical research, this ground zero is somewhat elusive, for the sources are few and enigmatic. The history of brewing before the Black Death is told mainly in regulatory materials: the provisions of the *Assisa panis et cervisie* as set out by the thirteenth century, the regulations by which towns and villages sought to control the trade, and especially the presentments of ale-tasters before their local courts.[3] In seeking to understand the lives of brewers in this early period, I have relied on the work of many local historians who have worked with these sources, but I have also examined thousands of presentments in dozens of jurisdictions, focusing particularly on about two dozen villages, towns, and cities. As map 1 shows, the sample thus comprised tilts toward the southeast, an almost inevitable skewing that reflects the distribution of extant archives. Nevertheless, neither the north nor the west are entirely unrepresented, and the sample includes pastoral, agrarian, and woodland villages; small towns;

Map 1   Location of Places Frequently Mentioned. Places in italics are part of the sample undertaken for this book (see the appendix).

regional cities; and the metropolitan center of London. The information I have collected about brewing in these places raises important questions about the history of regulation (as discussed in chapter 6) and interpretative methodologies (as discussed in the appendix). For now, let us focus on brewers and their trade.

Commercial Brewing, c. 1300

In late medieval and early modern England, brewers produced an essential beverage, a beverage that most people drank most of the time. Today, we drink ale and beer for taste and intoxication. Then, people also knew well the pleasures of drinking good ale, but in addition, they drank ale as a basic part of their diet. Children drank ale as well as adults, and it was consumed throughout the day, at breakfast as well as dinner.[4] People drank ale so regularly because other liquids were unhealthy, unsuitable, or unavailable; in a world where water was often polluted, where milk was converted into cheese and butter, and where wine was too expensive for most people, ale was the most readily available and safest beverage. In the southwest, people also drank cider, but even there ale was a basic part of most diets.

After 1350, per capita consumption of ale increased, and after 1400, beer began to compete with ale for English palates. But even before prosperity and beer began to expand the trade of brewers, English people drank ale in large amounts. Edward I had to provide his soldiers with about 1 gallon of ale each day, and this per diem appears to have been quite standard; it is found in household accounts, monastic corrodies, and even allowances for the poor inmates of hospitals.[5] Of course, the very poor sometimes could not afford ale, and they would, like the boy in *Aelfric's Colloquy*, drink "Ale if I have it, water, if I have it not."[6] But most peasants and laborers seem to have consumed ale on a regular basis. Ordinary folk certainly did not drink ale in the quantities enjoyed by those more privileged, and their ale was less strong and palatable. But there is considerable evidence to suggest that peasants of all sorts (smallholders, as well as their more prosperous neighbors) drank ale on a fairly regular basis.[7]

In aggregate terms, production of ale was already immense by the early fourteenth century. If everyone in England drank just a quart of ale a day, more than 17 million barrels had to be produced each year.[8] At this time, brewing was a fairly straightforward process that required widely known skills and widely available tools. Some brewers purchased malt, but others began by malting their grain. Barley, which would become the favored brewing grain of the sixteenth century, was by no means preferred in the early fourteenth century; many brewers used more oats than barley, and wheat and dredge (a combination of oats and barley) were also sometimes malted. The use of oats in brewing has been particularly associated with west country brewers, but in the thirteenth and early fourteenth centuries, even brewers in London preferred oats above all other grains.[9] Whatever grain was used, its malting was a long process; it was soaked for several days, then drained of water and piled into a couch, then carefully tended while it germinated, and finally cured in a kiln. For malting, a few tools were essential: a large vat or other vessel for soaking the grain, a trough or ladle for drawing off the water, shovels or forks for turning the grain in the couch, and a malt kiln. Only the last was a specialist tool, unlikely to be found in most households.

Brewing itself was a time-consuming task. First, the malt was ground (not too finely); then water was boiled; and then the two were mixed together, ideally with the malt and water running together into a mash tun. From the mash tun (or other vessel) was drawn off the wort, to which yeast and herbs were added. Within a day (or less), the ale would be ready for drinking. Most brewers drew off several worts from the malt, each successively weaker than the preceding one. Specialist tools (for example, troughs, malt mills, or mash tuns) eased the work of brewing, but ordinary household utensils were perfectly adequate. Most people could brew ale easily by purchasing malt, grinding it with a hand mill, boiling water in a pot, tossing in some malt, drawing off the wort into a second vessel, and adding yeast.

As a result of its accessibility, brewing was an industry of thousands of petty producers, not a specialist craft. These petty producers were themselves divided into two groups—those who brewed for consumption by their families (*domestic brewers*) and those who brewed for sale (*commercial brewers*). Most households could and did produce their own ale at least some of the time, and this work fell most often on wives. The wife of the late fifteenth-century Tyrannical Husband brewed at least once a fortnight; William Harrison's wife brewed once a month in the late sixteenth century; and even in the early seventeenth century, Gervase Markham offered extensive advice on domestic brewing in *The English Housewife*.[10] Because this brewing for use never merited the attention of aletasters, it is very poorly documented; for no period can we estimate its extent or reconstruct how it shared the burden of ale production with commercial brewing. But it would be a mistake to underestimate its importance.

Our most direct evidence of domestic brewing comes from elite households. In 1333–34, the household of Elizabeth de Burgh, Lady of Clare, brewed about 8 quarters of barley and dredge each week, each quarter yielding about 60 gallons of ale. Brewing varied by the season of the year, with vast amounts produced in December (when more than 3,500 gallons were brewed) and quite restricted production in February (only 810 gallons). The members of the Clare household drank strong ale throughout the year, imbibing with particular gusto during the celebrations of Christmas and the New Year.[11]

Elizabeth de Burgh's household might have seldom purchased ale, but most households, even aristocratic households, bought at least some of their brewed drink. Domestic brewing was an important source of ale for many households, but most probably alternated producing ale with buying it. Impossible to trace directly in extant records, this sort of dynamic interplay between domestic brewing and commercial brewing can be glimpsed in presentments for commercial brewing. *So many brewers sold ale so occasionally* that many of them must have sometimes brewed ale for sale, sometimes brewed ale for consumption, and sometimes mingled the two (both selling and consuming ale from any single brewing). In Brigstock (Northamptonshire) in the 1340s, for example, women paid about 200 amercements each year for selling ale, most selling only once or twice a year. Women such as Alice the wife of Thomas Baxster (who brewed for profit five times in three years) and Matilda the daughter of Adam Miller (who brewed five times in five years) probably supplied their families with ale by alternating brewing for use, buying ale, and sometimes selling ale.[12] This book is focused on the commercial brewers who sought to profit from making and selling ale, but domestic brewing is a critical—and unfortunately, largely undocumented—backdrop to this work.

Commercial brewing was very widespread, especially in the countryside. In Brigstock before the plague, more than 300 women—about one-third of the women who lived on the manor—brewed ale for sale. In Alrewas (Staffordshire) during the 1330s and 1340s, between 52 and 76 brewers sold ale each year (in a village with about 120 households). In Wakefield (Yorkshire) between 1348 and 1350, 185 women—accounting for almost one-third of all women —brewed for sale.[13] Commercial brewing was less pervasive in towns but still common. In Oxford, about 115 brewers worked in the early fourteenth century, serving a population of perhaps 10,000. In Norwich at about the same time, about 250 brewers sold ale to about 17,000 inhabitants.[14] In short, almost every other household brewed for profit in the countryside, and about 1 household in every 15 brewed for commercial purposes in towns.

So many people brewed for profit because they did so infrequently and in small amounts. In most communities, two sorts of brewers offered ale for sale: *occasional brewers* and *by-industrial brewers*.[15] Occasional brewers sold ale infrequently, probably combining, in many cases, domestic and commercial brewing. In other words, a wife might buy malt and brew it up, planning both to supply her family with ale and to turn a quick profit on the ale her family could not consume before it soured. In Brigstock, 273 brewers sold ale on this occasional basis, and although their individual contributions to the market were negligible, their aggregate effect was considerable; occasional brewers accounted for about one-third of the ale sold on the manor. In Alrewas and Wakefield, similar patterns prevailed.[16]

Occasional brewing of this sort might have solved some critical problems in the consumption and production of ale. Since ale was basic to the diet of ordinary people, each household required a large and steady supply; a household of five people might require about 1¼ gallons a day, or about 8¾ gallons a week. Yet ale was both time consuming to produce and fast to sour, lasting for only a few days.[17] Neighbors might have reacted to these constraints by alternating production among themselves. One household might brew one week (consuming some ale, selling the rest), another the second week, a third the following week, and so on.[18] To be sure, alternating production is not documented (except in inferences to be drawn from the presence of so many occasional brewers in the presentments of aletasters), and it was certainly neither formalized nor systematic. Yet, whether occasional brewers sought to alternate production with each other or not, they were certainly able to coordinate their production with another source of supply: namely, ale purchased from those brewers who worked more often in the trade.

These by-industrial brewers sold ale to their neighbors on a more reliable basis. Many women and men in medieval and early modern England worked in by-industries, that is, productive work pursued in the home as one of many employments, not a sole occupation. Commercial brewing was a very important by-industry. In Brigstock, for example, 38 brewsters worked frequently, and they accounted for almost two-thirds of the ale sold on the manor. Yet, as a rule, even these by-industrial brewers were not *professional brewers* (a distinction that will be developed more fully in the next chapter), for they were not committed to the trade on a steady and regular basis. Although they sold ale on many occasions, they brewed irregularly or even ceased brewing for long periods of time. Consider, for example, the wife of Richard Gilbert (we do not know her forename) who worked in brewing for nearly two decades. In some years, she sold ale all the time, but in other years, she sold ale only once or twice, and for five years in the midst of her brewing career, she abandoned commercial brewing altogether. The wife of Richard Gilbert pursued brewing not as a primary occupation but instead as a by-industry, a source of intermittent and supplemental income. Although few in number, these by-industrial brewers supplied most of the ale sold in early fourteenth-century Brigstock, Alrewas, Wakefield, and other rural communities.[19] In towns, commercial brewing was also divided between occasional and by-industrial brewers. In Oxford, for example, by-industrial brewers were an important but not yet dominant element among brewers.[20]

Because no accounts of commercial brewers survive before the sixteenth century, we can guess only roughly the amount of ale produced at each brewing. The upper limits are clear: about 8 quarters of grain, or 500 gallons of ale per brewing. This is what the Clare household usually brewed on a weekly basis, and the brewers of St. Paul's (London) worked at about the same level, yielding roughly 550 gallons each week.[21] The lower limits are less clear: perhaps little more than a dozen or so gallons at each brewing. In 1281–82, Robert Sibille the younger was amerced at the court of Kibworth Harcourt (Leicestershire) for brewing 4 bushels of malt and then selling the ale at an excessive price. At a yield of 10 gallons per bushel, Sibille would have brewed about 40 gallons, and he might have drawn even more from his malt than that.[22] Denise Marlere probably brewed at a similar level. Her largest vats—whose sizes she carefully specified in her will—held 12 gallons; if she used several of these to hold different strengths from one brewing, she might have brewed, say, 3 bushels at a time, producing as much as 36 gallons of weak ale. Some brewers produced even smaller amounts. When Oxford's aletasters compiled their list for June 1324, they occasionally noted amounts brewed and sold, most commonly just a quarter of ale (or 17½ gallons).[23] Indeed, even 100 years after the Black Death, many brewers produced at most a few dozen gallons of ale at a time. In 1454, the brewers of Elton (Huntingdonshire) had to be required to brew at least 2 bushels at each brewing (for a yield of about 20 gallons).[24]

Once brewed, ale was marketed in fairly rudimentary ways. Local selling was the rule, for ale—souring quickly and enduring badly the jostling, juggling, and changes in temperature of transport by ship, horse, or cart—was a poor candidate for long-distance trade. Only Lynn boasted an extensive export trade in ale, and only in a few instances did brewers even transport their ale to nearby towns or villages.[25] Direct marketing was also the rule. Tipplers—that is, men and women who did not brew ale but merely sold it—were active in a few towns and villages, but they were not as common as later.[26] Most brewers sold their ale directly to neighbors, either in *domo* or *extra domo*, that is, either for consumption in the brewer's house or for consumption off the premises. When offering ale for sale in their homes, brewers managed rudimentary alehouses where customers could drink, talk, and enjoy themselves. Sometimes customers also argued, as Sarah de Beltinge of Wye (Kent) found in 1311 when some customers at her *taberna* fought so fiercely that blood was drawn.[27] But alehouses were not so common as they would become after the Black Death, and most brewers sold their ale for consumption elsewhere. Customers brought their own pails or pans in which they carried the ale home. In a world where many households sold ale at least occasionally, a temporary sign of some sort, usually a branch or bush, told potential customers that ale was available within.

Although it is impossible to measure the profitability of brewing with much precision, profits were quite modest before the Black Death.[28] Because the assize stipulated prices for ale based on prices of grain, the potential for profit was always limited. In theory, if grain was cheap, ale was supposed to be cheap as well. In practice, however, prices for ale tended to remain more stable than prices for grain; as a result, brewers did better when grain was cheap and worse when grain was dear. Ale prices were more stable in part because the scale set by the assize allowed grain prices to fluctuate as much as sixpence per quarter before ale prices changed, in part because aletasters and other officers set ale prices only once or twice a year (after which grain prices could continue to change), and in part because these same officers were sometimes loath to raise or lower too dramatically the price of ale.[29] These pressures could translate into small profits for brewers, especially in years of famine or dearth. In the difficult years between 1300 and 1375, when grain was often unusually costly, brewers' profits must have been correspondingly limited.[30]

Although profits were generally low, they were better in towns than in villages. The *Assisa* allowed urban brewers to sell ale at much higher prices than their counterparts in the countryside—perhaps because brewers in towns were more essential to their localities, perhaps because they faced more expenses, or perhaps because they brewed stronger drink.[31] According to the *Assisa*, if an urban brewer bought barley at 20d. or 2s. per quarter, the ale brewed from it should sell at the rate of 2 gallons for a penny. A rural brewer who bought barley at the same price had to sell 3 (or even 4) gallons of ale for a penny. If this scale had been strictly observed, an urban brewer might have taken 9d. above the cost of raw grain from a brewing, and a rural brewer might have taken about 3d.

But this scale was not strictly observed.[32] As calculated at the local level, the prices set by the *Assisa* were loosely interpreted. The guiding principle of the *Assisa*—a sliding scale based on grain prices—was readily accepted, but the scale itself was less closely maintained. Some communities began very early to set different prices for different types of ale (a possibility not considered in the *Assisa*). In Coventry in 1278, for example, when a quarter of wheat or barley sold for 3s., the price of a gallon of ale was set at 1d., ¾d., or ½d., depending on quality.[33] And other communities required brewers to sell at even lower prices than those stipulated by the *Assisa*. In 1282, when Robert Sibille the younger was presented at the court of Kibworth Harcourt for selling his ale at too high a price, the stipulated price left him little room for profit. Having paid 2s. for 4 bushels of malt and required to sell 5 gallons of ale for 2d., he would have had to draw 60 gallons from his malt just to recoup his investment. His ale, in other words, would have been very weak indeed and his profits very low.

Moreover, the scale, as set by either the *Assisa* or local proclamations of the assize, considers only two elements (cost of grain and price of ale) of the profit-

and-loss equation. Brewers had many other expenses besides the cost of grain. They had to cover wear and tear on their equipment, costs for other materials (especially fuel and herbs), labor (their own and perhaps that of servants), and perhaps rental of space for brewing. The earliest records that specify such costs are from the late sixteenth century; then, William Harrison estimated that the cost of malt accounted for only half of his expenses, with fuel (20 percent), wages (12½ percent), wear and tear (8½ percent) and hops and spices (9 percent) accounting for the rest.[34] Early fourteenth-century brewers did not have to pay for hops, and their labor and fuel costs were surely lower, but like William Harrison and his wife, they had to pay for herbs or spices, and they also had to replace or repair worn utensils. Unlike the Harrisons, commercial brewers had more potential losses, especially ale that soured before sale and customers who failed to pay their debts. And they also had to pay for practicing their trade, either in amercements levied under the assize or in customary tolls on brewing or both.

Yet brewers had many ways to stretch their trade to make a profit. They could mix barley with other, cheaper grains, especially oats. They could draw as many gallons of ale from the malt as possible, taking 10 or even more gallons from a bushel. They could cheat their customers by selling weak ale in short measures. They could charge prices higher than those set by aletasters or jurors. Despite extensive and early regulation, the ale trade was never effectively controlled, and brewers had considerable leeway in trying to take a profit from their work.[35] With all these imponderable variables, actual profits could have varied very widely.

Consider, for example, the possible profits of brewers in Oxford during the early years of the fourteenth century.[36] In the late autumn of 1310, a jury gathered to review grain prices and to set ale prices accordingly. Stating that wheat had recently sold in the Oxford market for 8s., 7s.4d., or 6s.8d. a quarter (depending on quality); barley for 5s.; and oats for 2s.8d., it set prices for good ale at 1¼d. in *cuva* and 1½d. in *doleo*. The first price was the more standard of the two.[37] What profits could a brewer have expected from buying grain at these prices and then selling ale made from it at 1¼d. the gallon? For a brewing of 3 bushels of malt, the range of possible costs (shown in the four left-hand columns of figure 2.1) and receipts (shown in the four right-hand columns) was very broad.

The first two estimates of cost assume that an Oxford brewer would have brewed malt made from equal amounts of wheat, oats, and barley.[38] Cost 1 can be taken to represent a maximum figure; it adds to the price of malt an additional 10d. to account for the expenses of fuel, herbs, equipment, and wages (an adjustment based on the costs reported by William Harrison).[39] Cost 2 represents a minimum figure; it adds to the price of malt only an estimate for the price of fuel.[40] The next two estimates of cost assume a different ratio of grains in the malt, one similar to that employed at St. Paul's: two-thirds oats and one-sixth each for barley and wheat. This assumption produces a lower cost for malt, and hence slightly lower estimates for maximum (cost 3) and minimum (cost 4) expenses. The various estimates for receipts from sales of ale in figure 2.1 reflect the different number of gallons that a brewer might have drawn from 3

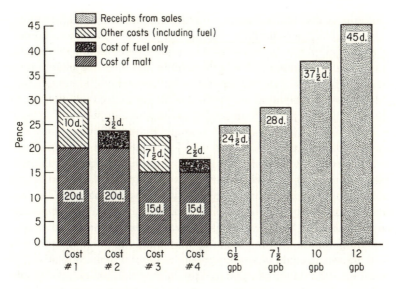

Figure 2.1   Estimates of Brewing Costs and Receipts in Oxford, 1310. Cost 1 is
based on brewing with malt containing equal amounts of wheat, oats and barley. It adds to the cost of malt an estimate for the cost of fuel, herbs, equipment, and wages. Cost 2 is based on brewing with malt containing equal
amounts of wheat, oats, and barley. It adds to the cost of malt an estimate for
the cost of fuel only. Cost 3 is based on brewing with malt containing more
oats (two-thirds) and less barley and wheat (one-sixth each). It adds to the
cost of malt an estimate for the cost of fuel, herbs, equipment, and wages. Cost
4 is based on brewing with malt containing more oats (two-thirds) and less
barley and wheat (one-sixth each). It adds to the cost of malt an estimate for
the cost of fuel only. Estimates of receipts from sales vary according to the amount
of drink drawn from a bushel of malt (gpb = gallons per bushel). Source:
Estimates based on data in H. E. Salter, ed., Mediaeval Archives of the University of
Oxford, vol. 2, Oxford Historical Society, pp. 151–152.

bushels of malt. Ale produced at a rate of 6½ gallons per bushel would have been
very strong, and 12 gallons of ale drawn from a bushel would have been very
weak. As figure 2.1 shows, these various estimates suggest that brewers either
could have made extraordinary profits or incurred extraordinary losses.

For Joan de Bedford and other brewers in Oxford in 1310, reality fell
between these two extremes. If Joan de Bedford had purchased a bushel each of
wheat, barley, and oats in the Oxford market in November 1310; if she had then
malted this grain and afterward brewed it into the "good ale" specified in the
proclamation (drawing about 7½ gallons from a bushel of her malt); and if she
had then sold it at the set price of 1¼d., she would have taken about 2s.8d. for
her pains, of which the grain would have cost her 1s.10½d. and fuel at least
3½d. more. In other words, Joan de Bedford would have taken 5d. over costs
for grain and fuel from her brewing; her other expenses would have lowered
this profit to just a few pennies. Of course, Joan de Bedford and her fellow brewers were not wholly at the mercy of the prices set by Oxford's jurors; she could

and did charge excessive prices. In so doing, she increased her retail profits by 6½d. per brewing, but she also raised her expenses by incurring each time an amercement of 3d.[41] In other words, the jurors might have allowed her a profit of a few pennies, and she took a few pennies more.[42] In a time when unskilled men earned no more than 1½d. per day and women could hope to earn ¾d. or 1d, this sort of profit was not negligible.[43] But to earn these small rewards, Joan de Bedford had to invest a great deal, to work hard over several days, and to gamble that in the narrow gap between the prices set by juries and the amercements levied by aletasters, she could win a few pennies from her trade.[44]

These few pennies were more than Joan de Bedford might have gained from working as a servant or unskilled laborer, but they fell below the sort of profits offered by more "skilled" work.[45] Skilled wage workers (almost all of whom were male) took 3d. a day or more for their labor, and artisans or merchants who worked out of their own shops did even better. Indeed, by any index of occupational status, brewing seems to have been an undistinguished trade. Skilled workers in medieval towns signified their status in many clear and public ways—the formation of a gild to organize the trade, the entry of people in the trade to the freedom (or franchise) of a town, or the presence among urban officers of men practicing the trade. In Joan de Bedford's time, brewing rarely merited such distinctions. In early fourteenth-century towns such as Oxford, Norwich, and London, wealth, prestige, and power came from dealing in wool, cloth, spices, or wine, not ale. In the countryside, where the trade in ale was more widespread and even less profitable, it was—as Christopher Dyer, comparing the medieval countryside to the modern third world, has noted—only "widespread poverty" that drove people into such low-profit activities as brewing.[46]

In the early fourteenth century, then, commercial brewing was a widely practiced and relatively unspecialized trade. Vast amounts of ale were produced and consumed, but production was ubiquitous, small scale, intermittent, and irregular. L. F. Salzman included brewing in his now classic survey of medieval industry, but if he had focused only on the trade before 1350, he probably would not have done so. Before the Black Death, commercial brewing was a marginally profitable trade that attracted little investment, little technological innovation, and little entrepreneurial interest.[47]

The Sexual Division of Labor in Brewing, c. 1300

This marginal trade attracted so few men that in the early fourteenth century, women dominated brewing. This is not to say that men were uninvolved in the trade, for they certainly did brew and sell ale. But few men brewed on their own, and most men, if active in brewing, worked alongside women. Before the Black Death, most of the brewing done in England—for domestic or commercial use—was done by women.

Today, when people are trained, employed, and recompensed as individuals, it is fairly easy to measure the number of women and men in a particular trade or profession. But such measurements are not so easy for the middle ages, when work was much less individualized. Most production and sale of goods—

cloth, shoes, clothing, foodstuffs, and other commodities—took place within the household, not in separate workplaces or shops. A trade was particularly associated with the head of household, but all the members of the household (husband, wife, children, servants) contributed to some extent. They did not share all tasks or work the same hours, and some were better trained or more committed to the trade than others. But as a rule, all helped when and as needed. To make matters even murkier, most households supported so many economic activities, by-industries as well as primary occupations, that they were "multi-occupational family unit[s]."[48] By-industries, of which brewing was perhaps the most popular, could also call on the labor of all members of a household. And the murkiness is made even more complete by the absence of the sort of records—diaries, account books, memoirs—that might provide details about how husbands and wives distributed their labor (and that of their children and servants) among the various employments of their households.

How, then, can we say so confidently that women dominated commercial brewing before the plague? Certainly, women probably called on the assistance of their families when they brewed ale. Husbands, children, and servants might have provided many brewsters with crucial help in purchasing supplies, fetching water, collecting wood for fuel, tending the fire and the wort, advising about taste and herbs, attracting customers, and even measuring ale and taking money. But the task of managing all these and other aspects of commercial brewing seems to have fallen on the shoulders of women. We have no private records that tell us this, but we can be certain of it because women were the people most often identified in public records—both in early legislation and in presentments under the assize—with the brewing trade.

Many early regulations and reports treat brewers as an exclusively female group—in other words, as brewsters only. In one version of the early twelfth-century customs of Newcastle, for example, the term *femina* described any brewer or baker; in a 1286 charter for Bakewell (Derby), the feminine term *pandoxatrix* signified any aleseller; and the Domesday entry for Hereford implied that brewing was done only by wives (*cuiuscumque uxor braziabat*).[49] Even in London, regulations and proclamations sometimes treated all brewers as female.[50] These were not merely local phenomena, for the thirteenth-century quasi statutes that regulated the ale trade also referred on several occasions to brewers as exclusively female.[51] To be sure, early references to brewers do not always treat brewers as female, and many laws and regulations refer to brewers in terms that either are neutral or explicitly include both sexes. Yet given the capacity of medieval Latin to refer to both sexes through such terms as *pandoxator* or *braciator*, the efforts of some clerks to feminize references to brewers are particularly striking. They suggest that in the fourteenth century and earlier, the trade was not merely *predominantly* female but indeed *exclusively* female.

Presentments under the assize of ale provide further confirmation that most brewers before the Black Death were women. On many manors, only women were accused of breaking the provisions of the assize. In Crowle (Lincolnshire) and Wye not even one man faced amercement as a brewer in the early four-teenth-century rolls sampled; in Brigstock, Ingatestone (Essex), Scalby (Yorkshire), Sutton (Cambridgeshire), and Wakefield, only a handful of men appeared among many, many women. Most were husbands of brewsters, cited once or twice for reasons that are unclear—perhaps the clerk wrote too hastily or perhaps the wife was temporarily unavailable. To be sure, on other manors, men predominated among those presented for infractions of the assize in the early fourteenth century. But as explained in the appendix, these presentments are often deceptive, citing husbands for their wives' brewing. In any case, what matters for the issue at hand is that on *some* manors there can be no doubt that brewing was exclusively women's work.

Both of these findings—that is, exclusively feminine language in some early regulations about brewing and exclusively female offenders in some early presentments of brewers—require the conclusion that although all members of a household might have helped in brewing, women took primary responsibility for it. This conclusion is verified by another trend in assize presentments: the virtual absence of unmarried males. In many villages and towns, singlewomen and widows brewed at least occasionally, and they sometimes produced a sizable proportion of the ale marketed in their communities. But bachelors seem either never to have brewed or to have done so very rarely. In only one instance —Richard Smith's analysis of late thirteenth-century Redgrave (Suffolk) and Rickinghall (Suffolk)—have large numbers of brewers been identified as never-married males. Yet Smith's method of identifying bachelors is problematic, and in any case, the men he identified as bachelors accumulated less than 4 percent of assize amercements.[52] Similarly, widowers seldom brewed; with few exceptions, a household's brewing ceased with the death of its wife. In Brigstock, only three men seemed to have continued the trade after the deaths of their wives, and in all three cases, they ceased brewing rather quickly.[53]

Some men did brew for profit before the Black Death, and some even took up brewing as their primary occupation. But their numbers were so few that in most towns, no freemen (that is, men admitted to the "freedom," or franchise, of a town) or only a very few identified themselves as brewers. In 1336–37, Alan de Munkton entered the freedom of York, stating that he was a brewer. Clearly, he brewed for his living, and perhaps he, like some other male brewers in late medieval York, worked in York's religious establishments.[54] In any case, of the thousands of men who entered York's freedom before the Black Death, Alan de Munkton was the only self-identified brewer, and he had few counterparts in other towns.[55] After the Black Death, more and more men would enter the freedom of York (and other cities), claiming brewing as their occupation. Seven male brewers entered York between 1350 and 1399, and dozens more entered in the fifteenth century. But the early fourteenth century was, with few exceptions, a time when women brewed.

Prosopography of Brewers, c. 1300

In the late thirteenth and early fourteenth centuries, the ale trade provided the households of both occasional brewers and by-industrial brewers with a critical source of supplementary income. Brewing was not highly profitable, but it

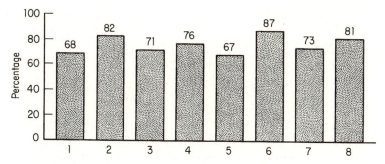

Figure 2.2   Percentage of Ale Sales by Married Brewsters on Selected Early Fourteenth-Century Manors. 1, Alciston (East Sussex), c. 1325; 2, Chedzoy (Somerset), 1329–49; 3, Cranborne (Dorset), c. 1330; 4, Norton Canon (Herefordshire), c. 1330; 5, Preston-on-Wye (Herefordshire), c. 1320; 6, Stockton (Wiltshire), 1306–44; 7, Sutton (Cambridgeshire), c. 1320; 8, Wakefield (Yorkshire), c. 1325. *Source:* See the appendix for information about the data collected for each of these communities.

was an accessible way to add modestly to household income. As we have seen, many households—indeed, in some villages, most households—profited from brewing at least occasionally. And although fewer households seem to have sold ale in towns than in villages, the ale trade was by no means confined to only a handful of urban families. In towns, as in the countryside, many people profited from brewing. As a result, brewers came from a wide variety of circumstances—poor and rich, itinerants and long-time residents, young and middle-aged and old, married women and singlewomen and widows. The typical brewster was anywoman. Nevertheless, certain broad characteristics do distinguish brewsters, particularly by-industrial brewsters, from other women in their communities.

First, most brewsters, like most adult women, were married. As figure 2.2 shows, proportions of married and not-married brewsters in the countryside varied widely, but married women accounted for the vast majority of brewsters. Singlewomen brewed in many villages, but they brewed very occasionally—only once or twice.[56] Widows also brewed for profit but seldom frequently. It seems, indeed, that even women who actively brewed while married often left the trade shortly after their husbands died (perhaps because of age or because they missed their husbands' assistance).[57]

Married brewsters also predominated in towns. The earliest extant list of brewers' amercements—an estreat roll from Wallingford in 1228–29—reports that about 80 percent of brewers were married women. This figure also prevailed somewhat later in Leicester, Norwich, and (as figure 2.3 illustrates) Oxford. Even in smaller towns, married women were still very prominent; in early fourteenth-century Tamworth, for example, they accounted for about two-thirds of brewsters.[58]

Given our lack of firm demographic data for pre-plague villages and towns, it is impossible to put these figures into a clear comparative context. We do not

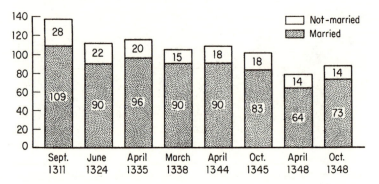

Figure 2.3   Married and Not-Married Brewsters in Oxford, 1311–1348.
Data from Oxford Assizes. Two extant lists (for September 1339 and
September 1340) were excluded because their data are incomplete. For
methods used to identify not-married women, see the appendix.

know how many women never married in early fourteenth-century England, and
although we know that the population included many widows (in Brigstock, for
example, they accounted for 12 percent of all women), we cannot reach a firm
estimate of proportions of married and not-married women in the population.
This is an "exasperating obstacle," and until better demographic data are available, it seems best to assume that the presence of married women and not-married women in the ale market roughly paralleled their presence in the general
population.[59] Most brewsters were married, but so too were most adult women.

In this light, it is important to recognize that although single and widowed
brewsters were in the minority and although they often brewed with less frequency than married brewsters, brewing nevertheless offered them an important resource. From the perspective of the aggregate ale trade in Brigstock, the
one time that the singlewoman Isabella Huet offered ale for sale might seem
insignificant. But from the perspective of Isabella Huet, that single instance of
commercial brewing might have loomed very large indeed.[60] Often living on
the very margins of subsistence, singlewomen and widows turned to commercial brewing—as they turned to gleaning or wage labor or spinning or prostitution or a host of other occasional activities—to patch together a living. As we
shall see in the next chapter, not-married women were able to include commercial brewing in their economic strategies less and less frequently after 1350.
So, although they seldom distinguished themselves as commercial brewsters
before the Black Death, singlewomen and widows then enjoyed an access to the
trade that their counterparts in later times would increasingly lack.

Most brewsters, then, were married. Most did not, however, brew throughout their married lives. The career patterns of by-industrial brewsters (our second characteristic) varied widely, reflecting the particular circumstances of each
individual brewster. Indeed, these varied careers suggest that neither reproductive duties nor family needs determined a woman's decision to seek income from
brewing. One might expect that women took up brewing when their repro-

ductive work waned, when—after many years of marriage—they were pregnant less often and caring for fewer small children. This seems not to have been the case, at least not invariably. One might also expect that women took up brewing whenever family needs demanded that they undertake such work, especially perhaps when a household full of children required more income. This seems also not to have been the invariable case.[61]

In the lives of individual women, these two expectations could, of course, collide; a woman with many small children might be distracted from brewing by their care but also need to take up brewing for their support. For such a woman, both considerations were important, but neither determined her response. Indeed, as she considered whether to brew or not, she probably had to think about much more than just her reproductive duties and her family's needs. First, she had to consider the labor resources of her household. A middle-aged wife with children old enough to assist her in small chores might reasonably undertake commercial brewing; a young wife with infant children or an elderly wife too frail for arduous work might reasonably forgo brewing. Similarly, a wife whose husband needed her regular assistance in his craft or other work might not brew, whereas other wives found brewing to be easily accommodated to the labor that their husbands required from them. Second, she had to consider alternative sources of income. Women had many ways to respond to the changing needs of their families—wage work, market gardening, other food trades, field labor, and the like. A wife to whom such alternative employments were available might have eschewed commercial brewing altogether.

In turning to commercial brewing, then, a married woman considered many possibilities. Did she have sufficient time after helping her husband and doing other chores? Could she get sufficient assistance from her husband or children or servants? Could she bring income into her household through other means? Women answered these questions in many different ways, and as a result, brewing patterns for married women—even those who brewed frequently enough to be considered by-industrial brewsters—varied widely in timing and consistency. Some women, like the wife of John Aldewyn of Havering (Essex), brewed for profit during their early married years, ceased brewing during middle age, and resumed brewing toward the end of life.[62] Other women did just the opposite, brewing most frequently during the middle years of marriage. Agnes the wife of Walter Tracy of Brigstock, for example, only began to brew frequently after she had been married for more than a decade, then brewed fairly intensely for several years, and then ceased serious work in the trade.[63] Still other women followed no discernible pattern at all. The wife of Hugh Brum of Brigstock, for example, brewed infrequently for many years with only a few interspersed years of intense activity.[64] Few women, to be sure, first began to brew late in life, but many started brewing as young wives and brewed thereafter according to household need and ability.

Perhaps the most common pattern was to limit commercial brewing both early and late, brewing for profit most often during the middle years of married life. Among the by-industrial brewsters whose histories can be reconstructed in Brigstock, most were married for about six years before they began to brew for

Table 2.1   Landholding by Brewers in Stockton, c. 1350

Amount of land held in rental	Number of households in rental	Number of times each household brewed
Virgate	3	15, 15, 16
Semi-virgate	16	0, 0, 0, 0, 1, 4, 6, 7, 7, 8, 8, 10, 11, 12, 17, 18
Smallholding/croft	5	1, 3, 5, 19, 24
Cottage	5	0, 1, 1, 3, 4

Source: BL, Add. Ch. 24394 (rental), and manorial rolls for Stockton (as detailed in the appendix).

profit, and most lived for about eight or nine years after they gave up the trade.[65] Another intriguing pattern, found by Maryanne Kowaleski in late fourteenth-century Exeter, has linked commercial brewing by wives to their husbands' trades. In Exeter, women were most likely to brew for profit when their husbands did not require their assistance. Because merchants, professionals, and men in the metal trades seem to have required less day-to-day help from women, their wives were more likely to brew than other women.[66] Kowaleski's findings suggest that the economic structures of brewsters' households might have shaped their careers more strongly than either their reproductive work or the general needs of their families.

A similar variation characterizes our third characteristic, the social status of brewsters within their communities. Zvi Razi has suggested, on the basis of his study of Halesowen (Warwickshire), that brewsters usually came from the most privileged households in their villages.[67] Richard Smith has argued the opposite, showing that most brewsters in Redgrave and Rickinghall came from the lowest echelons of rural society.[68] Most studies describe something between these two extremes, suggesting that commercial brewing was so widely practiced that it involved households from many different socioeconomic strata. As has been observed for manors in Huntingdonshire, southeast Durham, Staffordshire, and Devon, privileged brewers often dominated the ale market, but brewers of less distinguished status were nevertheless often involved in the trade.[69] As table 2.1 shows, much the same was the case for Stockton in the middle of the fourteenth century.

Indeed, even the seemingly contradictory data of Razi and Smith fit well into this pattern of dispersed involvement in brewing. Although Smith emphasizes "tendencies toward landlessness" among brewers, he also shows that brewing among those more privileged was both frequent and significant. Razi claims that "the ale industry in Halesowen was concentrated in the hands of rich villagers," but his own data show that some very marginal villagers were active in the trade. For example, Millicent King bore two bastard children and possessed only a cottage and garden, but for more than three decades (from 1317 to 1349) she brewed and sold ale on an exceptionally regular basis, suffering presentment

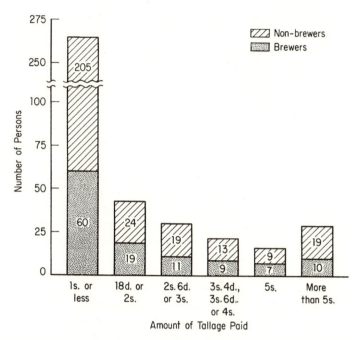

Figure 2.4   Brewers and Non-Brewers in the Leicester Tallage of 1286.
Source: Leicestershire Record Office, BR III/7/2 (cannemol list for
1287–88; in Leicester, the traditional toll on ale was known as the
cannemol) and BR III/4/27 (tallage for 1286). The transcription of the
second of these rolls in Mary Bateson, ed., *Records of the borough of Leicester*,
vol. 1, 1103–1327 (London, 1899), pp. 208–212, includes some errors
that have been corrected here. This analysis excludes 39 persons who
were assessed particularly heavily because of their involvement in the
trespass that occasioned the tallage. In most cases, brewers were linked
to tallage payers by coincidence of ward, as well as name. I thank
David Postles for suggesting that I compare these two records and
C.W. Harrison for helping me to replicate quickly my lost notes on
these documents.

for commercial brewing on at least 10 occasions each year. In Redgrave, Rickinghall, and Halesowen, as in other English rural communities, brewing was
widely dispersed across the social strata of rural England. Neither the very
wealthy nor the very poor were likely to be especially active in brewing, but
for a vast range of middling families, brewing was an accessible and frequently
used resource.[70]

Similar patterns prevailed in towns. In Leicester, 116 brewers were numbered among the payers of a tallage (or tax) in 1286. As figure 2.4 shows, they
paid roughly the same sums as their non-brewing neighbors, showing that commercial brewing in Leicester occupied poor, moderate, and wealthy households.
The average payment for brewers (2s. 1d.) was quite close to the overall average

(1s. 9d.). Similarly detailed information is not available for other towns, but it is quite clear that urban brewers elsewhere were neither particularly wealthy nor particularly poor. In York, of the 70 brewing households named in a 1304 survey, 45 lived in the city without (as far as we know) enjoying the perquisites of citizenship (a figure suggesting that many brewers were quite humble), but 18 acquired civic office (suggesting that other brewers achieved considerable civic prominence). In other towns, brewers were perhaps more marginal. In Oxford, only one early fourteenth-century bailiff was associated with the trade. In London, one late thirteenth-century ordinance suggests that brewers—particularly in fact, brewsters—were regarded as troublesome riffraff. Perhaps the more competitive economies of Oxford and London placed brewers at a disadvantage. In early fourteenth-century Oxford, for example, clothiers and merchants so dominated economic and political life that victualers, including brewers, could not compete with them. In towns where the victualing trades were more important, such as St. Ives with its annual fair, brewsters and their husbands were a more distinguished and powerful lot.[71]

Finally, many brewers were long-time residents of their towns and villages, but others were more mobile. In many communities, large numbers of brewers were transients, persons who cannot be identified with any of the permanent households in the area or who quickly disappear from any local records. Indeed, some fourteenth-century communities seem to have been visited by itinerant brewsters, who would arrive, brew briefly while residing in a local household (probably using the equipment of that household), and then depart. In Norwich, for example, the presentments of 1288–89 included two transient women (Margery *quae manet* in the home of Bartholomew de Chuham, and Basilla *manente* in the home of Gilbert le Taylor) who, as far as we know, never again brewed for profit in the town. The particular prominence of itinerant brewsters in some places—St. Ives during fair time and Redgrave during its market—reflected these unusually expanded opportunities for sales.[72]

Yet, despite the significant involvement of transient or quasi-transient persons in brewing, the trade was usually dominated by persons from more settled families. In Brigstock, over one-third of the village's by-industrial brewsters were new immigrants or soon-to-be emigrants, but almost two-thirds came from settled households. Brewsters from these settled households usually worked with much greater frequency than women from more transient families.[73] In short, the trade was certainly not closed to newcomers, but it was dominated by known, familiar faces.

Brewing, then, was such a ubiquitous trade that the circumstances of brewsters varied widely. We can say that by-industrial brewsters tended to be married, that they tended to brew during the middle years of married life, that they came usually from households of middling socioeconomic status, and that they were often long-time residents of their communities. Such a profile fits 20 of the 38 by-industrial brewsters in Brigstock, and these 20 women accounted for 34 percent of the ale sold in that community before the plague. They were women such as Alice the wife of John Pikerel who married by 1336, began brewing in 1340, and sold ale on a frequent basis for the next eight years.[74]

But this profile fits only a minority of brewsters in Brigstock and elsewhere. The 18 other by-industrial brewsters of Brigstock, accounting for 27 percent of local ale sales, led very different lives. They included women such as Margery the wife of Richard Mabli (whose family seems to have recently arrived in Brigstock), or Agnes the wife of Walter Tracy (whose family was very marginal in the village), or Sarra Soule (a singlewoman who brewed for nine years).[75] And, of course, a large number of women brewed merely occasionally, women from varied backgrounds and experiences who, nevertheless, contributed significantly to their local markets. In Brigstock, 273 such women accounted for 38 percent of the trade. They were women such as the singlewomen Isabella Huet and Alice Carpenter or the wives Alice Somenur and Alice Pikerel or the widows Edith Aylward and Edith Cocus.[76] For rural and urban women in the fourteenth century, brewing was a widespread skill and resource; some women were more likely than others to seek steady income from the trade, but the trade was not restricted in any sense to women of particular circumstances.

A Good Trade . . . for a Woman

In Western history, employments labeled as "women's work" have shared certain enduring characteristics across the centuries: low skill, poorly remunerated, and low status.[77] When women brewed in the early fourteenth century, brewing was such an employment. Making good ale certainly required skill, but because the skill was taught both informally and widely, brewing was neither an art nor a mystery. We might respect the brewsters of a village who could carefully prepare the malt, tend the wort, and spice the ale, but they excelled at work in which virtually all women were competent. Skilled they were, but they were not valued as skilled workers. Brewsters also made only modest profits from their work. Always restricted by regulation and amercement, profits were particularly limited in the early fourteenth century, when grain prices were high. And as a by-industry, commercial brewing lacked occupational dignity. Only a handful of people called themselves brewers in early fourteenth-century towns, and they had no gilds or other means of fostering occupational status and identity. Vast amounts of ale were produced and sold in England in the early fourteenth century, but the trade was so widely dispersed that it was, as we have seen, scarcely an industry. Nevertheless, brewing was—*by the low standards of women's work*—good work indeed.

First, it was work that could, in at least some instances, expand into larger and more profitable enterprises. Most brewsters sold ale just in their immediate neighborhoods, but a few supplied larger markets. Some brewsters sold to their manorial lords and ladies (as did the brewsters of Wistow in Huntingdonshire), others sold to their city governments (as did Richard Marsh's wife in Southampton), others benefited from sales to royal servants or officers (as did Agnes Shupton of York), and still others provided ale for the king's household.[78] In some cases, these brewsters produced and sold very large quantities of ale. Maud Elias of Hull, for example, sold 100 gallons of ale worth 6s.3d. to Edward I's household in 1301–1302. Only one other brewer in the town sold more.[79]

Brewsters' best opportunities for large sales came from two discrete sources: aristocratic households and markets or fairs. Elite households, often "actively hostile to the presence of women," seldom supported permanent live-in brewsters; instead, they patronized local women who steadily supplied their needs.[80] As a result, they could buy hundreds, if not thousands, of gallons from such local brewsters as Maud Elias. In the early fifteenth century, for example, the household of Richard Mitford, bishop of Salisbury, purchased about 125–150 gallons of ale *every week* from Alice Shepherd of Potterne.[81] Fairs and markets also expanded, albeit temporarily, the markets of brewers. In St. Ives, some brewsters seem to have worked only during fair time, but most of the profits of the fair went to the established brewsters on Bridge Street, who, it seems, simply expanded their operations to accommodate more customers.[82]

Second, commercial brewing both suited the needs of wives and enhanced their standing. For many wives, brewing for sale was one of many elements in an "economy of makeshifts." In medieval households, primary tasks were usually allotted to husbands and supplementary work to wives. A wife undertook a myriad of ancillary responsibilities: she supported her husband when his work required it (helping in the fields, at the workbench, or in the shop); she took primary responsibility for reproductive labor (both biological and social reproduction); and she pursued a variety of small, income-producing activities. These last employments might have been intermittent and unpredictable, but they were absolutely essential. The extra income that women brought home — whether selling miscellaneous home-produced goods, hawking the merchandise of others, working for wages, or even begging — probably often made the difference for their families between starvation and survival.[83] Brewing ale for sale (even occasionally, even unpredictably, even in small amounts) probably made this sort of difference in the lives of many families. Even occasional brewsters who worked in the trade on an infrequent and sporadic basis could hope thereby to provide a critical resource for their families.

Indeed, the medieval ale industry — a small-scale, low-investment, low-profit, low-skilled industry — suited especially well the economic needs of married women. Because ale soured quickly and transported poorly, it was unsuitable for large-scale, centralized businesses. As a result, wives who sought to sell ale on a modest and ad hoc basis could compete effectively in the trade. Because ale production involved widely known female skills, tools available in most households, and intermittent attention over long periods, it appealed to wives and mothers who sought inexpensive, quick, and flexible ways of supplementing their family economies. And because brewing for sale did not require long-term commitments of money or training, it suited wives who sought to juggle their productive work with other responsibilities. This is not to say that medieval wives "chose" brewing because they preferred work that was perceived as low skilled and low status and that yielded small profits. It is to say that given the ways in which married women were expected to accommodate their working lives to other demands, the medieval ale industry suited their circumstances.[84]

Moreover, although a brewster profited from a trade that had little public recognition in terms of skill or status, she probably accrued recognition for her work in ways that remain unrecorded in the dry archives of medieval manors and towns. She negotiated with grain suppliers, maltsters, waterbearers, servants, and of course her customers; she talked with local or civic officers about the quality, prices, and measures of her ale; she managed a complex business that involved both production and sales; and she brought income into her household. She might not have been recognized as a worker as skilled as a rural plowman or an urban gildsman, but she was probably recognized as a skilled housewife and a good provider for her family. Margery Kempe seems to have understood this when she took up commercial brewing—which she described as a task of "housewifery"—in order to maintain her social standing in Lynn.[85] She failed at brewing, but others were more skilled, more careful, or more lucky, and when they succeeded, they helped their families in notable ways. In Iver (Buckinghamshire), for example, men whose wives brewed were twice as likely as other men to hold local office. When such tangible rewards came from brewing, a married brewster could be well satisfied and well recognized. Thanks to her work, her family was better off.[86]

Needless to say, the status that a woman derived from brewing was limited in critical ways. Husbands had final control over the economic activities of their wives, including commercial brewing. As a result, husbands could tell their wives when, how, and to whom to sell ale, and they could also take the profits from brewing to use as they liked.[87] Moreover, the authority that women derived from brewing could be greeted with ambivalence and hostility as well as approval. As we shall see in chapter 7, many people felt anxious about the seemingly excessive power of brewsters. Because brewsters were noted for their cleverness in profiting from the trade, their ability to trick officers and customers, and their power to control infatuated or drunken men, they were sometimes seen as particularly disorderly and disobedient women. Both of these caveats—the authority of husbands over the work of their wives and the ambivalence with which many people viewed the success of brewsters—are important, but they do not belie the critical ways in which a woman might, within the constraints of her situation, profit both economically and socially from the brewing trade.

Third, commercial brewing contrasted favorably with women's other economic options. Compared to the trades of men, commercial brewing was perceived as low skilled and low in status, and it was poorly remunerated. But it offered more than most occupations open to women. Indeed, compared to other working women, brewsters stand out as particularly prosperous. In York, for example, among the elite group of women who achieved the freedom of York, brewsters were especially prominent.[88] Similarly, the poll taxes, although reflecting the post-plague circumstances of brewers, also show that brewing was, for women, an exceptionally good option. In these levies, not-married brewsters often paid higher taxes than other not-married women. In Howden in 1379, most not-married women paid the 4d. minimum, but brewsters usually paid 6d. or even 12d. In Oxford in 1381, most not-married women also paid the 4d. minimum, but brewsters paid from 3s. to 10s.[89]

Commercial brewing was more than unusually profitable work for a woman; it also seems to have opened up some exceptional public roles to women, especially in terms of legal capability. As a general rule, women could not serve as compurgators (that is, people who vouched in court for others), but in some borough courts, this rule was mitigated for brewsters, who were allowed to bring other women to swear on their behalf. In at least one town, Bury St. Edmunds, a brewster was permitted the unusual privilege of proving her innocence by swearing by her sole hand, without any compurgators whatsoever.[90] As another general rule, women did not hold public office, but in a few instances, female aletasters supervised the brewing trade.[91] These aberrations represent only very thin wedges for women into the legal and political lives of their communities, and they affected few women directly. They do suggest, however, that the brewing expertise of women was recognized and appreciated by their communities.

To a woman such as Denise Marlere, then, commercial brewing might have been limited in important ways, but it also offered significant opportunities. Denise Marlere was not recognized as a brewster in the public way that her husband was identified as a butcher.[92] She did not belong, as her husband did, to the gild merchant of Bridgwater. She never served, as her husband did, as a juror for the town. She worked in a trade that was less formal, less organized, and less professionalized than her husband's trade. Nevertheless, brewing was an important resource for their household. As a wife, she supplemented her husband's work with income from brewing and selling ale. As a widow, she continued to support herself and her dependents through the ale trade. And as a mother, she left to her daughter some of her most essential brewing tools. For Denise Marlere, as for many women in the time when women brewed, the ale trade at least partly supported herself, her husband, and her family. It was a good trade . . . for a woman.

CHAPTER THREE

NEW MARKETS,
LOST OPPORTUNITIES

Singlewomen and Widows as Harbingers of Change

In the market town of Howden in 1379, 9 not-married women—single-women, widows, and perhaps even some wives who, for whatever reasons, lived apart from their husbands—supported themselves in commercial brewing. One bachelor brewed for profit, and 11 married women also worked in the trade, but not-married brewsters accounted for nearly half of the commercial brewers in the town.[1] If you had wanted to buy ale in late fourteenth-century Howden, you might have purchased it from a married brewster or her husband, but you were just as likely to have bought ale from a singlewoman or widow who managed her own business.

Other not-married women in Howden might have envied the single-women, widows, and other female heads of household who were able to set themselves up in brewing. The vast majority of not-married women in the town worked in dependent and unskilled positions, as servants or general laborers. Among the poorest inhabitants, they usually paid the minimum 4d. in the poll tax of that year. Not-married women who brewed for profit were better off. They often lived independently, they pursued a relatively more skilled occupation, and they enjoyed a higher standard of living (paying usually 6d. or 12d. to the tax collectors of 1379). Although single and widowed brewsters were not as well off as many bachelors or married couples, they had good reason—if they compared themselves to other not-married women—to be satisfied with their lot in life.[2]

But other people in Howden might have pitied the not-married brewsters of their town. Compared to other brewers, they were not very prosperous. Single and widowed brewsters paid lower taxes than other brewers, indicating their lower status and lesser wealth. They also plied their trade with less help; only one not-married woman had a servant to assist her in brewing, but almost all married brewsters employed servants, as did the one bachelor in the trade.

And at least one not-married brewster in Howden probably did not live independently but instead resided in the household of her father. Of the establishments where you might have purchased ale in late fourteenth-century Howden, the houses of not-married women would have been the poorest and most humble.[3]

Perhaps enviable by the standards of other not-married women and perhaps pitiable by the standards of many of their married neighbors, the not-married brewsters of Howden exemplify the ambivalent experiences of all brewsters, whatever their marital status, in medieval England. For singlewomen, wives, and widows, as well as for deserted or deserting wives, single mothers, concubines, and other women, commercial brewing was a good option at a time when women rarely pursued high-status, high-skilled, and well-remunerated employment. This is what we saw in chapter 2. But within brewing, all women were not the same. A married brewster in Howden more often than not worked with her husband in the trade, enjoyed the assistance of a servant or two, and lived in a comfortable household. A not-married brewster more often than not worked alone in the trade, without the help of husband or servants or even children, and she probably lived in relative poverty.

These differences were critical not only in the work experiences of married and not-married brewsters but also in their ability to survive in the business. Over the course of the late fourteenth, fifteenth, and in some places sixteenth centuries, single and widowed brewsters slowly disappeared from the trade. Almost always a minority among the women who had profited from brewing before 1348, not-married women brewed less and less frequently in the centuries thereafter. By the sixteenth century, the only not-married women who brewed for profit in many places were widows of brewers who, in a time-honored tradition found in many crafts and gilds, carried on the businesses of their husbands. Their circumstances differed significantly from those of widows who, like Denise Marlere, had brewed in earlier centuries. Other not-married women still worked in the brewing trade in the sixteenth century, but they usually worked as tapsters who sold ale and as servants who worked in brewhouses, not as independent brewers.

Not-married brewsters were among the first women to leave commercial brewing, but they were not the last. The forces that eased singlewomen and widows out of brewing in the later middle ages eventually affected *all* women. Once not-married women could no longer set themselves up in brewing, a married brewster working independently of her husband had trouble doing the same, and a married brewster who worked in the trade together with her husband accrued less public recognition for her work. The fate of not-married women in brewing, then, both differentiates them from married women and prefigures the eventual destinies of all brewsters, whether married or not. As they left commercial brewing in the later middle ages, not-married women reacted more quickly than married women to the changing circumstances of the trade, but they followed a path that married women would also soon tread. In the broadest sense, the creation of this path is the subject of *all* the chapters in this book, but here we shall focus on the expanding commercial circumstances that over

the course of the late fourteenth, fifteenth, and sixteenth centuries created contracting opportunities for single and widowed brewsters.

Not-married Brewsters before the Late Fourteenth Century

As we have seen, even before the Black Death, not-married women tended to
brew less frequently than married women, and single and widowed brewsters
were more numerous in the countryside, where commercial brewing was more
widely dispersed, than in towns. After the Black Death, not-married brewsters
in some villages and towns faced new circumstances right away, but through most
of the fourteenth century, they retained a strong place in the trade. Who were
these not-married women and what sort of living were they able to get from
commercial brewing? Their marital status is rarely stated. We can infer that they
were not married from the nature of the listings in which they appear, but only
a few were explicitly identified as either unmarried daughters or widows.[4] It is
tempting to imagine from these few explicit identifications that not-married
brewsters were either young women supporting themselves before marriage or
old women supporting themselves in widowhood. Yet, although many young
maidens and old widows turned to commercial brewing for occasional support,
so did many other sorts of not-married women: lifelong singlewomen, young
widows with children, single mothers, deserted or deserting wives, concubines
of clerics or other men, even prostitutes. For example, in Norwich in 1288–89,
the 46 not-married brewsters in the town included 31 women identified by name
alone (such as Maud de Catton), 9 women identified as widows (such as Agnes
widow of Stephen de Aunston), 1 servant (*ancilla quae fuit serviens* William de
Welles), 2 lodgers (Margery *quae manet* in the home of Bartholomew de Chuham
and Basilla *manente* in the home of Gilbert le Taylor), 2 concubines of clerics (Alice
amica parsonis de Louthorp' and Alice *amica decani*), and 1 women who probably supported herself through prostitution, as well as brewing (her fine was excused *pro
amicitia carnali*).[5] We would like to know much more about the domestic circumstances of Maud de Catton and the other 30 women who, like her, were identified by name alone, but what we know of other not-married brewsters in her
town suggests that they had many life stories and circumstances.

This variety among not-married women might seem strange, but it sprang
directly from the circumstances of late medieval life. First, it was facilitated by
customs of marriage. Because people married relatively late, young women
often had to support themselves between childhood and marriage. Because all
people did not marry, some women supported themselves throughout their
lives, living alone or in association with other women. And because rules of sexual conduct and marriage were often ignored and overlooked, some women
lived with men as their concubines or common-law wives, and other women
lived apart from the men with whom they had once either been married or
borne children or both. Second, the various life circumstances of not-married
women were also facilitated by the high mortality of the age, a harsh fact that
left widows of all sorts—childless, with young children, with grown children;
young, middle-aged, old; rich, comfortable, poor—either to fend for them-

selves or to find new husbands. And third, the many different experiences of not-married women reflect also the housing arrangements of medieval communities, arrangements that could accommodate not-married women in many different ways. Some not-married women lived as servants or lodgers in the houses of others and some lived in their parental homes, but many others resided by themselves, with children and other relatives, or with other not-married women.[6]

Given their multifarious stories and circumstances, not-married women used commercial brewing in multifarious ways. A prostitute who sold ale on the side ran a very different business from a widow who sought to support herself and her children by selling ale in her neighborhood or from a daughter who hoped to build a nest egg through commercial brewing. Although most not-married women brewed only occasionally, some did work in the trade more consistently. For example, Emma Kempstere of Brigstock began brewing sporadically as a young woman in the second decade of the fourteenth century, and she turned to brewing more frequently as the years passed. As far as we know, she never married, but she became a regular supplier of ale to her neighbors in the 1330s and 1340s. Most by-industrial brewsters in Brigstock during these decades were married, but Emma Kempstere was able to hold her own in the ale market for a very long time indeed. In 1348, just before the plague arrived in the village (after which the extant records lapse), she was still selling ale to her neighbors on a very regular basis.[7] As a by-industrial brewster of not-married status, Kempstere was unusual, but she was not alone in Brigstock, in other early fourteenth-century villages, or indeed in towns. In Norwich, Margery de Brundall was cited for brewing in every leet but one between 1290 and 1313. In York, four not-married women who probably derived their main income from brewing entered the freedom of the city in the fourteenth century. In early fourteenth-century Oxford, many not-married brewsters—such as Maud London, who seems to have brewed about once a month from at least 1335 until 1348—seem to have relied heavily on profits from brewing. And according to the poll taxes, in addition to the nine not-married brewsters working in Howden in 1379, five such women brewed for a living in Oxford in 1381, three in Southwark, and three more in York.[8]

Nevertheless, women like Emma Kempstere, Margery de Brundall, and Maud London were exceptions; as a rule, most not-married women brewed only occasionally, and they were less likely than married women to brew on a by-industrial basis. In Howden and its region, for example, 25 not-married women were identified in the poll tax as brewsters, but 144 wives worked in the trade.[9] Why did married women predominate among by-industrial brewers? At least three factors seem to have contributed to the greater difficulties of not-married brewsters: the household basis of brewing, its time requirements, and its capital costs.

Ale was produced, sold, and sometimes consumed by customers not in special buildings constructed for these purposes but instead in homes and their surrounding curtilages or yards. As a result, the nature of a woman's household determined in part the viability of her brewing ventures. Married women were often better housed than singlewomen or widows, and they were able to call on the labor of children, husbands, and servants. These were not small advantages. A brewster needed space to brew and space to service customers. For single-women and widows, who often lived either as lodgers or servants in others' households or independently in small cottages or subtenancies, such space was sometimes unavailable. A brewster also needed labor assistance in meeting her many responsibilities: malting the grain (or selecting and buying the malt), fetching and preparing the water, collecting fuel, tending the wort, adding seasonings, advertising the availability of her brew, and selling to customers. For a woman who was not married or old or both, these multiple tasks would be onerous, perhaps sometimes physically impossible. A married woman was more likely than a singlewoman or widow to be able to marshall the labor of children to assist with some of the smaller chores (collecting wood, tending fires, and the like); she could hope for assistance from her husband with some of the more arduous tasks (such as turning the grain as it malted or hauling and pouring liquids); and she could also call on the aid of servants, who, although perhaps retained primarily for other work, might also assist in brewing. Quite simply, the household circumstances of married women were better able to support steady success in brewing than were the more limited labor and space resources of singlewomen and widows.

Wives also had strong advantages over most not-married women in controlling the timing and circumstances of their productive work. Most single-women and some widows worked as servants or laborers, and whether they lived in the houses of their employers or worked on a day-to-day basis, much of their time was not their own to manage as they saw fit.[10] Some servants brewed for their employers and a few others brewed on their own account, but with these exceptions, service and brewing were not very compatible. In contrast, although a married woman was certainly not a woman of leisure, she had much more control over her time. As she assisted her husband in his trade, nurtured children, gardened, raised poultry or pigs, cooked, and completed a myriad of other tasks, she could also brew and sell ale. Most married women, to be sure, did not add commercial brewing to their regular repertoire, but as highly adaptable and flexible workers, wives were better able to find time for brewing and selling ale than not-married women.[11] In other words, even by-industrial brewsters usually had to fit commercial brewing into a complex work pattern of other tasks and other employments, and in this circumstance, the flexible schedules of married women allowed them to accommodate brewing more easily than could those singlewomen and widows who supported themselves by hiring out their labor to others.

Finally, married women enjoyed another advantage over not-married women: they had access to more capital. To be sure, it was easy to brew occasionally without much capital investment. For example, almost three-quarters of the households in Exeter in 1377 brewed at least occasionally, a figure that suggests that most households—whether rich, middling, or poor—had the equipment, the supplies, and the skills necessary for brewing. But by-industrial brewing was another matter. A household that frequently offered ale for sale needed capital to meet a variety of costs: to purchase grain in times of dearth as well as abundance, to maintain equipment or add to it, and to hire servants to help in brewing or selling the ale. As a result, in Exeter, very few poor households sold ale on a regular basis, and richer households brewed much more frequently.[12]

These capital requirements offered real advantages to married women. As a working "partner" in a family economy who could rely in part on the greater earning power of males, a wife was better able than a not-married woman to meet the capital demands of frequent brewing. The so-called feminization of poverty is not a new phenomenon of the late twentieth century; even in the middle ages, not-married women were usually the poorest and most pathetic members of their communities. In late fourteenth-century Exeter, for example, not-married women were by far the poorest of all householders. Given their relative poverty, it is not surprising that most not-married women in the town brewed infrequently; only 3 of 41 (7 percent) brewed more than 10 times, compared to 136 of 484 married couples (or 28 percent).[13] As we have already seen for Howden, not-married brewsters had less personal wealth and employed fewer servants, and we can surmise that they also worked with less equipment, lived in poorer housing, and even perhaps ate less well.

In short, most by-industrial brewsters were married because their households better supported it, because their working lives better accommodated to it, and because their capital resources were more extensive. Of course, all married women were not the same, and the life circumstances of some wives supported by-industrial brewing better than others. Wealth made a difference; in Exeter, wives of merchants and professionals tended to brew more frequently than other married women, probably because they had more time, more servants, and more capital. Husbands' trades also made a difference; wives of braziers, goldsmiths, and other metal workers in Exeter brewed more often than wives of men in the clothing, textile, leather, and victualing trades, probably because they had to assist their husbands less often and therefore had more time to brew.[14] Of course, all not-married women were not the same. It seems likely, for example, that widows were often better able than singlewomen to pursue brewing on a by-industrial basis.[15] And it is quite clear that not-married brewsters in the countryside were better placed than their urban counterparts, who had to compete in a more professionalized and concentrated ale market. But as a general rule, singlewomen and widows were not as competitive in brewing as married women. Most not-married women brewed only occasionally and had to seek their primary livelihood elsewhere — in agriculture, service, huckstering, or other trades. Those few not-married women who did brew more frequently usually operated, as we have seen for Howden, more modest concerns than their married counterparts.

In most early fourteenth-century towns and villages, then, we would have found many not-married women working occasionally in the ale market and a few living by it. In a world where singlewomen and widows had limited opportunities for skilled and well-remunerated work, brewing stood out as an excellent option for women who lived without men. Not-married brewsters lived well, if judged by the standards of other not-married women. We have already seen that the not-married brewsters of Howden were more prosperous than other single-women and widows in the town. Oxford provides another example. In the Oxford poll tax of 1381, the nearly 250 not-married women in the town usually paid the minimum assessment of 4d. and seldom paid more than the average of 12d., but the few not-married brewsters in the town paid much larger sums: 10s., 4s., 3s., and 12d.[16] As these figures suggest, commercial brewing was a good option for not-married women, in an age when not-married women had few good options from which to choose. This is what John de Dachet understood when, in 1300, he left his daughter, Agnes, a brewhouse, which she was to use for eight years in order to establish herself in business. And Robert de Huttokeshatre made a similarly wise judgment when he, dying in the first outbreak of the plague, left a brewhouse to Joan the daughter of Henry Wyght for one year (after which it was to be sold).[17] As both men knew, singlewomen and widows had a hard lot in life and commercial brewing could somewhat ameliorate it. Yet times were changing.

The Commercialization of Brewing after 1348

After the Black Death, alebrewing expanded, becoming less domestic and more industrial. Occasional brewers disappeared, only the most prosperous by-industrial brewers survived, and a new breed of brewers—professional brewers—came to dominate the trade in many places. The slow transformation of brewing from a home-based, low-profit by-industry into a brewhouse-based, high-profit occupation did not occur in isolation; many other trades and crafts grew more professionalized and specialized during the later middle ages. Brewing, however, did change with particular rapidity and force.[18] Some aspects of the transformation of brewing are quite clearly demonstrated in extant sources, but they are difficult to trace in two respects. First, as one might expect, evidence of commercial change is more forthcoming for towns than for villages, and although some rural changes are well documented, other shifts can be only indirectly studied. Second, the story of the expansion of brewing after the Black Death is somewhat confounded by the introduction of beer, which began to be drunk in England in the late fourteenth century. Yet, beer was accepted by the English very slowly, and in most places, it was neither brewed nor drunk until the sixteenth century or later. Therefore, our discussion here will focus on commercial changes, from 1348 to 1600, associated with alebrewing alone. The very distinctive role of beerbrewing in the history of brewsters will be treated separately in chapter 5.

In the late fourteenth century, the market in ale expanded rapidly. Needless to say, after the devastation of the Black Death in 1348–49, brewers had fewer customers than before, but those fewer customers drank much more ale per capita than had their parents and grandparents. By the early fifteenth century, harvest workers at Sedgeford (Norfolk) consumed much more meat, much less bread, and nearly twice as much ale as they had in the thirteenth century. This pattern seems to have been typical not only of harvest workers but also of common folk throughout England. In the late fourteenth century, more grain went to brewing than ever before; alternative drinks (such as milk and cider) declined in popularity; and ale — a lot of ale — became a staple part of the diet of peasants, laborers, artisans, and others. As working people in both rural and urban areas began to enjoy a higher standard of living, they drank a good deal more ale.[19]

Ale consumption also seems to have increased among the landed and mercantile elites, especially consumption of purchased ale. By the late fourteenth century, wine competed much less effectively than before with ale. Indeed, so little wine was imported into England in the late fourteenth century that many gentle households must have gone without wine altogether and many noble households must have cut back sharply.[20] Moreover, just as elite households were consuming more ale than before, changes in estate management encouraged them to purchase ale rather than produce their own. As landowners began leasing their estates rather than managing them directly, they turned to the market to supply their victualing needs. They also settled down, stayed longer in fewer residences, and fostered considerably larger households. For brewers near these residences, the changed customs of the nobility and gentry often translated into regular and large orders for ale.[21] For example, the early fifteenth-century household of Richard Mitford, bishop of Salisbury, regularly purchased large amounts of ale from more than a dozen suppliers. In the 30-odd weeks from October 1406 to June 1407, just one of these brewers (a man known only as Warner) sold more than 1,500 gallons to the bishop's household.[22]

In short, as people from all social strata began to drink more ale more often, brewers had more business than ever before.[23] They also accrued higher profits. Because ale prices set under the assize were more stable than grain prices, brewers benefited from the strong harvests and low grain prices of the later middle ages. Grain prices were often high in the decades immediately after the plague, but by the 1370s, they began to fall. For brewers, falling grain prices meant higher profits. In London, for example, brewers were told to sell their best ale at 1¼d. in 1356, when barley cost more than 5s. a quarter; in 1375, when barley cost about 4s.9d. a quarter; and in 1387, when barley cost less than 4s. a quarter. In other words, London brewers in the 1380s spent on grain perhaps 80 percent of what brewers had spent in the 1350s, but they nevertheless were allowed to sell their ale at the same price. Some of the other costs faced by brewers were rising, such as the cost of faggots and labor. But since grain accounted for the single largest expense of brewers, its falling price, often uncompensated by falling prices for ale, seems to have worked to their economic advantage.[24]

Facing both larger markets and larger profits, brewers responded actively, creating a more industrialized craft and a higher status occupation. Needless to say, all brewers did not face similar circumstances, and as a result, brewing professionalized more slowly in the north and west and more slowly in villages than in towns. But as the demand for ale changed and the profits of the trade grew, brewing changed as well. These changes can only be sketched here, but they are quite clear for some towns and villages from as early as the mid-fourteenth century. In many parts of England, the prosperous and well-respected brewer of the seventeenth century had roots deep in the middle ages.[25]

After the Black Death, brewers began marketing their highly desirable product in more sophisticated ways, using mechanisms that had taken root earlier but only grew strongly after mid-century. To begin with, the trade divided much more sharply than before into alebrewers and alesellers. In towns such as Oxford, Norwich, London, Winchester, and Tamworth, tipplers—sometimes outlawed by town authorities and sometimes tolerated—became a fixture of the market over the course of the fourteenth century. In Oxford, by 1351, there were two tipplers for every brewer. In London a few years later, a proclamation set different penalties for brewers and tipplers. In the countryside, specialized retailing of ale grew more slowly, but many villages, such as Earl Soham (Suffolk) and Stockton (Wiltshire), boasted alesellers as well as alebrewers by the end of the century.[26] Usually supplementing the direct sales of brewers, tipplers expanded the amount of ale that any one brewer could hope to sell before it spoiled. In other words, most brewers continued to sell some of their product directly to customers, but thanks to tipplers, they were able to brew even more ale because they could market it indirectly.

In addition, more and more ale was sold, whether by brewers or tipplers, for immediate consumption in alehouses. Alehouses were not new in the late fourteenth century, but they seem to have grown much more popular in the decades immediately after the Black Death. Their growth created a new regulatory problem: the problem of brewers and tipplers who refused to sell their drink except to customers who consumed it on the premises. Complaints about refusals by brewers or tipplers to serve off-site customers, rare before the Black Death, proliferate in the late fourteenth century, in villages as well as towns. For example, a jury in Wye (Kent) in 1371 was interrogated about those brewsters "who are unwilling to sell ale outside their homes in sealed measures but only to those sitting in their alehouses (in tavernis suis), who use cups, dishes, and other unreliable measures, and who even sell their ale for 3d. a gallon." As this complaint suggests, brewers and tipplers preferred in-house sales because they could reap higher profits by using small, nonstandard measures and charging higher prices. Customers who sought the purchase of bulk supplies for consumption in their homes and law-enforcement officers who wanted to regulate both prices and measures might have protested, but throughout England, in-house sales of ale grew more common over the course of the late fourteenth century.[27]

In the countryside, brewers worked alongside tipplers, and both groups sold their ale for consumption not only in alehouses but also away from the premises. At least some rural tipplers also began to purchase their ale from urban suppliers. Shortly after the Black Death, brewers in Newcastle successfully penetrated the ale market in Whickham; villagers there were amerced for buying Newcastle ale not only for their own use but also for resale to their neighbors.[28] Unfortunately, this marketing of urban-brewed ale (or beer) in rural villages is very poorly reported in extant sources; we only know of the Newcastle ale sold in Whickham because the lord of Whickham considered himself defrauded of charges he could have levied on local brewers. The full extent of the competition that urban brewers created for rural brewers cannot be determined, but they rarely eliminated rural production of ale. The ale and beer of Newcastle,

London, Burton-on-Trent, and elsewhere might have been tippled in some villages, but almost without exception, local brewers continued to ply their trade.[29]

In towns, the proliferation of both tipplers and alehouses sometimes worked to separate the brewing of ale from its retailing. Many brewers continued to sell their ale directly to consumers in the later middle ages and after, but some brewers, especially in centers such as London, Southampton, and Lynn, began to concentrate on the wholesale trade. By 1408, the wholesale trade in London had expanded enough to prompt the city to issue new orders about larger measures—barrels and kilderkins. The order noted specifically that brewers sold ale "en groos" not only to the households of lords and gentry but also to hostelers and hucksters. By the sixteenth century, many urban brewers dealt solely in the wholesale trade or, at least, were required to do so. In 1478, Southampton, apparently trying to allow more of its inhabitants to make their living from the drink trade, proscribed its brewers (of both ale and beer) from trading in retail. Other towns issued similar orders in later decades.[30] No matter how loath urban brewers were to yield the retail trade entirely to tipplers, the wholesale trade offered bulk sales and, of course, large profits.

These new means of marketing ale were complemented by a more concentrated production of ale: fewer brewers sold ale more regularly. And as fewer brewers supplied a widening market, they began to specialize in brewing alone; a trade that had once involved many households intermittently began to involve only a few households consistently. When this happened, the *occasional* and *by-industrial* brewers of the early fourteenth century began to be replaced by *professional* brewers. The concentration of brewing into fewer hands has been observed in many late medieval villages and market towns—for example, in Holywell-cum-Needingworth and Warboys in Huntingdonshire; in Kibworth Harcourt (Leicestershire) and Alrewas (Staffordshire); in Stoke Fleming and other Devon villages; and in Havering (Essex).[31] Brewing was also concentrated into fewer hands in many contemporary towns—in Oxford, Norwich, Southampton, Colchester, Winchester, and London in the fifteenth century and in York and Leicester in the sixteenth.[32]

Population decline does not explain this trend. English population stayed low through most of the later middle ages, but even when it began to grow, the number of brewers did not increase. In 1500 fewer brewers were serving a population of roughly equal size to that in 1348. The cause is not clear. It is possible that occasional brewing was no longer attractive to its former practitioners. Perhaps the labor-short economy of the later middle ages offered so many opportunities for employment that fewer people turned to commercial brewing on an occasional basis.[33] But it is also quite certain that the growing size and complexity of the ale market sometimes squeezed out those who had once sold ale every now and then. In Oxford in 1501, for example, a system of rotating work among brewers was reviewed and maintained, despite vigorous complaints from smaller, part-time brewers that it hurt their business. In this instance, as perhaps in others, large-scale brewers who could promise their customers a regular and predictable supply triumphed over their more modest competitors.[34] Whatever the causes for the slow disappearance of occasional brewers in town and country, the results are clear: over the course of the late fourteenth, fifteenth, and in some cases sixteenth centuries, fewer brewers served larger markets. In a village such as Stockton, this meant that a population once supplied by a dozen or so brewers was served, in the early sixteenth century, by only one or two. And in a town such as Oxford, it meant that where 100 brewers had once worked in the fourteenth century, fewer than two dozen worked in the sixteenth.

As fewer people brewed, they also brewed more regularly. In the years before the Black Death, when many people sold ale on an occasional basis, even those few brewers who were more committed to the trade—those whom we have called by-industrial brewers—brewed for sale only intermittently. In some years a brewster such as the wife of Richard Gilbert in Brigstock sold ale regularly, in some years she sold not at all, and in some years she sold ale in one month but not in the next. This sort of irregularity disappeared as brewing became concentrated in fewer hands. The "common brewer" grew more and more important— that is, a brewer who, as noted in the manorial records of many late fourteenth-century and fifteenth-century villages and towns, brewed not once or twice or even three times but commonly (*communiter*). In 1390–91, for example, Robert Aylnot of Cuxham (Oxfordshire) paid a lump sum of 6d. for his ale toll; he was noted as a *communis brasiator*.[35] For Aylnot and many others in late medieval England, brewing was becoming a regular, not an intermittent, pursuit.

In part, brewers worked more consistently because their market was wider and more reliable. Since they could be sure of selling their ale, they made it available as often as possible. But also in part, brewers provided ale more consistently because their localities demanded it. With ale available for purchase from fewer outlets than had once been the case, it became imperative that those outlets stay in operation through all seasons of the year, in times of dearth as well as abundance, for the rich as well as the poor. In some places, brewers had to adhere to rotation schemes that ensured a regular supply of ale. In other places, brewers were ordered to continue in their trade, to pursue it to the exclusion of other occupations, or to provide ale at all times and to all customers.[36]

As the brewing trade narrowed to smaller numbers of practitioners who brewed more regularly, the trade became professionalized; that is, it became the primary occupation of at least some households. In the countryside, brewing was often incorporated into a professional commitment to victualing. In Hindolveston (Norfolk) in the 1370s, John de Folsham baked and his wife, Beatrice, brewed. In Stockton in the 1380s and 1390s, John Warner, who often brewed more frequently than any other person in the village, began also to work as a hostiller, baker, and general victualer. In Crowle (Lincolnshire) in the early fifteenth century, aletasters began to present not only brewers and bakers but also persons who profited simultaneously from both trades. In these and many other late medieval villages, brewing not only narrowed into fewer hands but also became incorporated into victualing in general. Victualers did not necessarily live by their trade alone—in the early fifteenth century, for example, Thomas Russhemere leased the demesne of Kempsey (Worcestershire) for 30 years before he began to profit regularly from milling, victualing, and brewing—but they often relied on it for regular and steady income.[37]

Professionalization was more rapid in towns, where some brewers began to focus on brewing alone, to the exclusion of other victualing trades. After the Black Death, more and more townspeople began to identify themselves as brewers when they entered the freedom of their towns, they called themselves brewers in their wills, they banded together to negotiate with local authorities about prices of ale and other matters, and they also formed themselves into gilds. In Norwich, for example, the first citizen identified as a brewer entered the freedom in 1414; the first self-identified brewer left a will in 1442; and by the early sixteenth century, the brewers of the town had formed some sort of gild to regulate their affairs.[38] To be sure, many urban households continued to combine brewing with other trades, particularly other victualing trades, but in at least some urban households, brewing became the prime and perhaps even sole employment.[39]

Late medieval brewers were not only fewer in number, more steady in their work, and more professionalized; they were also more ambitious in the scale of their operations, producing more ale, working in larger brewhouses, and employing more servants. Increased outputs are difficult to trace before the age of brewery accounts, especially in the countryside. For rural brewers, no evidence directly proves that brewing operations expanded after the mid-fourteenth century. As we have seen, most rural brewers before the Black Death probably expended only a few bushels of grain in each brewing, producing several dozen gallons at a time. When villages came to be served by fewer and fewer brewers in the late fourteenth and fifteenth centuries, each brewer probably produced more ale with each brewing, especially since population levels remained fairly steady for more than a century after the Black Death. In other words, it seems logical that Thomas Mascal, one of a handful of common brewers in Stockton in the late fifteenth century, produced more ale per brewing than did another Thomas Mascal, who 100 years earlier had been one of about two dozen brewers in the village and who had brewed for sale only intermittently—logical, but unverifiable from extant materials.[40]

Urban evidence is slightly more forthcoming. In both London and Lynn, increased output by some brewers in the second half of the fourteenth century began to differentiate them from their lesser colleagues. Two decades after the Black Death, some London brewers were producing so much ale that the city decided to treat large-scale and small-scale brewers differently. Those who brewed 5 quarters of malt a week or less were liable for fines of 40d., but those brewing more than 5 quarters of malt were liable for twice that amount. At about the same time, brewers in Lynn were also dividing into greater and lesser producers. Most Lynn brewers consumed only a few quarters of malt each week, but John Kep, the greatest of Lynn brewers, brewed 24 quarters a week, probably yielding between 1,500 and 2,000 gallons of ale (depending on strength).[41]

By the end of the fifteenth century, Kep's productivity was probably not exceptional, at least for brewers in major cities and towns. Our first extant set of brewers' accounts—a fragment from Oxford, circa 1506—shows regular yields of more than 1,000 gallons.[42] To be sure, 1,000 gallons might seem small compared to brewery production in later centuries, but it nearly doubled the production managed by St. Paul's, London, in 1340–41.[43] Since St. Paul's brew-house was large for its time, the unknown brewer of Oxford circa 1506 was probably exceeding by 10 times or more the yields of commercial brewers two centuries earlier. In short, over the course of the later middle ages, urban brewers began to produce ale in larger quantities, and it is likely that rural brewers did much the same (albeit on a comparatively smaller scale).

In seeking to produce more ale, brewers invested in larger premises and better equipment. Again, the rural evidence is less full, but there can be no doubt that urban brewers increasingly worked in surroundings that were more indus-trial and less domestic. By 1400, at least some London brewers managed quite substantial physical plants, far removed in equipment, size, and expense from the household operations of rural alewives. In 1407, the brewhouse of Stephen Hamme included not only a large number of movable items (vats, tubs, barrels, and the like) but also built-in equipment that could not be moved from the ten-ement (including leaden tubs, leaden taps, mash tuns, querns, and millstones). Hamme also kept tables and benches to accommodate his drinking clientele. Probably few brewhouses in early fifteenth-century London were built to purpose, but establishments like that of Stephen Hamme had been substantially modified for the production and sale of ale. They could also be quite expensive to equip and maintain. No valuation is appended to our description of Hamme's brew-house in 1407, but in 1486, a brewhouse that belonged to William Robinson contained equipment worth more than £22. Although the breweries of London worked on a scale unknown elsewhere, brewers in other late fifteenth-century towns had also invested heavily in their brewhouses and equipment. For exam-ple, in Oxford (where the right to brew for profit was, by then, attached to own-ership of certain brewhouses), the contents of a brewhouse were also valued, in 1496, at about £22.[44]

As urban brewers invested more in their physical plants and sought to pro-duce more ale per brewing, they also employed more servants. Even in the late fourteenth century some brewing households contained so many servants that they resembled what Caroline Barron has called "industrial units."[45] In towns such as Lynn, Ripon, Oxford, Southwark, Worcester, and York, brewers tended to employ more servants than their neighbors.[46] In London, hired labor had become so important to brewers that the trade faced a growing "servant prob-lem." In the wake of the labor shortages that followed the Black Death, brew-ers' servants demanded better wages, departed early from service, claimed an expertise in brewing that they lacked, and attempted to play one employer off against another.[47] In the early years of the fifteenth century, brewers' servants— by then, called journeymen—won their battle for a daily wage rate, obtaining either 3d. or 4d. per day, depending on the season; and by 1427–28, they were differentiated by skill, allowed to marry and live away from their employers' households, and numerous enough to threaten the brewers with a confederacy. Servants were, quite simply, essential to many brewers. In 1438, when the mem-bers of the Brewers' gild, armed with a new royal charter of incorporation, sought to restrict commercial brewing to themselves alone, they tried to cut off non-gild brewers by eliminating two crucial resources: water and servants.[48]

As a result of all these changes—the expanding demand for ale, its better marketing through tipplers and alehouses, the concentration of its production into fewer and more committed hands, and an expansion in the scale of production—the social status of brewers waxed, especially in towns. In 1381, brewers stood out from their neighbors, in both wealth and household size, in the poll taxes of Oxford, Southwark, York, and Worcester. They were not the wealthiest citizens of their towns, to be sure, but they paid higher taxes than the average, and they employed more servants than others. In Oxford, for example, brewers usually paid more than the average 12d. per person tax in 1381, a few brewers paid extremely high taxes, and one brewer employed more servants than anyone else in the town. At about the same time, Oxford brewers were gaining civic stature as well, enjoying a "spectacular increase" in those serving as town bailiffs and even rising, in some cases, to the mayoralty. By 1400, in other words, brewing in Oxford, which had once been dispersed throughout the town, was confined to a small number of relatively prosperous households. Over the course of the fifteenth century, brewing households grew even more prosperous and influential, and by the early sixteenth century, brewers were the wealthiest and most powerful people in the town.[49]

Rural communities had, of course, less developed status hierarchies, and it is correspondingly difficult to trace the standing of rural brewers; but it seems that rural brewers were less fortunate than their urban counterparts. In Birdbrook (Essex), Alciston (East Sussex), and other late medieval villages, brewers were probably slightly more prosperous than their predecessors before the Black Death, but they were not clearly distinguished from their neighbors.[50] And although some early sixteenth-century rural brewers could be very prosperous indeed, others lived in more modest circumstances.[51]

In some respects, the social ascent of brewers in the later middle ages was an effect achieved by the decline of other trades and the disappearance of occasional brewers.[52] But in other respects, the social rise of brewers was very real indeed. They profited from the strong demand for their product and the relative cheapness of grain. They benefited from the growing distinction between tippling and brewing, a distinction that sloughed onto tipplers the more unsavory associations of the drink trade. And they took advantage of the very real need for their product to squeeze others out of competition (as in Oxford in 1501). By the early sixteenth century, brewers' gilds controlled the trade in such towns as London, Oxford, and Southampton, and by the mid-sixteenth century, brewers were serving regularly in urban offices throughout England.[53]

Yet it would be a mistake to think that the numerous part-time brewers of the early fourteenth century had been replaced, by 1500, by a few wealthy owners of industrial complexes. In many parts of the countryside, commercial brewing remained a widely practiced and domestically based trade well into the sixteenth century. In Crowle, for example, numerous brewers—both occasional and by-industrial—continued to serve their neighbors at the end of the fifteenth century, not-married women continued to brew to some extent, and brewers directly marketed their ale in the village without the intervention of alesellers. Even in some cities, brewing became professionalized only minimally before the end of the sixteenth century. In York, for example, commercial brewing was still widely practiced; still home-based; and still pursued by not-married women, as well as wives, at the very end of the century.[54] But it would also be a mistake to think that little changed in the occupation of brewing over the course of the later middle ages. The professionalization of brewing was often more evident in urban than in rural settings, and it was especially clear in major brewing centers such as London, Southampton, and Lynn. Changes elsewhere were more modest and sometimes much delayed, but changes did occur. In Stockton, for example, where about a dozen brewers (including many not-married women) had worked before the Black Death, only one or two common brewers (none of them not-married women) worked by the fifteenth century. Slowly but surely, brewing changed after the Black Death from a home-based industry pursued intermittently by many occasional or by-industrial brewers to a brewhouse-based industry pursued by a few professional brewers.

Not-married Brewsters and the Commercialization of Brewing

When the brewing trade expanded and became commercialized in the centuries after the Black Death, all brewsters—wives, as well as widows, single-women, and other not-married women—found themselves in new and challenging circumstances. As we shall see in the next chapter, married women and their husbands began to renegotiate their respective contributions to commercial brewing, and over time, brewing ceased to be a by-industrial trade of wives and became a professional trade of husbands. The shifting balance of brewing activity between wives, on the one side, and husbands, on the other, rested on domestic decisions that are exceedingly difficult to trace in the extant documentation. Yet gild records provide one means of sorting out the new terms under which married couples worked in the more profitable brewing industry of the later middle ages. This is what we shall examine in the next chapter.

The changes that are so subtle for married brewsters, however, are much clearer for single and widowed brewsters. After 1348, not-married women ceased brewing in large numbers. In Stockton, for example, brewing by single-women and widows constituted roughly 20 percent of the ale trade in the late thirteenth century, 13 percent in the early fourteenth century, 11 percent in the decades after the Black Death, and only 6 percent in the early fifteenth century; by the second half of the fifteenth century, commercial brewing by singlewomen and widows had virtually disappeared. In the town of Norwich, not-married brewsters accounted for 16 percent of brewers in 1288 but only 7 percent by 1390. Of course, change was less rapid in some communities than in others; for example, not-married women (especially widows) still accounted for about 1 of 10 brewers in York in the 1560s. Yet what happened in Stockton and Norwich eventually also happened elsewhere, even though the exact timing and extent of change varied; in towns and villages throughout England, not-married women brewed for profit less and less frequently over the course of the late fourteenth, fifteenth, and sixteenth centuries.[55]

In part, the slow disappearance of single and widowed brewsters was a function of the disappearance of occasional brewers. As brewing became a professionalized trade, occasional brewers—among whom not-married women were disproportionately numbered—turned their attentions elsewhere. Yet the withdrawal of not-married women requires fuller explanation, for at least some of them had once brewed frequently for profit in the century before the Black Death. What happened to the fifteenth-century counterparts of by-industrial brewsters such as Emma Kempstere, who had plied her trade in early fourteenth-century Brigstock? Why did women like her not join the ranks of professional brewers in late fifteenth-century Stockton or Norwich? They did not because they usually could not. Commercialization—whether in a few towns before the Black Death or in a variety of urban and rural communities thereafter—worked to the disadvantage of not-married brewsters. In the expanding ale market of the later middle ages, not-married women lacked two essential requirements for success in the trade: investment capital and managerial authority.

As we have already seen, even before the Black Death, the capital demands of by-industrial brewing were sufficiently high to discourage many not-married women, perhaps especially in towns. After 1350, this particular form of discouragement intensified. As brewing expanded in the later middle ages, those who invested more capital in their enterprises fared best. Brewers who managed larger premises, worked with better equipment, and hired more servants had strong advantages over smaller brewers. They could supply their customers with better ale on a more regular basis, and they could better garner the favor of officers empowered to regulate the trade.[56] The capitalization of brewing was not unique among late medieval industries, but it was particularly intense. In early sixteenth-century Oxford, brewhouses were the "nearest approach to an industry involving substantial capital investment and production" in the town.[57]

In addition to needing capital to invest in premises, equipment, and labor, brewers also needed capital to carry customers' debts. In the countryside, customers might owe brewers only a shilling or two, but although small, these debts could remain unpaid for a long time or, indeed, forever. In a common pattern that troubled many brewers, customers such as Thomas Wright of Wakefield (Yorkshire) delayed or avoided payment by moving from one brewer to another. In January 1349, Wright owed Annabel Hughet 18d. for ale, but four months later, he had accumulated another unpaid debt of 20d. with another brewer in the area.[58] In towns, customers' debts could run to much larger amounts; in a six-month period in 1368, for example, Richard Markeby of London ran up a debt of 46s. for ale purchased from Alice the wife of Jordan de Barton.[59] In both town and country, the burden of debt probably increased as brewers began to supply tipplers, as well as private customers. Since tipplers purchased large quantities from brewers, they ran up larger debts than retail customers. In the early fifteenth century, for example, the huckster Alice Norwell owed the brewer John Godyng 5 marks for ale she had purchased from him and then resold.[60]

These expanding capital needs placed not-married brewsters at a severe disadvantage, for capital—in the form of cash or credit—was not as readily available to not-married women as to either men or married women. It is a commonplace that women controlled fewer resources in both land and movable wealth than men, a commonplace that is writ large in every tax roll and rental for preindustrial England. But it is a commonplace that had very real effects on the lives of late medieval and early modern singlewomen and widows. Inheriting less property than men, obtaining less training for skilled work than men, and earning lower wages than men even for similar work, not-married women were, quite simply, poorer than men. Faced with a changing brewing industry that required more capital investment, they had less capital to invest.[61]

This was true, as we have already seen, of the not-married brewsters of Howden, who, compared to other brewers in the town, were quite poor. Consider, for another example, the not-married brewsters of late fourteenth-century Southwark, women who lived in a ideal time and place for taking advantage of the commercial expansion of brewing. (In the next century, this suburb would become a center of commercial alebrewing and beerbrewing for both local consumption and export.) In 1381, of 24 brewers (all brewers of ale), 3 were not-married women. None of these brewsters had the sort of wealth that would be needed to exploit the new commercial opportunities of the day; Margery Bruwer paid only 4d. in the poll tax of that year, Alice Jolyf 12d., and Joan Saundres 12d. But some of the male brewers (or male heads of brewing households) were quite wealthy: William Weston and his wife faced a 5s. assessment, as did Thomas Hosyar and his wife; 10 others were assessed between 3s. and 4s., 4 at 2s., 3 at 12d., and 2 at 8d. Clearly, some men headed brewing establishments as modest as those of brewsters, but other men controlled the biggest and wealthiest brewhouses in late fourteenth-century Southwark. These men and their wives would have the investment capital to exploit the expanding ale trade (and eventually, the beer trade as well).[62]

Compared to other brewers, not-married brewsters lacked not only cash in hand but also access to credit. Brewers often used credit to finance their operations, either through loans of money or through deferred payments for goods or services. In 1391, for example, the London brewer John Thromyn owed over £3 to William at Mille for 13 quarters of malt bought between Michaelmas and Pentecost.[63] Credit was a basic and essential feature of commercial life in both town and countryside. Over the course of the fourteenth, fifteenth, and sixteenth centuries, credit changed: moneylending outpaced deferred payments; fewer creditors controlled more credit; credit increasingly went to specialized projects in industry, trade, and agriculture; and Londoners controlled more and more of the market for credit. But throughout the period, the extension of credit was based on mutual trust.[64]

This mutual trust was less readily available to not-married women than to others.[65] Singlewomen and widows were poor credit risks, economically as well as legally. The poverty of not-married women undermined their credit: since they owned less, they could borrow less. And the law of contracts rendered all women, including single and widowed women, bad risks. Although legal conventions seemed to favor not-married women over wives, no woman was as reliable a debtor as a man. A married woman could not make contracts at all unless she enjoyed the special privilege of acting as *femme sole*, that is, unless she had arranged to be treated by the courts as if she were a not-married woman, exempt from the authority that husbands customarily exercised over wives. A widow or singlewoman was as personally responsible as a man for her own contracts. In actual practice, however, not-married women were not as legally responsible as men since the possibility of their eventual marriage confounded the enforceability of their contractual obligations; debts contracted by single-women and widows were sometimes shifted when they married onto their new husbands.[66] The liability of husbands for the debts of their wives, whether contracted before or after marriage, might have added masculine probity to female contracts, but it could also lead to long and convoluted suits at law. This is what happened, for example, to Gilbert le Brasour in 1305 when he sought to recover a debt of 13s. 10d. from Mabel, the wife of John le Heymonger; although Mabel le Heymonger was a huckster who traded as a *femme sole*, she successfully evaded Gilbert le Brasour's suit by the simple device of refusing to answer without her husband. Mabel le Heymonger made contracts on her own account, but she was not—as Gilbert le Brasour discovered to his inconvenience—a legally responsible debtor.[67] At a time when the collateral for many debts was not property but trustworthiness, the legal status of female contracts rendered women—single-women and widows, as well as married women—less trustworthy than men.

So, not-married women lacked "credit" in both senses of the term, not only owning less property with which to secure loans but also possessing less reliable contractual authority. As a result, their ability to obtain loans was quite restricted. As Maryanne Kowaleski's analysis of 4,526 debt cases in late fourteenth-century Exeter shows clearly, "the mere fact of being female" significantly shaped credit. Even unenfranchised and poor men took on much larger debts than most women. Women tended to borrow from other women, they tended to contract debts more for domestic uses than for business concerns, and they obtained much smaller loans than men (averaging one-third to one-half the amount obtained by men). And in a world where women borrowed much less than men, not-married women borrowed even less than married women; in Exeter, for example, singlewomen and widows took on especially small debts—only 4s.6d. on the average, compared to 6s.4d. for all women and 14s. for men.[68]

Handicapped by their limited access to capital in the form of either cash or credit, not-married brewsters faced another growing obstacle in the later middle ages. As brewing expanded, it came to require a level of managerial authority that not-married brewsters could seldom command. Late medieval brewers hired, as we have seen, exceptional numbers of servants, males as well as females. In late fourteenth-century Oxford, for example, brewers employed about three male servants for every two female servants (although at least some of the female servants worked in tippling, not brewing). In Southwark at the same time, brewers seem to have employed nearly equal numbers of female and male servants. But the work forces of brewhouses slowly changed, with more and more brewers served by many males and only one or two females. In London by the 1420s and 1430s, brewers' servants were numerous, troublesome, and almost exclusively male. All servants who worked as "chief brewers" or "second brewers" in the actual manufacture of ale were male, and the only female servants worked in huckstery, that is, as sellers of the ale brewed by their employers.[69]

This expansion and masculinization of service in brewing boded ill for not-married brewsters, who seem to have found it very difficult, if not impossible, to maintain authority directly over such a work force. As P. J. P. Goldberg has noted in his analysis of the late fourteenth-century poll taxes, women who ran businesses employed fewer servants than men and especially few male servants.[70] We might wonder why this was so. Did women lack the capital to establish such businesses? Did social teachings about male authority and female dependence undercut the authority of female mistresses over male servants? Did sexual scandal and innuendo inhibit the employment of males by women?[71] Yet causes aside, the results are clear and important: not-married women were unlikely to manage enterprises that employed many servants, especially many male servants. As brewing became just such an enterprise, it became less and less suitable for not-married women.

The growing commercial disadvantages of not-married brewsters were probably aggravated by popular anxieties not only about brewsters but also about women who lived apart from the authority of men. These anxieties were not new in the late fourteenth century, but they may have either intensified or been felt in new ways. As depicted in a wide range of cultural media, brewsters were seen as untrustworthy, disorderly, and unreliable tradeswomen (a subject we will examine more fully in chapter 7). Not-married brewsters might have particularly suffered from these characterizations because they had "not any man to control them," because, in other words, the nefarious behaviors associated with their sex were not mitigated by the governing presence of a husband. Certainly, most representations of disorderly brewsters show them either without husbands or with ineffectual husbands. Moreover, not-married women, whether in brewing or other trades, were also the subjects of considerable anxiety, which in at least some cases took real form. In 1584, for example, a jury in Manchester noted that unmarried women baked, brewed, and pursued other trades "to the great hurt of the poor inhabitants having wives and children." Complaining that these women "abus[ed] themselves with young men" and provided an "evil example," the jury ordered that no singlewoman should pursue an independent trade, or in the terms of the order "be at their own hands or keep any house or chamber."[72]

In the late thirteenth and early fourteenth centuries, married women had worked more than singlewomen and widows as by-industrial brewers because their domestic situations, their work patterns, and their access to small amounts of capital offered important advantages. As brewing slowly expanded after the Black Death, the first two advantages waned in importance. By the fifteenth century, some urban brewers were working in brewhouses, not homes, and they were following their trade as an occupation, not as a by-industry juggled with other duties. But the third advantage of married women, access to capital, waxed in importance. And a new factor, management of large numbers of male servants, came into play. Whenever and wherever these changes were felt, not-married brewsters, who had always worked at more of a disadvantage—cultural as well as economic—than their married counterparts, slowly left the trade. In the expensive and well-served brewhouses of late fifteenth-century London, Southampton, Oxford, and other towns, wives were often active, but not-married women were rarely found.[73]

To be sure, not-married women still worked in the ale and beer trade in the fifteenth and sixteenth centuries, but they worked less as independent brewsters and more on the margins of the trade. Some began to work as sellers rather than producers. Oxford provides an early example of this trend, for as not-married women brewed less frequently in early fourteenth-century Oxford, they began to work as alesellers more frequently. Roughly equal numbers of not-married women brewed and retailed ale in Oxford in 1311, but 40 years later, three such women worked as tipplers for every one who worked as a brewster. In most cases, not-married women followed either brewing or tippling throughout their careers, suggesting that few individual women were forced to substitute tippling for brewing and that, instead, each succeeding generation of not-married women found brewing less viable and tippling more feasible. Only a few women, such as Gillian de Walton in the 1330s, actually moved between brewing and tippling. Without doubt, Gillian de Walton preferred to brew the ale she sold, for direct brewing lowered her costs and increased her profits. But when she could not brew, she sold ale brewed by others. What happened precociously in Oxford happened elsewhere during the following decades; as brewing became less accessible to not-married women and as aleselling became more distinct from ale-brewing, some women—especially singlewomen and widows—began to support themselves in tippling, not brewing.[74]

By the sixteenth century, one particular sort of not-married women, widows, predominated among women who found employment by tippling ale and managing small alehouses. As both Peter Clark and Keith Wrightson have noted, almost all women licensed to keep alehouses after 1552 were widows.[75] In part, the preponderance of widows who kept alehouses reflects anxiety about other not-married women. Worried about prostitution and similar activities in alehouses, magistrates judged an older widow a better risk than other women (as will be considered more fully in chapters 6 and 7). Yet in part, this preponderance of widows also reflects efforts to alleviate their poverty. As the Privy Council noted in 1596, it behooved local communities to support the alehouse licenses of "the ancienter sort of honest conversation . . . that have no other means to live by."[76] By allowing widows to run small alehouses, some communities tried to keep widows and their dependents off parish relief.

Other not-married women, particularly singlewomen, found paid employment in brewing. As servants of brewers, not-married women tippled the ale of their employers, carried ale on their backs to the houses of clients, worked in the process of brewing itself, and undertook a myriad of other tasks associated with the trade.[77] Brewers hired unusually large numbers of servants, and at least in the fourteenth century, many of them were women. But female service in brewing declined in both opportunity and status. As a service hierarchy developed within brewhouses, female servants were excluded or employed for only the least skilled and least desirable tasks. In many late fifteenth-century and sixteenth-century brewhouses, many types of workers were employed (clerks, brewers of various skill levels, drayers, coopers, and others), but usually only one or two women found work (invariably as unskilled workers).[78]

If some not-married women (particularly widows) tippled ale or sold it in alehouses and some others (particularly singlewomen) found employment in brewing, a few others (exclusively widows) supported themselves by running brewhouses. These widows might seem to be a remnant of past traditions of not-married brewsters, but they were not. Instead, the widows who worked in brewing after the trade became professionalized, worked in such different ways than before that they represent change, not continuity. In most male trades, widows had long enjoyed well-recognized claims to continue the businesses of their husbands.[79] As brewing became more profitable, more professionalized, and more practiced by men, this traditional option became available to brewers' widows, as it had been available in previous centuries to the widows of other tradesmen and merchants. In other words, although widows sometimes still brewed for profit in 1600, as in 1300, their relationship to the trade differed fundamentally in the two periods. In the earlier period, widows supported themselves by following a woman's trade; in the later period, widows supported themselves by continuing their husbands' trade.

Denise Marlere, who brewed as a widow in late fourteenth-century Bridgwater, exemplifies earlier patterns of brewing by widows. Marlere brewed in widowhood as a continuation of a trade she had pursued as a wife. When married, she had probably supported her husband in his work as a butcher, raised children and maintained the domestic needs of the household, brought in money by a variety of means, and brewed for profit. After her husband, Nicholas, died (sometime after 1389), she continued to profit from brewing, as she had done in the past. Denise Marlere brewed because brewing in late fourteenth-century Bridgwater was a woman's trade.

Yet as brewing commercialized in the fourteenth, fifteenth, and sixteenth centuries, widows like Denise Marlere ceased brewing, and other sorts of widows—widows of male brewers—became associated with the trade. In 1558, for example, when the alebrewer Mitchell Alleson died, his wife, Joan, took over the business. When she remarried two years later, her new husband, Lawrence Stringer, became associated with the trade; and although she might have assisted him in private, only he paid quarterage to the gild, took apprentices, and otherwise participated in the formal life of the trade. When Lawrence Stringer died in 1570, the twice-widowed Joan Alleson, alias Stringer, again took over the brewhouse and assumed all the perquisites of gild membership that were available to her. When she died in 1574, she passed on the brewhouse that Mitchell Alleson had left in her custody some 16 years earlier to their two sons, Ralph and Henry, and Ralph took over the business. Joan Alleson brewed as a continuation of her husband's trade. She brewed because, in late sixteenth-century London, brewing was a man's trade that widows were expected to maintain for both their own support and the eventual inheritance of their children.[80]

As a broad outline, this sketch of the late medieval expansion of brewing and its effects on singlewomen and widows necessarily obscures nuances, exceptions, and other perspectives. By focusing on the places and regions where these changes first occurred, we have seen their earliest manifestations rather than their last effects. Since brewing did not expand everywhere at the same time, these late medieval changes were, for some places and regions, part of their sixteenth-century and even seventeenth-century histories. Later change did not necessarily parrot early change. When brewing in a town such as Manchester expanded and capitalized at the very end of the sixteenth century, it was influenced by factors—such as the power of London brewers and the attraction of beer—that had had little importance in the expansion of brewing in fifteenth-century Oxford. Also, by focusing solely on the ale industry, we have isolated important commercial factors at the expense of obscuring a critical technical factor. As we will see in chapter 5, the introduction and gradual acceptance of beer accelerated the commercialization of brewing and contributed its own peculiar challenges for women in the trade. And finally, by focusing on not-married women, we have differentiated women according to marital status but obscured socioeconomic differences among brewers. Just as not-married brewsters found it hard to compete in the newly capitalized brewing industry of the later middle ages, so did poor women regardless of marital status, as well as poor men.

Yet we have traced, in those places where brewing expanded early and without the influence of the new technology of beerbrewing, an important pattern. As brewing commercialized and capitalized, the presence of women in the industry waned and the presence of men waxed. At least initially, marital status might have mattered more than sex. Neither not-married women nor bachelors competed well in the expanding ale trade of the later middle ages. Married women maintained their hold over much of the trade, and they were joined, in increasing numbers, by their husbands. In a sense, this might seem like nothing new; even in the pre-plague years, most by-industrial brewers had been married women. But in two important senses, this was very new indeed. First, not-married brewsters lost the small foothold they had once had in the trade; fewer and fewer singlewomen and widows brewed for profit, either as occasional or as by-industrial brewers.[81] Second, as we will consider more fully in the next chapter, married women developed a different relationship to commercial brewing. What had once been a by-industry pursued independently by wives became a primary occupation of many households and an occupation that, although perhaps more shared between husbands and wives than other occupations, was nevertheless identified particularly with the male head of household.

A Lost Opportunity, Not a Lost Trade

As commercial brewing changed over the course of the later middle ages, the occupation of brewing was so transformed that in many places it bore little resemblance in 1500 to what it had been in 1300. In Oxford, the few, wealthy, and powerful brewers of the Tudor town worked in a virtually different trade from the hundred or so brewers of the pre-plague town. Although both brewed ale for sale, they brewed and sold in entirely different circumstances. For Oxford brewers in 1300, brewing was a home-based by-industry that required little capital, little knowledge of markets and marketing, and little hired labor. For Oxford brewers 200 years later, brewing was a brewhouse-based industry that required capital, marketing strategies, and the employment of large, diversified work forces. Given the transformation of brewing over these centuries, it is not really accurate to characterize the experiences of not-married women as one of *exclusion* from a trade they had once practiced. Instead, not-married women, who had sometimes worked in the by-industry of brewing as it was practiced in early fourteenth-century Oxford, were *unable to gain access* to the new capitalized industry of brewing as it had come to be practiced in early sixteenth-century Oxford. What had changed was not the status of women's work but instead the skill, status, and profitability of brewing.

As not-married women left brewing, they supported themselves through other sorts of work that had been traditionally available to them. In some cases, they took up occupations that required skills but were not remunerated as skilled work (that is, occupations that were similar to commercial brewing before the Black Death). As stocking knitting and lace making developed in England, many not-married women (and many wives) found employment in producing such goods. Not-married women also worked in other aspects of victualing—in making cheese, gardening for market, raising poultry, and huckstering foodstuffs in cities and towns. Other not-married women supported themselves in less legal ways, profiting from smuggling or prostitution or petty thievery. And of course, many not-married women, particularly singlewomen, worked as domestic servants in town or country, and others received wages as common day laborers. Some of the employments of early modern singlewomen and widows were comparatively new (such as lace making), but others (such as domestic service) were very traditional indeed. Most important, whatever the work of not-married women in 1600, it was viewed (like the work of their forebears in 1300) as low-skilled and low-status work, and it yielded (like the work of their forebears in 1300) poor remuneration. Low in perceived skill, low in conferred status, low in pay or profits, this is the sort of work that not-married women had found in brewing in 1300—good work for a woman but still quite humble. Although brewing no longer offered such employment by 1600, not-married women found similar work elsewhere. In the midst of the changing world of England after the Black Death, the work status of singlewomen and widows had stood still.

CHAPTER FOUR

WORKING TOGETHER

Wives and Husbands in the Brewers' Gild of London

In the history of brewing, an understanding of the work undertaken by wives and husbands is critical but elusive. Living in a society where work was structured more around households than individuals, many wives and husbands shared the tasks of brewing for profit. They worked together—sometimes with the assistance of servants and children—to collect supplies and materials, to brew up the ale or beer, and then to market it either retail or wholesale. Some wives and husbands might not have shared this labor at all, but many others certainly did. For them, brewing was a family affair, not an individual pursuit. Yet the structure and significance of this family affair shifted in most towns, and many villages as well, between 1300 and 1600. In 1300, it was most common to buy ale from married brewsters who supervised their families' work in the trade, work that was (more often than not) a by-industry that supplemented other household employments. By 1600, it had become more common to buy ale or beer from married male brewers who supervised work that constituted the primary occupation of their households and that sometimes employed more hired than familial labor.

We have already considered this contrast as exemplified by the histories of Denise Marlere and Joan Alleson. Working in the late fourteenth century, Denise Marlere might have benefited from her husband's assistance in brewing, but both they and their neighbors seem to have known that Nicholas was the butcher and Denise the brewster (no matter how much one assisted the other). Working in the mid-sixteenth century, Joan Alleson might have assisted her husband, Mitchell, in brewing and certainly stood in his place after he died (later ceding that place temporarily to her second husband, Lawrence Stringer), but if Mitchell had not been a brewer, she probably would never have worked in the trade. By the late eighteenth century, wives of brewers—such as Hester Thrale—still helped their husbands keep accounts and manage breweries, but they did not necessarily even follow the trade as widows. When her husband died in 1781, Hester Thrale was advised that "it was madness to carry on with no boy to inherit," and she sold the business a few years later.[1]

Yet as the balance of responsibility for commercial brewing slowly shifted from wives to husbands, it shifted in very subtle and largely undocumented ways. Our public records focus so often on householders as the persons legally responsible for domestic employments that they obfuscate the realities of brewing by wives and, in the end, the realities of brewing by husbands as well. In other words, for a village whose aletasters regularly named householders in their presentments, we cannot trace any shift in marital responsibilities for brewing: husbands were named in 1300, 1400, 1500, 1600, and later. And for a village whose aletasters once named individual brewers but later shifted to naming householders, we might suspect that this shift reflected new divisions of familial labor in brewing but we cannot be certain of it. Indeed, aletasters' presentments sometimes began to list husbands rather than wives for reasons entirely unrelated to brewing itself, such as the arrival of a new clerk.[2] Private records, which might help us to see what lay behind public identifications of brewers, simply do not exist. In an ideal archive, we might find letters or diaries or memoirs of brewsters whose husbands either did or did not become more involved in their trade. But most brewsters (and most male brewers as well) were illiterate, and the earliest private records we have for brewers are not domestic or personal memorabilia but instead business accounts from sixteenth-century brewhouses run by men.

We cannot, in other words, examine directly the changing ways in which wives and husbands worked together in commercial brewing. But in one unusual source, we can trace some ways in which wives and husbands negotiated their responsibilities in the trade. In February 1418, William Porlond was appointed clerk of the Brewers' gild of London, and he began immediately to record information about the gild in a book which he kept from his initial appointment until his death in 1438. He recorded not only miscellaneous petitions, arguments, and accounts but also information about the personnel of the gild. As if eager to fill his new post well, Porlond kept especially careful records in the early years of his tenure. For the first seven years of his book (1418–25), we have complete lists of members; and for 1420–21 in particular, we know who paid quarterage (or annual dues) to the gild, who attended the gild breakfast, who wore the gild livery (distinctive clothing) of either hood or gown, who feasted at the gild dinner, who joined the gild as new members, and who acquired the freedom of the city through the gild. Porlond's careful records during the early years of his clerkship are especially useful because two additional sets of information were generated by a bitter dispute in 1419–20 between brewers and the mayor, the legendary Richard Whittington (who was much hated by the brewers of his day): a census-like list of brewers compiled by the city, and a special collection among brewers to raise funds for their fight against the city (carefully recorded as a *taxatio voluntaria* in Porlond's book).[3]

Porlond's records show that about one-third of the members of the Brewers' gild were women and, indeed, that most of these women were wives. Some wives joined the gild as individuals, while their husbands pursued other trades, but many other wives joined the gild jointly with their husbands. From this extraordinary book, then, we are able to observe how wives and husbands participated—separately and together—in the day-to-day operation of a nascent professional organization for brewers, and by extension, how they might have participated in the day-to-day operations of their families' brewhouses. As we shall see, wives and husbands worked together in brewing in early fifteenth-century London, but they did not, it seems, work in equivalent ways. The slow professionalization of brewing, of which gild formation was a critical part, was pushing husbands to the forefront and wives into the background.

Gild Formation and Women

When William Porlond began to keep the Brewers' records in 1418, commercial brewing in London was already a highly developed and organized trade. Brewers were a diverse group. Some managed large establishments; others brewed in only small amounts. Most brewed ale; a few brewed beer. Many focused on the retail trade; others profited from the wholesale market. Some brewed as a by-industrial supplement to other work; others pursued brewing as a primary occupation. In addition, the trade was shared among several distinct occupations: brewers, to be sure, but also hostelers, cooks, pie bakers, and hucksters. Hostelers served their guests with ale they either purchased from brewers or brewed themselves. Cooks, pie bakers, and hucksters usually regrated ale; that is, they bought ale, which they then hawked through the city for a profit. Cooks and pie bakers sold ale along with other foodstuffs; hucksters often specialized in retailing ale alone.[4] In 1406, the city agreed that the mystery of brewers, an organization whose history stretched back to a fraternity founded by John Enfield in 1342, could supervise all persons working in the ale trade—brewers, hostelers, cooks, pie bakers, and hucksters. The gild empowered by this agreement slowly expanded its supervisory powers until, in 1438, it obtained at the great cost of more than £141 a royal grant of incorporation. This incorporation permanently altered the balance of power between city and gild. Thereafter, the city and the gild acted as more or less equal partners in negotiating the terms of the market in ale and beer—prices, supervision, quality, measures, and the like. Yet, although the Brewers' gild had thereby acquired extensive supervisory powers over its trade, it was not among the most distinguished gilds in the late medieval hierarchy. Perhaps not ranked at all before 1400, it placed only twenty-sixth of 65 gilds in 1487.[5]

When the Brewers received their incorporation in 1438, they lagged several generations behind London's more prestigious trades. As early as 1328, 25 mysteries in London already elected their own officers, and many other trades—including skinners, girdlers, goldsmiths, and tailors—received royal charters from Edward III. Yet compared to brewers in other cities, London brewers were precocious. Several generations after the brewers of London had received their charter from Henry VI, brewers' gilds were still rare in other English cities. By 1500, brewers in Hull, Norwich, Oxford, Coventry, Newcastle, and Southampton were getting organized, but most did not fully incorporate until the next century. In Southampton, for example, brewers were organized enough to accept responsibility for part of the town's fortifications in the fifteenth century, but they were not incorporated until 1543.[6] In many other towns, brewers' gilds did not incorporate until the late sixteenth century or even seventeenth century: 1574 in Leicester, 1575 in Winchester, 1578 in Northampton, 1579 in Exeter, 1586 in York, 1607 in Chester, and 1624 in Lincoln.[7]

In London and in other towns, gilds did not encompass all commercial brewers. Given the great diversity of those associated with the trade, many who brewed only as a by-industry—perhaps many wives, and certainly many hostelers and cooks—avoided gild membership. Hucksters and servants were regulated by the gild but not always part of it.[8] As a result, many persons involved in London's ale market evaded full involvement in the gild, not paying quarterage, not wearing livery, or eschewing both. When the city compiled its list of brewers in 1419–20, it named 290 persons; of these only about two-thirds (185) had any association with the gild in that year.[9] The gild, in short, represented the upper crust of the brewing trade, and its membership excluded many humble brewers, many part-time brewers, and all alesellers.

Not surprisingly, women numbered disproportionately among those excluded from (or avoiding) gild membership. Of the householders named in the city list, females failed to associate with the gild with much greater frequency than males (roughly one-half of brewsters, as opposed to one-fourth of male brewers).[10] Some brewsters, such as Beatrice Tye and Alice Gildsborough, never joined the gild or otherwise participated in its activities. And all tapsters worked without such association. Forced to endure the fines and regulations of the gild, these brewsters and tapsters must have seen the gild as a supervisory body, not an associational opportunity. In 1419–20, for example, the gild's list of those selling with false measures included more women than men. Only two of these women might have belonged to the gild, and many others were nameless, identified only, for example, as a "huckster by the stocks" or "a tapster in the cellar at the end of Bread Street."[11]

These nameless women—some of whom were married and others who were not—remind us that for many tapsters and some brewsters the formation of a gild promised more ill than good. Gilds helped to professionalize a trade, supporting those who pursued it full time and undercutting those who worked on a part-time or by-industrial basis. Gilds also created their own public and political structures from which women, even those economically very active and successful in the trade, were generally excluded. And gilds often sought to restrict participation in a trade, particularly undermining the work of singlewomen, widows (save for widows of gildsmen), and other not-married women.[12] Most brewers' gilds were no different from other gilds in these respects. In Chester, the brewers' gild tried to monopolize the trade, particularly hurting poor widows and aged citizens who sought to make a small living from the trade. In Oxford, the gild limited the ability of widows to stay in the trade and also forbade the employment of women to transport ale to customers. In Leicester, the gild formed by the city in 1574 was made up of men whose wives brewed, not the

Table 4.1   Women and Men in the Brewers' Gild of London, 1418–25

Year	Females % (no.)	Males % (no.)	Total number
1418–19	35 (78)	65 (142)	220
1419–20	31 (77)	69 (169)	246
1420–21	35 (76)	65 (142)	218
1421–22	37½ (99)	62½ (165)	264
1422–23	42 (131)	58 (181)	312
1423–24	42 (144)	58 (196)	340
1424–25	41 (152)	59 (218)	370

Source: Quarterage lists found in GL, Ms 5440, fos. 2–4, 47–49v., 63v.–64v., 67v.–69, 82–83v., 115v.–117v., 131–133.

brewsters themselves.[13] In almost all of these gilds, the membership was all male or included just a handful of women. In short, most brewers' gilds in sixteenth-century England were, like most gilds in other trades, gilds of men.

But in early fifteenth-century London, women, particularly married women, were very active as members of the first brewers' gild in the realm. Indeed, women constituted roughly one-third of gild members. As table 4.1 shows, the proportion even rose slightly over the early years of Porlond's book. In accepting quarterage payments from large numbers of widows, singlewomen, and wives, the Brewers' gild followed a practice unique in the city. Most other London gilds tolerated no female members at all; this was true of the Grocers in 1373, the Coopers in 1439–40, and the Weavers in 1456.[14] The Brewers' gild would have been exceptional, then, in accommodating *any* female members, even if in only small numbers, but among the Brewers, one woman was in the gild for every two men. In this most unusual of circumstances, how did women and men—or, since most gild members were married, how did wives and husbands—share the responsibilities and opportunities of gild membership?

Wives and Husbands in the Brewers' Gild of London

The number of women in the Brewers' gild has been consistently underreported since William Herbert in 1834 counted 39 women among those who wore the livery of the Brewers in the fifth year of the reign of Henry V.[15] I have been unable to replicate Herbert's count, but it is wrong; the quarterage lists from 1418 to 1424 show between 78 and 152 women who paid dues each year. The main difference between my figures and those of Herbert (and the many modern historians who have followed him in this regard) is that I counted the wives. Although many women and men paid quarterage as individuals (usually paying 12d. a year), most people paid as married couples, jointly rendering 2s. each year. Hence, some women (mostly widows but also some wives and a few singlewomen) belonged to the gild as individuals in the early 1420s, but dozens of other women participated in the gild together with their husbands and paid,

Table 4.2   Representation of Households in Quarterage Payments to the Brewers' Gild of London, 1418–25

Year	Households represented by female alone % (no.)	Households represented by male alone % (no.)	Households represented by married couple % (no.)	Number of total households
1418–19	11 (17)	51 (81)	38 (61)	159
1419–20	9½ (18)	59 (110)	31½ (59)	187
1420–21	11 (18)	53 (84)	36 (58)	160
1421–22	9 (17)	46 (83)	45 (82)	182
1422–23	9 (18)	34 (68)	57 (113)	199
1423–24	11 (23)	34 (75)	55 (121)	219
1424–25	9 (22)	37 (88)	54 (130)	240

Source: Quarterage lists found in GL, Ms 5440, fos. 2–4, 47–49v., 63v.-64v., 67v.-69, 82-83v., 115v.-117v., 131-133.

just like their husbands and just like individual members, 12d. dues each year. In other words, Porlond's quarterage lists provide two sorts of information: they tell us what people belonged to the gild (as broken down by sex in table 4.1), but they also tell us in what form each household attached itself to the gild (whether through a man, a woman, or a married couple).[16]

As table 4.2 shows, roughly 10 percent of the businesses represented in the gild in the early 1420s were run primarily by women.[17] Marital status alone does not explain why some women paid quarterage as individuals, for not only widows and singlewomen but also wives did so. Of the women who paid quarterage on their own in 1418–19, more than half were widows. In some cases, widows managed brewhouses that, once a by-industry to the main occupations of their husbands, had taken on new economic importance in widowhood (that is, they worked in brewing, as had Denise Marlere in late fourteenth-century Bridgwater). In some cases, however, widows of brewers managed brewhouses that had been and continued to be the main economic resource of their households (in other words, some substituted for their dead husbands, as would the widow Joan Alleson in the 1570s). The predominance of widows among women who joined the gild unaccompanied by husbands increased over the seven years covered by Porlond's early lists. In the quarterage of 1424–25, more than two-thirds of women paying separate quarterage were widows. Singlewomen also joined the Brewers' gild but not as frequently as widows—perhaps as many as four in 1418 and two in 1425. As a rule, not-married brewsters, whether widowed or never married or otherwise alone, remained in the gild for quite short periods of time, often only a year or two.[18]

Wives also sometimes maintained gild membership without their husbands, and in the 1418–19 quarterage list, four wives did so. In most cases, it is likely that these wives were running brewhouses as by-industries, as concerns sepa-

rate from the occupations of their husbands. Agnes Bugge, the wife of the draper
Stephen Bugge, for example, paid sole dues to the gild throughout the 1420s.
When Stephen Bugge died in 1429, he bequeathed what he called his brewhouse
(*totum tenementum meum bracineum*) to Agnes, and deeds indicate that he was, in fact,
the legal owner of the property. Yet his failure to join the gild and his clear
involvement in the drapery trade suggest that Agnes was the primary manager
of the brewhouse. Similarly, when John Amwell, skinner, died in 1425, his will
noted that his wife, Joan, who had joined the fraternity in 1422–23, supervised
a brewhouse, which he then bequeathed to her. Like Stephen Bugge, John
Amwell never joined the Brewers' gild.[19]

In other cases, wives who paid quarterage as individuals might, in fact, have
been representing the primary occupation of their households, not by-industries
ancillary to their husbands' occupations. Idonea Hatton, wife of Roger Swanfield, was the sole member of her household who paid quarterage for five years
between 1418 and 1423. During these years, however, her husband seems to
have been actively involved in the brewhouse, and in 1424, he also joined the
gild as a full member.[20] Similarly, most of the men who belonged as individuals to the gild represented a conjugal business. Nicholas Fuller paid quarterage
for himself alone until, after several years, his wife was brought into the gild. In
other words, among those who paid quarterage alone, some women and most
men were representing marital brewhouses. Why a wife such as Idonea Hatton
or a husband such as Nicholas Fuller maintained individual gild memberships is
usually unclear, but in many cases, their spouses eventually joined under pressure from the gild to regularize their relationship to the trade.[21]

Insofar as quarterage payments can suggest the actual nature of brewing in
early fifteenth-century London, the data in table 4.2 suggest that although some
brewhouses were managed by individuals—widows, singlewomen, some married women and married men in dual-trade households, and perhaps some
bachelors—most brewhouses in London were managed jointly by wives and
husbands. Over the years covered by Porlond's early quarterage lists, the gild was
increasingly able to profit from this fact; by 1422, more than half of the brewhouses represented in the gild paid double quarterage, for both wife and husband. We cannot know why some brewhouses were represented in the gild by
husbands only, others by wives only, and still others by both wives and husbands, but we can know that most of the most profitable brewhouses in London
(that is, those represented in the gild) demanded the attention of a married couple. Although some not-married women supported themselves by brewing and
some wives brewed as a by-industry, most commercial brewing in early fifteenth-century London was a family affair.

Whether working with their husbands or working at brewing as a by-
industry, married women often reaped considerable profits from the ale market.
The economic clout of married women in the brewing trade is particularly evident in their contributions to the *taxatio voluntaria* through which the gild raised
money for its fight against Richard Whittington. Of the three wives noted as
paying quarterage as individuals in 1419–20, two contributed to this levy (albeit
through their husbands, at least as rendered by Porlond in his listing), and they

contributed quite large sums. Stephen Bugge, the husband of gildswoman Agnes Bugge, offered the largest contribution of all (20s.), and Roger Swanfield, the husband of gildswoman Idonea Hatton, paid a quite respectable 6s.8d. Of the 59 married couples in the gild, an exceptionally high number (39, or 66 percent) contributed to the tax, and they offered exceptionally generous sums. These patterns of contribution to the *taxatio voluntaria* indicate that married women—whether pursuing brewing as a by-industry (as Agnes Bugge probably did) or brewing in cooperation with their husbands (as Idonea Hatton probably did)—were often quite successful at their work.[22] Indeed, some were so successful that they were able to break into the profitable trade with the Crown. Wives were actively involved in brewing in at least 19 of the 24 brewing concerns to which the Crown owed money in 1420–22. In other words, about 4 of every 5 brewhouses involved in the lucrative royal trade in ale were managed, at least in part, by a married woman.[23]

Many of these married brewsters seem to have worked quite separately from their husbands. Their success, in other words, might have been enhanced by the financial and social assistance of their husbands, but it was not necessarily a result of the husbands' direct day-to-day involvement. Agnes Bugge's husband, Stephen, might have contributed on her behalf to the *taxatio voluntaria*, but he worked in another trade altogether (drapery). Their arrangement was not unusual; men in at least 20 percent of the households covered by this analysis were involved in other trades, and many of the women in these households must have been primarily responsible for the brewing undertaken therein. For example, John Russell and his wife, Alice, both belonged to the Brewers' gild, but since John was a grocer, it is likely that Alice took primary responsibility for the commercial brewing done in their household. Like John Russell, many of these husbands were involved in victualing or other trades related to brewing; indeed, the most common occupation was that of maltman. Yet most husbands of married brewsters worked in trades entirely unrelated to brewing; Agnes Bargon's husband was a tallow chandler, Cecilia Bedwell's a whittawer, and Agnes Flete's a capmaker. By-industrial brewing by wives sometimes complemented husbands' occupations, but it was more often than not pursued quite separately.[24]

Yet, although wives successfully managed their brewhouses (either on their own or together with their husbands) and although wives joined the gild in large numbers, they did not partake fully with their husbands in the associational life of the gild. Their husbands were full members, enjoying all the perquisites of gild life, but wives were, at best, only partial members, enjoying a quite limited range of the opportunities offered by the gild. The different experiences of women and men in the Brewers' gild tell us about how this gild (and other gilds like it) sought to limit the participation of women. But it also indirectly speaks to critical changes in the ways in which wives and husbands worked together in commercial brewing. In London in the 1420s, wives continued to work in brewing in large numbers, but their work was increasingly hidden behind the public personalities of their husbands.

For a young man embarking on a career as a brewer, the gild offered a set of very clear and hierarchical opportunities. After proving himself in service, he could expect to become free of the gild, paying usually 6s.8d. to gain thereby not only civic enfranchisement but also the right to wear the livery of the Brewers. Yet, after gaining his freedom, he often would continue to work for others, and it was not until he was able to marry and establish his own brewhouse (if at all) that he might move to the next stage of the gild hierarchy. At that time, he could acquire (usually for a fee of 3s.4d.) entry to the fraternity of Brewers. With entry to the fraternity came the obligation of paying annual quarterage and the right to join others in the gild's annual feast. Eventually, a very successful male brewer might expect to advance still further, attaining invitations to the special meals held for the "more noble" of the craft and being chosen to serve in gild offices. Essentially, then, a young male brewer faced a gild of three tiers: (1) those free of the gild and in livery, (2) those admitted to the fraternity, and (3) those selected for participation in the governance of the gild.[25] For a young woman, the situation looked very different, and in essence only the second tier was open to her (and only partly open at that).

With very few exceptions, the first tier was closed to women, probably because freedom and livery were so closely associated with civic life, ceremony, and politics. Hence, the gild was never a route to civic enfranchisement for women. Of the 24 persons who acquired the freedom between 1419 and 1421, not one was a woman, and the same absolute exclusion of women from the freedom recurs throughout Porlond's book. Although one brewster styled herself as a "freewoman" of the city in her will, her status came from widowhood, not the gild.[26]

Similarly, the public declaration of association that came through wearing the livery of the gild—either the hood worn by lesser brewers or the gown worn by greater brewers—was also rarely undertaken by women, regardless of marital status. By wearing livery, brewers publicly expressed gild association and solidarity; livery was worn at funerals of gild brothers and sisters, at gild functions (both within the Brewers' hall and also outside it), and on civic occasions (when all gilds would gather in their liveries). The wearing of livery was so important that it was replaced every two years, a quite frequent turnover considering the cost: individual men usually paid 6s. (for the cloth for a hood) or about 20s. (for the cloth for a gown). Although no precise rules seem to have determined who did and did not wear livery, the general practice is clear: only men wore livery, and they wore it from the time that they gained the freedom of the craft. Porlond's records occasionally noted women who wore livery, but few women did so. Six women took livery in 1418–19; no women in 1420–21; three women in 1422–23; and in most subsequent years, a mere handful of women (and sometimes none at all) purchased or received livery. With only one exception, all of these women took material for wearing the lesser livery of the hood.[27]

Who were these few women who were listed among the hundreds of men who received livery cloth? In some cases, these women were completely unexceptional—ordinary women who, usually with their husbands, paid quarterage to the gild. In other cases, however, women wore livery because of the status of their husbands; masters' wives often received livery cloth, as occasionally did

William Porlond's wife and female servant. And in perhaps the most telling cases, women who wore livery were exceptional in their own right, either boasting long-standing attachments to the gild or paying for their own entry into the fraternity (a payment that was, as we shall see, rare for women). These women —some married, some not—seem to have managed businesses on their own.[28] In other words, women were most likely to wear livery in two quite distinct circumstances: (1) as the proud wives of officers of the gild or (2) as brewsters who, whether married or not, belonged to the Brewers as individual gildswomen. Women were least likely to wear livery if they were ordinary wives, married to men not distinguished by gild office and working in brewing together with their husbands.

In any case, the wearing of livery by all these women was clearly unusual. Unlike most men who regularly purchased livery cloth every two years, most women who received livery cloth took it on only one occasion. Perhaps these women wore their livery so seldom that they did not need to replace it; perhaps they thought it too expensive to replace; perhaps they found that having livery was an unnecessary extravagance. And, of course, we must remember that, unlike most men, most women never wore livery at all. When Emma Canon, Katherine Wygeyn, and William Porlond's servant Rose took livery cloth in 1422–23, they were among 224 men who did so. Or to put it another way: in the livery distribution 1420–21, none of the women who paid quarterage donned the livery of the gild, but 9 of every 10 men did. In practice, women were the only group in the gild who regularly failed to wear livery.

The position of women in the second tier of the gild progression for men— entering the fraternity, paying quarterage, and attending the annual feast—was certainly better, although somewhat awkward. Most women entered the fraternity by virtue of their husbands' entry (and the standard entry fee of 3s.4d. remained unchanged for both married couples and individuals). Women rarely paid separately for entry, but they could do so; Joan Amwell and Katherine Wygeyn entered the fraternity in 1421–23, Gillian Scot entered in 1429–30, and Joan Sturmyn did the same in 1430–31. These patterns suggest that entry involved not individuals as much as households. In other words, entry to the fraternity registered a new brewhouse (or an old brewhouse under new management), and the names associated with such entries suggest that these new brewing concerns were run by married couples, and occasionally unmarried men or brewsters (not married as well as married). Certainly, it seems clear that the women who entered the fraternity alone managed separate brewhouses. Joan Amwell's husband was a skinner, and Joan Sturmyn's husband was a tailor; both men seem to have been completely uninvolved in the commercial brewing of their wives. Gillian Scot was probably a singlewoman. Katherine Wygeyn was actually married to a brewer (William Termeday), but they were treated so discretely in gild records that they probably managed two brewhouses. In any case, women such as Joan Amwell, Joan Sturmyn, Gillian Scot, and Katherine Wygeyn were exceptional; most women entered the fraternity in tandem with their husbands.[29]

The obligation to pay quarterage accompanied, of course, entry to the fraternity, and whether women formally entered the fraternity or not, they were liable for quarterage payments. As we have seen, women paid quarterage in large numbers, accounting in the early 1420s for roughly one of every three members of the gild. With entry to the fraternity and payment of quarterage, gild members also became eligible to attend the annual feast of the gild, an important event in the festive year, in which both gildswomen and gildsmen participated. In 1421, 155 persons attended the annual dinner, including 36 wives who came with their husbands and 6 women who attended alone. This annual dinner, called "Our Feast" in the accounts, usually entailed substantial feasting, musical and dramatic entertainment, and some transactions of gild business. Masters' accounts were sometimes settled at these dinners, and the feast probably also included politicking, possibly elections to gild offices (this was certainly true in later years) and discussions about gild policies. Women probably participated either not at all or only informally in the political aspects of the annual dinner; since women could neither serve in gild offices nor gain civic enfranchisement through the gild, it is unlikely that they participated in electoral processes. It is even possible that women and men sat in different rooms at these dinners (as was done in some gilds).[30]

In any case, women, although present at these dinners, did not attend as regularly as men. Women accounted for one in three members of the gild but only one in four persons at the annual dinner. Not-married brewsters attended in especially reduced numbers, and although wives attended in larger numbers than other women, they were still more likely to miss the dinner than to attend it. Thirty-six wives ate with their husbands, and a few others feasted alone, but 77 men came to the dinner unaccompanied. Costs might partially explain the comparatively low attendance of women. The dinner was not free to members, and women, interestingly enough, paid lower charges than men. Most men alone paid 16d., most married couples paid 2s., and most women alone paid 12d. This lower charge might reflect the gild's expectation that women would consume less food than men, but since some men also paid 12d., it seems probable that the lower charge reflects a qualitative decision about the ability to pay. Certainly, many poorer members of the gild—and perhaps especially, therefore, not-married women—might have skipped the dinner because, despite the reduced charge, they were unable or unwilling to pay. Whether excluded by policy or poverty, singlewomen and widows were almost entirely absent from this annual celebration of the gild, and wives attended in quite reduced numbers.[31]

As members of the gild, women also contributed to the exceptional tax of 1419–20, the taxatio voluntaria to raise money for the gild's fight against Richard Whittington. Porlond's notations about this collection, however, obfuscate the contributions of wives to this effort; he noted in his list only husbands, not wives. Yet we can reach two conclusions from his records. First, not-married women were either especially poor brewsters or especially unenthusiastic supporters of the gild in its moment of crisis. More than half of the members of the gild contributed to this collection, but of 15 widows and singlewomen, only 2 chipped in. And although 5 other women (who were not members of the gild) contributed to the tax, female contributors were far outnumbered by men (9 women versus 146 men). Since female contributors tended to offer much smaller sums than men, poverty seems the likeliest explanation. Second, some wives, especially those who belonged to the gild without their husbands, were strong supporters of the cause. Through their husbands, Agnes Bugge and Idonea Hatton contributed very large sums to the *taxatio voluntaria*, reinforcing our sense that they (and others) were very successful brewsters. These large contributions also underline the commitment of at least some women to the gild as an institution. Not-married brewsters and poor brewsters might have eschewed membership in the gild and resented the gild's supervision of their trade, but other brewsters, particularly married brewsters and brewsters who managed profitable concerns, supported the gild with enthusiasm.[32]

The third and final tier of gild life, participation in gild politics, seems to have been entirely closed to female members. Through most of the 1420s, the gild was governed by four masters, who remained in power for two-year terms; then, in 1429, the term was shifted to a single year in order (among other rationales) to allow younger members to enjoy the honors and benefits of mastership. Yet, although the gild sought by this change to open office to as many able members as possible, only men were judged able; no woman ever served as a master of the gild. Moreover, women seem not to have participated in general decisions about gild life and policy, for as a 1388 report explicitly explained, the Brewers promulgated new ordinances by the agreement of brothers alone. The political disability of women in this specific case is scarcely surprising, and since gild office was generally reserved for only the most successful men, many men, as well as all women, never achieved mastership. But men could at least aspire to gild office and know that, if clever, judicious, and lucky, they might achieve their goals. And men could also at least participate in the general decisions of gild life. For women, such aspirations were impossible. Women joined the gild and supported it with the same quarterage payments as those rendered by men, but they were always part of the governed, never part of the governors.[33] This was as true of married as of not-married women.

Women also did not attend the "power event" of the gild year—the annual breakfast. Porlond noted that the breakfast held on 20 May 1421 was a "*jantaculum nobilioribus artis predicte*," and his list of attenders entirely bears out this description; only an elite subset of the membership attended the gild breakfast. Of the 40 men breakfasting together on 20 May (another 12 were invited but failed to attend), many were past, current, or future officers in the gild; many were involved in the lucrative ale trade with the Crown; most wore the more prestigious gowned livery; and many contributed quite substantial sums to the *taxatio voluntaria* of 1419–20. While they breakfasted, these men conducted gild business—adjudicating quarrels, dispensing alms, reviewing accounts, appointing clerks, and the like. In return, they seem to have feasted at the expense of the gild, and feasted very well. Most members of the gild were excluded from this feast, but the only group consistently excluded was that of women. Among men attending the breakfast in 1421 were some who wore only the lesser hood of the Brewers' livery, some who ran only modest brewhouses, and some who had not even paid quarterage in that year to the gild. Yet although some male brewers of modest status and marginal attachment to the gild attended the breakfast, no brewster—no matter how successful in trade—joined the feast. For example, the long-standing gildswoman and successful brewster Idonea Hatton did not attend the breakfast; instead, her husband, who would not join the gild for four more years, feasted with 39 other men.[34]

William Porlond's detailed notes about the Brewers' gild in 1418–25—who gained civic enfranchisement through the gild and then wore the liveries of hood and gown; who paid quarterage to the gild, feasted at the gild dinner and contributed to the *taxatio voluntaria*; who held office and attended the elite annual breakfast—offer a remarkably clear picture of life in a late medieval gild. Women's place in the brewing trade was certainly exceptional, for, unlike other gilds, the Brewers' gild admitted women in large numbers. Yet women were not full members of the gild. They might best be described as *working* members rather than *corporate* members. In most cases, women associated with the Brewers' gild to the extent necessary to follow their trade, but they were not involved in the many rituals and customs through which the gild defined and asserted its corporate solidarity. These rituals and customs were not minor matters but were instead essential to the life of both gild and city.[35] In part, women seem to have been excluded from certain functions, such as admission to the freedom or feasting at the annual breakfast. In part, however, women also seem to have failed to distinguish themselves as enthusiastic members of the gild, for they attended the annual dinner less frequently than men and they responded to the special call of the *taxatio voluntaria* less readily than men. These two trends doubtless complemented each other, as women, offered only a partial membership in the gild, failed to support it as fully as men (a failure that probably seemed to justify, if justification had been needed, their lesser status as partial members).

Working Together

What does the ambivalent place of women in the Brewers' gild of London tell us about how wives and husbands might have worked together in brewing? A hundred years before William Porlond began to keep the records of the Brewers' gild, this question might have seemed nonsensical. At that time, brewsters so predominated in London that civic ordinances sometimes specified brewers by using exclusively feminine terms.[36] By the early fifteenth century, however, the brewing trade was more thoroughly mixed, pursued by men as well as by women. In most cases, as we have seen, women and men shared the trade within a conjugal household, with a wife and husband together managing a brewhouse. And as we have also seen, these conjugal brewhouses were among the most successful enterprises in London's ale trade. When wives and husbands worked together in brewing, how did they divide their labor and responsibilities?

One answer to this question is quite clear. In terms of public activity in the trade, husbands had more responsibilities than their wives. To be sure, married women enjoyed a public presence in brewing, as members of the gild, that was itself quite unusual; in most trades, gild membership was not open to women at all, except for widows of dead gildsmen. So, married brewsters, because of their ability to join the Brewers' gild, enjoyed a public confirmation of their work that was not enjoyed by women who worked with their husbands in weaving or drapery or cooperage or most of London's other skilled trades. Yet the scope of this public confirmation was narrowing. In both the gild and the brewhouse, husbands increasingly took on a public role that encompassed the work of their wives. In the day-to-day life of the gild, as we have seen, husbands participated in crucial activities that excluded their wives—meeting at the gild breakfasts, wearing the gild livery, and otherwise expressing the corporate solidarity of the gild.

In the day-to-day life of brewhouses, husbands seem to have similarly assumed public responsibility for commercial brewing. When Porlond noted only men in his list of creditors of the Crown in 1420–21 and 1421–22, he translated conjugal enterprises into male brewers. And when city clerks ignored all wives in compiling their list of brewers in 1419–20, they attributed to men activities that were either partly or wholly their wives'. In an important sense, these sorts of practices were not new. Because the city compiled its 1419–20 list in order to make brewers liable for future infractions, it focused on the responsible person under the law—the husband. This was a common and long-standing practice in many places. Yet the principle behind this practice— the principle that a householder was responsible for the actions of his or her dependents—had not always been applied to brewsters, and as husbands in London and elsewhere grew more and more involved in the daily activities of commercial brewing, it seems to have been applied more regularly. In short, the trend was towards a sort of "shadow economy" within the brewing industry. Married women increasingly worked in the shadow of the public presence of their husbands, who—whether they worked in the trade or not—personified in public the brewer in the household.

In the 1420s, the Brewers' gild was newly established and not yet incorporated, the brewing trade was expanding but not yet highly capitalized, and the technological innovation of beerbrewing was known but not widely practiced. In subsequent decades, the shift toward a greater public presence for men and a lesser public presence for women reached fruition. By 1437–38, individual gildswomen accounted for only 6 percent of the membership of the Brewers' gild, and only singlewomen and widows (no wives) paid sole quarterage. By 1500–1501, wives no longer paid quarterage at all (even with their husbands), and the only women then admitted to membership were, it seems, widows (of whom 13 accounted for 7 percent of gild members). This status quo—only a few widows among the largely male membership of the gild—continued through much of the sixteenth century, although in some years, no women at all belonged.[37] Wives were no longer gildswomen, but in at least some instances, they were still brewsters. As late as 1544, Richard Pickering, a member of the Brewers' Company (as the gild was then known), told the mayor and aldermen that he could not answer their inquiry about the yields of brewing because "he committeth the whole charge thereof to his wife." Joan Pickering was not a member of the gild.[38]

What this increasing privatization of wives' brewing meant in terms of the day-to-day management of a brewhouse is hard to say. It seems likely that the public presence of "brewers" like Richard Pickering gave them a certain authority within the brewhouse, as well as outside it. Pickering might have found it convenient to tell the mayor and aldermen that he gave the "whole charge" of brewing to his wife, but he might have taken on some tasks in the business, especially tasks that suited his greater public role. He might have directed and managed the servants; he might have contracted formal agreements with suppliers and customers; he might have arranged loans and accepted debts. In other words, he might have assisted his wife by doing things that she—as a woman and more particularly, a *married* woman under coverture—found hard to do. Joan Pickering might have understood better than her husband the secrets of brewing and the mysteries of the trade, but it was Richard Pickering who could join the gild, agree to the contracts, give orders to the servants, and otherwise advance her trade. To judge by the wealth of conjugal brewhouses in the 1420s, a division of labor of this sort worked very well indeed.

In a very important sense, gild formation was itself a critical part of this growing privatization of the work of married brewsters. Gilds provided a new and especially powerful forum that extended into new areas the old practice of subsuming a wife's brewing into the person of her husband. As a brewers' gild confirmed the dignity and honor of the trade, it tended to highlight the work of men and obscure the work of women. As a brewers' gild regulated itself and negotiated with civic officers, it replicated in its own administration the male-only hierarchy of civic governance. As a brewers' gild sought to reduce a widespread and diverse trade to manageable proportions, it favored large businesses and frowned on small enterprises, which were so often managed by women. And as a brewers' gild sought to enhance its place within local hierarchies, it celebrated its male membership in public displays and public processions. Gilds of brewers, like gilds in almost all other trades, boded ill for the work of women, wives as well as widows, singlewomen, and others.

Yet other forces also encouraged the eclipse of married brewsters, and these forces could be felt in towns without brewers' gilds, as well as in the countryside. When not-married brewsters began to leave the trade from the late fourteenth century, married brewsters were almost certainly affected. As long as it was not unusual to buy ale from a singlewoman or widow, wives could maintain a public presence in the trade. But when not-married brewsters in London and elsewhere slowly gave up the trade, individual brewing by any woman, including a wife, might have come to seem more unusual and anomalous. For example, although not-married brewsters were not very active in early fifteenth-century London, they nevertheless constituted the bulk of the women who belonged to the Brewers' gild in their own right. As long as single and widowed brewsters, no matter how poor, were active enough to obtain membership in the gild, they created a place in the trade for all women, regardless of marital status. In other words, the Brewers' gild might have accepted so many female members (wives, as well as singlewomen and widows) in part *because of the work of not-married women in the trade.* When widows such as Denise Barthorp and single-women such as Emma Canon worked in brewing and maintained memberships in the gild, they created a critical and unusual female space, a female space that accommodated married as well as not-married brewsters. Without Barthorp and Canon, it is less likely that married brewsters such as Agnes Bugge and Idonea Hatton would have been able to maintain individual memberships in the gild. Indeed, as we have seen, when the presence of not-married brewsters in the gild declined from the 1430s, the presence of married brewsters declined as well. As this London example suggests, it seems likely that single and widowed brewsters—who had no choice but to maintain some public presence in the trade because they had no husbands to take on "public work" for them—created a critical public presence for all brewsters, whether married or not. When single-women and widows ceased brewing, married women might have found themselves less able than before to take on public roles in the trade.

The slow commercialization of the ale trade also contributed to the privatization of brewing by wives. As successful brewing came to demand more capital, more management, and more commitment of time, wives responded more effectively than not-married women because they could rely on their husbands to assist in critical ways. But when commercialization brought husbands into brewing, it undercut the work of wives. As brewing came to require more legal, contractual, and managerial authority from its practitioners, husbands stood more often in the stead of their wives. In contracting loans, hiring and directing servants, and negotiating sales, husbands helped their wives, but they also accrued public recognition. And as brewing became more profitable and more professionalized, it became an attractive occupation, not merely a modest by-industry. Instead of assisting their wives in a by-industry, more and more husbands—like many of the men in the Brewers' gild of early fifteenth-century London—worked with their wives in the occupation of brewing. What had been the work of women became work appealing to men as well; brewing became, in other words, a good trade for men. When this happened, by-industries pursued by wives slowly became occupations pursued by husbands.

Because of the extraordinary records kept by William Porlond, we have been able to trace some aspects of how wives and husbands worked together in brewing in early fifteenth-century London. This is a very specific time and place, especially since London was so unique a city within the realm. But we have traced in the Brewers' gild of early fifteenth-century London a trend that occurred elsewhere in due course—in towns with brewers' gilds, in towns without such gilds, and in villages. In all these places, husbands slowly took on more public roles in the trade, and wives receded into the background. Gilds contributed to this trend, but so, too, did the decline of not-married brewsters and the commercialization of the trade. As we shall see in chapter 6, regulation of brewing also played a critical role. This division of labor between wives and husbands proved to be very profitable for many conjugal brewhouses, but it slowly undermined women's work, whether public or private, in the trade. In the late eighteenth century, Hester Thrale sold the family brewery after her husband's death because she knew that a man had to run it, no matter how much that man might rely on the private advice and work of his wife and other female kin. In the late sixteenth century, Joan Alleson would probably have found this notion bemusing. And in the late fourteenth century, Denise Marlere would probably have laughed outright at such an idea. Many things changed in brewing as it was practiced in the times of Denise Marlere, Joan Alleson, and Hester Thrale; one critical change was that the public business of brewing slowly came to be associated with men alone.

CHAPTER FIVE

NEW BEER,
OLD ALE

Why was Female to Male
as Ale was to Beer?

In late fourteenth-century Lullington (Sussex), several dozen people brewed for profit. Although some sold ale regularly, brewing was not very professionalized, and most brewers in Lullington in the 1370s brewed for sale on only an occasional basis. Singlewomen and widows probably accounted for about one-third of all brewers, the rest being married women or men. One hundred years later, the brewing trade looked very different. Instead of dozens of brewers, only a handful worked in Lullington, and they often brewed "commonly" throughout the year. Among these common brewers were a few not-married women, but most brewers by the 1470s were married couples. By this time, common brewers also worked alongside other professional victualers, usually two butchers and a baker.

Within a few decades, the face of brewing in Lullington would change yet again. In the 1480s, ale (brewed with malt, water, and yeast) began to face a new competitor in Lullington—beer (brewed with malt, water, yeast, and hops). At first, beer was merely sold in Lullington, but by the 1520s it was regularly brewed on site. The introduction of this drink coincided with other changes in Lullington's brewing trade: the separation of selling from brewing; the slow disappearance of by-industrial brewers; and eventually the triumph of common victualers, who baked bread, brewed drink, and managed alehouses. By 1551, three men (and probably their unnamed wives)—Richard Colvyle, John Bennet, and Richard Compere—seem to have managed alehouses from which they sold virtually all the ale, beer, and bread purchased in Lullington.[1]

The introduction of beer—first sold and later brewed, as well as sold—was a crucial part of these changes in Lullington. To be sure, beer was not the only factor that transformed the trade in Lullington, but its introduction helped to encourage the slow emergence of a small group of professional, male brewers. Initially seen as a foul source of adulterated ale, the use of hops in brewing came

late to Lullington and the rest of England. The story of its slow acceptance by
English brewers and drinkers is a story of urbanization, immigration, capitalization, and professionalization. It is also a story of masculinization, for beerbrewing was seldom pursued by women. Although the first person to *sell* beer
on Alciston manor (of which Lullington was a part) was a woman, neither she
nor any other woman was ever cited for *brewing* beer for sale to their neighbors.
In London in the 1430s, some brewsters of ale still belonged to the Brewers' gild
on their own account, but all of the beerbrewers associated with the gild were
either men or married couples. In York at the same time, women occasionally
entered the freedom as alebrewers, but never as beerbrewers. In Southampton,
alebrewing remained long associated with women, but with the exception of a
few beerbrewers' widows, beerbrewing was a male trade.[2]

In its strong association with men, beerbrewing might not have discriminated sharply among women of different marital statuses. At a time when the
commercialization of alebrewing was working more to the disadvantage of not-
married than married women, beerbrewing seems to have been remarkably inac-
cessible to *all* women, singlewomen, wives, and widows (save, of course, for the
widows of beerbrewers). To be sure, it is very difficult to trace the ways in which
husbands and wives might have negotiated work in beerbrewing differently from
work in alebrewing; wives were seldom associated with beerbrewing in the
extant records, but since they were also seldom associated with alebrewing by the
late fifteenth century, it is almost impossible to trace distinctions between the two.
Yet wives of beerbrewers might have been less active in their husbands' trades
than were wives of alebrewers. First, the symbiotic relationship between not-
married and married women in brewing suggests, given the virtual absence of
references to beerbrewing by not-married women, that married women were
also less active in the trade. Second, it seems telling that the only two cases of
women in sixteenth-century London still privately managing breweries (even
though men took public responsibility for their trade)—the case of Joan Pickering and her husband, Richard (discussed in chapter 4), and the case of Joan Bellows and her son, Roger (discussed in the notes)—both involved the production
of ale, not beer.[3] We cannot be sure, but it seems likely that married, as well as not-
married, brewsters found beerbrewing less accessible than alebrewing.

The coincidence of the rise of beerbrewing in England with the decline of
brewsters is a specific instance of an important general trend: the association of
new technologies with men. This link can be found in brewing outside of England—for example, in late medieval Denmark, men controlled the trade in
highly valued German beer and women were restricted to selling less valued
Danish beer.[4] It can also be traced in other branches of food production and
sales—for example, in dairying, women were marginalized as the trade grew
more sophisticated and organized.[5] And it can even be found in activities far
removed from either brewing or victualing—for example, in medicine, the
introduction of new tools and methods facilitated the dominance of male physi-
cians over female healers.[6] Since in so many cases the development of new technologies resulted in increased male involvement, it seems that we might be right
to conclude that technology has a "masculine face."[7] Yet, as we shall see in this

chapter, such a conclusion would be premature, misjudging both the origins of technological changes and their effects.

More than two decades ago, Sherry Ortner examined a similarly general trend in her path-breaking essay that asked, "Is female to male as nature is to culture?"[8] Ortner answered her question affirmatively, arguing that the association of female with nature and male with culture was a tenacious and pervasive characteristic of human societies. Yet in the most critical part of her argument, she concluded that this seemingly universal fact is rooted not in biology but in culture. As she put it, "the whole scheme is a construct of culture rather than a fact of nature." In other words, women are not, in fact, closer to nature than men, but they are so *perceived*. In this chapter, we will reach a similar conclusion about the gendered associations of ale and beer. Although beer and the new technologies it encouraged were controlled almost exclusively by men, the explanation lies not in biology but in history. Women rarely brewed beer for profit not because of some innate connection between masculinity and technology but instead because of social, legal, and economic barriers that limited their access to beerbrewing.

In the thirteenth and fourteenth centuries, only one drink—ale in English, *cervisia* in Latin—was prepared by England's brewers. Made with only malt, water, and yeast, English ale was sweeter and less stable than beers brewed on the continent, where hops were added to the process.[9] By seething the wort with hops, continental brewers were able to produce a beverage that, although more bitter to the taste, drew more alcoholic content from less grain, carried much more easily, and lasted longer.[10] These advantages did not begin to attract English interest until quite late. Hopped beer might have been known in England as early as the late thirteenth century, when Richard Somer was selling Flemish ale (*cervisiam flandr'*) in Norwich.[11] But if this Flemish ale was really what would later be called beer, it was not readily accepted. For almost 100 years after Somer offered his drink for sale in Norwich, no beer seems to have been bought or sold in England, much less brewed.

By the late fourteenth century, however, circumstances began to favor the introduction of beer and the new brewing technologies it encouraged. From the 1370s, merchants in towns along the eastern and southern coasts of England— Lynn, Norwich, Colchester, London, Winchelsea, and other ports—began to import and sell beer.[12] About two generations later, certainly by the 1430s, beer began to be brewed, as well as sold, in England.[13] And in 1441, beerbrewing was sufficiently widespread to require royal supervisors of the trade.[14] Three factors (each with its own implications in terms of women's access to this new technology) especially encouraged English adoption of beer in the late fourteenth and early fifteenth centuries: trans-channel trade and migration, expanding commercial opportunities, and military requirements.

Beerbrewing as an Alien Trade

From its first use as "Flemish ale" in England, beer was an alien drink, produced by aliens and drunk by aliens.[15] The link between beer and aliens lasted a very long time, indeed. More than 150 years after beer began to be sold in England,

Andrew Boorde noted, "Ale for an Englishman is a natural drink. . . . Beer . . . is a natural drink for a Dutchman."[16] When, a century after Boorde, beer had become the preferred drink of most English people, John Taylor still maligned it in firmly nationalistic terms: "Beer, is a Dutch boorish liquor, a thing not known in England, till of late days an alien to our nation, till such times as hops and heresies came amongst us, it is a saucy intruder into this land."[17] Only in the eighteenth century did the distinction between English ale and Dutch beer finally pass out of common currency.

This distinction lasted so long because it was a very real one. The English only slowly acquired a taste for beer, and even after native markets for beer were firmly established, beerbrewing itself remained a trade dominated by aliens. Even in the late sixteenth century, when more and more Londoners were drinking beer in preference to ale, many beerbrewers in the city either were alien or relied on the help of alien servants. In short, the introduction of beer presented English brewers, males as well as females, with a fierce new competitor: the alien brewer. In the long run, Englishmen met this competition better than Englishwomen.

When first consumed in England in the late fourteenth century, beer was brewed on the continent, imported into English towns, and sold for local consumption. The main consumers of this new drink—which was much more bitter than ale and hence not immediately appealing to English drinkers—were the "Dutch" (an inclusive term then used for persons from both the Low Countries and Germany). We have no records that can tell us how many aliens visited or resided in England in the late fourteenth century, but as Caroline Barron has recently noted, England then offered many attractions to immigrants from the Low Countries who wished to escape "floods, warfare, taxation, hunger, poverty, and violence." By the mid-fifteenth century, more than 16,000 aliens, most of them "Dutch," worked in England.[18]

The thirst of these newcomers for their native drink was initially slaked with imports from continental breweries. Southeastern towns such as Great Yarmouth, Norwich, and Winchelsea not only had established trade routes along which beer could flow but also boasted nonnative residents probably eager to avoid the sweetness of English ale by buying imported beer. By the end of the fourteenth century, Great Yarmouth was bringing in 40–80 barrels of beer each month.[19] Most of the trade then rested in the hands of aliens, who both imported and tippled the drink.[20]

After 1400, alien beerbrewers began to settle in English towns, but only a few beerbrewers (if any) worked in most English towns until the end of the fifteenth century. A beerbrewer started working in Shrewsbury in 1409; another joined the freedom of York in 1416; and in 1424–25, London brewers prepared a complaint about "aliens nigh to the city dwelling [who] brew beer and sell it to retail within the same city."[21] In 1436, a year marked by anti-alien activity after the Duke of Burgundy deserted the English cause, brewers in London were few and mostly alien but prosperous and powerful. When more than 200 members of the Brewers' gild contributed to the relief of Calais in that year, a special contribution came from seven beerbrewers, who, although most were aliens in a foreign land, contributed much more money on the average than did native alebrewers.[22] They also successfully sought royal protection when threatened by the anti-alien sentiment of the day. In June of that year, reacting to rumors that beer was poisonous and unhealthy, the king ordered London to allow beerbrewers from Holland and Zeeland and elsewhere to continue to ply their trade without harassment.[23]

There were probably even fewer alien beerbrewers elsewhere in England. When more than 1,800 aliens certified their loyalty in the wake of the Burgundian crisis, only 6 (living in Scarborough, Boston, Norwich, Walberswick, London, and Barnstaple) worked as beerbrewers.[24] And when aliens began to be regularly taxed in 1440, only a few beerbrewers cropped up in most returns.[25] Even in 1483, when beerbrewers (along with merchants) were singled out from other aliens for special assessments, they were few in number and largely confined to a handful of cities: Norwich (3), Ipswich (5), Hull (3), London (8), Exeter (1), Oxford (1), and the cinque ports (3). Except for Norfolk, Suffolk, and Essex, alien beerbrewers seldom worked outside of the main towns. Only a few English beerbrewers, who relied on the help of numerous Dutch servants, appeared in the listings.[26] By that time, an export trade in English beer had developed (reversing the directional flow of beer across the channel), and this trade was almost entirely in the hands of aliens.[27]

One hundred years later, beer drinking was much more widespread and English brewers had more part in its production, but beerbrewing remained a trade with substantial alien involvement. By the late sixteenth century, beer was drunk not only in major cities in the southeast but also in many smaller towns: Leicester, Coventry, Oxford, Chester, Winchester, and elsewhere.[28] It was still, however, not popular in the northern towns; in 1543, the Council was informed that beer shipped to Berwick could not be sold there because "here they care for no beer."[29] Beer was also finding drinkers in rural villages, although the infiltration of beer into the countryside was a much more prolonged and scattered process. In Sussex, the first suggestion of beer consumption in inland villages dates from 1472–73; by 1500, "beer was being sold almost everywhere" in the county.[30] But Sussex was a coastal county with ports closely tied to trade with the Low Countries, and in many villages elsewhere, no beer was sold until well into the sixteenth century or beyond. In South Tawton (Devon), beer apparently did not replace ale until 1649, and in Ottery St. Mary (Devon) only ale was being sold as late as 1681.[31] Yet at the same time that beer was competing with ale in many sixteenth-century towns and villages, it was triumphing both in London and among the propertied elites. By the late 1560s, most of London's companies (as gilds were then called) consumed beer, not ale, at their annual banquets and other meals.[32] In the households of the gentry and nobility, beer was also the primary brewed beverage, and ale had come to be seen as an "old and sick men's drink."[33] As John Grove put it in 1630:

WINE: I, generous wine, am for the Court
BEER: The City calls for Beer.
  ALE: But ale, bonny ale, like a lord of the soil in the Country shall
      domineer.[34]

In London, where the citizens called for beer, alien beerbrewers still controlled much of its production. In 1585, the Privy Council estimated that about half the beerbrewers in London were aliens, and they were about right.[35] A decade earlier, when the city surveyed brewers' weekly outputs, grains in stock, and anticipated deliveries of grain, more than half of the beerbreweries in London were either owned or operated by aliens. This 1574 survey, which includes most members of the Brewers' Company and probably all the large breweries, lists 34 beerbrewers (operating 32 breweries); about a dozen were aliens, and another half dozen employed alien servants. Among the 58 alebrewers in the survey, none were alien, and none employed alien servants.[36] Indeed, alien influence was still so strong in beerbrewing that the Company had, a year earlier, agreed that it would restrict the entry of "Flemings and strangers" into its ranks.[37]

In short, from the introduction of beer into England in the late fourteenth century through the Elizabethan era, beerbrewing was a mystery known especially to aliens. Their presence in beerbrewing, although much lessened by the end of the sixteenth century, remained strong throughout. In 1607 a petition set out the advantages of London's alien brewers: their reliance on alien ships and servants, their control of foreign markets, their failure to contribute to common charges, and their convenient wharves along the Thames. These advantages might have been more imagined than real, but alien beerbrewers were still sufficiently numerous, prosperous, and distinctive in 1607 to merit such complaints.[38]

Alien influence in English beerbrewing had important consequences for the place of women in the trade, consequences that can be traced most clearly in urban records (and particularly the records of London). When aliens began to market and then brew beer in English towns, it was a product that was, with very few exceptions, produced and sold by men. This was in part because the Dutch brought to England their own industrial and trade traditions, traditions of a beerbrewing industry that was already highly masculinized. By 1400, brewing centers in Germany and Holland boasted beerbreweries that worked on scales almost unimaginable by English alebrewers; the largest breweries in Utrecht produced about 680 gallons at a time, in Hamburg about 1,350 gallons. Commercial brewers in England would not reach such levels for another 100 years and more.[39] Continental beerbreweries were also very closely regulated and taxed by their governments, and they were supported by well-organized gilds of brewers. At a time when English alebrewing was just beginning to expand and organize, some Dutch and German beerbrewers already managed large, expensive, and profitable industrial complexes.

Given these circumstances (whose later replication in England we shall, in large part, trace in this book), it is scarcely surprisingly that German and Dutch beerbrewers were wealthy, respected, powerful, and *male*. Wives might have assisted their husbands in beerbrewing (as wives assisted their husbands in many trades), but beerbrewing in towns such as Hamburg and Utrecht was a high-status trade of male householders. In early fifteenth-century London, as we saw in the last chapter, women accounted for nearly one-third of the members of the Brewers' gild, and many of these women brewed independently. In Ghent at the same time, the only women noted in the gild records were a few widows of deceased brewers, and they were often, it seems, only briefly associated with the trade. In Cologne, women who sold beer or produced traditional beers (made, like ale, without hops) were associated with the gild, but even they were not members of the *Brauerzunft*, the organization for those who brewed the more prestigious and profitable hopped beer. If women had once independently brewed hopped beer for profit in towns such as Ghent and Cologne, by 1400 that day was long past.[40] Widows sometimes managed their deceased husbands' breweries, and daughters sometimes inherited the breweries of their fathers, but women's involvement in continental beerbrewing came through family, not work. In short, alien beerbrewers brought to English towns their growing sense that (as Munich brewers would phrase it later) "brewing is a learned art and given to men alone."[41]

Moreover, relatively few Dutch women either visited or settled in England in the fourteenth through sixteenth centuries. Contemporary surveys explicitly excluded some alien women (such as those married to Englishmen) and might have overlooked others, but there can be no doubt that the vast majority of immigrants were male; in the surveys of the early 1440s, only 1 woman appeared for every 10 men.[42] Faced with the costs, challenges, and risks of cross-channel migration, very few women were among the aliens who brought to England the art of beerbrewing. To some extent, then, beerbrewing was a male trade because it was introduced through an immigration skewed heavily in favor of males.

Dutch beerbrewers also employed very few women, many fewer than alebrewers. Brewers of both ale and beer hired unusually large numbers of servants, and in both sorts of breweries, a service hierarchy seems to have developed quite early. In the early fifteenth century, for example, the alebrewers of London drafted regulations for servants that reveal a complex structure — distinctions between servants more and less skilled; between servants who lived in and lived out; between servants hired by the day and those hired by the year. Most alebrewers' servants in London seem, by that time, to have been male, but in other localities, alebrewers probably still employed many women (as they had, for example, in both Oxford and Southwark in 1381).[43]

Alien beerbrewers, in contrast, hired almost no women to help run their establishments. In the late fifteenth century, dozens of alien servants worked for beerbrewers, but very few of them were women. For example, John Evinger managed a beerbrewery in Tower ward in 1483 in which he employed 11 alien servants. Only one was female (and she was married to one of the male servants). Since Evinger, his wife, and all their servants were Dutch, immigration patterns contributed to this custom of male-dominated service. But cause and effect is not clear. Did Dutch brewers hire males because only males immigrated? Or did only males migrate to England because only they could find employment? In any case, Evinger was typical; other alien beerbrewers in London employed either only male servants or, as he did, one female servant among many male servants. English beerbrewers followed suit; of the two Englishmen who brewed beer in late fifteenth-century London, both employed Dutch servants, all of them males.[44]

The distinctive employment practices of alien beerbrewers did not escape English notice, but complaints were directed at the preferential employment of *alien* servants, not *male* servants. As late as 1607, English brewers were still accusing alien beerbrewers of employing only servants from their homelands (unless they employed an English clerk just to get business from English customers).[45] Given differences of language and custom, this preference of alien beerbrewers for alien servants might have been understandable, but it was never welcomed by the English, who sometimes grudgingly tolerated it as an unpleasant necessity and sometimes outrightly discouraged it. In 1530–31, beerbrewers were explicitly exempted from previous rules that allowed aliens in handicrafts to keep no more than two servants; but in 1540, they were implicitly included in new restrictions against employing more than four alien servants.[46] In any case, gender was never an issue. In 1567, for example, when Elizabeth I allowed 31 beerbrewers in London to keep four alien servants beyond the limits set by the 1540 statute, she required them to hire Englishmen as their master brewers and under-brewers.[47] In other words, insofar as alien beerbrewers were encouraged to hire native-born workers, they were encouraged to hire males in highly skilled positions.

All of these factors—the imported tradition of a male craft of beerbrewing, the scarcity of immigrant Dutch women, and the practice of hiring few female servants in beerbreweries—ensured that Englishwomen had relatively few informal opportunities to learn beerbrewing from Dutch immigrants. Indeed, Englishwomen seldom even learned the craft through marriage, for Dutch immigrants rarely married native women. Also, since the Dutch formed their own religious fraternities and, by the sixteenth century, often worshipped in their own churches, Englishwomen would not have come into much contact with them through religious worship and celebration.[48] Englishmen complained about the closed society of Dutch immigrants (about, for example, their unwillingness to hire English servants). But Englishmen had more opportunities to learn from the Dutch: they sometimes gained employment in Dutch beerbreweries; they learned about the Dutch through military service; they worked with Dutchmen in gilds and wards; they socialized with Dutchmen in the streets and alehouses. Women had many fewer such opportunities, and in the informal social world of urban women, a Dutch beerbrewer's establishment might have seemed alien in more ways than one.[49]

Beerbrewing and Commercialization

Beer might have first come to England to satisfy alien palates, but it spread only because of native enthusiasm for the new drink. This enthusiasm grew in part from market forces; as the growing demand for brewed drink after 1350 created challenges of production and distribution, these challenges were more readily met by beer than ale. Yet the solutions reached by brewing beer instead of ale created new challenges of their own, challenges that men met more readily than women. Hence, the changing commercial environment of late medieval England was a second major factor that not only promoted the transition from ale to beer but also shaped female access to the new craft.

As we saw in chapter 3, the market for ale expanded after the Black Death, with people of all social strata drinking more ale more often. In response to this expanding market, brewers trafficked ale in new ways, relying more than before on tipplers and encouraging more consumption in alehouses. Yet as long as brewers produced ale rather than beer, they responded only partially to the opportunities presented by the growing demand for their product. Because ale soured quickly, brewers could not risk producing large batches of drink that might decay before it could be sold. They added various spices—one writer recommended ginger, gillyflower, mountain thyme, and curcuma—to strengthen ale and to mask its souring, but they could not slow the decaying process (except by resorting to the expensive option of using more malt to brew stronger ale).[50] Because ale also carried so poorly, brewers could serve customers only in their immediate localities. Some ale was transported by ship, barge, cart, or even packhorse, but most brewers sold within very restricted ranges. And because ale required a relatively low yield ratio, it was costly to brew. Brewers made a profit from selling ale, to be sure, but their profits were narrowed by high production costs, especially for malt. The commercial changes of the later middle ages might have encouraged brewers to produce more and to distribute their product more widely, but the perishability of ale and the high costs of alebrewing restricted their ability to respond accordingly. All these restrictions were loosened by brewing beer instead of ale; beer lasted longer, traveled better, and cost less to produce.

Beer's stability and long life offered great advantages over ale. Timing was critical in all brewing. As Thomas Tusser put it, "Too new is no profit, too stale is as bad."[51] Ideally, both ale and beer were sold when solidly "stale"—neither new and unmatured nor old and soured.[52] This ideal moment varied with strength; if a brewer produced an exceptionally strong batch of either ale or beer, it took longer to mature, but once properly stale, it lasted longer in that state. A stronger batch also transported better, with less chance of going off as a result of the jostling, sloshing, unpredictable temperatures, and other accidents of transport. By adding hops, beerbrewers produced a stronger beverage with improved longevity and portability. As the Elizabethan social commentator William Harrison noted, "the continuance of the drink is always determined after the quantity of the hops, so that, being well hopped, it lasteth longer."[53] Beer was usually not ready for sale until about a week after brewing, but it improved with age and could be kept for as long as a year.[54]

Adding hops to the brewing process also gave beerbrewers more drink for their grain. Alebrewers generally drew about 7½ gallons from a bushel of malt, brewing their drink strong in order to improve longevity. Yet, because seething the wort in hops assisted both fermentation and preservation, beerbrewers were able to achieve the same effect with less grain. Reginald Scot claimed in his enthusiastic book on hops, "whereas you cannot make above 8 or 9 gallons of indifferent ale out of one bushel of malt, you may draw 18 or 20 gallons of very good beer." He was roughly right. Yield ratios varied widely from brew to brew, as brewers sought to produce beers or ales of weak, ordinary, or strong composition. But beerbrewing generally yielded more drink for less grain. In 1502, for example, Richard Arnold's recipe for brewing beer indicated that a brewer could draw 60 barrels of single beer from 10 quarters of malt (or about 27 gallons per bushel). At York in 1601, the difference was recognized in legislation: victualers were enjoined to use a half quarter of malt when brewing beer but a full quarter when brewing ale. To produce as much beverage of the same strength as an alebrewer, a beerbrewer had to purchase about half the malt.[55]

To achieve this higher yield, beerbrewers did, of course, incur extra costs for both hops and fuel, but their yields far offset these extra expenses. William Harrison's wife, Marion, spent 10s. on malt, 2d. on spices, 4s. on wood, and 20d. on hops; if we assume that half of her fuel costs went to boiling water initially (a process required in brewing both ale and beer) and half to seething the wort in hops (required only in beerbrewing), brewing beer rather than ale cost her an additional 2s. for wood and 20d. for hops. For that additional 3s.8d.

(about 25 percent of her total costs for materials), she more than doubled her brewing output, producing about 20 gallons from every bushel of malt.[56] This was a nice saving for a domestic brewer such as Marion Harrison, but for a commercial brewer, these higher yields from beerbrewing were even better news: they translated into higher profits. As a report to Elizabeth I noted in 1589, her beerbrewers enjoyed "greater gains than alebrewers having a good help from their headcorn and hops."[57]

Initially, the lower production costs of beerbrewing were reflected in its cheaper price. In 1418, for example, the drink supplied to the English army in France cost 30s. for each tun of ale and 13s.6d. for each tun of beer.[58] In most localities through the early sixteenth century, beer continued to be priced somewhat more cheaply than ale, an initial advantage that might have helped make beer attractive to English drinkers. But as the English began to prefer beer to ale, the price differential between the two drinks began to narrow, and it eventually disappeared altogether. By the mid-sixteenth century, ale and beer were equivalently priced in London, Hereford, Leicester, and many other places.[59] Beerbrewers, able to brew with much less cost than alebrewers, were able to sell their drink at the same prices and to reap, therefore, much higher profits. This was precisely the nature of the complaint made to Elizabeth in 1589; because of hops, the beerbrewers who served her household made higher profits than her alebrewers.

In short, the introduction of beerbrewing enabled enterprising brewers to respond more effectively and more profitably to the expanding markets of the late fourteenth, fifteenth, and sixteenth centuries. By brewing beer, they could sell larger amounts, they could cover larger territories, and they could produce more beverage with less cost.[60] But not every brewer could take advantage of these opportunities, for beerbrewers needed more resources than alebrewers. On the face of it, brewing beer was not necessarily costlier than alebrewing since the methods were much the same; beerbrewing simply added another stage to the process. To brew ale, water was boiled, poured over ground malt, let stand for a time, drained off, cooled, and finally, yeast and seasonings were added. To brew beer, an intermediate stage was needed: water was boiled, poured over ground malt, let stand for a time, drained off, *seethed for an hour or two with hops,* cooled, and finally, yeast and seasonings were added. Yet, despite the slight differences between the two processes, beerbrewing usually required more tools, more material, more labor, and more stock.

Although it was possible to brew beer with the same tools used to brew ale, beerbrewing was much easier with additional equipment. As with alebrewing, a single copper and single heating source (either an open fire or a closed furnace) could suffice for beerbrewing, being used both for boiling the water initially and later seething the wort in hops. This was how Marion Harrison brewed three batches of beer from the same malt, alternating boiling and seething the first, second, and third batches in her one furnace (she might have had several coppers). But additional coppers and heating sources (one set for the initial boiling of water and a second set for seething the wort in hops) made beerbrewing much easier. So, too, did furnaces (which allowed for more careful seething) and additional gutters, troughs, pails, and sieves (or better yet, double-bottom vats). And because beerbrewers needed to store their drink longer, they also kept more barrels and kilderkins than did alebrewers.[61]

To brew beer instead of ale, a brewer also had to buy hops and additional fuel. Neither of these commodities cost as much as malt, but they were not cheap, and they were not always readily available.[62] Beerbrewing was also so much more labor intensive that beerbrewers always employed more servants than did alebrewers.[63] And because beer needed to mature before sale, beerbrewers had to be able to maintain larger stocks than did alebrewers. If a beerbrewer invested, say, 3s.4d. in a quarter of malt and a few more shillings on wood, hops, and other materials, at least a week and probably more than a month had to pass before any profit on that investment could be realized. Yet an alebrewer could fully realize a profit within just a few days. Because the turnaround time on investment was much more immediate for ale, an alebrewer was able to manage on much smaller outlays of capital.

An enterprising brewer who switched from ale to beer faced not only higher costs for equipment, supplies, and overhead but also higher risks.[64] Seething the wort with hops introduced risks that alebrewers avoided: the hops might be of poor quality, the seething might be mistimed, or the long maturing process might go awry. The larger scale of beerbrewing also introduced risk, for a batch that went awry was more costly than a fouled brewing in an alebrewery. Yet the most serious risk that afflicted beerbrewers was a human one: bad debts. Although all brewers provided credit to customers and had to absorb unpaid debts, these were an especially acute problem for beerbrewers, perhaps because their larger operations produced customers with larger debts. In the late fifteenth century, London beerbrewers tried novel methods of discouraging indebtedness: they offered a discount to customers who paid in cash, and they agreed among themselves not to serve any customers indebted to other brewers (this last idea was quashed by the city).[65] Throughout the sixteenth century, beerbrewers complained constantly (and much more than alebrewers) about bad debts. Their complaints seem to have been very real. When Roger Mascall died in 1573, he left more than £1,400 in "desperate and doubtful debts" owed by more than 200 people. He had more of his wealth in bad debts than in assets.[66]

Table 5.1   Weekly Outputs of Alebreweries and Beerbreweries in London, 1574

Malt expended each week (quarters)	Alebreweries (number)	Beerbreweries (number)
4−9	20	0
10−19	34	0
20−29	3	2
30−39	1	8
40−49	0	6
50−59	0	5
60	0	6
70	0	3
80	0	1
90	0	1

Source: BL, Cotton Faustina C II, fos. 178−188.

Unfortunately, comparing the relative costs of alebrewing and beerbrewing is more an exercise in logical deduction than a direct comparison of business records. Ideally, we might compare the inventories and accounts of alebreweries and beerbreweries to see how the former ran on less capital than the latter. Or, just as ideally, we might trace in the account books of one brewery the capital costs of switching from the production of ale to the production of beer. But such records are not available. Nevertheless, our evidence, although fragmentary and inferential, points in one direction only: beerbrewing offered larger markets and higher profits, but it required more capital and entailed more risk. The differences between the two types of brewing are clearly illustrated by the more modest operations run by alebrewers in late sixteenth-century London. In 1574, London undertook a survey of its brewers, their weekly outputs, and their stocks of malt. On the average, beerbrewers produced about four times as much each week as did alebrewers (48 quarters versus 12 quarters); indeed, only the grandest alebrewers matched the malt use of even the most modest beerbrewers. As table 5.1 shows, a very clear distinction separated professional alebrewers from professional beerbrewers in sixteenth-century London: the latter simply ran much larger establishments.[67]

What did all this mean for women? The technological advantages of beerbrewing offered effective responses to the late medieval commercialization of the drink trade, but they also rendered beerbrewing less accessible to women. Instead of a modest trade that a singlewoman or widow might turn to for support or that a wife might pursue as a by-industry, beerbrewing worked on a grand scale, with larger capital costs, higher risks, and expanded markets. As we saw in chapter 3, the expanding market for ale in the later middle ages discouraged not-married brewsters. As the technological advantages of beerbrewing began to offer new responses to this market, married as well as not-married brewsters found themselves less able to work than before. On the scale of commercialization that beerbrewing made possible, women quite simply could not compete with men: they lacked the necessary capital, they lacked ready access to distant markets, and they lacked managerial authority.

We have seen that capital investment was already an important factor in late medieval alebrewing, and it became an even more critical requirement for success in the new trade of beerbrewing. Indeed, some brewers grew so rich that they profited not only from their investment in the trade but also from their ability to manipulate grain supply and to force out smaller brewers.[68] Yet capital was not as readily available to women as to men; as we saw in chapter 3, women suffered from more limited cash resources and also less access to credit. Most brewsters who might have sought to expand into beerbrewing would have faced severe restrictions on their ability to raise investment funds for new equipment, new supplies, or extra labor. These restrictions were severe enough, but as beerbrewing expanded, they were exacerbated by a third limitation: the inability of women to form partnerships as easily as men. Partnerships were unusual in brewing until the mid-sixteenth century. Thereafter, they became more common, particularly in the very largest beerbreweries. In 1574, four of the larger beerbreweries of London were managed by partners, and by 1580, partnerships were becoming so popular in the city that the gild ordered that no brewer could be in more than one partnership at a time.[69]

Yet as more brewers, especially, beerbrewers, used partnerships to raise capital for their growing businesses, women were placed at a disadvantage. For most women, hindered by both contractual disabilities and poor resources, partnerships were not a viable option. In purely technical terms, some women — singlewomen, widows, and wives designated as femmes soles — could contract business partnerships. But other women, especially wives, who were usually femmes coverts, could not. Without a contract, no partnership. And in practical terms, probably few women, except some fortunate widows, possessed sufficient property to be desirable business partners even if they could contract such arrangements. Yet most propertied widows seem to have invested their resources in loans, not partnerships.

Perhaps most important, a partnership with a woman could lead, as Wassell Webling learned the hard way, to difficult and costly disagreements. When Nicholas Webling died about 1567, he, like many of his contemporary beerbrewers, lacked confidence that his wife could manage his business on her own. So he arranged for his brother, Wassell (who was only in his teens), to join his wife, Elizabeth, in the trade. Wassell and Elizabeth agreed to share equally the expenses and the profits of the brewery. But Wassell was nervous about the possibility of Elizabeth's remarriage, and he pressured her to promise that if she should take another husband, he would not participate in their business. The legal force of such a promise, which was never given, is doubtful. But, in any case, Wassell had good reason for his disquiet: Elizabeth did remarry, relations between Wassell and Elizabeth and her new husband, Thomas Dolman, did deteriorate, and the partnership ended badly in a bitter court suit.[70] To be sure, many partnerships between men ended in misunderstandings, but as the Webling-Dolman case illustrates, partnerships with women increased that possibility; since a female partner might introduce a new party — that is, a new husband —

to the arrangement, the potential for disharmony grew. Probably worried by such experiences, men seem to have shied away from partnerships with wealthy widows (or even wealthy singlewomen). None of the partnerships in beerbrewing reported in 1574 included women, and aside from the unhappy case of Wassell Webling and Elizabeth Dolman, almost all brewing partnerships in the sixteenth century seem to have been between men only.[71]

Women were also less competitive than men in a second commercial arena that grew in importance with beerbrewing: market relations, both inland and overseas. For beerbrewers, overseas trade was crucial for both supplies and sales. Since hops were not cultivated in England until well into the sixteenth century, beerbrewers had to rely for more than a century on hops imported into Southampton, Poole, London, and elsewhere. Once overseas markets for English beer developed in the late fifteenth century, beerbrewers used these same ports not only to obtain hops but also to send their beer back across the channel. Over the course of the sixteenth century, the export trade grew to be so important that many London brewers relocated their businesses on the Thames. By 1590, 20 great breweries along the Thames sent 26,400 barrels of beer abroad each year.[72] Access to this overseas trade was shaped by both nationality and gender. Aliens so long controlled the export market in beer that, even as late as 1607, the English were complaining that Flemish beerbrewers excluded them from it. Yet men also controlled it, even more exclusively than aliens. Although a native-born male brewer occasionally exported beer to the continent, no brewster ever did.[73] Male control of beer export was not exceptional, for the involvement of women in overseas trade was generally very low; one study has suggested that less than 2 percent of importers were female (and most of these were widows winding up the overseas trade of their husbands).[74]

In the home market, beerbrewers also sold their drink in more complex ways than did many alebrewers. Beerbrewers often marketed their product directly to consumers, but they also sold in wholesale quantities to shipowners, military provisioners, channel islanders, and private customers. In 1542, for example, beerbrewers in Southampton were able to supply 650 tuns of beer to Jersey and another 575 tuns to Guernsey and Aldeney.[75] This sort of trade was large and profitable; it was also a trade pursued by men, not women. Wholesale distribution required resources that few women could command: capital for investment in stock, contacts with shipowners and factors, familiarity with royal officers and regulations, and knowledge of customers and markets in distant places. As a result, to give just one example, among the hundreds of traders involved in overland transport from Southampton in the fifteenth and sixteenth centuries, only a mere handful were women.[76]

Perhaps more important, wholesale distribution required business relations of mutual trust and obligation, relations unlikely to be fostered, because of both social prejudice and legal constraint, between a man and a woman. For example, John Smythe, a shipper working out of Bristol in the mid-sixteenth century, relied primarily on one beerbrewer to supply his ships. Thomas Heynes always had beer in stock when Smythe needed it, he was always ready to receive back from Smythe beer unused at the end of a voyage, and he was always willing to carry debt and accept payment in kind. In return, he got good business from Smythe, sometimes more than £50 of business in one year alone.[77] Even if a woman had commanded the capital necessary to carry on a venture the size of Heynes's, she would have had difficulty cultivating and sustaining an exclusive trade relationship with a shipper such as Smythe, for she would have lacked both social and legal credibility. In social terms, she was handicapped by misogynous ideas about women in general and brewsters in particular, ideas that suggested (as we shall see in chapter 7) that brewsters were particularly unreliable and untrustworthy people. In legal terms, she lacked, of course, the contractual authority of a man. As with overseas trade, male control in the domestic whole-sale market for beer was unexceptional; very few women worked as wholesale merchants in any kind of commodity.[78]

Successful beerbrewing required capital resources few women could gather and market relations that also eluded most women; it also required a level of managerial authority that women could seldom deploy. Beerbreweries were dis-tinguished from alebreweries by their large staffs of male workers—just the sort of work force over which women rarely exercised authority. One estimate from 1636 suggests that a beerbrewer employed almost two dozen workers, includ-ing three clerks, a master brewer and an underbrewer, four tun men, a stoker, a miller, two coopers, six draymen, two stable workers, and a hog man.[79] As Margery Draper found after her husband died in 1576, exercising authority over these men was a difficult matter. John Draper left his beerbrewery to his wife, and within a year, she was embroiled in a difficult suit brought by Thomas Hob-son, a clerk responsible for accounts. Draper had two complaints against her employee: he was cheating her, and he had "most shamefully, wickedly and hor-ribly" attempted to force marriage on one of her daughters. We don't know how this suit was resolved, but it suggests that some employees in beerbreweries run by women (that is, by widows of beerbrewers) might have exploited the par-ticular vulnerabilities of their mistresses to advance themselves in the trade.[80] As Margery Draper found, women seem to have been less able than men—because of gender roles, social prejudice, sexual anxiety, or a combination of these fac-tors—to exercise authority over the large and masculine labor forces found in some fifteenth-century and sixteenth-century ale breweries and in virtually all beerbreweries.

In short, the commercial changes that made beer such a marketable prod-uct in late medieval and early modern England inhibited the ability of women (as well as many poor men) to profit from the trade. Singlewomen and widows, belonging to the poorest and most vulnerable segment of England's population, were unlikely beerbrewers; they could not invest their meager resources in a new trade that required more money, more risk, more contacts, and more ser-vants. Wives, who so often pursued brewing as a by-industry subsidiary to the trade of their husbands, were also unlikely beerbrewers, for they lacked suffi-cient capital, legal status, and social stature. The only women associated with the new technologies of beerbrewing were widows of beerbrewers, and even they were, as we shall see, more likely than not to eschew the trade. So, at a time when some women continued to profit from the less demanding costs and markets of alebrewing, many fewer profited from a new beerbrewing industry that required its brewers to have ready access to various forms of capital, numerous contacts in diverse and farflung markets, and firm control over a large and largely masculine labor force.

Beerbrewing and Military Provisioning

A third and final factor not only encouraged the shift from ale to beer but also worked to exclude women from the beer trade: military provisioning. In theory, soldiers throughout this period were responsible for securing their own food, but in practice, provisions had to be made readily available for purchase and preparation by troops in the field. Armies were too large to live off local supplies (whether seized or purchased), and hungry soldiers fought badly, if at all. As Barnaby Rich noted in 1581, valiant men will willingly risk their lives in battle against pike or musket or cannon, but few will happily subject themselves to famine.[81]

Provisions were secured in a variety of ways. The armies of Edward I were fed by living off the land, by purveyance (that is, the compulsory sale of goods to royal officers), by private entrepreneurs who undertook to provide supplies for purchase, and by supplies organized by magnates. All of these expedients were used by Edward I's successors, but purveyance and entrepreneurial supply were particularly important, for example, in Edward III's provisioning of Calais. Over time, supplies provided by merchants slowly superseded purveyance, and by the end of Elizabeth's reign, military provisioning was largely in the hands of private contractors; victualers undertook with the Crown to purchase supplies, transport them to the field, and distribute them to the troops. Ship provisioning, which grew in importance with the growth of English naval power, also came to require mercantile cooperation so that ships could be quickly supplied for voyages of many weeks.[82]

Brewed beverages, either ale or beer, were a critical part of this victualing of the army and navy. In 1295, Edward I had written to Chester to secure ale for his army at Conway, and every one of his successors had to worry similarly about providing troops with sufficient drink.[83] Commanders knew to pay attention to the complaints of their men, for a lack of good ale or beer created low morale at best and mutiny at worst. Henry VIII, for example, learned early about the importance of a steady supply of good drink. In 1511, John Stile wrote the young king from Spain that "the greatest lack of victuals that is here is of beer, for your subjects had liefer for to drink beer than wine or cider, for the hot wine doth burn them and the cider doth cast them in disease and sickness."[84] In 1512, an expedition in Spain led by Thomas Grey, Marquis of Dorset, faced a mutiny shortly after the beer ration dried up.[85] And in 1513, the Lord Admiral ordered that no beer for ships was to be brewed in the west country because sailors objected to drink made from oaten malt and preferred London beer above all others.[86]

Although the need for good ale and beer was clear, meeting that need was difficult. Securing bulk supplies of drink was hard enough, but transporting those supplies to the troops and maintaining their freshness were even more challenging. In 1340, for example, when the people of Great Yarmouth had to fit out 30 ships manned by 1,510 sailors for 40 days of service between England and Flanders, they had to supply over 60,000 gallons of ale (or as the record explicitly states, 1 gallon for each man each day).[87] At a time when an alebrewer might produce only 60 to 120 gallons per brewing, this was a daunting demand. By shifting from ale to beer, suppliers eventually eased these sorts of logistical challenges. Because beer cost less than ale, carried better than ale, kept better than ale, and was more readily available on the continent than ale, beer very early replaced ale as the primary drink of English soldiers and sailors.[88]

In facilitating this early shift from ale to beer, the victualing of Calais was critical. When Edward III secured Calais in 1347, he won a great strategic victory and created severe logistical challenges. Until 1361, the garrison of more than 1,000 men in Calais endured a state of continuous warfare with the French, and even with supplies from the English-controlled countryside around the town, the garrison could not feed itself. Most of the food was brought from England, secured either through purveyance or through merchants who were encouraged to bring their wares to the town.[89] Even after hostilities eased in the 1360s, the provisioning of Calais remained a critical strategic concern. In 1403, for example, the mayor and bailiffs of Sandwich were ordered to allow three ships "laded with ale and other victuals" to pass immediately to Calais.[90] Even as late as 1555, Calais was regularly exempted from statutory restrictions on the export of victuals from England.[91]

Under these acute provisioning requirements, beer quickly won a new market in Calais. Shipped directly from the Low Countries, beer was introduced early and readily accepted. Indeed, such quantities were being brought to Calais by 1397 that the town appointed a broker to manage "ale of Holland, Eastland, Zeeland, and other places, also called beer."[92] A few years later, when the mayor of Calais asked parliament for control of the sale of basic foodstuffs in the town, the assize of beer was included (for the first time in English records) along with the assizes of bread, wine, and ale.[93] At a time when only small amounts of beer were being imported into only a handful of English towns, beer was already an important commodity in the garrison town of Calais.

The use of beer in military provisioning spread rapidly beyond the confines of Calais. At the siege of Rouen in 1418, Londoners sent more beer than ale to the troops.[94] Ale and beer were supplied together to the armies of the fifteenth century, but by the early sixteenth century, beer had edged out ale entirely. In 1487, ale was specified for the last time in a royal proclamation about the victualing of an army or fleet, and thereafter, almost all correspondence about the provisioning of the forces of Henry VII and his successors dealt with beer only, not ale.[95] In 1492, Henry VII began to build at Portsmouth what would become a very extensive complex designed solely for brewing beer for the navy.[96]

What effect did this early and strong demand for beer in military provisioning have on the relative presence of women and men in beerbrewing? First, the sheer scale of military demands for brewed drink—ale as well as beer—favored the sort of capitalized, large-scale industry that was more available to men than to women. For example, when Great Yarmouth had to come up with more than 60,000 gallons of ale on short notice in 1340, men more readily than women possessed the capital and contacts needed to profit from the demand. One woman, Joan Hikkeson, sold 400 gallons to the bailiffs, but the bulk of the supply came from two men, Peter Grymbolp and John Gaytor, who each sold 30,000 gallons to the town.[97] These figures illustrate in the specific context of military provisioning what we have already seen for beerbrewing in general; a brewster might try to profit from the military market by brewing larger quantities herself or by buying supplies from her neighbors for resale, but she operated on such a small and local scale that she could not compete with the greater economic and social resources of men. Hence, it is not surprising that in towns such as Southampton, where provisioning ships was an early and profitable trade, beerbrewing very quickly grew into an industry controlled by wealthy and powerful men. In sixteenth-century Southampton, women still brewed ale on occasion, but they were never part of the lucrative industry of brewing ship beer.[98]

Second, among the brewers who accompanied armies, males seem to have been more common than females. Beer had to be purchased outright for the navy, but the army was sometimes served by malt that was then brewed in the field by brewers who worked in garrisons or moved with the army.[99] Of course, women traveled with armies in large numbers. Many of them were wives or widows of soldiers, and they usually supported themselves as sutlers (that is, sellers of provisions to the soldiers), prostitutes, nurses, and laundresses. Their presence was critical for military morale and maintenance. Even Leicester's disciplinary code of 1585, which sought to exclude as many woman as possible from the army, nevertheless recognized that wives, nurses, and laundresses had to be tolerated among camp followers.[100]

Yet, despite the presence of women in military garrisons and on military campaigns, brewing beer for the troops seems to have been a male preserve. On the one hand, some commanders actively discouraged beerbrewing by women. Lord Bridgewater was so worried about the prospect that a "poor wench" was the brewer at Ludlow Castle in 1641 that he wrote his constable about the matter; the constable promised to "find out a man to do it" in the future.[101] Bridgewater probably worried so much about a woman selling beer because he assumed, for reasons we will examine in chapter 7, that women and drink were a disorderly combination; other commanders, eager to maintain order among their troops, might have similarly sought to discourage brewsters and tapsters from serving their men. On the other hand, such outright discouragement was sometimes unnecessary, for the very process of military recruitment favored male brewers. Brewers were found and shipped out much like soldiers, and they were, in at least some cases, expected to fight as soldiers as well. In 1522, a memorandum about the provisioning of Berwick noted that brewers could also, if necessary, serve as gunners.[102]

Military demands for drink, then, not only encouraged a rapid shift from ale to beer but also facilitated the greater involvement of men in beerbrewing. Both the army and navy needed to be able to secure, on short notice, vast quantities of good-quality drink that would not sour either in transport or during storage. Beer responded to these needs more readily than ale, and when troops began to consume beer in the late fourteenth century, they were usually served by male brewers. When the army and navy were supplied by commercial brewers, it was men who commanded the resources necessary to supply huge amounts of drink on short notice. When the army was supplied by resident brewers who worked in garrison or field, these brewers were also usually males who could, in some cases, combine brewing with soldiering. The military trade in beer developed early, and it developed in ways that seem to have hastened the exclusion of women from beerbrewing.

Why Was Female to Male as Ale Was to Beer?

When the inhabitants of Lullington and other English villages took their first sips of beer, they had not, as we have seen in this chapter, encountered the "irresistible social force" of technological change.[103] Beer offered new possibilities for producing and marketing brewed drink, but these new possibilities were not inevitable results. Commercial change both preceded and facilitated the technological change from ale to beer; beerbrewing, long known in England, gained a foothold only when the expanding markets of the late fourteenth century created a climate that favored the cheaper, longer-lasting, and more easily transported beer. In other words, technology was not "a sine qua non for successful commercial change" in brewing in fifteenth-century and sixteenth-century England.[104] In the early fourteenth century, the English were not ignorant about beer and the techniques of its production; instead, they eschewed beer and preferred their sweet ale. Beer gained a following among the English only when other circumstances—the growth of alien populations in England, the expanding markets of the later middle ages, and the demands for a reliable supply of drink for soldiers and sailors—encouraged them to drink and later to brew the bitter beverage they called beer.

The first person to sell beer in the area around Lullington was a woman: Joan Eversfield, who in 1488 worked as a huckster of both ale and beer in Telton. Yet for women, the advent of beer boded ill. To be sure, women became proficient brewers of beer for consumption by their own families. Marion Harrison certainly knew all the tricks of making beer, even if she brewed only for her family and never for profit. And to be sure, a few women profited—as did Joan Eversfield—from selling beer that had been brewed by others. But women seldom brewed beer for profit. Singlewomen almost never did so, and wives also seem to have been less associated with commercial beerbrewing than with alebrewing. Only widows brewed beer, but they were invariably widows of beerbrewers, not just widows. When women like Elizabeth Webling and Margery Draper took over their husbands' businesses, they were not brewing as women had brewed in the past.

Indeed, these widows of beerbrewers illustrate a critical point about the relationship between women and beerbrewing: this relationship was structured in ways that might look "natural" but were in fact familial. As we have already seen in the case of alebrewing, reproductive work cannot explain women's declining role in the trade. Not-married brewsters—that is, those women with the least reproductive responsibilities—gave up the trade before all other women, and the extent to which married women brewed ale for profit seems to have been more determined by their husband's trades than by their own biological clocks. In the cases of both ale and beer, many of the obstacles that late medieval brewsters encountered—such as inadequate capital or insufficient managerial authority—seem to have been partly rooted in the conjugal family. In other words, because so many legal and social practices in late medieval England anticipated that male householders would be responsible for their dependent wives, children, and servants, women therefore had less contractual authority than men, more limited access to capital, and narrower networks of friends and associates. Needless to say, these distinctions might seem "natural" at times, but they were based in legal and social institutions that grew up around particular family structures. They reflected custom, practice, and tradition, not biology.

Widows of brewers particularly emphasize this point because they illustrate how powerfully familial concerns could shape women's access to the trade. Because their involvement in commercial brewing came from family, not work, widows of brewers were relatively unaffected by distinctions between ale and beer. In the late sixteenth century, the only women associated with the Brewers' Company of London were brewers' widows, and in a most interesting pattern, these widows seem to have been the only women for whom the challenges of beerbrewing were surmountable. They were, in other words, the exception that proves the rule.[105]

Of the brewers named in the 1574 survey, 18 alebrewers and 10 beerbrewers left wills while their wives were still alive. They made remarkably similar provisions for their wives: in roughly equal proportions, a few explicitly left breweries to their wives and rather more trusted to their wives the execution of their wills.[106] The wardens' accounts of the Brewers' Company suggest a similar equivalency. Four of 10 beerbrewers' widows maintained their husband's gild connections. Mary James enjoyed exceptional wealth; she regularly offered £8 each year for the poor of the gild, and in 1592–93, she was reported as brewing 120 quarters a week (only three breweries surveyed by the company produced more). Seven of 17 alebrewers' widows took up membership in the company, and although none could compete with the weekly output of Mary James, several were very active businesswomen. The only distinction between widows of alebrewers and beerbrewers was one that also distinguished their husbands: beerbrewers (men as well as their widows) took fewer apprentices than alebrewers.[107]

Most widows, it should be emphasized, did not succeed their husbands as members of the Brewers' Company; some might have nevertheless been allowed to pursue their husband's trade, but others clearly either gave it up or passed it along to sons.[108] And some widows who did continue their husbands' interests encountered, as did Elizabeth Webling and Margery Draper, less than full success. In any case, among the minority of widows who maintained the breweries and gild associations of their husbands, the brewing of ale or beer seems to have made little difference. This is not surprising. Widows of skilled men were different from other women, able to claim access to crafts and trades that were, save for widows, resolutely controlled by males. Even in crafts that excluded women from all training and participation, widows were able to accede to the businesses of their husbands.[109] In other words, the involvement of widows in beerbrewing, as well as alebrewing, shows how family expectations could override, at least in part, a host of other social, economic, and legal practices. Because these widows were standing in the stead of their husbands, they had access to resources (such as capital and credit, as well as already established links with suppliers, wholesalers, and customers) that most other women lacked, and because they were substitutes for their husbands, they also exercised forms of authority (such as taking and sponsoring apprentices) that eluded other women. These few widows brewed beer not because they were women but because they were stand-ins for deceased brewers.

Women in London, Lullington, and elsewhere were not automatically excluded from the technologies of beerbrewing. Instead, they faced a host of factors that made them less able than men to take up the opportunities posed by brewing beer instead of ale. These factors were neither natural nor linked in an essential way with the reproductive and domestic tasks undertaken by many women. In the changing environment of the later middle ages, some people were not as readily able as others to penetrate the new trade of beerbrewing. These disadvantaged people—people who, for example, lacked access to alien traditions of beerbrewing or who lacked ready capital for investment—were more often women than men. Not all women faced such obstacles, and not all men were free from them. But women more often than men encountered a complex web of factors—legal, economic, social, political, ideological—that made them less able than men to respond to the opportunities presented by brewing beer instead of ale. These factors, not any simple biological determinism that kept women at home in by-industries and sent men out to profit from mercantile ventures, ensured that beerbrewing as it developed in late medieval England was a trade of men.

It seems, then, that if technology has a "masculine face" that face is ensured not by technology itself but rather by the particular social forces that accompany any new technology. Technological change occurs in specific contexts (for example, late medieval England) that both facilitate the acceptance of that change (for example, the development of beerbrewing in England) and shape its effects on social relations (for example, the exclusion of women from beerbrewing). There was nothing natural or inevitable about the exclusion of women from beerbrewing in England or, by extension, about the exclusion of women from other industries undergoing technological change. The pattern might seem general or even near universal, but it is rooted, as Sherry Ortner suggested long ago, in human actions, not human biology.

CHAPTER SIX

GENDER RULES

Women and the Regulation of Brewing

Historians of women can only be grateful for the very close regulation to which commercial brewing was subject from a very early date. Because local officers wanted not only to ensure an honest trade in ale but also to extract income from it, we know more about brewing than any other aspect of women's work in the middle ages. But medieval women themselves felt little gratitude. Some women, such as Gillian wife of Richard Pykard, actively resisted supervision. In 1275, when the aletasters of her hamlet in Wakefield manor (Yorkshire) came to look over her work, she brazenly told them that she would sell ale against their regulations, adding that she cared not at all about the orders of the bailiffs or even the earl.[1] And some women, such as the brewsters of Exeter, even joined together to object to what they considered to be unreasonable restraints on their trade. In 1317, they were so upset by the proclaimed prices at which they had to sell their ale that they took down their ale signs and refused to sell at all.[2] Yet such protests, whether individual or collective, were not very common, and most brewsters seem to have endured regulation as a necessary fact of the trade. None of them, however, could have welcomed the persistent efforts of aletasters, bailiffs, and others to interfere in the small profits they made from brewing and selling ale.

Male brewers also sometimes resisted and often endured the regulations to which the trade was subject. But the force of regulation fell more heavily on women than on men, and often more heavily on singlewomen and widows than on wives. To be sure, as regulators sought to ensure good supply, to control quality and prices, and to extract revenues from brewers and other victualers, they were not primarily motivated by issues of gender or marital status.[3] Yet in seeking these ends, officers reinforced norms of gender hierarchy and household structure. Regulatory schemes drew, naturally enough, on existing government structures, thereby introducing into the specific context of commercial brewing the general political and legal disabilities of women vis-à-vis men. They also built on and complemented the commercial, technological, and organizational trends, which, as we have already observed, disadvantaged brewsters. In other words, the force of regulation did not transform brewing from an industry hospitable to women into an industry hostile to them, but it helped the process along. Although brewsters seem never to have protested explicitly against the masculine tilt of regulation, they would have been better off without it.

The regulation of brewing in medieval and early modern England is a story of a complex interplay among seigneurial perquisites, local administrations, and royal interests. From Anglo-Saxon times, lords and ladies had often taken a gallon or two from every batch of ale that their tenants brewed for sale. This charge—most commonly called a *tolcester*—was basically a toll levied on commercial brewing.[4] From at least the twelfth century, local authorities began to subject commercial brewers to closer control, especially through an assize of ale that regulated the quality, prices, and measures of their products. This assize was proclaimed nationally in the thirteenth century, but it was a local phenomenon in both origin and practice. From the late fifteenth century, civic officers began to experiment with licensing schemes, and royal officers began to try to control the trade more closely by appointing national overseers, encouraging monopolies, and eventually (in the mid-seventeenth century) levying an excise on ale and beer. These regulatory schemes—some seigneurial, some civic, some royal—adapted to one another in a confounding variety of ways.

In sorting out how these various schemes affected the participation of women and men in the brewing trade, this chapter combines general observation with case study. It also spans the chronology of this book, taking us back to the time when women brewed in the early fourteenth century and forward to the time of male-controlled breweries in late sixteenth-century cities. We will begin by considering the broad implications of the two most influential regulatory schemes: first, the assize of ale and, second, efforts to license brewers. After reviewing the general implications of these regulatory measures, we will consider their practical force in one specific context: the town of Oxford. In Oxford, where brewers were subject to exceptionally close supervision from a very early date, women quickly ceased to be competitive players in the brewing trade.

The Assize of Ale

The early history of the assize of ale is obscure, but it seems to have been constituted by local measures and to have remained local in both definition and enforcement. Several thirteenth-century quasi statutes (*Assisa panis et cervisie, Judicium pillorie,* and *Statutum de pistoribus, etc.*) gave broad force to the assize of ale, but they validated existing practices rather than created new ones. Impossible to date precisely, these texts both drew on local ordinances and relied on local enforcement.[5] As a result, when jurors—such as those in early fourteenth-century Southampton—were asked whether the assize of ale "be well kept in all points," what they considered to be the assize of ale was more defined by local practice than by national statute.[6] Yet despite the importance of local definition, certain essential aspects of the assize were enforced in most jurisdictions.

As early as Domesday, localities sought to regulate ale sales and punish erring brewers. The unusually detailed Domesday entry for Chester reported that anyone (*vir sive mulier*) giving false measure paid a fine of 4s., and anyone making bad ale was either placed in a cucking-stool (*in cathedra ponebatur stercoris*) or fined 4s.[7] A few decades later, Newcastle-on-Tyne set punishments for any woman (*femina*) who offended in sales of bread or ale. By the second half of the twelfth century, local orders began not only to regulate brewers but also to speak expressly about an assize that brewers were to observe. In Tewkesbury, burgesses faced fines *pro assisa fracta*; in Walsall, forfeitures were set *pro assisa panis vel cervisiae fracta*; and in Egremont, twelve burgesses were to determine *assessum panis et cervisiae*.[8] By the early thirteenth century, the officer who became so critical to enforcement of the assize of ale, the aletaster, was already working in some places.[9]

As a result, by 1266–67 (the traditional date for the quasi statutes), critical aspects of the assize of ale had been long established. Through the assize of ale, localities already monitored the measures, quality, and prices of ale; they subjected brewers to fines, forfeitures, and even corporal punishment; and they relied on jurors, aletasters, and other local officers to supervise the trade. The quasi statutes articulated some of these practices more fully. They specified how prices should be calculated according to both the cost of grain and the location of sale (urban ale cost more than rural ale), how jurors should be interrogated about the assize, and how offenders should be punished.

At about the same time that these texts were formulated, manorial and civic officers began to keep more detailed records than before, records that allow us to observe closely how local officers enforced the assize of ale. Enforcement varied within each jurisdiction, but a few features were very common. First, the assize itself—that is, the determination of the proper price at which ale could be sold—was often set by a jury, which reviewed current costs of grain or malt and set prices accordingly for various strengths of ale; these prices were determined at least once a year (usually the autumn) but often more frequently. Second, special officers, usually called aletasters, enforced the assize in most localities. They monitored the sale of ale on a day-to-day basis, tasting ale before it was sold (assuming that the brewer summoned them, as required) and altering prices as necessary. They also presented brewers at court, recommending amercements based on the nature of each brewer's offense. Third, as actually enforced, the assize fluctuated between punishing brewers and de facto licensing them. In many jurisdictions, the assize was used to punish dishonest or incompetent brewers, but it also licensed through amercement all brewers (even those who had brewed well).[10]

By 1300, then, commercial brewers throughout England could expect to be supervised through the assize of ale. Jurors set fair prices for their trade; officers tasted their ale, checked their measures, monitored their prices, and supervised their sales; and local courts extracted from them not only amercements for breaking the assize but also de facto licensing fees. After 1350, many communities began to monitor brewers even more closely; they required brewers to advertise the availability of ale so that all could have equal access to it, and they punished brewers who favored in-house customers over those who wished to take ale away for consumption elsewhere.[11] By 1500, some communities had extended their supervision still further, trying to regulate the supply of ale (by requiring brewers to brew in all seasons and at all times) and trying to constrain disruptive alehouses (by limiting opening hours and prohibiting games).[12] These new provisions sometimes fell under the umbrella of the assize of ale, but its essential core remained unchanged: through the assize of ale, brewers paid small amercements to practice their trade, but they were also punished for bad measures, poor quality, unfair prices, and other undesirable trading practices.

Although focused on the ways in which brewers might cheat their customers, the assize of ale was not solely an early instance of consumer-protection legislation. The quasi statutes might have been designed to protect one consumer above all others: the royal household, which because it purchased large quantities of ale as it moved about the realm, needed to be protected from inflated prices.[13] And certainly, the assize was a source of considerable income to those who held the right to its enforcement. In this sense, the assize of ale was merely a different form of taxing brewers, either a replacement or supplement to the tolls that brewers had long had to pay to ply their trade.[14] Indeed, courts more often profited from amercements of cheating brewers than they prevented the cheating itself. In some rural jurisdictions—for example, on the manors of Ingatestone (Essex), Crowle (Lincolnshire), and Hindolveston (Norfolk)—the impulse for profit so overrode the need for supervision that money was taken not only from brewers but also from aletasters (who were amerced for supposedly failing to do their duty).[15]

Although the assize of ale sought to regulate all brewers, its regulation affected female and male brewers differently, and in some respects, it also differently treated not-married and married brewsters. To begin with, the assize, as a seigneurial perquisite enforced by local courts, involved many officers who did many things, but all of these officers were male. When juries had to consider the cost of grain and set prices for ale in the coming months, only men served. When aletasters had to monitor day-to-day work in the trade and report their findings in local court, only men served (with a few rare exceptions). And when mayors, bailiffs, collectors, or other officers helped to regulate the trade, only men served. In most of the towns and villages of early fourteenth-century England, therefore, a trade that was virtually all female was supervised by an all-male officialdom. Thereafter, as more and more men took up the trade, they were able to aspire not only to commercial brewing but also to participation in its regulation.

In a legal sense, this is scarcely surprising, for women had little part in any public aspect of medieval governance. But in a practical sense, the absence of women from the regulation of the ale trade is very surprising indeed. After all, brewing was a widespread female skill. In villages and towns across England, men drank ale (and doubtless appreciated the difference between good and poor ale), but women actually brewed the stuff; they knew how to squeeze the most out of the malt, how to disguise a weak ale, how to predict whether a brew would sour or stay true. Women, in short, knew better than men the skills and secrets of which every aletaster needed to be informed. But legal custom prevailed over practical experience; only men supervised the ale trade since, although men could be expected to know less about brewing than women, only they were fully competent legal and political actors.

This bifurcation created in many medieval communities an ale trade of male supervisors and female producers, but it occasioned no contemporary comment, probably because it was seen as the consequence of the "natural" governance of women by men. It did, however, produce noteworthy strains, strains that testify to women's particular expertise in this trade. Some women acquired exceptional legal privileges by virtue of their brewing skills. The borough of Torksey, for example, recognized women's brewing knowledge by allowing any woman accused of selling ale falsely to acquit herself by the supporting testimony of her female neighbors.[16] And some women acquired exceptional political privileges through their knowledge of brewing, even serving on occasion as aletasters.[17] Yet these sorts of special privileges, born of the strain of excluding from specific legal and political activities the people most skilled to participate, were highly exceptional. As an almost universal rule, men supervised commercial brewing, and women, although they brewed, sold, and bought ale, had no authority over the ale market.[18]

As we will consider more fully in chapter 7, this sexual division of labor between male regulators and female brewsters might have encouraged the displacement of popular anxieties about the trade onto women alone. In other words, since men tried without much success to regulate a trade pursued by women, it was perhaps easy for people to imagine that the abuses of the trade — bad ale, deceptive measures, excessive prices, and the like — were peculiarly female abuses. In any case, the possible ideological effects of this sexual division of labor were enhanced by practical effects; in at least some instances, the office-holding capabilities of men offered them (or their wives and other female kin) substantial advantages over other brewers. Sometimes, officers were excused from brewing amercements, as were jurors in fourteenth-century Exeter.[19] Sometimes, officers tried to conceal brewing from which they profited, as did some jurors in Halifax (Yorkshire) in 1314.[20] And sometimes, officers used their authority to coerce business, as did William Crompe, an early sixteenth-century mayor of Canterbury, who promised light supervision to tipplers who purchased ale from him and his wife.[21]

To be sure, these sorts of abuses were worrisome, and as a result, office-holders were often proscribed from brewing. But such efforts were limited and ineffective. No legislation, for example, ever addressed the very common problem of men who, as aletasters, supervised their wives' commercial brewing. In the brewing trade, the potential for abuse — officers avoiding amercements, paying only minimal sums, hiding the brewing of female kin, and even coercing business — was always strong. Since not all men were officers, not all men profited from official malfeasance. Yet many men of quite modest status served as jurors and aletasters. Only two groups were excluded from the potential profits of combining regulation of brewing with brewing itself: poor men and their families, and not-married women.[22]

When male aletasters stood before their courts and named brewers, they sometimes added a second sort of distinction between men and women: they identified brewers differently according to sex and marital status. By virtue of its close regulation, brewing provided women with a public recognition of their work that was both frequent and regular; at their local courts, brewsters could expect that aletasters or other supervising officers would discuss, review, and assess their work. In a village such as Brigstock, brewsters were named (and amerced) every three weeks, year after year. No other work undertaken by women—selling eggs, spinning wool, weaving cloth, even hiring out their labor—was as regulated and therefore as publicly recognized. Needless to say, we should not overemphasize the importance of the publicity afforded brewers by assize presentments. Certainly, all brewers would have preferred to escape the notice of aletasters (and the amercements they levied), and just as certainly, brewers enjoyed public recognition for their work in many spheres other than their local courts. A successful brewster might accrue public prestige for her work through her neighbors' observations, her customers' satisfaction, her family's contentment, and even her day-to-day dealings with aletasters and other officers. Presentment under the assize of ale was only one of many public acknowledgments of a brewer's work, and not a very desirable one at that. Nevertheless, we also should not underestimate the public importance of the matters brought before local courts. Unlike modern courts, the sorts of legal forums to which assize presentments were brought—manorial courts, views of frankpledge, mayors' tourns, and the like—were public gatherings attended by many local people on a regular basis; indeed, many of these courts required *all* tenants or inhabitants to attend *all* meetings. So when an aletaster rose before his court and named brewers, he spoke to his community, not to a small group of professional administrators and clerks.

In speaking before the court, an aletaster did not always (as discussed more fully in the appendix) name the actual brewer; instead, in some jurisdictions and at some times, he named husbands for the brewing done by their wives. These presentments, which focused on householders rather than individual brewers, were not universal, and in many jurisdictions, aletasters regularly cited married brewsters in their own names. Moreover, when they did occur, these householder-focused presentments merely manifested more general practices in the specific context of the assize of ale. They reflected not only long-standing legal principles about the husband's right to act as his wife's guardian but also the very real balance of economic power in medieval households. In other words, the assize of ale did not cause the legal subsumption of wives under their husbands, but it did provide yet another forum for the expression of this principle. This particular aspect of the enforcement of the assize of ale took hold in only some medieval jurisdictions, and it affected not at all most singlewomen and widows, who were almost always named as being directly responsible for their work as brewsters.

The assize also seems to have differentiated between women and men in one final respect: its punishments. Both men and women were subject to amercement, and both men and women sometimes had amercements forgiven because of poverty or other incapacity. But corporal punishment was another matter; it seems not only that women were more liable to corporal punishment than men but also that they often suffered a specifically female form of punishment. In the quasi statutes attributed to Henry III, corporal punishments were stipulated for both bakers and brewsters who repeatedly offended against the assize. A recalcitrant baker was to be punished on the pillory (*debet subire judicium pillorie*). In other words, his (or her) head or arms (or both) were to be locked into a wooden frame in a public part of the village or town. The punishment for a recalcitrant brewster was somewhat more obscure: she was subjected to the *trebuchetum vel castigatorium* in one text and to the *judicium tumbrelli* in the others. It seems that a brewster was to be punished in some sort of cart, and from other sources, we can surmise that she was most likely to be punished in what was more commonly called a cucking-stool. In other words, she was to be seated at one end of a pivoting bar, and from this location, she was exhibited to her neighbors, carried about town, and/or ducked into a pond, river, ditch, or other body of water.[23]

The cucking-stool was the common fate of female scolds in the sixteenth and seventeenth centuries.[24] In earlier centuries, when its use and terminology were more varied, it was clearly employed to punish not only scolds and whores but also brewers, and especially brewsters. Some records indicate that both male and female brewers were subjected to these punishments; this was true at Chester in 1086, Preston circa 1200, and late fourteenth-century Milverton (Somerset).[25] In at least some instances, the critical distinction seems to have been the *trade* rather than the *sex* of the offender—bakers on pillories and brewers on cucking-stools.[26] Perhaps cucking-stools were originally associated more with brewers than with women, but since most early brewers were female, the punishment was then extended to women guilty of other offenses (such as scolding or whoring). Or perhaps cucking-stools were always associated more with women than men and were extended particularly to brewing (and male brewers as well as brewsters) because of the extensive presence of women in this particular trade.

In any case, it seems quite clear that brewsters suffered the cucking-stool more often than male brewers. First, many records quite explicitly treat these corporal punishments as being inflicted on brewsters alone. Although the quasi statutes often spoke of brewers of both sexes (*braciatores*), the language shifted tellingly to only brewsters (*braciatrices*) in the sections detailing corporal punishments.[27] Similar language was used in mentions of cucking-stools in specific towns and villages. In medieval Hereford, an offending alewife was to sit on the *gongestol*; in London, she suffered on the *thewe* (a punishment "ordained for women"); and at Kibworth Harcourt (Leicestershire), the reeve was ordered in 1342 to make a *tumberellum* for brewsters (*braciatricibus*) selling against the assize.[28] Second, even when male brewers were also subject to these punishments, they could escape them more readily because they were better able than brewsters to pay large amercements, bribe officers, or otherwise avoid their just due. For example, at Chester, Preston, and Milverton (all places where the possibility of male punishment in this manner was clearly acknowledged), brewers could escape the cucking-stool by paying large fines. A man was more likely than a woman (and a married brewster more likely than a not-married brewster) to be able to come up with the 4s. required in Chester or the heavy fine (*meliorem finem quem poterit*) expected in Preston or the 4d. to 12d. paid in Milverton. Third, we know from other uses of these punishments that they were normally applied to women only. As John Spargo noted from his long list of references to cucking-stools, men were occasionally paraded or exhibited on cucking-stools, but they were never ducked in water.[29]

Corporal punishment of any sort—whether pillories, cucking-stools, or other humiliations—might not have been very common. In late thirteenth-century Tamworth, for example, of more than 500 offenses involving sales of foodstuffs, only 1 resulted in corporal punishment. In Milverton, the threat of the cucking-stool seems to have been reserved for only the very worst offender (*pessima brasiatrix*). Since it was more profitable to amerce brewers than to punish them on cucking-stools or pillories, many officers avoided the latter in favor of the former. As Helen Cam has noted, brewing offenses were so often "winked at" for a small fee that many jurisdictions never even possessed the required pillory and cucking-stool.[30] But at least some officers sometimes did not wink at erring brewers, and although our documentary evidence of corporal punishments is quite sparse (since they generated no income, they were recorded less frequently), it is sufficient to indicate that brewsters were punished on cucking-stools in both town and country through the late medieval and early modern centuries.

Whenever officers resorted to corporal punishment of brewers, then, it seems that cucking-stools were sometimes reserved for brewsters (as well as for other female offenders). Yet if the cucking-stool was more a female punishment and the pillory (or other fates) more often reserved for men, the distinctions in the middle ages were still fluid, and their significance is hard to gauge. After all, men *were* subject to physical chastisement, just perhaps not as often and not the same sorts of chastisement. Perhaps male brewers were often, like bakers, placed in pillories or whipped or otherwise physically punished.[31] These are not enviable punishments, and like the cucking-stool, they offered their victims uncomfortable, public occasions for ridicule and scorn.

William Harrison was of the opinion that cucking-stools were just "a little washing in water," which failed to deter offenders.[32] But as an upright and well-respected cleric, he seems to have underestimated the dreadfulness of punishment on a cucking-stool. To brewsters, it seems to have been a very frightening prospect indeed. In mid-fourteenth-century London, an alewife apparently so feared *la thewe* that she bribed the mayor to be put on it at night, when few would witness it.[33] In Montgomery, town officers expected that merely the sight of what was locally called the "goging-stool" might so frighten an erring brewster that she would immediately swear to brew truly in the future.[34] One four-teenth-century poet used the cucking-stool to chide brewsters:

> Hail to you the brewsters with your gallons
> Potels and quarts, over all the towns.
> Your thumbs bear much away, shame have the trickery;
> Beware of the cucking-stool, the lake is deep and dirty.[35]

The assize of ale remained an important source of profit in most jurisdictions through the later middle ages. Presentments under the assize, which survive in abundance from the late thirteenth century, often become less full and less reliable during the late fifteenth and early sixteenth centuries (although they survive in some jurisdictions well into the seventeenth century and beyond).[36] In part, the decline of assize presentments reflects changes in the courts to which aletasters reported; by the early sixteenth century, many manorial jurisdictions had become perfunctory or even moribund. In part, however, the decline of assize presentments reflects new regulatory factors. Promulgated immediately after the Black Death, the Statutes of Labourers infringed on local supervision of the ale trade and created a precedent for more centralized supervision.[37] Gilds of brewers, which began to be formed in the fifteenth and sixteenth centuries, sometimes took over from civic authorities the supervision of the ale trade.[38] Beer, which grew tremendously in popularity over the course of the fifteenth and sixteenth centuries, was technically not covered by the provisions of the assize of ale. And the *Act for licensing alehouses* in 1552, which required all alehouse-keepers to be licensed by justices of the peace, shifted supervision of the drink trade further away from local courts. Whenever and wherever the assize of ale remained in force, however, it provided an exceptionally elaborate system of trade regulation, a system to which virtually all brewers were subject. Yet, although all brewers, were subject to the assize, it fell more heavily on brewsters, who were more likely than their male counterparts to have no part in the enforcement of the rules of their trade, to have their work obfuscated by presentments made under the assize, and to suffer frightening and humiliating punishment on cucking-stools.

Schemes to License Brewers

The assize of ale functioned as a de facto licensing system, but the licensing schemes that began to develop in the fifteenth and sixteenth centuries went far beyond the assize. Whereas the assize enabled officers to license brewers *post factum*, these new schemes usually licensed brewers to ply their trade in the future. Whereas officers had used the assize to extract fees from *all* who had brewed, these new schemes sought to limit brewing to small numbers of common brewers. Whereas the assize had not distinguished between small and large producers of ale (save sometimes to amerce some brewers more than others), these new schemes favored large brewers over their more modest competitors. And most important for our purposes, whereas brewing by women had been tolerated (even if sometimes obscured) under the assize, these new licensing schemes more strongly favored male over female brewers.

Like the assize of ale, licensing schemes mingled together not only central and local initiatives but also the regulation of brewers and tipplers. The earliest central initiatives regulated aleselling, but since many alesellers brewed their own product, these schemes indirectly licensed many brewers as well. In 1495, a statute directed against beggars allowed justices of the peace to take bonds for good behavior from those alehouse-keepers of whom they approved and "to reject and put away" others. These measures were expanded in 1552 with a statute establishing clear procedures for licensing alesellers that endured, with minor emendations, for centuries. By empowering magistrates to suppress aleselling "in such town or towns and places where they shall think meet and convenient," the statute allowed not only licensing of alesellers but also the limitation of their number.[39] Alesellers were to be licensed by justices of the peace, offering both bond and surety for their honest pursuit of the trade. In many villages and towns, this system became the primary means of licensing both tipplers and brewers.

In some towns, however, tippling and brewing were discrete occupations by the sixteenth century, and in these places, brewers were licensed in different ways. Royal schemes to license brewers were not very successful.[40] At the local level, however, schemes for licensing urban brewers developed earlier and somewhat more successfully. By the end of the fifteenth century, Oxford was supplied with ale through a carefully controlled rota of fewer than two dozen brewers; only they were to brew, and they were to brew only according to a preset schedule. In 1532, Norwich ordered that "no person within the said precinct shall set up any brewery of ale or beer for sale without license of the mayor and the wardens of the trade." In 1562, York licensed "honest citizens" to brew or sell malt liquors. By 1566, brewers in Nottingham were required to be licensed. In 1578, Lyme Regis licensed seven common brewers to brew and sell malt liquors in the town. In that same year, the "great brewers" of Northampton obtained the right to restrict brewing to themselves alone. In 1599, Leicester, which had tried in the past to regulate its brewers through a city-organized gild, agreed to require all common brewers to be licensed by the mayor and aldermen. Even in London, where the Brewers' gild helped the city regulate the trade, the city occasionally used bonds from its brewers to try to control them more effectively. In an ad hoc fashion, then, towns began to control brewers through licensing: they empowered only certain persons to brew; they sought oaths from brewers to follow their trade faithfully; they required bonds and sureties to ensure brewers' observance of rules about quality, prices, and other matters.[41]

These local licensing schemes were not very effective. They usually failed to prevent brewing (or selling) by unlicensed persons, and they often fell out of use within just a few years. Indeed, sometimes brewers actively resisted licensing schemes.[42] Yet although these efforts to use licenses to create a well-regulated brewing industry were ultimately unsuccessful in many respects, the very process of licensing worked to discourage female brewing and encourage male brewing. When mayors, aldermen, constables, justices of the peace, and other officers tried to create a tightly controlled, closely regulated, and easily taxed market in malt liquors, they envisioned a small cadre of common brewers who were respected, honest, prosperous, and reliable. Men fulfilled these requirements better than women.

To those issuing licenses, women had at least three strokes against them. First, the association of the female gender with disobedience, disorder, and disruption encouraged licensing officers to prefer male brewers to brewsters. As we shall see in chapter 7, justices of the peace, mayors, and others had seemingly good reason to assume that an establishment managed by a man would be better regulated, more orderly, and quieter. Second, the legal disabilities of women, particularly wives, encouraged officers to license men, who could be more readily called to account. And third, the relative poverty of women undercut their civic responsibility. As many officers doubtless observed, women more often than men left amercements and fines unpaid.[43]

Despite these obstacles, some women did secure licenses, especially licenses for alehouse-keeping. Because alehouse-keeping constituted what Keith Wrightson has called a "system of circulating aid," parishes willingly supported the licensing petitions of laborers, artisans, smallholders, and widows. If these people profited from selling ale, they might not become so impoverished as to become the responsibility of their neighbors.[44] Most licenses went to men (many of whom might have been standing in for their wives), but a significant minority—roughly 10 percent—were issued to women.[45] With these licenses, alehouse-keepers not only sold ale or beer but also often brewed the drink they sold. Women licensed to keep alehouses, in other words, were much like the by-industrial brewers of the fourteenth century: they brewed the ale they sold, they produced on a small scale for immediate consumption, and they often worked at other occupations in addition to alehouse-keeping.

Yet the women licensed to keep alehouses in the sixteenth century and later constituted not only a small minority of licensees but also a small minority of a particular sort: they were almost invariably widows. Few married women were licensed to brew or sell ale; if they worked in the trade, their husbands secured the alehouse licenses for them. Also, few singlewomen were licensed to keep alehouses. Indeed, some places actively opposed the work of any but elderly women in the brewing trade. In 1540, Chester ordered that no woman between the ages of 14 and 40 could keep an alehouse or tavern. In 1584, a jury in Manchester complained that singlewomen who baked and brewed not only took trade from men with families to support but also "abused themselves" with young men (because they had "not any man to control them").[46] Poor, elderly widows, whom no one wanted on parish relief, were excellent candidates for alehouse licenses, which allowed them to make a small living. But never-married women were to seek their living elsewhere, and wives, if they worked in the trade, were to work under the supervision of their husbands.

In both conception and practice, the licenses that some towns began to issue to brewers differed in fundamental ways from licenses for alehouse-keeping. If the latter preserved, in part, the by-industrial brewing of the middle ages, licenses for brewing looked to the future, not the past. Building on the economic and social changes of the later middle ages, schemes to license urban brewers envisioned a small group of prosperous, reputable citizens who made their living primarily (if not exclusively) by brewing, especially by selling drink wholesale to private households, civic groups, alehouses, inns, and other institutions. Indeed, as was sometimes explicitly recognized in discussions about these schemes, they disadvantaged small brewers in favor of large brewers. In contrast to alehouse licenses, which often helped the working poor survive, brewing licenses did just the opposite: in the interest of better supply and tighter regulation, they favored the rich over the poor.

Needless to say, the desire to license a few, prosperous common brewers had implications for townswomen who sought to profit from brewing. Not-married and married brewsters were affected in different ways. We have already seen how singlewomen and widows fell behind as the trade became more capitalized, centralized, and professionalized. Licensing added a further hurdle to the already considerable obstacles they faced. Once common brewers were able to restrict their trade (even if only in theory) to a licensed handful of their fellows, they had even more power. The implications for brewsters were so momentous that the replacement of petty brewers by common brewers was sometimes conceptualized in gendered terms; in early seventeenth-century Weymouth, "ale-wives" were ordered to cease brewing and to buy all their ale from common brewers.[47] When singlewomen, widows, and other not-married women continued to brew in such circumstances, they worked in a "shadow economy," either enduring small fines for brewing without proper authorization or hoping to work on a scale small enough to escape the notice of licensing authorities. In other words, urban schemes to license brewers pushed not-married women even more toward the margins of the trade.

The case of Alice Everard in fifteenth-century Oxford illustrates the practical implications of licensing for independent brewsters. In 1434, the commissary of the university, troubled by disorders in the brewing trade, assembled 19 brewers, ordering them to better regulate their brewing, appointing two inspectors over them, and requiring each to swear to brew honestly in the future. Their names were carefully listed for future reference (and six more names were subsequently added to the list). All the brewers fully identified on the commissary's list (some were identified by surname only) were male. But some women were still active in the trade. Five years after this public assembly, the brewster Alice Everard was brought before the commissary for refusing to brew weak ale to sell at reduced prices to the poor, and she was, for this offense, proscribed from brewing in the town (*ab arte pandoxandi est perpetuo suspensa*). As far as we can tell, Everard was a singlewoman or widow who supported herself, at least in part, by commercial brewing. What did it mean for such a woman that she was excluded from the 1434 assembly and from the implicit licensing that it afforded? On the one hand, it meant very good things: she did not have to suffer the commissary's wrath, swear to brew honestly, or probably endure as much regulation of her trade. On the other hand, it also boded ill for Everard's work: since she was not at the assembly, she lacked legal recognition of her trade, she lacked solidarity with her fellow brewers, and she even lacked the reassurance that a public oath of honesty might have offered to her customers. Long before 1434, the most competitive brewers in Oxford were men (many perhaps assisted by their wives or even standing in for them), but the assembly of that year added legal recognition to the economic and social advantages that they already enjoyed.[48]

For married women, the licensing of common brewers had a slightly different effect: it contributed further to the public association of their work with their husbands. In York, for example, a licensing scheme in 1562 replaced married brewsters with their husbands, virtually inverting the sex ratio of publicly recognized brewers in the town. A few years before this scheme was introduced, almost all recognized brewers in York were female; when the chamberlains collected the customary "brewsters' fine" in 1559, they looked (as had their predecessors) to the women of the town—to many wives, to some widows, and perhaps also to a few singlewomen. Yet this focus on brewsters changed with the 1562 licensing scheme. The project involved alesellers as well as brewers, and it sought to limit involvement in the ale and beer markets to persons "specially allowed." Proceeding parish by parish through the wards of the town, this scheme licensed 139 persons, of whom only 14 (mostly widows) were female. Of course, the dozens of women unnamed in this list had not ceased to brew for profit between 1559 and 1562; instead, they had ceased to be recognized as brewsters by their city.[49]

In other words, when the governors of York licensed "honest citizens" to brew or sell malt liquors in 1562, they seem to have determined that the wives, widows, and singlewomen who had long paid brewsters' fines to the city were poor risks in their newly organized system, and they turned, whenever possible, to male guarantors for brewsters. They turned, in most cases, to the husbands of women who actually brewed: to Reynold Batty instead of his wife, to Henry Bothe instead of his wife, to William Brown instead of his wife, and so on through dozens and dozens of married brewsters. York's new licensing program was not particularly successful, and it had to be reiterated and reviewed in subsequent years. But it had one clear effect; thereafter, whenever civic officers considered the brewing trade, they thought about heads of brewing households, not actual brewers, and hence, they thought about men more often than women. As a result, when the chamberlains again collected the traditional "brewsters' fines" in 1565, they named 84 brewers, of whom only a few (again, mostly widows) were female. After the licensing scheme of 1562, the civic face of brewing in York became a male face.

For Reynold Batty and his wife, it probably mattered little (or not at all) how York's officers recorded their household's involvement in commercial brewing; whether he was cited or she or even both of them, they endured the same supervision and paid the same fines. Certainly, there is no evidence whatsoever that wives in York (or elsewhere) objected to the way that licensing schemes identified their own brewing with their husbands. This new practice was, after all, merely an extension of old practice; when magistrates or other officers licensed husbands for the brewing done by their wives, they were thinking much like aletasters who had named husbands in their assize presentments. Yet no matter how seemingly "natural" and accepted was the guardianship of husbands over the property and work of their wives, this practice affected all brewsters in negative ways. By reinforcing the notion that male brewers were more publicly responsible, it made more difficult the work of not-married brewsters in the trade. And by partly hiding from public view the brewing that wives were often still performing, it devalued the work of married brewsters. Moreover, these new licensing schemes extended the old practice of householder-focused presentments in two respects: they invariably cited husbands for wives (whereas assize presentments did so only in some times and places), and they licensed

husbands for *anticipated* actions by their wives (rather than, as in assize presentments, making husbands liable for the *past* actions of their wives).[50] In short,
licensing schemes helped to create the public male brewers of many sixteenth-
century towns. These men possessed all the public attributes of professional
brewers: they became free of their towns as brewers; they belonged to brewers'
gilds; they were licensed to follow the trade. But when pushed, some of these
"brewers" admitted, as did Richard Pickering in London in 1544, that their
wives knew more about the trade than they did.[51]

In restricting the trade in ale or beer to specified "honest citizens," most of
them male, York was seeking what many municipalities throughout England
sought in the sixteenth century: a tightly controlled, closely regulated, and easily taxed market in malt liquors. As long as the trade was widely dispersed
among women, this control was elusive. But by restricting the market not only
to smaller numbers of brewers but also to brewers who either were male or
were answerable through males, this control seemed more feasible. This search
for a well-regulated brewing industry never reached its ultimate goal, but the
search itself shaped the sexual division of labor in the trade. In seeking to control the trade, York's officers in 1562—like their counterparts elsewhere—shud-
dered at the prospect of many poorly regulated brewsters and warmed to the
prospect of a few easily regulated male brewers.

The Regulation of Brewing in Oxford

Because the regulation of brewing relied so heavily on local officers and local
practices, it varied considerably from place to place. Brewers in urban areas
tended, not surprisingly, to be subject to earlier and closer supervision than rural
brewers. Faced with the pressing need to ensure adequate supplies of good quality ale at affordable prices, many late medieval towns strictly monitored brewers and their trade. Yet even in some towns and cities (York is a good example)
regulation of brewers remained fairly relaxed well into the early modern era.
In Oxford, the story was very different, for there brewers were subject very early
to exceptionally close supervision. As a result, Oxford provides a telling illus-
tration of the effects of regulatory measures on the sexual division of labor in
the trade.

In early fourteenth-century Oxford, brewing was closely supervised and
rapidly developing. Close supervision grew from town-gown tensions over the
trade. By royal command, town officers were forced to cooperate with the university in regulating brewers, and after 1324, the town even had to share with the
university the profits of the assize. It might seem that this awkward situation would
have benefited brewers most of all since town officers (to whom fell the day-to-
day burden of enforcement before 1355) resented university demands for a well-
regulated market.[52] In actual practice, however, Oxford's brewers seem to have
been remarkably well supervised, despite—or more likely, because of—continuous university complaints about poor enforcement. In a series of extant rolls for
various years between 1311 and 1351, we can follow the careful regulation of the
Oxford ale market. Twice a year, four aletasters moved house by house through

Table 6.1   Brewing and Tippling in Oxford, 1311–51

	Brewers		Tipplers	
Date	All households	Female-headed households	All households	Female-headed households
September 1311	139	28 (20%)	118	26 (22%)
June 1324	112	22 (20%)	73	18 (25%)
April 1335	116	20 (17%)	118	33 (28%)
March 1338	105	15 (14%)	152	37 (24%)
April 1344	108	18 (17%)	161	42 (26%)
October 1345	102	18 (18%)	130	33 (25%)
April 1348	78	14 (18%)	117	29 (25%)
October 1348	88	14 (16%)	129	46 (36%)
October 1349	59	14 (24%)	99	37 (37%)
May 1350	45	8 (18%)	89	25 (28%)
October 1351	33	5 (15%)	69	16 (23%)

Source: Oxford Assizes. Excluded from these figures are a few households for which a clear distinction between brewing and tippling could not be established. Because the figures for brewers include a few persons of unknown sex, they differ slightly from those shown in figure 2.3.

the wards of Oxford; their work was supplemented by assessors (who determined the amercements due from each brewer) and collectors (who actually received the amercements). The first extant roll reports on more than 250 households involved in the ale market in 1311: stating the name of the householder, noting whether members of the household had brewed *and* sold ale or merely sold it, indicating the price of the ale sold, and specifying an amercement.[53]

This contentious but fairly rigorous regulatory climate was complemented by the unusual economic circumstances of a university town. Queen's College seems to have had a brewhouse as early as 1340, but most of the halls of the medieval university relied on local brewers for their supply of ale.[54] Because of large numbers of thirsty scholars (about 1,500 at the beginning of the fourteenth century), brewers in Oxford could sell their wares easily.[55] In this climate of close regulation and strong demand, the ale trade in Oxford developed precociously. First, brewers early developed a strong commitment to the trade. Even in 1311, by-industrial or perhaps even professional brewers (it is not possible to distinguish between these groups in the Oxford listings) accounted for one of every four brewing households and almost half of the ale sold in the town. These by-industrial or professional brewers dominated the market more with each passing decade, so that by the 1340s many fewer brewers were controlling the ale market of the town (see table 6.1). Second, brewers began early to rely on tipplers. In 1311, when brewers in towns such as Norwich, Exeter, and Leicester rarely used tipplers to help market their drink, about equal numbers of brewers and alesellers were working in Oxford. Tipplers became even more important in the Oxford market as the decades passed. By 1348, about three alesellers worked for every two brewers in the town.

In this closely supervised and expanding market, the place of brewsters, wives, as well as singlewomen and widows, was slipping. Married brewsters faced a regulatory situation that particularly emphasized the public responsibility of their husbands. The practice of citing husbands for brewing done by their wives was certainly not uncommon (especially in towns), but it was especially entrenched in Oxford. As the aletasters proceeded through the wards of Oxford, they almost never named a married brewster, and in so doing, they were following not merely custom or practice (as elsewhere) but also an order.[56] Responding to complaints from the university, Henry III and later Edward III stipulated that Oxford householders were to be responsible for any harm done to scholars by their dependents. Edward III specifically ordered that burgesses had to be responsible for any members of their household (*pro familia sua et servientibus suis*) who sold wine or other foodstuffs to scholars.[57] As far as I have been able to determine, this order was unique to Oxford, and it probably reflected the peculiar strains of the Oxford food market, with townspeople using any means to profit from their trade with the university. This regulatory response to the unusual strains of the Oxford market had a clear effect on wives: earlier and more completely than married brewsters in other places, wives in Oxford found their brewing obfuscated by the legal authority of their husbands.

Singlewomen and widows also found themselves at a disadvantage in Oxford's ale market, for they seem to have abandoned the trade even earlier than elsewhere. In 1311, 20 percent of households active in brewing were headed by women, but this proportion fell to about 17 percent by the 1330s and 1340s (see table 6.1). At the same time, not-married women were increasingly relegated to the less prestigious and less lucrative side of the ale market—to tippling rather than brewing. In 1311, about one in five households in tippling was headed by singlewomen or widows; by October 1348, they accounted for about one in three establishments of this sort. In both cases—fewer female-headed households involved in producing ale and more such households working in retail only—the trends were slight but consistent. Hard numbers might tell the story more clearly. In September 1311, 28 singlewomen or widows brewed commercially; in October 1348, only 14 did so. In 1311, 26 singlewomen or widows worked as tipplers; in 1348, 46 did so.

Over the course of the four decades before the plague, then, fewer and fewer households in Oxford profited from commercial brewing, husbands accepted extensive public responsibility for brewing by wives, and not-married brewsters were being squeezed into the least profitable sectors of the trade in ale. In the immediate wake of the Black Death (which arrived in Oxford in November 1348), these trends were exacerbated and intensified. Oxford was devastated by the plague, losing at least one-third of its population, and the brewing trade reacted sharply.[58] The market for ale contracted, the profitability of the trade became less predictable, and many brewing households went out of business. As table 6.1 shows, by 1351 brewing had been reorganized. Just three years after the Black Death, the number of brewers in the town had fallen by almost two-thirds, tipplers were much more common than brewers, and fewer female-headed households were involved in both brewing and tippling. These trends suggest that the adversity of the plague encouraged not only a more rapid professionalization of brewing (fewer households brewed, and they supplied ever-larger numbers of retailers) but also a more rapid decline in the number of not-married women in the trade, especially in brewing per se.

Then, in 1355, regulation of brewing in Oxford took a dramatic turn, a turn that would shape the trade well into the seventeenth century: the university obtained from Edward III sole jurisdiction over commercial brewing in the town.[59] Thereafter, town officials had no legitimate voice in the regulation of brewers and their trade. In supervising the brewing trade, the commissary and his officers had unambiguous objectives. They wanted to ensure that their scholars were regularly supplied with ale of good quality, reasonable price, and true measure, and they expected to enhance the university's treasury with amercements and fees. Unlike town officers, who were sometimes themselves involved in brewing or who sought, as good citizens, to promote the brewing trade of their municipalities, the university had little sympathy for those who produced and sold ale. Instead, it sided unequivocally with customers. For the commissary and his officers, their task was simple: brewers were to be regulated as closely as possible to ensure that their scholars were well and properly served. Over the next few centuries, brewers in Oxford were regulated with an intensity perhaps unique to their town.

Almost all the records of the university's administration of the assize of ale in its first decades are lost, but we do know that the university employed its own aletasters and that receipts from ale amercements remained high.[60] We also know that the trade had come to be dominated by prosperous citizens who managed large and profitable brewhouses. The 29 householders who reported brewing as their main occupation in the poll tax of 1381 enjoyed considerable wealth and prestige. Walter Wycombe and his wife, Alice, employed more servants (11) than anyone else in town, and they also paid one of the town's highest assessments (10s.). Other brewers had smaller households and more modest resources, but they were, as a group, more prosperous than other townspeople. At the same time, brewers were also acquiring greater political power. Only one brewer had served as bailiff before the plague; after 1350, brewers served frequently not only as bailiffs but also as mayors, aldermen, and royal commissioners.[61]

Not-married brewsters retained a place in the trade, but it was a restricted one. Of the 29 households that brewed in 1381, 5 were headed by not-married women (17 percent). In other words, widows, singlewomen, and other not-married women still controlled about the same slice of the ale market that they had held in mid-century. Yet, more than brewing per se, not-married women in 1381 were finding work in two other aspects of the trade: aleselling and service in brewhouses. About a dozen worked as tapsters in 1381, and another 18 worked as servants for brewing households. Nevertheless, in both retailing ale and serving brewers, not-married women were outnumbered by men, who seem to have commanded not only more work of this sort but also better work. All of the hostelries in Oxford were headed by men, most servants in brewhouses were male, and almost all the servants who were able to command high wages from their masters were male.[62]

In the mid-fifteenth century, when our records become more full, brewers in Oxford were prosperous but subject to ever-closer supervision. Critical aspects of this supervision were set in 1434, when Christopher Knollys, commissary of the university, called the town's brewers before him in St. Mary's church. Angered by brewers' inadequate service to scholars, townspeople, and the poor, Knollys ordered them to so regulate their brewing that everyone would be reliably supplied with ale. He appointed two inspectors, and he required each brewer to swear solemnly to brew good ale and observe the assize. Nineteen brewers (all males, as far as we know) swore to abide by these terms of work, and six other brewers (all males) later joined the group.[63] This meeting foreshadowed all the essential changes that would characterize brewing in fifteenth- and sixteenth-century Oxford: brewers would be very closely regulated by the university; they would professionalize further and form a gild; they would effectively exclude women from their ranks.

By the end of the fifteenth century (if not well before), Knollys's vague effort to ensure a regular supply of ale—his requirement that at least a few brewers bring forth ale each week—had evolved into a rigid system of rotating production.[64] Every alebrewer was subject to this system, each taking a turn assigned by the university. They produced ale on a regular 15-day rotation, with two brewers bringing forth ale on most days.[65] Their place in the rota was attached to specific brewhouses, an arrangement that minimized nuisance, eased supervision, and controlled the number of brewers in the town.[66] Eventually, the university not only assigned brewers to a brewhouse and a place in the rota but also explicitly licensed them, a system that extended even further the university's control over the trade.[67]

This brewers' rota was a regulator's dream. By requiring that brewers produce ale according to a set schedule, the university was able to ensure, first, that brewers could not manipulate supply and demand to their advantage and, second, that scholars and townspeople would always have a plentiful supply of ale. Under the rota, brewers became less like entrepreneurs and more like servants; they made a predictable living by producing ale on a schedule set by the university. Not surprisingly, brewers protested against the rota, but the university prevailed.[68] As the university itself put it, the rota benefited "the university and the town, because through it, we will have a greater abundance of ale, so that if the ale of one brewer be not good or healthy, it is possible to take healthier ale from another, rejecting that which is not good."[69]

Yet this rota also squeezed smaller brewers out of the ale market. At the very end of the fifteenth century, some poorer brewers complained to the university that the 15-day rota was too short for them. Claiming they were unable to sell their ale within the shorter 15-day cycle unless they brewed small quantities (a claim that suggests that they sold more by retail than by wholesale), they asked that the rota be extended over more days. This suggestion brought vigorous complaints from wealthier brewers, but in 1501, when the town was largely deserted because of an outbreak of the plague, a longer (18-day or 20-day) rota was attempted. It resulted in shortages of ale in August and September. Hence, in the interest of ensuring a steady supply of ale and under strong pressure from wealthier brewers, the university responded by reimposing the 15-day rota.[70]

In insisting on this shorter rota, the university hurt small and part-time brewers, albeit indirectly and with hesitation. Within a few years, petty brewers in the town would be hit even harder. In 1516, the chancellor promised to restrict the number of brewers in the town to only 16, and in 1534, the town ordered that brewers (and other victualers) work in only one food trade.[71] Supported by wealthy and full-time brewers, these orders were justified by the purported impoverishment of not only brewers in Oxford but also the Oxford populace in general. Whatever the real motivation behind these orders, their effect was clear: they buttressed the power of a small group of professional brewers in the town.[72]

These professional brewers were both wealthy and powerful. Henry Ivory, who had protested especially hard (*maxime*) against the longer rota, ran a brewhouse whose contents—leaden tubs, vats, tuns, and a variety of minor utensils—had been valued a few years earlier at more than £21.[73] Ivory brewed on alternate Fridays, and although we do not know how much he produced at each brewing, the chance survival of a fragment from a contemporary brewer's account suggests that he might have brought forth as much as a thousand gallons of ale. In this much mutilated account, the anonymous brewer recorded customers (ordinary persons, as well as colleges and halls), the quality and quantity of the ale they purchased, the porters who delivered the ale, and paid receipts. The business was large and predictable; brewing after brewing, the same customers received deliveries of many gallons of ale. The account suggests that a large-scale brewer like Henry Ivory ran a prosperous business that accommodated to the university's rota by serving dozens of regular customers every fortnight.[74] Men like Henry Ivory were as powerful as they were prosperous. In the civic hierarchy of early sixteenth-century Oxford, brewers replaced merchants and clothiers as the most powerful men in the town.

As the social and political status of brewers grew, so did their trade solidarity, and here, too, university regulation played an important role. In the fifteenth century, brewers had attempted to organize themselves, and on at least some occasions, the university had vigorously opposed confederation. At other times, however, the university tolerated and perhaps even encouraged corporate action by the brewers of the town. The inspectors empowered in 1434 were brewers themselves, as probably also were the guardians responsible for assigning a rota of brewing in 1462. And on various occasions, the university concluded agreements with the brewers as a group, acknowledging their de facto incorporation. Certainly, the brewers were organized as a gild by the early sixteenth century (if not before), but our first firm information about the structure of a brewers' gild in Oxford dates from 1521.[75]

On the first of June in that year, the chancellor issued an incorporation for the brewers that was designed, as the preamble claimed, to ensure that brewing was profitable enough to keep the town well supplied with ale. Its specific regulations show that the university, far from being threatened by the prospect of a brewers' gild, intended to use incorporation to further its regulatory power over the trade. Virtually forcing this incorporation on the brewers (who were liable to forfeit £40 if they refused to accept it), the chancellor specified that only 20 brewers could work in the town, limited the gild's self-governance, stipulated prices to be charged for ale, and threatened to levy high fines for failure to provide an adequate supply. All 20 brewers swore "upon a book" to follow these and other stipulations.[76]

From the mid-fourteenth century, then, the university played a vital role in creating a professional group of brewers in Oxford. The number of brewers in the town fell, and their wealth and social influence expanded. By the early sixteenth century, no more than two dozen brewers produced most of the ale sold in Oxford, and they were the richest and most powerful occupational group in the town.[77] As brewing became a more restricted and prestigious trade in Oxford, the place of women within it became even more circumscribed. Indeed, since the extant records speak so predominantly of men, it is difficult to determine the extent to which women were participating in commercial brewing, if at all. If many singlewomen or widows, such as Alice Everard, still brewed on a modest and unregulated scale, they were not reported in our sources. And if wives still worked privately at the trade, their husbands took all public recognition for that work. Despite the limitations of the extant sources, however, it seems quite clear that brewing in sixteenth-century Oxford had become fundamentally a trade of men.

In this trade of men, at least one group of women—widows—still retained a place. In 1447, one brewer's widow was numbered among the 20 brewers in the town; in 1501, 6 widows (some perhaps recently bereaved in the plague then ravaging the area) were included among the 23 brewers in the 15-day rota established that year; and throughout the rest of the sixteenth century, a few widows appeared in most brewing rotas.[78] Yet the ability of widows to brew for profit was restricted in two ways. First, like brewers' widows in London, they seem to have been excluded from corporate activities; although they were allowed to profit from brewing, they did not join other brewers in gild activities or negotiations with the university.[79] Second, their right to brew was attached to their households (and brewhouses), not to their persons. As stated in the incorporation of 1521, a widow could continue to brew *as long as she did not remarry*; if she remarried, a child or apprentice was to step into her former husband's place. Brewing by widows in Oxford, then, did not continue past traditions of female brewing as much as it adapted to new conditions of male brewing. When a widow such as Joan Chilham had brewed for profit in mid-fourteenth-century Oxford, she had worked in a trade in which women predominated, a trade from which she could readily profit in widowhood. When a widow such as Agnes Trederf of mid-fifteenth-century Oxford brewed for profit, she was continuing her husband's trade, tolerated of necessity by her late husband's colleagues. In other words, Joan Chilham had brewed because the trade was accessible to her *as a woman*; Agnes Trederf brewed because the trade was accessible to her *as the widow of a brewer*.[80]

Aside from widows, very few not-married women seem to have brewed in Oxford after the Black Death. Alice Everard brewed at least briefly in the mid-fifteenth century, and almost 200 years later, the singlewoman Elizabeth Keit was allowed to replace her father in the brewers' rota (although for only a few months). If other singlewomen brewed in the town, we do not know of it.[81] Singlewomen were probably discouraged from brewing by two complementary aspects of the university's regulation of the trade. On the one hand, they were marginalized by regulatory policies that focused on male brewers. As discussed above, when a woman such as Alice Everard was overlooked by university officers, she might have avoided unpleasant regulation but she also failed to accrue public recognition and approval of her trade. On the other hand, the university—by restricting the number of brewers, by insisting on a shorter rota for brewers, and by forming a gild of brewers—assisted in the development of a brewing trade that was large scale, profitable, and prestigious, that is, a trade in which singlewomen and widows could not compete very effectively. Not-married women, who traditionally turned to brewing on a small-scale and occasional basis, had no ready place in a system of rotated brewings, large brew-houses, full-time brewers, and organized gilds. If singlewomen still brewed in Oxford in the fifteenth and sixteenth centuries, they worked at a level so insignificant that they were not even counted among the lesser and poorer brew-ers (*inferiores et pauperiores pandoxatores*) who were forced to accept the 15-day rota in 1501.

Because the Oxford records so consistently cite husbands for brewing that was, at least in the early fourteenth century, done by their wives, the changing place of wives in the brewing trade after the mid-fourteenth century is difficult to assess. Yet the participation of wives in brewing probably fell. The university's encouragement of a brewing trade dominated by a few large-scale brewers undercut home-based production in general and women's work in particular. Consider the university's restriction of commercial brewing to a specified set of brewhouses, each operated by one brewer only: this rule discouraged part-time brewers (who might have shared resources) and encouraged the development of well-stocked brewhouses such as that leased by Henry Ivory. Consider the rota imposed by the university: this system favored large-scale brewing, discouraged part-time domestic production, and encouraged the brewing of huge quantities of ale in quasi factories. Finally, consider the hiring patterns of Oxford's brewers: from the mid-fourteenth century on, brewers hired exceptionally large numbers of servants, and increasingly these servants were males. Indeed, on at least one occasion, brewers attempted to restrict female employment in their trade.[82] All of these developments suggest that as brewing became less tied to domestic production and more reliant on male labor, wives had a lesser role in the trade than before. Certainly, by the sixteenth century, Henry Ivory and other male brewers in Oxford were so strongly and so professionally identified with the trade that it is hard to imagine that they—like Richard Pickering of London (who, after all, called himself a mercer in his will)—actually passed along to their wives the actual work of managing their brewhouses.

Nevertheless, women did manage to retain a strong position in one aspect of the brewing trade, its retail market. Even in the early seventeenth century, women remained prominent among the tipplers of Oxford.[83] In continuing to

find work as tipplers, women in Oxford remained, in a sense, in the same position they had held 300 years earlier. In 1300, many women made small and
occasional profits from brewing and selling ale out of their homes. In 1600, some
women also made small and occasional profits from selling ale out of their homes.
In the intervening three centuries, however, brewing itself had changed. Under
regulatory pressure from the university and in response to the changing economy of Oxford, the brewing trade had become consolidated and professionalized; whereas many people had made a small profit from brewing in 1300, a few
people made quite large profits in 1600. It was not accidental that those many
people in 1300 were mostly female and those few in 1600 were mostly male. As
the production of ale became more regulated in Oxford, women retained only
a small place in the least lucrative and least prestigious sector of the trade.

Few (if any) women, then, brewed in sixteenth-century Oxford in ways similar to brewsters in the early fourteenth century. Widows were allowed to maintain the trade of their husbands (with restrictive conditions), and wives might
have assisted their husbands in the trade, but the sexual balance of power in the
trade had shifted away from women in favor of men. How much of this shift was
recognized by contemporaries or was even intentional is hard to say. Indeed, the
Oxford records contain two enigmatic cases that suggest quite contradictory conclusions about the attitudes of male brewers toward female involvement in their
trade. The first is a perplexing and incompletely reported case of a widow encouraged to cease brewing. In 1511, the society of brewers (*societas artis pandoxatorie*) in
Oxford agreed to pay 13s. to the widow Joan Dodicott if she would leave the
trade. This offer, which seems to have been unique, was later quashed by the university when Dodicott's fellow brewers failed to pay up.[84] The second is almost a
mirror image of the first, for it tells of a widow who was encouraged to stay in
brewing. In 1593, when the brewhouse of Widow Robinson fell into disrepair,
her spot in the rota was shifted only temporarily (until she could again brew), and
all the other brewers of the town agreed to contribute 6d. from each brewing
toward her upkeep.[85] Why Dodicott was discouraged from brewing and Robinson supported is impossible to say; more than 80 years separate these two cases,
which were probably, in any case, partly shaped by individual personalities and
circumstances. What both cases suggest, however, is that whether Oxford's male
brewers welcomed women in their trade or not, the women whom they so
encountered were few, widowed, and anomalous in a trade of men.

In imposing a rota of brewings, in limiting the number of brewers allowed
in the town, and in incorporating a brewers' gild, the university encouraged the
development of a small, professional cadre of wealthy male brewers. These
changes were not, of course, caused by university regulation alone. On the one
hand, the university was not all-powerful, and it had, at times, to negotiate with
both town and brewers in regulating the trade. On the other hand, regulatory
measures (whether from the university, town, or gild) were complemented by
economic forces, some unique to late medieval Oxford and others more generally felt throughout the realm. Yet it is worth noting, in conclusion, that one critical factor that promoted the expansion of brewing elsewhere — beer and beerbrewing — was largely absent in Oxford. Beer found a market in Oxford only

comparatively late. Although one beerbrewer worked in the town in the late fifteenth century, beer did not gain a strong foothold in Oxford until the 1570s (it was even proscribed in the 1521 incorporation of brewers).[86] In Oxford at least, the technical advances and economic benefits of beerbrewing—its longer life, its greater portability, and its cheaper production—cannot account for the slow exclusion of women from the trade. Economic changes played an important part, but the firm, steady, and self-interested regulation of the university also contributed to the development in the town of a profitable and prestigious industry controlled by men.

Brewsters and Regulation

In the unusually close regulation endured by its brewers, Oxford was exceptional, not typical. Yet what happened particularly clearly there also happened elsewhere: regulation of brewing undermined women's place in the trade. Kings and queens, lords and ladies, mayors and aldermen, bailiffs and aletasters, all of these people regulated the brewing trade, and few of them explicitly stated a preference for male brewers over brewsters (although some occasionally did). Nevertheless, their attempts to regulate the trade, whether successful or not, put brewsters at a disadvantage. For singlewomen, widows, and wives, the intervention of almost any regulatory body in their work as brewsters boded ill. As changes in the market, changes in the product, and changes in the organization of the trade fostered a masculinization of brewing, so, too, did changes in its regulation. To be sure, regulators allowed a place for women, but the place was usually a humble one. Women worked as brewsters when the trade offered small profits in the early fourteenth century, but thereafter women increasingly found less independent work in brewing and more work as tipplers or poor widows supported by alehouse-keeping and, in a few cases, as widows of brewers who carried on their husbands' trade.

The force of regulation in brewing expanded and intensified with the development of the English state. A trade that had been carefully supervised in the thirteenth century was even more closely regulated in the sixteenth century. This intensification of regulation certainly hurt brewsters, but the thirteenth century was no golden age of unregulated women's work. Even then, the enforcement of the assize of ale placed male supervisors over female brewsters, offered women less room for legal maneuverability, threatened women with the particularly terrifying prospect of the cucking-stool, and encouraged husbands to take public responsibility for brewing done by their wives. Although brewsters' work might have been less regulated in the thirteenth century, it was also less profitable. Later developments—such as regulatory cooperation between gilds and governments, the licensing act of 1552, and various urban schemes for licensing brewers—further discouraged brewsters, but they built on an already firm foundation. Moreover, the force of regulation intensified earlier in some places than others—in towns earlier than in villages and in towns such as Oxford and London earlier than elsewhere. All regulatory projects were not found everywhere; schemes to license common brewers were almost exclusively based in towns, perhaps in part because urban common brewers increasingly supplied drink to tipplers in surrounding villages.

Yet running through all these regulatory schemes were certain common themes: an assumption that governance was the business of men alone; a divi-[1] sion of the world into householders, on the one hand, and their numerous [2] dependents, on the other; and a belief that women were naturally more dis-[3] obedient, disorderly, and disruptive than men. Viewing their society in this way, bailiffs, mayors, aletasters, and others considered a trade pursued by numerous brewsters—not married as well as married—to be inherently uncontrollable, and as the trade began to attract more and more male participation, they welcomed the prospect of a handful of more easily controlled male brewers. Why they viewed the world in this way is the subject to which we now turn.

CHAPTER SEVEN

THESE THINGS MUST BE IF WE SELL ALE

Alewives in English Culture and Society

In 1948, Felix Frankfurter, writing a majority opinion for the Supreme Court of the United States, drew on his memory of the traditional English "alewife, sprightly and ribald," to review a Michigan law that proscribed women from selling liquor unless they worked in establishments owned by their husbands or fathers. Noting that the equal protection clause of the Fourteenth Amendment to the U.S. Constitution "did not tear history up by the roots," Frankfurter accepted that "bartending by women may . . . give rise to moral and social problems." Living hundreds of years and thousands of miles away from the "historic calling" of alewives, Frankfurter drew on his cultural memory of them to conclude that women who serve liquor, especially women who are unsupervised by fathers or husbands, are unruly, disruptive, and troublesome. Armed with such assumptions, one of the greatest jurists of the twentieth century allowed a law to stand that discriminated on the basis of not only sex but also marital status.[1]

Four hundred years earlier, the city fathers of Chester had not been guided by a written constitution that promised equal protection, nor had they been informed by Enlightenment ideas about reason, justice, and equality. But they shared with Frankfurter a fundamental distrust of women in the drink trade, who, they thought, promoted "wantonness, brawls, frays, and other inconveniences."[2] Concerned that these activities would hurt the city's reputation, in 1540 they ordered that no woman between the ages of 14 and 40 years could keep an alehouse. They presumably hoped, by limiting alehouse-keeping to women thought to be either too young or too old for sexual activity, to clean up the ale trade and expunge its association with prostitution. What the state of Michigan would attempt by relying on the authority of husbands and fathers, the city of Chester attempted by relying on the biological clock. But the guiding assumption in both cases was the same: when women sell liquor, disorder and promiscuity will result.

This chapter explores how this assumption played out in the lives of Englishwomen between 1300 and 1600. Three questions guide this exploration. First, what sorts of ideas about alewives—that is, women who either brewed or sold ale—were part of the common cultural currency of preindustrial England? To answer this question, we will examine representations of alewives found in a variety of cultural media.[3] Popular as well as elite, rural as well as urban, serious as well as entertaining, these images portray alewives as disorderly, untrustworthy women. Second, what social and ideological forces encouraged this popular distrust of alewives? In answering this question, we will trace three threads that created a particularly negative image of women who sold intoxicating beverages: antipathy toward victualers of all sorts (males as well as females); fears about the drunkenness, gluttony, and sexual misbehavior associated with alehouses; and misogyny. Although the first two explain why people disliked brewers and alesellers, only the third explains why people focused their dislike on brewsters and tapsters. Third, what do these representations of alewives tell us about ideological inhibitions on women in the ale trade? This question will take us into the complexities of what Gabrielle Spiegel has called the "social logic of the text." These representations of alewives were more than just cultural artifacts embedded in specific sites of cultural and ideological production; they were also "textual agents at work," agents that generated social realities as well as springing from them.[4] As we shall see, the "work" of these texts changed as the brewing industry changed. In the fourteenth century, alewives were represented as dishonest and alluring traders, but by the sixteenth century, when male brewers and beer competed for customers with brewsters and ale, alewives were also represented as old-fashioned women who marketed foul drink. In both these instances and in many others, representations of alewives displaced anxieties about the trade in general onto female traders in particular, and in so doing, they worked to inhibit commercial brewing by women.

Representations of Alewives

The best-known depiction of a brewster is John Skelton's Elynour Rummyng in *The Tunning of Elynour Rummyng*, a poem probably written in 1517.[5] This is a well-received poem (then as well as now), written by a poet-priest renowned for the satiric temper of his verse. Literary critics laud the descriptive power, wit, and irony of *The Tunning of Elynour Rummyng*. Yet its portrait of the alewife Elynour Rummyng, for all its artistic force and wit, is strikingly vicious and nasty.

Twisting the traditional catalog of a woman's beauty, Skelton describes Elynour Rummyng in careful detail as a grotesquely ugly woman: her face bristles with hair; her lips drool "like a ropy rain"; her crooked and hooked nose constantly drips; her skin is loose, her back bent, her eyes bleary, her hair gray, her joints swollen, her skin greasy. She is, of course, old and fat.[6] She is also religiously suspect, accepting rosaries as payment for ale, swearing profanely, learning brewing secrets from a Jew, entertaining a customer who "seemed to be a witch," and dressing up on holy days "after the Saracen's guise" and "like an Egyptian." Indeed, the poem is rife with allusions not only to witchcraft but also to inverted religious rites, including a blasphemous mock communion celebrated with ale.[7] As Skelton says quite straightforwardly at one point, "the devil and she be sib."

This is bad indeed, but Elynour Rummyng is more to Skelton than merely an ugly woman of doubtful Christian faith. She is also depicted as a highly unscrupulous tradeswoman. Skelton tells us that she adulterates her ale: she drools in it; she sticks her filthy hands in it; she allows her hens to roost over it, using their droppings for added potency. Skelton also implies that Elynour Rummyng cruelly exploits her customers' enthusiastic need for her ale: she bargains hard; she accepts as payment inappropriate goods (wedding rings and cradles, as well as rosaries); she encourages indebtedness. And Skelton describes her establishment as roughly run and wholly unappealing: pigs run farting and defecating through the house; fights break out; embarrassed customers—all women, most of them *gross* women—slink in through the back door.[8]

There are, of course, many ways to read *The Tunning of Elynour Rummyng*, especially its depiction of the title character. Skelton's poem is fast-paced and humorous, it draws heavily on literary conventions, and it strongly reflects his satiric temper. His depiction of Elynour Rummyng can be seen as harmless or even affectionate absurdity, as class-based humor created for a courtly audience, or as satire directed against drink and drunkenness.[9] Yet it is also possible to read the poem, for all its humor and affection and for all its attacks on other subjects such as the popular classes or public drunkenness, as a biting critique of a brewster, a critique that suggests that she and her brew and her alehouse were to be avoided at all costs. This sort of criticism was not new in Skelton's time, and it did not end with *The Tunning of Elynour Rummyng*; Skelton's audience easily laughed and responded to his jibes because it was, in a sense, familiar with the text.

Perhaps the earliest and most common representation of an alewife in English culture shows her condemned to eternal punishment in hell. This characterization is most fully developed in the Chester mystery cycle, a series of plays performed on Corpus Christi (and later, Whitsun) from at least the early fifteenth century.[10] A brewster appears at the end of play 17, *The Harrowing of Hell*, after Christ has emptied hell of all deserving souls. The brewster alone remains, bewailing her fate:

> Sometime I was a taverner,
> a gentle gossip and a tapster
> of wine and ale a trusty brewer,
> which woe hath me wrought.
> Of cans I kept no true measure.
> My cups I sold at my pleasure,
> deceiving many a creature.
> Though my ale were nought.
>
> And when I was a brewer long,
> with hops I made my ale strong;
> ashes and herbs I blend among
> and marred so good malt.
> Therefore I may my hands wring,

shake my cups, and cans ring.
Sorrowful may I sigh and sing
that ever I so dealt.

Taverners, tapsters of this city
shall be promoted here with me
for breaking statutes of this country,
hurting the common weal,
with all tipper-tappers that are cunning,
mis-spending much malt, brewing so thin,
selling small cups money to win,
against all truth to deal.[11]

As the play closes, Satan welcomes the brewster, one devil rejoices in her addition to their entourage, and another gleefully promises to marry her. The sins that win the Good Gossip of Chester a special place in hell are all commercial crimes: she uses short measures (dealing in cups and cans, not standard measures), she adulterates her ale (with hops, ashes, and herbs), and she sells poor-quality drink. This scene, in a play performed by the cooks and innkeepers of Chester (men who competed with alewives in the drink trade), was perhaps itself derived from a popular midsummer tradition called "cups and cans." On midsummer day, the innkeepers and cooks marched in a procession of other traders, preceded by a devil and a woman clanging the illegal cups and cans used by so many brewers and alesellers.[12]

The tale of the Good Gossip has often been interpreted as either a crude addition to the play or a needless comic interlude, but as R. M. Lumiansky has argued, it illustrates well the central point of the play—that Christ will protect the righteous—and might have been an integral part of The Harrowing of Hell from the beginning.[13] Thus, the Good Gossip served as a general warning to all of Chester's citizens that they, too, if unrighteous, could suffer eternal damnation. Yet she also delivered very specific warnings to the tradespeople of Chester; although herself a woman, she reminded the gildsmen of Chester that they needed to deal honestly with their fellow citizens. And of course, in both her representation and her speech, she directly warned Chester's brewers, taverners, and alesellers of their likely fate in hell.

The hellish fate of brewsters and tapsters was a potent and unusually popular representation. Its earliest extant depiction occurs in the Holkham Bible Picture Book, a text produced by a lay artist between 1325 and 1330 for a lay purchaser. There, the Last Judgment shows a male baker, a cleric, and an alewife being carried by devils to a boiling cauldron. The alewife waves a jug over her head, suggesting that she cheated her customers with false measures.[14] Similar images are found on misericords in Ludlow (Shropshire) and Castle Hedingham (Essex) and in a late fifteenth-century boss in Norwich cathedral.[15] Condemned alewives also feature prominently in Dooms (or depictions of the Last Judgment) painted on the walls of late medieval parish churches. Indeed, in singling out social problems for artistic comment, these Dooms depict alewives more often than any other victualers or traders. In paintings surviving in nine separate parish churches, alewives are shown in hell, waving their jugs, exposing their breasts, drawing foul brews, and embracing demons. As Jane Elizabeth Ashby has noted in her study of these Dooms, several of the alewives stand out from other condemned souls because of their especially cheerful and happy countenances; they are delighted, it seems, to find themselves in hell.[16]

At the same time that representations of damned alewives were circulating in England, William Langland paused twice in *Piers Plowman* to name and describe the activities of two brewsters.[17] In a lengthy description of the seven deadly sins, Langland depicts the wife of Covetousness as cheating in two trades: cloth-making and brewing. In just a few lines, this woman is described (by her husband) as breaking almost every possible rule for the production and sale of ale — providing poor-quality ale to the poor, hiding her best ale for preferred customers only, charging exorbitant prices, and measuring with nonstandard cups:

> I bought her barley malt   she brewed it to sell.
> Penny ale and pudding ale   she poured together
> For laborers and for low folk   that was kept by itself.
> The best ale lay in my bower   or in my bedchamber,
> And whoso tasted thereof   bought it thereafter
> A gallon for a groat   no less, God knows:
> And 'twas measured in cupfulls   this craft my wife used.
> Rose the Regrater   was her right name;
> She hath holden huckstering   all through her lifetime.[18]

Rose the Regrater partly functions in the poem as an illustrative appendage of the sins of her husband, Covetousness. But she also represents, in very vivid and specific terms, a brewster who should never be trusted by her customers. With her weak ale, her unfair prices, and her deceitful cups, she is a sister to the Good Gossip of Chester, a roughly contemporary figure.[19] To be sure, Langland also illustrates Rose the Regrater's duplicity (and the allied duplicity of her husband) through her work as a weaver (in which she uses loosely spun yarn and false weights). But in both his description of Rose the Regrater and his literal naming of her, he emphasizes her work as a brewster and tapster. For him, there could be no better wife for a greedy man who lied and cheated for profit than a woman in the drink trade.

Once done with *Avaricia*, Langland turns to *Gula*, where he immediately describes another alewife, Betoun the Brewster. She runs an alehouse that foreshadows in its rowdiness and grossness the yet nastier establishment of Elynour Rummyng.[20] But she also is distinguished by her skills as a temptress, skills that recall the sin of Eve. As Glutton is heading piously to church, Betoun the Brewster entices him into her house and away from religious worship.

> Now beginneth Glutton   for to go to shift
> And carries him to kirk-ward   his fault there to show.
> But Betoun the brewster   bade him good-morrow
> And asked of him with that   whitherward he would.
> "To holy church," quoth he   "for to hear Mass,

And after will be shriven   and then sin no more."
"Gossip, I've good ale," quoth she   "Glutton, wilt thou try it?"
"Hast thou aught in thy bag?   Any hot spices?"
"I have pepper and peony   and a pound too of garlic,
And a farthing's worth of fennel-seed   for fasting days."
Then goeth Glutton in   and great oaths come after.[21]

The fictional Betoun the Brewster, like the fictional Elynour Rummyng, is a wicked woman, an unchristian encourager of vice, and a profiteer at the expense of others. Indeed, she might even have hosted, as Elynour Rummyng certainly did, a mock mass in which drinking songs were substituted for hymns, a cobbler stood in for the priest, the ale pot circulated as a chalice, and Glutton's own vomit signified penitential restitution.[22]

William Langland was concerned about much more than erring alewives, and his *Piers Plowman* abounds with criticisms of related behaviors: he ridicules drunkenness, he dislikes immoderation in all forms, and he distrusts victualers of all types and both sexes. For Langland, the ale trade brought together all these vices, and for Langland, the ale trade was best personified by two female characters: the cheating Rose the Regrater and the tempting Betoun the Brewster.[23]

John Lydgate, poet to the court of Henry V, did not share all the moral concerns of William Langland, but he, too, commented on the wiles of alewives. Lydgate complained about another common type: the sexually alluring woman who tempted her customers to spend money on drink by flirting with them. He criticized one alewife directly:

Gladly you will, to get you acquaintance
Call men to drink, although they therefore pay;
With your kissing though that you do pleasance
It shall be dearer, ere they go their way
Than all their ale, to them I dare will say.
Thus with your ale, and with your cheer so sly,
You them deceive, that in you most affie [trust].

To Lydgate, the flirting alewife was a source of pain and dismay, as well as undue debt. As he particularly emphasized in a sarcastic antiphrasim that he appended to this first poem, the attractive but unattainable alewife epitomized duplicity and inconstancy.[24]

As established parts of the canon of English literature, *The Tunning of Elynour Rumming*, *The Harrowing of Hell*, *Piers Plowman*, and the poems of John Lydgate are much-studied texts whose nuances and ambiguities have led to many different interpretations and many long-standing controversies. In reading the representations of alewives found in these texts in particularly negative terms, my argument stresses a characterization ignored in much of this literary criticism, sometimes complementing and sometimes confounding past interpretations. My argument also stresses the potentially large audiences for these works. Skelton wrote often for courtly audiences, and it is certainly possible that *The Tunning of Elynour Rumming* was originally crafted for the amusement of Westminster courtiers, not humble peasants or artisans. Yet it is just as possible that *The Tunning of*

Elynour Rummyng was written for a wider and more popular audience, as suggested not only by its vocabulary, syntax, and meter but also by its particular suitability for oral presentation.[25] Whatever Skelton's intended audience might have been, his poem attracted wide popular attention; it was reprinted on several occasions in the sixteenth and seventeenth centuries, it was included in the libraries of such ordinary people as the mason of Coventry, whose books were cataloged by Robert Laneham in 1575; and it was sufficiently well known to merit allusion in later popular texts, such as Ben Jonson's *A Tale of a Tub*.[26] Lydgate, like Skelton, was a poet connected to the royal court, but his two ballads addressed to a teasing alewife were clearly some of his more casual efforts.

William Langland, a married clerk who lived in London for at least part of his adult life, wrote for more humble audiences, and the many extant manuscripts of his *Piers Plowman* have usually been traced to men who worked as clerks or administrators. But as Caroline Barron has recently noted, "the appeal of Piers Plowman was very wide, perhaps even wider than has yet been suggested."[27] The authors of *The Harrowing of Hell* in the Chester cycle are, of course, unknown, but like Langland, they wrote in an urban milieu about matters both urban and rural. Their audiences would have included both the townspeople of Chester who supported the cycle and people from nearby villages who came to the town for the festivities.

Moreover, the representations of alewives found in these canonical texts vibrated with particular social force because they were not alone. When parishioners gazed up at the walls of their churches to see alewives cavorting happily with devils, their understanding of such images was partly shaped by a wide range of other popular representations of alewives as sinful, tempting, disgusting, and untrustworthy women. In ballads, tracts, popular prints, pamphlets, and other media, ordinary people expressed a fearful dislike of alewives that was as fully intense as the representations of Skelton, Langland, and Lydgate.

Among the many ballads and tracts that survive in printed form from the sixteenth and seventeenth centuries are several that describe alewives in very unflattering terms. *Jyl of Brentford's testament* tells about an alewife who bequeathed farts to all and sundry (including the poor clerk who wrote out her will).[28] *The Good-fellows Counsel* complains about a fat alewife who connives to get her customers to eat and drink more than they either need or can afford.[29] *The Kind Beleeving Hostess* describes a alewife who deceives her husband, cheats her customers, encourages debt, and keeps whores as servants (in the end, the ballad promises that she'll get her due, for the singer has run up a large debt that he has no plans to pay).[30] And *The Industrious Smith* tells the story of a simple smith who is undone by his aleselling wife. Hoping to improve their lot in life, he suggests that his wife take up aleselling. When she does, the poor smith "was never so troubled before," for the alehouse brought disorder, drunkenness, debt, and cuckoldry. To his every complaint, his wife responds reassuringly with the refrain of the ballad: "Sweetheart, do not rail, these things must be, if we sell ale." In the end, the smith loses not only the alehouse by which he had hoped to thrive but also his smithy.[31]

Other popular media tell still more tales about alewives. Mother Bunch narrates *Pasquil's Jests*, an early seventeenth-century book of humorous stories, where she is described as a brewster of great size, great appetite, and great age. Her ale was potent in more ways than one:

> She raised the spirits of her spicket, to such height, that maids grew proud, and many proved with child after it, and being asked who got the child, they answered they knew not, only they thought *Mother Bunch's* ale and another thing had done the deed, but whosoever was the father, *Mother Bunch's* ale had all the blame.

Written with strong humor and some affection, the portrait of Mother Bunch draws on characterizations we've already encountered—physical grossness, sexual danger, and uncleanliness:

> She was an excellent companion, and sociable, she was very pleasant and witty, and would tell a tale, let a fart, drink her draught, scratch her arse, pay her groat, as well as any Chemist of ale whatsoever. From this noble *Mother Bunch* proceeded all our great greasy Tapsters, and fat swelling Alewives, whose faces are blown as big as the froth of their Bottle-ale, and their complexion imitating the outside of a Cook's greasy dripping pan. . . .[32]

The very name of another seventeenth-century alewife, Mother Louse, implies a similar lack of sanitation. Yet Mother Louse is mostly ridiculed for her great age and old-fashioned clothing. Pictured in front of her rough-and-tumble establishment (Louse Hall), she replies to her critics:

> You laugh now goodman twoshoes, but at what?
> My Grove, my mansion house, or my dun hat?
> Is it for that my loving Chin and Snout
> Are met because my teeth are fallen out?
> Is it at me, or at my ruff you titter?
> Your Grandmother, you rogue, nere wore a fitter.[33]

One final example: *The Tale of Beryn*, a near-contemporary spin-off of Chaucer's *Canterbury Tales*, begins with a lengthy prologue relating how the Pardoner was out-conned by a tapster, Kit. Like Lydgate's teasing alewife, Kit is unfaithful to men, falsely mourning a dead lover and falsely flirting with the Pardoner. Indeed, she is the ultimate trickster. The Pardoner confidently hopes to beguile Kit into bed and then steal her money, but her plots outdo his. Triumphing over all his schemes, Kit takes the Pardoner's money, shares his feast with others, arranges a sound thrashing for him, and of course offers her sexual favors to another man. In Kit's hands, the Pardoner suffers a fate that seems to befall all men who trust in "tapsters and other such."[34]

As these many examples show, representations of alewives in late medieval and early modern England are found in a wide variety of media, and they come from a wide range of social milieux. Court poets created these images, as did married clerks, gildsmen, artisans, and peasants. Their receptive audiences included courtiers, as well as clerics, townspeople, and peasants, and their representations enjoyed popularity for a very long time. Already fully developed by the early fourteenth century, the representation of an alewife singled out among other sinners for eternal damnation endured well into the seventeenth century. In 1600, a reforming mayor in Chester suppressed the midsummer enactment of "cups and cans" with its alewife and devil, but it was revived in 1617.[35] Suspicious of the honesty, neighborliness, and faithfulness of women in the drink trade, people seem to have delighted for centuries in this representation of the special sinfulness and certain damnation of alewives.

Precious few positive celebrations of alewives and their trade offset these many nasty depictions. I cannot pretend to have unearthed all representations of alewives from English cultural media over more than three centuries, and I have found many minor representations that I have not described here.[36] But I have located only two substantial representations of good alewives that might offset the many negative representations of their more wicked sisters. Both are quite late, and both are positive in ambivalent ways. The first, a drinking song performed in *The Knight of the Burning Pestle* (1613), celebrates Jillian of Berry as an ideal alewife for the drinking man: she welcomes all, she offers good ale and beer, she charges nothing, and she kisses freely. This ideal was, of course, impossible (what alewife could stay in business without charging for her drink?), and its impossibility might have indirectly maligned real alewives, who were less welcoming and less willing to offer drink without charge. In any case, it was an ideal for drinking men only, one that would have had considerably less appeal for either their wives or their neighbors.[37]

The second comes from Donald Lupton's early seventeenth-century survey of English places and characters. He offers a fairly straightforward portrait of a brewster who

> if her Ale be strong, her reckoning right, her house clean, her fire good, her face fair, and the Town great or rich, she shall seldom or never sit without Chirping Birds to bear her Company, and at the next Churching or Christening, she is sure to be rid of two or three dozen Cakes and Ale by Gossiping Neighbours.

Lupton sympathetically understands the business of a brewster, yet even his positive description includes many now-familiar complaints about alewives: that their ale is substandard; that they connive (in this case, with justice's clerks) to avoid legal supervision; that they are falsely friendly; that they flirt with their customers.[38]

Aside from these two ambivalent cases, I have found no celebrations of alewives: they are not praised for the essential product they provide; they are not honored for their good trade and fine ale; they are not held up as epitomes of good wives and good neighbors. Instead, brewsters and tapsters are represented in late medieval and early modern England as nefarious traders, filthy people, and likely candidates for eternal damnation.

Social Analogs

These characterizations of Elynour Rummyng, the Gentle Gossip of the Chester cycle, Rose the Regrater, Mother Bunch, and others of their ilk speak to a widespread and popular distrust of women in the brewing trade. What were the sources of this distrust? And why was it focused particularly on alewives, rather than on *all* brewers and alesellers? Attacks on alewives drew on three complementary traditions: distrust of the trading practices of all victualers, fears about the sins and disorders caused by excessive drinking, and hatred of women.

In late medieval and early modern England, victualers were tolerated because they did essential work, but they were constantly suspected of abusive practices: adulterating their products, selling poor-quality foods, using false measures to cheat their customers, and charging unfairly high prices. Hence, William Langland not only maligns cheating alewives but also complains about the unruliness and irregularity of all brewers and all victualers. He urges officers

> To punish on pillories   and punishment stools
> Brewers and bakers   butchers and cooks,
> For these are this world's men   that work the most harm
> To the poor people that   must buy piece-meal.[39]

Other texts echo Langland's concerns about the trading practices of all victualers, male as well as female. Geoffrey Chaucer depicts the Cook in *The Canterbury Tales* as a slightly unsavory, drunken fellow whose foodstuffs are of dubious cleanliness and quality.[40] John Gower describes all victualers as lowly types, who cheat even their friends and neighbors at every opportunity.[41] And Barnaby Rich avers that bakers and brewers sin ten times more than usurers, especially in their abuse of poor customers.[42]

Yet complaints about male victualers were much less virulent than complaints about alewives specifically. First, they seem to have been less common. Aside from brewing and dairying, men participated actively in most victualing trades, and given the predominance of men in such trades as butchering and fishmongering, their representations (negative or positive) are surprisingly few and far between. Second, negative representations of male victualers are milder, more abstract, and less personal than those of alewives. Langland's depiction of Rose the Regrater is much more riveting than his other comments about victualers or brewers; he names Rose, he locates her within a household, and he details her trickery with careful specificity. Chaucer might ridicule the slovenly habits of his Cook, but he also tells us that the Cook is a competent tradesman, skilled at preparing meat, judging ales, making stews, and baking pies. Gower criticizes all victualers, but he reserves special condemnation for female victualers, who, he tells us, deceive and trick their customers much more than do men. As a general rule, representations of male victualers are disparaging only about their business practices; no slighting mention is made of their physical appearances, their establishments, their piety (or lack thereof), their sexuality, or their very salvation. Men actively pursued many victualing trades and suffered much complaint from suspicious customers, but there is no male equivalent of Elynour Rummyng or the Good Gossip of Chester or Mother Bunch.[43]

Moreover, male brewers not only escaped the nastiest criticisms of their trade but also benefited from unambivalently positive representations. William Harrison had no doubt, it seems, that men brewed trustily and that women sold duplicitously. He speaks glowingly of how male brewers "observe very diligently" the water used in brewing and how a "skillful workman" can alter his proportions to make better beer. Yet he denigrates alewives, describing how they encourage excessive drinking by adding salt or rosin to ale and advising his readers how they might foil such devices.[44] When popular authors began to celebrate the labors of both merchants and artisans in the late sixteenth century, male brewers were sometimes singled out for special praise.[45] One playful song was devoted exclusively to *The Praise of Brewers*. It begins:

> There's many a clinking verse was made
>   In honor of the Black-smiths trade,
> But more of the Brewers may be said
>   Which no body can deny.

Rife with puns about brewing, the song describes one brewer's martial triumphs over the Scots and Irish and bemoans his death (and the loss of his strong beer).[46] I have found nothing in a similarly positive vein for brewsters.

The vulnerability of alewives to particular criticism was also enhanced by the disorder that could attend the sale of ale or other alcoholic products. Ale and beer were essential foodstuffs, consumed as basic liquid refreshment by persons of all ages and all classes, and used in both cooking and healing. Yet ale and beer differed fundamentally from other foodstuffs in their inebriating effects. These effects might have been desired and sought by some customers, but they were vigorously opposed by civic authorities, who wanted orderly houses and quiet lanes, and by church authorities, who equated drunkenness with the sin of gluttony. Sermons depicted alehouses as "deadly rivals" to the church, a rivalry clearly emphasized by Langland in his description of Betoun the Brewster enticing Glutton away from confession and holy mass.[47] Proverbial teachings maintained that "the tavern is the devil's schoolhouse," an idea echoed not only in the many depictions of alewives in hell but also in Skelton's comment on Elynour Rummyng that "the devil and she be sib."[48] And local authorities attempted to control alehouse behavior by prohibiting games, drunkenness, and prostitution, just the sorts of behavior deplored by Langland, Skelton, and the authors of various ballads.[49] Among all victualers, then, brewers of both sexes suffered special opprobrium because the food they sold was a potentially sinful one.

All victualers were suspected of cheating in their trade, and all brewers and alesellers were censured for causing drunkenness and disorder. But brewsters and tapsters suffered from these suspicions more than male victualers, male brewers, and male alesellers. In part, the particular association of brewing abuses with women might rest in their early presence in the trade; because most brewers in the early fourteenth century were women, cultural representations of brewers were perhaps set in a female form. Also, these negative representations of alewives might reflect the sometimes sexualized circumstances of ale-selling in which women and men played well-known games. Yet neither cultural traditions nor sexual practices suffice to explain why women were so consistently and so continuously singled out for particular reproach. The missing piece is misogyny.[50] Because of long-standing traditions about the natural unfaithfulness, wickedness, and unreliability of women, alewives were marked out from other victualers and brewers for special suspicion and attack. In other words, because alewives were women, they—not male brewers and not male tipplers—bore the brunt of popular anxiety about cheating and disorder in their trade.

Like all women, alewives were deemed untrustworthy. If Adam was deceived by Eve, Samson by Delilah, David by Bathsheba, even Robin Hood by the wicked prioress, how could a simple man hope to escape the deceit of a conniving alewife? As one contemporary lyric taught about women:

> Their steadfastness endureth but a season;
> For they feign friendliness and work treason.[51]

John Gower could so confidently assume that female victualers cheated more readily than male victualers because his misogynous culture taught him just that.

Like all women, alewives were seen as temptresses who drew men into sin. Betoun the Brewster, Kit, and the paunch-bellied hostess were, after all, daughters of Eve, tempting customers into excessive consumption and excessive expenditure. Just as Betoun the Brewster enticed Glutton away from mass and into her alehouse, so other alewives were seen as tempting unwitting customers into sin and debt. In *The Tale of Beryn*, Kit responds to the Pardoner's news that he is fasting by setting a pie before him and encouraging him to "Eat and be merry."[52] If ale and beer generated sin, women were thought to help the process along.

Like all women, alewives were seen as sexually uncontrolled, driven by "beastly lust" and "foul delight."[53] A tense sexual ambivalence runs through representations of brewsters and tapsters. Some dwell on the disgusting physical appearance of alewives, such as Elynour Rummyng, Mother Bunch, and Mother Louse, with whom few men would willingly lie down.[54] Others emphasize the duplicitous sexuality of alewives who, like the alewife of Lydgate's ballad, tease and flirt with customers only to get their business. Still others associate alewifery and whoredom; the alewife Kit in *The Tale of Beryn* seems ready to sleep with almost any man. And still other representations malign alewives not just for teasing and whoring but also for adultery. The foolish industrious smith is made a cuckold by his wife, who admonishes him not to complain for "These things must be, if we sell Ale."[55] In all of these representations, the potent mixture of sexuality and drink is blamed on alewives; it is the woman, neither her male customers nor her husband, who bears responsibility for the teasing, the adultery, and the whoring.

Perhaps most important, like all women, alewives were deemed prone to disobedience. Walter Map wrote, "Disobedience . . . will never cease to stimulate women"; Chaucer dwelt repeatedly on the disobedient and disruptive power of the Wife of Bath over her husbands; a popular proverb taught simply that "a woman will have her will."[56] This misogynist theme had particular resonance for brewsters and tapsters since their work threatened the ideal of a proper patriarchal order. In flirting with customers, alewives undermined the authority of their husbands; in handling money, goods, and debts, they challenged the economic power of men; in bargaining with male customers, they achieved a seemingly unnatural power over men; in avoiding effective regulation of their trade, they insulted the power of male officers and magistrates; and perhaps most important, in simply pursuing their trade, they often worked independently of men. A "good" alewife flirted and managed and bargained and traded in the interests of her husband and household, maintaining all due deference and subordination. But even a "good" alewife had the potential power, through her trade, to subvert the "natural" patriarchal order.[57]

It is no wonder, then, that representations of alewives dwelt on fearful images of willful and self-governing women. The undoing of the industrious smith is his inability to rule his wife. We are told at the outset, "And though he were very discreet and wise/Yet he would do nothing without her advise." Humiliated in a variety of ways, the smith is eventually insulted (in perhaps the unkindest cut of all) by a customer who will pay only his wife, saying, "I owe you no money, nor none shall you have/I owe to your wife, and her I will pay."[58] We learn similarly of the kind believing hostess that she is entirely unruled by her husband:

> To speak, poor man, he dares not;
> My Hostess for him cares not;
> She'll drink and quaff
> And merrily laugh
> And she his anger fears not.[59]

In these and other representations, alewives disobey not only their husbands but also all men. They fail to obey statutory rules and regulations (as did Elynour Rummyng, Rose the Regrater, and the Good Gossip of Chester). They lack respect for God and his church (as exemplified by Betoun the Brewster and all the alewives left in hell). They make complete fools of their male customers, encouraging them to misbehave and lose control (as did Elynour Rummyng, Betoun the Brewster, and Lydgate's alewife). And they encourage other women to be disobedient to their husbands; the alewife Tipple was a companion to Strife, the wife of the downtrodden and beaten Tom Tyler, and Elynour Rummyng managed to urge even a "housewife of trust" to barter the goods of her family in exchange for ale.[60] Indeed, the entirely female world of *The Tunning of Elynour Rummyng* suggests where an alewife's power can lead: a chaotic world without men in which women, not just alewives but *all* women, are in control.

European misogyny, then, found an ideal field for expression in popular antipathy toward alewives. Represented in so many cultural artifacts of late medieval and early modern England, anxiety about brewsters and tapsters sprang in part from two sources quite independent of misogyny—dislike of victualers and concerns about the drunkenness, gluttony, and sexual license of alehouses.

Yet it was misogyny that directed these two anxieties toward women and added further to people's dismay. Misogynous ideas about the natural weaknesses and disorders of women suggested that brewsters would cheat more than male brewers, would temptingly lure men into the gluttonous and sexual sins of ale-houses, and would flagrantly resist the rule of men. If alehouses were "the devil's schoolhouse," then women were the devil's schoolmistresses—disobeying men, deceiving them, leading them into both gluttony and lechery, and of course profiting at their expense.

Social Meanings

These representations did not, of course, directly harm the business of alewives. It would be absurd to suggest that *The Tunning of Elynour Rummyng* convinced customers to avoid the brewhouses of women and patronize the brewhouses of men. Few poems are so powerful and few audiences so susceptible to poetic suggestion.[61] Moreover, the brewing trade was not so clearly divided between men and women that customers could readily choose to take their custom to one group rather than the other. Yet it would also be absurd to suggest that *The Tunning of Elynour Rummyng* was art alone, entirely lacking any social force.[62]

Like any representation, these depictions of alewives as unsavory people and untrustworthy traders resonated in diverse and multiple ways. There were certainly benevolent sides to these images. Poems like *The Tunning of Elynour Rummyng* offered good entertainment, and while they were read or recited or discussed, customers would drink and laugh and stay to drink again. Such poems also might have defused tension about alewives and their business. In chuckling over Elynour Rummyng and her adulterated ale, foolish clientele, and grotesque ale-house, customers might have assured themselves that their own lot was better. Their hostess was nicer, cleaner, kinder, and more honest than Elynour Rummyng, and they were neither as desperate nor as disgusting as her fictional clientele. These sorts of reactions to the poems, ballads, plays, or other media that maligned alewives might have actually eased an alewife's trade, helping her to keep customers happy, content, and drinking. Yet these benevolent effects played alongside quite malevolent resonances. For while these poems, ballads, and plays provided both amusing entertainment and reassuring contrasts for customers, they also articulated concerns that could seriously undermine the businesses of brewsters and tapsters.

The attitudes betrayed in these representations might have inhibited the trade of alewives in many ways: they socially marginalized the alehouses run by alewives; they implied that alewives were particularly likely to cheat and deceive their customers; they suggested that the drink sold by alewives was particularly filthy and adulterated; and they dangerously associated alewives with disorder, heresy, and witchcraft. In everyday life, these sorts of accusations carried real force. In 1413, the brewster Christine Colmere of Canterbury lost all her trade when Simon Daniel told her neighbors that she was leprous; although the charge was false, her customers left her for fear of contaminated ale.[63] In 1641, an unnamed widow who brewed for the garrison at Ludlow castle lost her trade because, despite her fine reputation, a male competitor spread false rumors about her person and her business.[64] As both Colmere and this unnamed widow learned, a brewster's trade could be damaged by words alone. What they lost through specific slander, other alewives—who worked in a world abounding with images that ridiculed them and maligned their trade—might have lost through more general opprobrium.

Yet as the brewing trade changed, so, too, did representations of alewives. Our earliest sources betray a strong anxiety about cheating by alewives, and this anxiety found further expression well into the seventeenth century. By that time, however, new concerns were also developing in representations of alewives, for after about 1500, anxieties about cheating were often supplemented by worries about foul products and disorderly alehouses. It is difficult, given the paucity of sources and the idiosyncrasies of their survival to the present day, either to assess or to explain the importance of this seemingly "new" emphasis on the filthiness of alewives and their products. For example, a stronger emphasis on physical caricatures of alewives after 1500 might reflect discursive conventions (especially the effect of *The Tunning of Elynour Rummyng* on later depictions of alewives), sexual anxieties (especially about singlewomen or widows still in the trade), social conventions (especially about witches, scolds, and other undesirable women), or a combination of these and other factors. Moreover, changes in representations of alewives are subtle, not definitive; the mid-seventeenth-century Mother Louse draws on newer emphases on the filthiness of alewives, but she also echoes (in her plans to deceive the excisemen and her promises of "bigger pots and stronger ale" in the future) past complaints about cheating alewives.

Nevertheless, no matter how subtle these representational changes and no matter how obscure their origins, their social meanings were partly rooted in the changing circumstances of the drink trade. In the early fourteenth century, when the ale trade was modest and home-based, nasty depictions of alewives might have served mostly as safety valves, releasing social tensions over female predominance in such a crucial trade. Representations of alewives as conniving cheaters feature strongly in this earlier period, when ale, unchallenged by beer, was most often sold for consumption away from a brewster's shop or home. In the early sixteenth century, when brewing was more profitable and more attractive to men, nasty images of alewives might have more directly discouraged women from working in the trade. New representations of the foul ale and disorderly establishments of alewives belong to this period—when beer challenged ale for the palates of English drinkers, when proliferating alehouses created severe regulatory problems, and when small-scale producers of ale worked alongside professional brewers of ale and beer.

Early representations of alewives pick up on many themes, such as their tempting of innocent customers (Betoun the Brewster) or their sexual teasing (Kit in *The Tale of Beryn*). But, as seen in depictions of Rose the Regrater, the Good Gossip of Chester, and other unnamed condemned alewives who brandish their illegal pots, cheating by alewives was especially emphasized in the earliest representations. These depictions of alewives as duplicitous tradeswomen were particularly dangerous because they were very true to life: they maligned alewives for the very offenses that were most common and most worrisome to customers. Brewers often cheated with impunity: they diluted their ale, altered their measures, and demanded higher prices, and on most such occasions, neither customers nor officers were any the wiser. Indeed, given contemporary imprecisions of coinage, measures, and quality control, some level of fraud by brewers was probably unavoidable. All communities tried to regulate their brewers and force them to conform to specified standards of price, quality, and measure, but full conformity by brewers was, in fact, quite rare.[65] Not surprisingly, most communities seemed to have been resigned to a certain level of nonconformity, making brewers pay standard fines or licensing fees and tolerating a little bit of fiddling by them behind the scenes.

So all alewives were not innocent tradeswomen, falsely accused of cheating when they were only trying to make reasonable profits in roughly honest ways. Some alewives did cheat, and some cheated egregiously. In 1364, for example, Alice the wife of Robert de Caustone of London sold ale in a cleverly disguised false measure. Adding 1½ inches of pitch to an unsealed quart and laying rosemary on top to conceal her subterfuge, she created a "quart" measure that was so fraudulent that even six of her quarts did not make a true gallon.[66] Yet, although some alewives cheated excessively, not all alewives were guilty of such offenses, and more important, these offenses were not peculiar to women.

It is, of course, impossible to pinpoint the incidence of cheating in any trade (either then or now). Yet there is no reason to assume that women in the drink trade cheated more than men. Our best measure of the phenomenon of cheating by brewers and tipplers comes from reports that the aletasters of Oxford filed in 1324. In June of that year, when they moved through the wards of the city, the aletasters noted at each house whether ale had been sold at the proclaimed price and whether it had been of sufficiently good quality. They checked, in other words, for two common tricks of the trade: charging excessive prices and selling weak or mixed ale. The aletasters seem to have collected their information by interviewing each brewer or aleseller on his or her premises, tasting the ale (if available), and collecting information from neighbors. Their presentments name either not-married brewsters or men (who in most cases probably represented either their wives or a married couple active in brewing). In other words, these presentments can tell us whether singlewomen and widows were more likely than married couples, bachelors, or married women to be adjudged guilty of charging excessive prices or selling weak ale. They suggest that, in fact, not-married women cheated with roughly the same regularity as did other brewers and tipplers (see table 7.1).

These figures can be only suggestive, for it is impossible to know whether singlewomen and widows in the drink trade were treated differently from other brewers and alesellers in Oxford. Perhaps their rate of cheating is accurately reported, but it might be overreported by aletasters especially suspicious of women or, indeed, underreported by aletasters especially willing to overlook or forgive women's petty offenses. As always, there is an immeasurable interpretative shortfall between transgression and legal response. Nevertheless, these

Table 7.1   Offenses of Brewers and Tipplers in Oxford, 1324

Offenses:	Not-married women		Men/couples		Total	
	Number	Percent	Number	Percent	Number	Percent
None	19	47½	63	43	82	44
One	18	45	68	46	86	46
Two or more	3	7½	16	11	19	10
Total	40	100	147	100	187	100

Source: Oxford Assizes for 1324.

Note: One case with incomplete information has been excluded from these calculations.

figures do lead to two safe conclusions: cheating was common among all brewers and alesellers, and it does not seem to have been particularly prominent among women "ungoverned" by male householders.

Yet, despite what was very likely a rough parity of cheating between women and men in the ale trade, most representations of the trade depict cheating brewers as women, implying that the trade would be well regulated and justly pursued if confined to men. Anxiety about cheating was displaced onto just one segment of the trade: women (and perhaps especially *not-married* women, who, if they lived without male masters or householders, seemed to be particularly unregulated and uncontrolled). In other words, descriptions of the false trading practices of a brewster such as Rose the Regrater both *expressed* and *aroused* the anxieties of ordinary people about their reliance for an essential foodstuff on a trade that could only be minimally regulated. Customers worried that brewers and tipplers would cheat them, and Rose the Regrater and others like her did just that. Stories about Rose the Regrater and other dishonest alewives might have inhibited a real alewife's ability to manipulate her trade in customary ways; since her customers anticipated being cheated, she was perhaps able to cheat them less effectively. These stories might also have discouraged customers from frequenting the premises of real alewives; since they expected an alewife to be especially dishonest, customers might have taken their trade, if given the choice, to a male brewer or tippler or, at least, to a married alewife well-governed by her husband.

By the sixteenth century, representations of alewives not only impugn their honesty but also malign their foul ales and their disorderly alehouses. Alewives had always been depicted as adulterating their ale, but by the sixteenth century, they were also accused of preparing their ale in foul and unclean ways. Both Rose the Regrater and the Good Gossip of Chester had mingled strong and weak ales together. Later alewives foul their brews in ways that are more disgusting than illegal. Eleanor Rummyng's ale contains her drool; filth from her "mangy hands"; dung from her roosting hens; and snot from her nose, which, Skelton tells us, was "Never stopping/But ever dropping." Lest readers miss the point that the aptly named Mother Louse runs an unclean establishment, her picture and poem are accompanied by an escutcheon showing three quite realistic lice, with an ale pot at the crest and the motto "three liese passant." The notion that alewives brewed their ale without any concern for cleanliness or health reached parodic proportions in the early seventeenth-century depiction of Mother Bunch. Her famous ale, known all over England, comes directly from her "most precious and rich nose."

Representations of disorderly alehouses date back to the fourteenth century, but they also grew more vivid and more common over time. Glutton sates his desire for food and drink at Betoun's alehouse; many later characters obtain at alehouses not only food and drink but also sexual play and, perhaps, sexual satisfaction. Lydgate's alewife teases him to distraction; the tapster Kit in *The Tale of Beryn* flirts shamelessly with the Pardoner; and the wife of the industrious smith flaunts her lovers before her befuddled husband. Other representations depict alewives as procuresses or harborers of prostitutes. When the industrious smith finds his maidservant in bed with a customer, his wife reassures him, as always, that "these things must be if we sell ale." The kind, believing hostess keeps two whores, Bess and Dolly, to service her customers, and she offers to procure other women as well.

These representational shifts accompany, of course, very real changes in the circumstances of the ale trade in the fifteenth and sixteenth centuries. First, in 1350, ale had no real competitors, but by 1500, beer was vying with ale for English drinkers. Suggestions that alewives were old-fashioned and unclean might have spoken directly to this new dichotomy. Beer, brewed in cities such as London and Southampton, was a product of upright gildsmen and large brewhouses, and it was drunk by sophisticated, urban drinkers. Ale, brewed in the houses of countrywomen and drunk by simple folk, was comparatively unregulated, uncontrolled, and old-fashioned.[67] Second, in 1350, most ale was sold for consumption elsewhere, but by 1500, alehouses were a ubiquitous feature of the English landscape. Much loved by English alewives and English drinkers, alehouses generated considerable social problems: drinking late at night or on Sundays; corruption of servants and apprentices; games, gambling, and other amusements; prostitution; and of course, disorderly drunkenness.

When Skelton, then, located Elynour Rummyng in a rural alehouse, he was doing more than representing a common type. He was also playing with contrasts between ale and beer, town and country, petty producers and gildsmen, and of course women and men. If Elynour Rummyng had sold beer purchased from a supplier in London, the poem might have retained its critique of drunkenness but lost much of its class-based and gender-based humor. In brewing ale herself and selling it in her alehouse, Elynour Rummyng represents what so many other alewives came to represent in the media of the time: old-fashioned, poor countrywomen; bad, unregulated ale; disorderly and troublesome alehouses.

Of course, these representations held much truth. By the sixteenth century, the women most likely to hold alehouse licenses on their own account were poor widows. Their ale, brewed in private homes in small amounts, was much harder to regulate than beer. Increasingly, both they and their customers were rural yokels, not artisans or merchants or gentry. And their alehouses, often poor and rough, seem to have fostered a variety of traditional activities that troubled and worried their social "betters." But as with cheating, so with foul ale and disorderly houses: these problems were not generated by alewives but were ubiquitous in the drink trade, associated as much with the trade of men as with the trade of women.[68]

Consider, for example, the supposedly upright brewers of London in the sixteenth century. By that time, brewers of beer and ale in the city were a small, prosperous, and well-regulated group. With a gild representing their interests to both city and Crown, they had a strong professional identity; and since their gild admitted only the occasional widow to membership, they protected their trade from much female influence. Yet their trade was as plagued as that of rural alewives with adulterated or badly brewed products and with disorderly houses and drunken clients. From the reports of the city, we learn that these wealthy and prestigious gildsmen regularly cheated in their measures, sold unwholesome ale or beer, charged unfair prices, brewed strong beer that encouraged drunkenness, tolerated disorderly houses, kept unclean premises, and wantonly disobeyed city orders.[69] The trade was so badly managed that in the 1590s a professional informer, Hugh Alley, found that he could largely support himself by initiating suits against erring brewers.[70]

Yet, although professional London brewers, just like rural alewives, sold adulterated drink and fostered drunken disorder, anxieties about these aspects of the drink trade focused largely on alewives. In other words, representations of alewives brewing foul ale and managing foul houses displaced *general* concerns about the trade onto this *particular* group of traders. They suggested that if women did not brew or sell drink, good products would be bought from responsible proprietors who ran sober establishments. The Brewers' Company of London seems to have understood this dynamic quite well. Its incorporation charter of 1639 spoke harshly of women who "are not fit" to sell ale or beer and promoted in their stead "men that are members of this company and have been trained and brought up in the trade, mystery and art of brewing."[71]

Sexual misconduct in alehouses was, of course, another matter. If alehouses had been free of women, much of the sexual disorder associated with the drink trade would have disappeared. Without women serving heterosexual men, there would have been no teasing tapsters, no adulterous alewives, no whores working out of alehouses. These associations of female aleselling with unruly female sexuality reflect a basic tension in the trade of alewives. To attract customers into their houses and sell drink to them, alewives needed to be pleasant and amusing. As *Choice of Inventions* put it:

> A man that hath a sign at his door,
>   and keeps good Ale to sell,
> A comely wife to please his guests,
>   may thrive exceeding well. . . .

Yet an alewife who was too comely or too friendly ran into trouble. She offended male customers who misconstrued commercial friendliness as genuine flirting (as Lydgate had done); she risked adultery (or the appearance of adultery); she suffered the ire of local authorities seeking to root out disorderly houses. The preceding verse ends:

But he that hath a Whore to his wife,
    were better be without her.[72]

Of course, the heterosexual dynamic of alehouses involved men as well as women; both played the game, both profited from it, both sinned, but only women were usually blamed. This dynamic also often involved women who were employees, not proprietors. The alluring woman of an alehouse was sometimes its owner and sometimes the owner's wife, but she was often a daughter or a maidservant or a prostitute allowed to work out of the premises. Thus, Lupton notes that a prosperous hostess had to be sure that she or her daughter or her maid would kiss her customers "handsomely."[73] Thus, the very first task of the industrious smith when he decides to open an alehouse is to hire a maidservant to attract customers:

They sent for a wench, her name it was Besse
And her they hired to welcome their guests.[74]

And thus, in court records, keepers of alehouses were regularly admonished to be "honest" and tolerate no whores. In 1380, for example, Robert Lovington and his wife, Amy, welcomed whores into their alehouse in Bridgwater and thereby lost their license to tipple.[75] In other words, sexual misconduct in alehouses did not rely on the sex of the proprietor. Yet, although brewers and alehouse-keepers of both sexes used young women to attract customers to their trade, the sexualized nature of aleselling was associated with brewsters and tapsters only. As Margaret Fiske of Norfolk said in 1578, "there cannot be any alewife thrive without she be a whore or have a whore in her house."[76]

When English people, then, considered the trade in ale or beer in their communities, they saw many problems. In the fourteenth century, they saw brewsters who, working and selling out of their homes, often cheated their customers in subtle and nefarious ways. By the sixteenth century, they still fretted about cheating, but they also worried more than before about unhealthy brewing, disorderly alehouses, and sexual license. These were real concerns and real problems. But their representation in English cultural media took problems common to *all* brewers and suggested that they were specific only to *female* brewers. The cultural repertoire of late medieval and early modern England suggested that all the problems associated with brewing—cheating, foul products, disorderly houses, and a host of other uncontrollable disruptions—were caused not by the trade itself but by the presence of women in the trade. Very real anxieties about the trade were displaced in a very unrealistic fashion onto just *female* brewers and *female* alesellers.

Misogyny and Brewsters

In the midsummer procession at Chester, this displacement took literal form, with the goodly innkeepers and cooks of the city preceded in their march by a cheating alewife and her devil. What did bystanders make of this scene? We know that they must have focused much of their attention on the alewife's cheating for they called this part of the procession "cups and cans" after the emblems of duplicity that she carried. For some, she might have signified the unregulated trade of tapsters, as contrasted with the better trade of innkeepers and cooks. But for others, she might have chastised the innkeepers and cooks as well as the tapsters, for she did, after all, precede their company. In other words, the cheating alewife of "cups and cans" could represent not only the corrupt trade of women but also the corrupt trade of all brewers and even all victualers. Needless to say, these representations were not mutually exclusive.

Of course, the cheating alewife of "cups and cans" was only part of the cultural package of the time, and by focusing on her and her analogs in this chapter, I do not mean to suggest that there was an unremitting attack on the work of women in brewing and aleselling. As we have seen, many representations of alewives were fond as well as critical, funny as well as judgmental. Some of those who watched "cups and cans" might have pondered neither cheating alewives nor cheating victualers but might instead have merely enjoyed the jangling vessels, the outrageous devil, and the pageantry of the procession. Others might have seen the alewife as an emblem of their own good alewife, who, if she cheated a bit and flirted a bit, was still a good neighbor and a good friend. They might have laughed with her instead of taunting her.

We cannot stand with the good folk of Chester and judge how they reacted to their "cups and cans," and to an important extent, this search for a true "reaction" is illusory in any case. If we had stood in Chester's streets in 1540 watching the crowd react to the alewife and her devil, we would have seen many reactions: laughter, anger, disgust, boredom, perhaps even fear. Some might have called out encouragement to the alewife; others might have pelted her with rotten food and pebbles. By 1617, to all these reactions was probably added another: embarrassment among some citizens that such an old-fashioned custom had been revived in their city. The cheating alewife of "cups and cans" does not represent straightforward misogyny in either its origins or its effects. Instead, she illustrates the powerful ways in which misogyny mingled with other traditions and other discourses.

In the year 1540, the mayor of Chester, Henry Gee, oversaw a series of measures designed to eliminate female disorder. First, in the order mentioned at the outset of this chapter, aleselling was proscribed for women between 14 and 40 years of age. As explained in the new ordinance:

> Whereas all the taverns and alehouses of this city have and be used to be kept by young women otherwise than is used in any other places of this realm, whereof all strangers resorting hither greatly marvel and think it an inconvenient use whereby not only great slander and dishonest report of this city hath and doth run abroad in avoiding whereof and also to eschew as well such great occasions and provocations of wantonness, brawls, frays and other inconveniences as thereby doth and may ensue daily among youth and light disposed persons as also damage unto their masters and owners of the taverns and alehouses. . . .[77]

Alewives, in other words, threatened the trade of the city, damaged its reputation, fomented disorders, corrupted the young and weak, harmed masters, and
even hurt the owners of alehouses and taverns. Whether Gee's order to restrict
female tippling was very effective or not, it was certainly not forgotten; it was
repeated in later decades and, on at least a few occasions, firmly enforced.[78]

The second order followed hard on the first, and it sought to restrain traditional celebrations associated with childbirth and churching. Complaining
about the great waste of the costly dishes, meats, and drinks brought to women
in childbed (gifts that were then reciprocated by the new mother at her churching), this ordinance proscribed such gift giving and limited attendance at
churchings to the midwife, mother, and sisters of the new mother.[79] Coming
almost immediately thereafter, the third order regulated women's headgear.
Although somewhat confusing in its phrasing, this ordinance sought to limit
excessive wearing of caps, kerchiefs, and hats; to allow only hats of white or
black; and to distinguish singlewomen from married women and widows.[80]

These new orders were promulgated in May, the first two on the twelfth,
just four days before Whitsun. So, when the good folk of Chester laughed at the
condemned alewife in the Whitsuntide plays of that year and watched "cups and
cans" in the midsummer procession, they might have laughed and watched in
different ways from before. They especially might have appreciated more
intensely the disorderly dangers that arose from women, for Henry Gee and his
brethren had just determined that the work of women, the festivities of women,
and even the very clothing of women were threatening enough to the polity to
require firm and careful regulation. In 1540, "cups and cans" confirmed the
sober judgment of Chester's best citizens that women, especially women in the
ale trade, must be restrained and controlled.

But before 1540, "cups and cans" had already spoken to these issues, and
the legislation of that year merely expressed in a new (and perhaps more powerful) forum some of the premises of this traditional rite. Henry Gee, growing
up in Chester and serving as its mayor once before in 1533–34, had probably
seen "cups and cans" on many occasions. He almost certainly did not walk home
from the midsummer procession of 1539 determined to reform the ale trade in
Chester because of what he saw on that day in the procession of innkeepers and
cooks. But he just as certainly was not ideologically removed from the premises
of "cups and cans." In his legislation of May 12, 1540, Henry Gee expressed the
same ideas as those acted out annually in "cups and cans": both saw women as
disorderly, and both displaced the problems of the drink trade onto women
alone. One did not cause the other, but both were imbricated within a complex
discourse that drew heavily on misogynous ideas. To be sure, this discourse was
informed both by anxieties about all victualers and by worries about drunken
disorders, but it was also critically shaped by assumptions about the seemingly
natural duplicity, disobedience, and disorderliness of the female sex.

In the other chapters of this book, we have seen how women slowly lost
their place in the brewing trade. In chapter 3, we saw how singlewomen and widows were unable to respond effectively to the expansion of commercial brewing after the Black Death. This was in part because both legal rules and social cus-

toms made it difficult for women to employ men, to foster trade relationships with men, or even to exercise authority over them. In chapter 4, we traced how women were sometimes excluded from gilds of brewers and sometimes subordinated within them. This was in part because gild prestige relied on the virtual exclusion of women from public participation in the trade. An all-male gild was so important that by the sixteenth century—as illustrated by the Pickering household—some women still brewed, but only their husbands belonged to the gild, only their husbands represented the public face of brewing. In chapter 5, we saw how women were unable to gain access to the new skills and new requirements of beerbrewing when it was brought to England by Dutch traders and settlers. This was in part because these beerbrewers brought with them from the continent a tradition of brewing as a highly skilled male profession, an art that was "given to men alone." In chapter 6, we examined how mayors and constables and justices did their best to discourage female brewing and encourage male brewing. This was in part because they thought, with Henry Gee, that women were special sources of disorder. Is there a relationship between all these obstructions, on the one hand, and misogynous representations of alewives, on the other? Of course. The alewife and her devil in "cups and cans" expressed in one forum what Henry Gee expressed in another. Fortified by their common misogynous ideology, both saw alewives as culpable for the abuses of the trade, and both therefore imagined that a trade run by men would be a trade better run.

CHAPTER EIGHT

WOMEN'S WORK IN A CHANGING WORLD

"If a venture prospers, women fade from the scene."[1] These few words seem to describe well what we have observed in the history of brewing. In 1300, brewing was a ubiquitous trade that required little specialized skill or equipment, conferred minimal trade identity, and offered only small profits. As such, it was accessible to women, and compared to the other, even more limited economic options of women, it was a good trade for them. By 1600, brewing in many places had been transformed into a specialized trade that required training and investment, conferred social prestige and gild status, and offered considerable profits. As such, it had ceased to be a trade of women and had become a trade of men. Brewing had prospered; brewsters had faded away.

Yet, brewsters did not just fade away, taking their part in a predetermined fugue of the sexes. Brewsters faced changing circumstances, reacted to them, and made history. Historians of women once described such histories in terms of *victimization* or *agency*, asking whether women were passive victims of men or active agents in shaping their own lives. Were women forced out of brewing? Or did they choose to leave it? Neither question adequately addresses the experiences of brewsters. Certainly brewsters and the men with whom they lived and worked made choices, but their choices were shaped and defined by the world around them. As Marx noted long ago, women and "men make their own history, but . . . they do not make it under circumstances chosen by themselves."[2]

In the case of brewing, those circumstances shifted dramatically against women in the centuries between 1300 and 1600. As commercial opportunities expanded after 1348, women had only small amounts of capital to invest in new equipment, limited authority over large work forces, and few contacts for obtaining supplies and opening new markets. As gilds offered brewers new ways to negotiate with civic authorities and express their trade status, wives found themselves second-rank members in organizations run by their husbands. As beer began to replace ale in the English diet, brewsters suffered from poor access to the new technology of beerbrewing and from an inability to respond effectively to the commercial opportunities it offered. As brewing and aleselling came under ever-closer government regulation, women's modest enterprises were deemed more disorderly and problematic than the larger enterprises run by men. As all of these changes in the trade proceeded, women suffered from cultural representations that implied that all the problems associated with the production and marketing of brewed drink were caused by brewsters alone. Taken together, these changes tilted the scales against brewsters and in favor of male brewers. In such circumstances, if a woman ceased brewing and took up, say, lace making, she adjusted and accommodated to new circumstances, but she neither freely chose to leave the trade nor was a victim of direct exclusion from it. If a man began to assist his wife in brewing and perhaps eventually to take over primary responsibility for it, he reacted to new opportunities, but he did not thereby baldly force his wife to leave the trade.

If brewsters were neither free agents nor powerless victims, how can we best understand their history? In this book, the history of brewsters has been told in two different ways—as a story of change in a specific area of women's work and as a story of continuity in the general state of women's work.[3] Both of these histories are firmly based on fact. Women's work did change (women no longer brewed as much as in the past), and women's work did stay the same (women still worked in the least appealing sectors of the economy). Yet these two histories can lead to very different understandings of the experiences of brewsters.

The story of change is the older and to some the more compelling. Between 1300 and 1600 brewing was transformed, and the effects of this transformation on women seem, at first glance, to fit the paradigm of a dramatic and negative transformation in women's work. In 1300, brewing in a town such as Oxford was a localized, small-scale industry that required little capital investment, yielded small profits, and could be pursued within the home; it was, therefore, a classic sector of women's work, characterized by low status, low skill, and low remuneration. Women predominated in the trade. By 1600, brewing in Oxford was closely regulated by the university and gild; access to the trade was restricted to a handful of persons; and the successful pursuit of brewing required capital investment, technical skill, and social clout. It had become, therefore, a capitalized and professionalized trade in which men predominated. To be sure, women still worked in the Oxford ale trade in the sixteenth century; as widows of brewers, they sometimes continued to manage their family businesses (as widows of skilled tradesmen had, of course, also done in the earlier centuries), and as poorer women, they worked in the lowest levels of the trade (especially as alesellers and ale carriers). But by 1600, those women still working in brewing were far outnumbered by men, who as either brewery owners or skilled brewery workers reaped the main profits from the trade. Brewing, then, seems to fit the model of a women's trade that was taken over by men as it became capitalized and industrialized.

In providing an example of a dramatic and negative transformation in women's work that accompanied a major turning point in economic history, this first history of brewsters contributes to a very old tradition in women's history. Indeed, the notion that the transition from a "medieval" to a "modern" economy resulted in a dramatic loss for working women remains one of the most enduring themes of women's history. Articulated early in the twentieth century by Alice Clark, this thesis of decline has been embraced by medievalists and early modernists alike.[4] From Eileen Power (who wrote in 1926 of a "rough-and-ready equality" between medieval women and men) to Caroline Barron (who has recently depicted a "golden age" for women in late medieval London), medievalists have repeated and elaborated Clark's positive assessment of women's roles in the medieval economy.[5] Although early modernists such as Keith Snell, Bridget Hill, Michael Roberts, and Margaret George sometimes disagree about the precise date of the decline, most agree that the period after 1500 witnessed some version of "woman's descent from paradise."[6]

Yet the history of brewing offers no evidence of a medieval "rough-and-ready equality" between the sexes or of a medieval "golden age" for women. When women brewed, it was a humble employment, offering little prestige and little profit. Compared to the other sorts of work available to women, brewing was a good option, but compared to the sorts of work available to men, it was a poor option indeed. The history of brewing also offers no evidence of a "descent from paradise." Brewsters worked less frequently in 1600 than in 1300, but they had not lost a high-status trade; they had, instead, failed to participate in an "ascent to paradise," failed to hold on to the once modest trade of brewing as it grew in profits and prestige.[7] The history of brewsters shows, first, that even the best women's work in the middle ages was humble work (belying any notion of a golden age) and, second, that the enduring characteristics of low status, low skilled, and low profit describe women's work in 1300, as well as in 1600 (belying the notion of a transformation in women's work status). Indeed, the history of brewsters suggests that those who have emphasized a dramatic change in women's work have mingled two things best kept separate: the experiences of women and women's *status*. Many things changed in the experiences of women who sought to profit from brewing, but their status as workers remained quite low.

If history-as-change inadequately describes the experiences of brewsters, history-as-continuity might help us to better understand what happened to the brewsters of late medieval England. We have seen that the history of brewsters is also a story of remarkable stability in women's status—of women "standing still" in a time of opportunity and expansion. When commercial brewing became more profitable, more complex, and more respectable after the Black Death, a brewster such as Denise Marlere had the opportunity to expand her business and increase her profits, and she might well have done so. But fewer and fewer Denise Mareleres brewed for profit in the later middle ages. Instead of exploiting the opportunities presented by the expansion of brewing, women left the trade, and they remained stuck in low-status, low-skilled, and poorly remunerated work. Before 1348, brewing in Oxford lacked all the accouterments of a recognized craft: it was a widely dispersed by-industry, not a trained occupation; it had no gild; it was rarely associated with the wealthy and most powerful householders of the town. After 1348, brewing slowly acquired these trappings. But as brewing grew more distinguished, women's work stayed the same. In 1600, women in Oxford seldom brewed, but they still found work in widely dispersed, low-skilled, and low-profit employments; singlewomen were virtually excluded from the formal trades of the town, wives assisted their husbands as best they could, and widows took over the businesses their husbands left behind.[8]

This second way of telling the history of brewsters emphasizes that although some of the forms of women's work changed between 1300 and 1600 (for example, women worked less in brewing and more in lace making), its *substance* remained the same (that is, women's work remained characteristically low status, low skilled, and low profit). Perhaps pressures for continuity—for maintaining the low work status of women—were so strong that brewsters could not retain their predominance in the trade once it began to expand. Perhaps brewsters, who seem in some respects to have been ideally positioned to profit from changes in the ale market after 1350, were in other respects profoundly disadvantaged. If, in addition to telling a story of brewsters who left their trade, we also see their history as a story of women who could not exploit new opportunities, how might we better understand their lives? What factors explain the inability of most women to respond effectively to the late medieval expansion of the brewing trade?

In understanding the stability at the center of the history of brewsters, biology has no explanatory power. Strength differentials between the sexes were certainly not an issue, for brewers physically exerted themselves less in 1600 than they had in 1300. In 1345, the singlewoman Emma Kempstere probably had to haul by herself the water, fuel, and grain that she used to brew ale in Brigstock; as far as we know, she hired no servants or laborers to help in her work. After the Black Death, however, brewers' households were notable for their extensive reliance on hired labor. A brewer such as Walter Wycombe of Oxford might have consumed more water, fuel, and grain than Emma Kempstere, but he had servants (specifically, 11 servants) to do the hauling for him. In his work as a brewer, he spent more time managing servants than physically laboring himself. Indeed, there was an inverse correlation between the physical demands of brewing and women's work in the trade; as brewers shouldered less physical work, women left the trade.[9]

Reproductive labor similarly seems to have not inhibited women's work as brewsters. To be sure, some women stopped brewing because, as the trade expanded and became more professionalized, it suited less well the sort of work they—as wives and mothers with many other responsibilities—sought. Most brewsters did not just work in commercial brewing and nothing else; they also labored as helpers in their husbands' trades, as mothers to their children, and as housekeepers for their families. As a result, many women were "eternal amateurs" in the productive tasks, such as brewing, that they pursued on their own.[10] Juggling these tasks with the demands of both their husbands' trades and their own domestic responsibilities, these women needed work that was readily available, work that, in other words, had minimal requirements for training, investment, or even time. As long as brewing was a humble trade, wives could brew whenever and wherever they had time free from other duties. When brewing changed into a more profitable and more demanding trade, some of these wives found it less amenable to their needs.

Yet nothing biological ordained that wives had to assist in their husbands' trades (rather than the other way around) or that the necessary work of women in reproducing life had to be extended beyond pregnancy and lactation into child care, cooking, and cleaning. If some young wives ceased brewing when it no longer accommodated well to their responsibilities toward husbands and children, those responsibilities were every bit as historical as the introduction of hops by foreign brewers in the fifteenth century.[11] Few wives, in any case, seem to have done so. As with matters of physical strength, so with reproductive labor: there was an inverse correlation between reproductive work and women's work in brewing. Women with the least reproductive responsibilities—that is, singlewomen and some widows—left the trade first.

If biology did not shape the inability of women to compete in the expanding brewing trade of the later middle ages, family certainly did. On the one hand, whether a woman worked in brewing or not was strongly shaped by her marital status. In the fourteenth century, singlewomen and widows were the least successful and most vulnerable brewsters. They might have enjoyed a legal credibility denied to wives, but they lacked economic, social, and political clout. By the sixteenth century, the only women who brewed in many towns and villages were widows, but they were one particular sort of widow, that is, widows of brewers. On the other hand, whether a wife worked in brewing or not might have been strongly shaped by family considerations. Pregnancy, lactation, and child care seem not to have mattered, but at least sometimes the husband's trade mattered a great deal. In Exeter and perhaps elsewhere, wives of men in trades that demanded less female assistance brewed more regularly than wives of other tradesmen.[12] In other words, wives brewed not when they were free from childbearing or child care but when the other *economic* demands of their households gave them time to pursue the trade.

The most subtle familial influence on the history of brewsters has been the hardest to trace, that is, the shifting contributions of wives and husbands to commercial brewing. As long as brewing was a by-industry, it was women's work, used by many wives to supplement the income of their husbands. Yet as brewing developed into a more desirable occupation in the later middle ages, more men took up the trade, using it as the main source of income for their families. This shift has been very difficult to trace, and for a very long time indeed, some men—such as Richard Pickering in mid-sixteenth-century London— seem to have relied on the expertise and knowledge of their wives. At some point, however, married brewsters became helpful wives of brewers. When Hester Thrale advised her husband about the running of his business in late eighteenth-century Southwark, she was a good wife, not a brewster, and the same seems to have been already true of the widows who took over their husband's breweries in late sixteenth-century London.

Although it is difficult to trace this shift in either specific or general terms, at its heart lay presumptions about family, household, and economy that were enshrined in law. It was expected that male householders would take responsibility for the activities of their wives, children, and servants. It was also expected that husbands would pursue, if possible, a skilled occupation, with wives playing a supporting role—not only assisting husbands in their work but also bringing in additional income through ancillary activities. Legal practices recognized these expectations in a variety of ways. Courts noted that husbands controlled the circumstances of the brewing done by their wives; husbands could tell their wives when to brew or to whom to sell their ale, and they controlled the income produced from brewing. Courts also sometimes cited or even licensed husbands for their wives' work as brewsters, concealing in an important forum the actual work being done by women. And courts seldom extended to wives the proprietal and contractual powers that their husbands enjoyed, making it difficult for married brewsters to secure credit, form partnerships, or otherwise extend their businesses. Like family, the law critically shaped the ways in which brewsters responded to changes in their trade.

Economic factors also help to explain why brewsters were unable to take full advantage of the late medieval expansion of the market for brewed drink. In the late fourteenth century, those who best responded to new opportunities in the brewing trade commanded capital resources, which allowed them to invest in new premises, better equipment, and more hired labor. These expanding capital demands placed women at a severe disadvantage, a disadvantage that can be seen most clearly among women who lacked ready access to the greater economic resources of men, that is, singlewomen and widows. When beerbrewing began to compete with alebrewing in the fifteenth century, its capital demands were so extensive that almost no women, except widows of beerbrewers, were associated with the art of producing this new hopped drink. In addition to the obstacles raised by women's more limited access to capital and credit, the commercialization of brewing raised other challenges—the need to manage large, male work forces; the need to maintain strong trade links with suppliers and customers; the need to raise capital through partnerships—that men met more readily than women.

Politics was also important, although perhaps not in the way that has been conventionally assumed by those historians who have described a sort of dialectic between family and state. In an article that has profoundly shaped the field since it was first published in 1973, Jo Ann McNamara and Suzanne Wemple argued that the power of aristocratic women declined with a "loss of family power" in feudal relations from the twelfth century.[13] Their notion that a politics based on kinship and family worked to the advantage of aristocratic women has since been elaborated by (among others) Suzanne Wemple's own work on Frankish women, Marion Facinger's studies of French queenship, Pauline Stafford's work on Anglo-Saxon queens, and even Joan Kelly's examination of women in the Renaissance. It has also recently been extended into the study of less privileged women, living in both towns and villages. In a sophisticated study of the civic status of women in five late medieval cities, Martha Howell has suggested that townswomen lost "the civic status they had once borne as members of families" when the commune (based on individuals) replaced the brother-

hood (based on families) as the associational basis of urban life. In a study of
English villagers in the seventeenth century, Susan Amussen has argued that the
decline after 1660 of a family-state analogy (which made the power of fathers
equivalent to the power of kings) created an ever-wider divergence in the experiences of women and men.[14]

Yet for those interested in how structures of family and state shape the lives
of women, the history of brewsters and the regulation of their trade offers a cau-
tionary tale. It might seem that families shield women from the powers of the
state, but brewsters could not escape "the state" from within the shelter of "the
family."[15] Even in the early fourteenth century, when brewing was a family-
based business pursued largely by wives, the force of regulation fell more heavily on women than on men. And even at this early date, the regulation of brewing reinforced in the political realm the private dependency of women within
the family. After all, one of the hallmarks of medieval and early modern regulation of brewing — the tendency to seek out householders as more reliable and
more liable than their dependents — distinguished in critical ways between most
women (that is, wives) and most men (that is, husbands). Although "the state"
and "the family" might have been competitive systems of power in some
respects, they mutually supported the power of men. Alice Clark thought of a
medieval state as "composed of self-contained families consisting of men,
women, and children, all three of which are essential."[16] Yet, as the history of
brewsters shows, medieval polities saw husbands as very different from their
wives and children. Some of the greatest difficulties that some brewsters faced,
such as their inability to participate in the regulation of their trade and their
inability to secure licenses for brewing, grew from political distinctions between
householders and their dependents.

Finally, ideology also limited the extent to which brewsters were able to
respond effectively to the new opportunities of the later middle ages. Ideology
shaped the world of brewsters in some very general ways. Because it was
expected that women would be always governed by men, familial, legal, economic, and political structures accommodated best to women who were dependents of husbands or fathers. Although wives and daughters had less autonomy
than their husbands and fathers, they also avoided certain responsibilities and
enjoyed the protection of a male householder. Singlewomen, widows, and other
women who headed their own households had more legal recognition than
wives and dependent daughters, but they were also more vulnerable in social,
economic, and political matters. Ideology also shaped brewsters' lives in very
specific ways. Attacks on the brewing trade drew on some non-misogynous
sources, but they also tapped misogynous traditions, which taught that women
were more sexually voracious, more duplicitous, and less trustworthy than men.
The cultural media of late medieval and early modern England suggested that all
the problems associated with brewing — cheating, foul products, disorderly
houses, and a host of other uncontrollable disruptions — were caused not by the
trade itself but by the presence of women in the trade.

If we seek, then, to understand why so few women in the fifteenth and sixteenth centuries followed the lead of fourteenth-century brewsters such as

Denise Marlere, we need to begin by looking at family structures, legal customs, economic circumstances, political imperatives, and ideological presumptions. These factors affected some women differently than others, but they affected all women to some extent. These factors shaped the lives of men, as well as women, but they constrained most women more than most men. The brewsters of medieval and early modern England might have "stood still" in the midst of enormous economic change, but their immobility was not of their own making. At every turn, they found themselves unable to respond as effectively as men to the new opportunities available in their trade.

Yet brewsters did not passively withdraw from the trade. Some brewsters unhesitatingly protested against regulation: they complained about prices set too low by juries, they resisted prying aletasters, and they sought to avoid detection and punishment. In most cases, brewsters protested as individuals, but sometimes they resisted as a group.[17] Yet we have no records of brewsters explicitly objecting to the obstacles they faced *as women*—no strikes by brewsters denied full membership in a gild, no complaints by brewsters that men were given licenses they were denied, and no lamentations by brewsters about legal rules that prevented them from borrowing money or forming partnerships. Many brewsters might have accepted as natural the obstacles that they faced; if others resented the growing advantages of men in the trade, their comments are lost to us.[18] Whether they protested or not, brewsters did react to changing circumstances. Some, like Gillian de Walton in mid-fourteenth-century Oxford, ceased brewing and took up tippling. Some, like Emma Canon in early fifteenth-century London, associated as closely as they could with the gilds that began to regulate their trade. Some, like Alice Everard in mid-fifteenth-century Oxford, operated as far as possible outside of the recognized organizations and regulations of the trade. And some, like Joan Pickering in mid-sixteenth-century London, continued to brew even when their husbands assumed all public responsibility for the trade. As the brewing industry expanded in the later middle ages, women were unable to retain their dominant place, but because some women searched out new ways in which they could continue either to brew or to profit from selling drink, women were not thrust out of the drink trade altogether. They retained within it a place different in form but similar in substance to the work of women in past times—they worked as servants in brewhouses; they tippled ale brewed by others; they assisted their husbands in the trade; and in villages and towns less touched by changes in the trade, they still brewed and sold their old-fashioned ale.

The continuity that lies at the heart of the history of brewsters also lies at the heart of the history of women. Historians of women need not "go on endlessly repeating and proving the obvious, that is to say, the grossly unjust treatment that women have received over thousands of years at the hands of males."[19] But historians of women do need to investigate the forces behind this obvious fact, that is, to explain how the oppression of women has endured for so long and in so many different historical settings. This problem—the problem of historicizing patriarchy—has inspired considerable fear and loathing among historians, but it must be addressed.[20] The power of patriarchy in our lives today rests, in part, on our failure to understand how it has worked in past times. As long as we refuse to study patriarchy as a historical force, we will fail to understand its workings and we will be subject to its power. Let us end, then, by considering what the history of brewsters might tell us about the history of patriarchy.

First, two caveats. In the minds of many people, the term *patriarchy* is strongly associated with blaming men.[21] Some readers might have already sighed to themselves, "Oh dear, here comes the part where she blames it all on men!" Others might have anticipated the same result but reacted quite differently: "Oh good, now she's going to prove that it is all the fault of men!" I intend to satisfy neither group. Men are certainly implicated in patriarchy; some men have vigorously supported its tenets and institutions, and most others have benefited from its power. But not all men have gained equally from patriarchal structures, and some men—for example, homosexual men in some societies— have suffered directly from misogyny and patriarchy. In any case, women have not been innocent of collusion with patriarchy; some have supported it, some have benefited from it, and most have raised their sons and daughters to conform to it.[22] In investigating patriarchy, then, I am not interested in a simplistic history of nasty men who oppressed virtuous women. Instead, I am interested in understanding how the substantial power of men over women has been maintained, even in times of otherwise dramatic change.

The term *patriarchy* is also sometimes associated with a feminism that falsely elides differences among women, assuming that white, middle-class, heterosexual women can speak for all women.[23] In recent years, feminist scholars have learned a great deal about differences among women, slowly coming to appreciate that these differences are not mere divergences from a white, middle-class, heterosexual norm. The differences that matter (for example, those based on race, class, sexual orientation, and world region) are signified by vast imbalances of power, and I most certainly do not intend to replicate them in suggesting that we study in new and more subtle ways the subject of patriarchy.

Nevertheless, as we more fully appreciate differences among women, we also must not forget differences between women and men. We need, in other words, to develop new ways of considering how the history of women, *as women*, has been different from the history of men, *as men*. In late medieval England, some women had more capital or status than some men; some women wielded more political power than some men; some women enjoyed ethnic or sexual privileges denied to some men. But within each group of men and women— whether the group was structured by commonalties of class, power, ethnicity, or whatever—women as a group were disempowered *compared to men of their group*. Peasant women held much less land in their villages than did peasant men; townswomen did not enjoy the same benefits of gild association as did their fathers, brothers, and husbands; and women of the landed classes did not sit on privy councils, serve as justices of the peace, or attend parliament. We might argue about whether this disempowerment of women vis-à-vis comparable men has always been the case, but it certainly was the case in England between 1300 and 1600. In asking how patriarchy worked in these centuries, I might highlight differences between women and men, but I do not thereby obscure differences among women.[24]

With these caveats in mind, I have sought, in trying to relate the history of brewsters to the history of patriarchy, to study the ways in which the institutions and structures of a past time worked to maintain male privilege and female disadvantage. I have conceptualized this object of study—"patriarchy"—as a social formation, rooted in the structures of human societies. Although I have spoken of the concept in the singular, I know that its manifestations must be multiple. That is, just as the concept "capitalism" has led to the study of many forms of capitalistic enterprise, so the concept "patriarchy" will help us to elaborate its many different forms and manifestations. I have also assumed that the study of any single form of patriarchy must consider not only how it changed over time but also how it affected different people in different ways.

This case study of brewsters has not, by any means, provided all the perspectives necessary for a history of patriarchy, either generally or in the specific instance of England between 1300 and 1600. But it has forged a path that will, I hope, be much extended, widened, branched, redirected, and crossed in the future. As a preliminary report in the project of historicizing patriarchy, it critically complicates our understanding. Patriarchy has too often been understood in simplistic terms. Antifeminists have usually argued that male dominance is unavoidable, locating the roots of patriarchy in biological differences or functional imperatives. Feminist scholars have also tended to emphasize single causes for the perdurance of patriarchy, arguing that its roots lie in psychological need, misogynous ideology, economic structures, or sexual practices.[25] More recently, feminists have begun to propose more complicated analyses of patriarchy, but these have been limited by their modern focus. Sylvia Walby's model of a "private patriarchy" contrasted to a "public patriarchy" relies so exclusively on English history since 1800 that it cannot be readily adapted for premodern societies. Patricia Hill Collins's notion of a "matrix of oppression" critically melds different systems of oppression, but it is based heavily on the dynamics of race relations in the contemporary United States.[26] This study of brewsters takes us back further in time, and it shows us a patriarchy that is highly changeable, complex, and capacious.

For brewsters, patriarchy was not rooted in any single cause; it was everywhere. The wide dispersal of patriarchal power into many locations seems to have been a critical part of its force and endurability. Brewsters faced no single "committee of patriarchs" determined to force them out of the trade. Instead, the forces arrayed against them were more subtle and more diffuse. We have studied these forces under the distinct headings that best break down the history of brewing: commercial and economic disadvantages, technological hurdles, gild formation, regulatory constraints, and cultural assumptions. But we have also considered them more abstractly: family, law, economy, politics, and ideology. At every turn, brewsters faced institutions whose customs, rules, and assumptions hindered their trade.

What might have been particularly confounding about this situation was that none of these institutions existed solely to keep women in their place. Gilds were not formed with the explicit intention of excluding women from the trade; beerbrewing did not remain an alien trade just to keep its secrets from women; the rules that limited the contractual authority of wives were not designed solely to keep women down. In a sense, patriarchy was an effect of many institutions, but neither the sole effect nor the sole intention of any one. To be sure, when John Enfield began to gather the brewers of London into a fraternity, he might well have frowned on the brewsters in his trade, and the gildsmen who succeeded him certainly did little to encourage women's participation in their association. But the gild offered many things in addition to male privilege—solidarity with other brewers, better regulation of trade, stronger bargaining with the city, and protection for those who fell on hard times. Some of these benefits appealed to brewsters, as well as to male brewers, and if male privilege was part of the package, it might have seemed an amorphous or ancillary part.

English patriarchy in these centuries was, then, particularly strong because it sprang from many sites, all of which, while buttressing patriarchy, also served other critical functions. Brewsters were, in a sense, disabled by many institutions, all of which both were and were not patriarchal.[27] The force of these institutions was further strengthened by the flexibility of some patriarchal effects and the endurability of others. Consider how as gilds emerged as a powerful force in brewing, they easily took up and adapted assumptions about male governance that were already manifested in culture and law. Ideas once applied to domestic and government structures were adapted to nascent gild administrations. This new application drew on both existent ideology (for example, the assumption that men should rule) and existent structures (for example, the reliance on heads of households, who were usually male). Or consider how representations of brewsters, always negative, took on new emphases as the trade changed. When beer began to compete more effectively with ale, alewives were depicted not only as disorderly and dishonest but also as producers of adulterated, disgusting, and unhealthy drink. These new depictions drew on existent images of bad brewsters, but they emphasized (to the detriment of women in the trade) new problems and new competitions in brewing.

Yet if new representations that disempowered women emerged with exceptional rapidity and creativity, they also drew on misogynous forces that endured remarkably well across time. Some of the patriarchal sites examined in this book—economic practices, legal customs, and ideological constructs—have displayed exceptional stability. Women's low status in the economy remained intact despite vast changes in a trade they had once pursued virtually to the exclusion of men. Legal mechanisms for regulating brewers shifted and changed, but they nevertheless always handicapped women in special ways. Misogynous ideology provided long-standing themes from which representations of brewsters could be drawn and redrawn. The interplay in the history of brewsters between flexible and enduring sites of patriarchal power raises intriguing questions about their relative force. Did certain institutional sites of patriarchy change so little because they were essential? Or were the essential sites those that were more flexible and adaptable? Or did the two work hand in hand?

In addition, the force of patriarchy fell on brewsters in many different ways; brewsters were excluded from some activities, segregated within others, and divided against themselves.[28] Exclusion was a powerful means of patriarchy. Brewsters were excluded from the regulation of their trade, from many gilds, and sometimes from the trade altogether. But segregation also worked effectively to limit brewsters. They belonged to the London gild in the early fifteenth century but were not full members; they brewed ale more readily than beer; they fell from brewing into aleselling but not out of the trade altogether. And the old adage of "divide and conquer" also worked against brewsters, for differences among them were critical to their slow withdrawal from the trade. Not-married brewsters, especially unable to take advantage of commercial expansion, left the trade much earlier than married women; but virtually all women eventually left brewing, in part because the departure of singlewomen and widows undermined the position of married brewsters. The experiences of brewsters suggest that recognition of differences among women is essential not only for nuance and clarity but also for understanding, ironically enough, the experiences of *all* women. Because different brewsters left the trade at different times, the slow masculinization of brewing was perhaps obfuscated and facilitated. Patriarchal adjustments to the changing profitability of brewing—new regulations about brewing by singlewomen, the establishment of new gilds for husbands of married brewsters, or the development of new depictions of brewsters as foul and filthy workers—might have been especially effective because they harmed some brewsters more than others.

In a case study of this sort, many questions can be considered, but many others must be left unexamined. We have been unable to see, for example, how moments of crisis affect patriarchal powers, a question of considerable importance for the project of historicizing patriarchy. We have also been unable to place much emphasis on the differences of class and race that are so important in the histories of women. And we have not been able to examine important aspects of the private lives of brewsters—their sexualities, their domestic arrangements, their personal aspirations. Nevertheless, this study has illuminated, for one historical setting, some critical aspects of patriarchal power: its multiplicity; its production as an effect of essential social institutions; its flexibility; its endurability; and its powerful strategic use of exclusion, segregation, and division. It is my hope that by investigating historical circumstances such as these, we can come to understand and overcome the forces that have harmed and still do harm the lives of women and men.

I think about women's history now very differently from that autumn day in 1987 when I was first asked by a student, "How is that any different from today?" When I look back across the centuries of women's history, I see a sort of dance in which women and men—many different sorts of women and men—move across the room, alter their steps, and even change partners, but *always* the men are leading. I'm interested in the new positions, new steps, new partners, but I'm even more interested in the continuity of male control of all of these various dances. What has kept women from ever taking the lead or even sharing it? In the history of brewsters, the answer lies, as we have seen, not in biology, not in organized male malice, and not in social necessity, but instead in the historical interplay of many patriarchal institutions: family organization, legal practice, economic structures, political imperatives, and cultural presumptions. Faced by these, brewsters might have made good ale, but that was not enough.

INTERPRETING PRESENTMENTS UNDER THE ASSIZE OF ALE

M‍ost aspects of women's work in medieval and early modern England remain undocumented and hence unstudied by historians. Chance references tell us that women predominated in certain types of work, such as dairying, gleaning, spinning, and caring for the sick. Yet we know very little about such female occupations. The one exception is commercial brewing, for which considerable documentation survives. In most medieval communities, commercial brewers endured strict supervision under the provisions of the assize of ale, both as articulated by the thirteenth-century quasi statutes and as worked out in local practice. Enforcing standards of measurement, quality, and pricing under the assize, local officers reported their findings to manorial or civic courts. Their reports, often made every three weeks, provide lists of commercial brewers that span decades or even centuries, and they are sometimes supplemented with information about frequency of brewing, types of ale, and the activities of tipplers. Few medieval trades were as carefully regulated and, hence, as well documented as the brewing trade.

Yet, although presentments of brewers under the assize of ale provide a voluminous source of information about commercial brewing, they also present considerable interpretative challenges. This appendix explains how these challenges were resolved for this study, especially in chapters 2 and 3. Needless to say, many other primary sources used in this book—such as literary and artistic texts, civic ordinances, gild records, and brewing accounts—have also required careful evaluation. Also, many of the subjects considered in this book—such as cultural representations of alewives, regulation of brewers by gilds, and most aspects of brewing in the sixteenth century—have not required much use of assize presentments. In focusing on assize presentments in this appendix, I do not mean to imply either that the interpretation of all the other sources used in this book is more straightforward or, indeed, that only commercial brewing as reported under the assize has been considered in this book. Put simply, assize presentments merit special treatment because their use requires careful explanation. Section I discusses method and interpretation, explaining how conclusions about brewers were derived from presentments under the assize. The subsequent two sections provide information about the rural and urban communities included in the survey of assize presentments.

I. Interpreting Assize Presentments

In most communities, local officers (often called aletasters or aleconners) supervised commercial brewing and presented brewers at court sessions. As discussed in chapter 6, this supervision antedated the thirteenth-century quasi statutes but thereafter fell within their limits. The *Assisa* regulated the prices set for ale, which were to vary according to both the cost of grain and the place of sale. Brewers were to be amerced for their first three offenses and punished physically thereafter. These limited statutory provisions changed in actual practice, with officers usually supervising not only the price of ale but also its quality and measurement. Brewers were therefore liable for punishment if they committed any of three offenses: selling ale in false or illegal measures, selling ale of poor quality, or selling ale at excessive prices. Brewers could also incur punishment for trying to escape supervision by, for example, failing to summon the aletasters or selling without proper publicity. Yet as the scope of enforcement widened, the scope of punishment narrowed. Local courts infrequently punished brewers on the cucking-stool or by similar public humiliations, preferring instead to profit from amercements.

Presentments varied. For example, this is how the brewers of Woolhope (Herefordshire) were presented on 29 July 1344:[1]

> The tasters of Donnington present that John le Brut (i) [and] Gilbert de Culham (i) brewed and broke the assize. *Assize* 12 pence....
>
> The tasters of [Wool]Hope present that Alice de Pokemore (i), William de la Broke, Alice de Stonhull (i), Idonea de Stonhull (i), Thomas le Bruchere (i), William le Bailiff (i), Richard de Neuconer (i), Adam de Ravenhull (i), [and] Geoffrey le Knyght (i) brewed and broke the assize. [The tasters of] Brockhampton [present that] Margery de Dene [and] Margery Richardson (i) [brewed and broke the assize]. [The tasters of] Putley [present that] Walter Comyn (i) brewed etc. [The tasters of] Buckenhill [present] nothing. *Assize* 5 shillings.

A few months later, on the first day of December 1344, brewers and alesellers in Ingatestone (Essex) were presented in a slightly different manner:

> Richard ate Hyd and Thomas Hamekyn, tasters of ale, in mercy because they did not do their office. *Mercy* 4d.
>
> The wife of Richard Osebarn in mercy because she brewed and sold against the assize. *Mercy* 3d.
>
> Alice Geroldis in mercy for the same. *Mercy* 4d.

The wife of William Synoch in mercy for the same. Mercy 3d.

The wife of Stephen le Tannere in mercy for the same. Mercy 4d.

William Morisce in mercy for the same. Mercy 2d.

Hawise Huckestere, regrater, [in mercy] because she sells against the assize. Mercy 2d.

William ate Halle and Thomas Morisce, tasters of ale, in mercy because they did not do their office. Mercy 4d.

Beatrice Jurdonys in mercy because she brewed and sold against the assize. Mercy 4d.

Margery Coppyngho in mercy for the same. Mercy 3d.

The wife of Thomas Tayllour in mercy for the same. Mercy 2d.

Margery Forys in mercy for the same. Mercy 2d.

The wife of John atte Strate in mercy for the same. Mercy 3d.

The wife of William ate Halle in mercy for the same. Mercy 3d.

The wife of William Wodeward, regrater, in mercy because she sold against the assize. Mercy 4d.

Katherine Bullis in mercy for the same. Mercy 2d.

The wife of Thomas Loncrote in mercy for the same. Mercy 4d.

The wife of John ate Welle in mercy for the same. Mercy 2d.

As these examples from Woolhope and Ingatestone suggest, there is a certain numbing familiarity about assize presentments, for they seem always to provide long lists of names with petty fines and little further information. Yet there are also important differences in how jurisdictions regulated their brewers and in how that regulation changed, even within one jurisdiction, over the course of time. Furthermore, although presentments of brewers seem to be straightforward and clear, their proper use in historical analysis is complex. Three critical questions had to be resolved in order to use these presentments to reconstruct commercial brewing in late medieval and early modern England.

Do these presentments tell us about all brewers?

Designed to regulate commerce in ale, the assize of ale never encompassed domestic brewing; women who produced ale for consumption by their families were neither presented nor regulated by aletasters. In terms of its coverage of commercial brewers, presentments under the assize raise two possibilities: they include either all commercial brewers or only those who broke the assize. The difference is critical, for the former allows us to treat assize presentments as fully encompassing commercial brewing whereas the latter suggests that assize presentments provide a limited view of the trade.

Three considerations suggest that assize presentments incompletely report on commercial brewing. First, in some jurisdictions, brewers obtained long-term licenses to ply their trade, and these offered some immunity from presentment under the assize. At Alciston (Sussex) in 1445, for example, William Coby paid 6d. to brew wherever and whenever (*totiens quotiens*) he pleased unless he brewed very improperly (*nisi graviter delinquerit*).[2] If long-term licenses such as these allowed many brewers to escape presentment by aletasters, presentments provide inadequate coverage of the trade. Second, some aletasters, like those in Ingatestone in 1344, were fined for official malfeasance. If aletasters really neglected their duties, their presentments incompletely report the trade in ale. Third, the wording used in most presentments of brewers indicates that only offenders were noted. In Woolhope and Ingatestone (and in almost all other jurisdictions), the aletasters presented persons who had "brewed and broken the assize" or "brewed and sold against the assize." If we take the court record literally, only offending brewers, not all brewers, were presented.

None of these considerations, however, seriously limits the coverage of commercial brewers found in most assize presentments. Long-term licenses were neither common nor long in duration. William Coby's long-term license, which lasted just one year, was one of only a handful issued in mid-fifteenth-century Alciston.[3] In pre-plague Brigstock (Northamptonshire), for another example, brewers purchased only 48 long-term licenses but paid 3,796 amercements for breaking the assize. In addition, long-term licenses did not permit brewers to disappear from the written record, for they were carefully noted in court rolls, and they also did not preclude presentment of offending licensees.[4] Most important, many jurisdictions seem to have issued no long-term licenses at all, requiring all brewers to be subject to regular amercement; of the 19 rural communities included in the sample, brewers secured long-term licenses in Brigstock and Alciston alone. In short, the occasional issuance of long-term licenses does not seriously undermine the coverage of assize presentments.

Dereliction of duty by aletasters also presents only a minor problem. Aletasters could fail to make thorough presentments in many ways—missing a particular brewing, forgetting specific cases when they came before the court, overlooking cheating by family and friends, or pricing ale as stronger or weaker than its true quality deserved. Supervising the ale trade was an onerous duty at which most aletasters inevitably fell short, at least occasionally. In addition, as discussed in chapter 6, supervising the ale trade could be a profitable occupation, with some aletasters accepting bribes or favors from brewers and others overlooking brewing done in their own households. As a result, in some rural jurisdictions, aletasters were regularly amerced for generally failing at their job. Yet, these amercements were so standardized that they suggest a financial arrangement rather than a supervisory problem. In Ingatestone, for example, aletasters were amerced with as much regularity as brewers from the very first surviving assize presentments in 1292 until the 1480s. Amercements of aletasters were more a source of profit for lords than a comment on the quality of their work.[5]

Despite the inevitable pitfalls (and potential profits) of regulating the trade in ale, aletasters had to be generally honest for a simple reason: their work was very public. Because any ale offered for sale was publicly announced, an aletaster who supervised brewers was, in turn, supervised by their customers. He knew that if his presentments were flawed, local juries or tithingmen or other officers might correct them. In Ingatestone, for example, aletasters were sometimes amerced more than the standard sum precisely because they had committed specified errors.[6] Indeed, public oversight of aletasters was so compelling that some aletasters presented themselves or their own wives for brewing; William ate Halle did so in the Ingatestone presentment transcribed above.[7] In short, despite complaints about official malfeasance and despite regular amercements of aletasters in some jurisdictions, it seems likely that aletasters presented most brewers most of the time.

The formula that stated that all named brewers had "brewed and broken the assize" was also a profitable fiction. Despite this formula, all brewers—those who brewed properly as well as those who brewed badly—usually faced amercement. In some cases, brewers were presented but not amerced unless they had traded against the assize. In late thirteenth-century Preston-on-Wye (Herefordshire), for example, most brewers paid amercements of 6d. in each court, but sometimes a man paid nothing because he (or his wife) had observed the assize (*quia tenuit assisam*).[8] In other cases, all brewers were amerced just for plying their trade, but those who offended against the assize paid especially large amercements. In early fourteenth-century Chedzoy (Somerset), for example, aletasters presented brewers twice: once for brewing and once for using false measures.[9] And in some other cases, all brewers were fined not according to the offense but according to the frequency of brewing. In fourteenth-century Stockton (Wiltshire), for example, brewers were liable for 4d. per brewing; if a brewster produced five batches of ale (good or bad), she paid 20d.[10] Although technically levied "for breaking the assize," these amercements functioned as a de facto licensing system.

These sorts of patterns imply that although offending brewers often paid more in amercements than other brewers, all brewers were presented by aletasters at their local courts. Presentment-as-licensing explains the long-term licenses occasionally purchased by brewers in Alciston, Brigstock, and elsewhere, for such licenses would have had no purpose in a system that amerced *offending* brewers only. Presentment-as-licensing also explains the numbing repetition of supposedly erring brewers that is a feature of all lists of assize presentments. At Earl Soham (Suffolk), for example, Walter Bele or his wife, Agnes, were presented for "brewing and breaking the assize" at every court held between 1356 and 1376. The Beles were not flagrantly cheating their customers year after year; instead, they managed an established brewing business and paid a small licensing fee to follow the trade. Indeed, a few years after the Beles ceased brewing, the court of Earl Soham abandoned the fiction of amercements under the assize. Thereafter, brewers were simply noted as having brewed and having, hence, paid stated sums.[11]

The origins of the practice of amercing all brewers for supposedly "breaking" or "selling against" the assize are obscure, but two factors might have played a role. First, aletasters had good reason to suspect *all* brewers of misconduct *all* the time. Indeed, given contemporary imprecisions of quality, measurement, and coinage, most brewers probably broke the assize on a regular basis (whether willfully or not). In such circumstances, an aletaster could best perform his (or rarely, her) office by charging all brewers with the seemingly inevitable effect of commercial brewing, that is, an infraction under the assize of ale. Second, presentments under the assize complemented and sometimes replaced earlier tolls on brewers. These tolls had various names—tolcester, can-nemol, alesilver—and were found in a variety of jurisdictions (urban as well as rural). As a rule, they were levied on all commercial brewers within the juris-diction who, simply by virtue of pursuing their trade, were liable for payment in either cash or ale. In Cuxham (Oxfordshire), for example, commercial brew-ers paid either 1 d. per brewing or a gallon of their ale. These ale tolls sometimes coexisted with assize supervision, sometimes superseded it, and sometimes were replaced by it; but in all cases, they created a strong precedent for amercing all brewers, regardless of the legality of their trade. In other words, although the assize of ale sought to punish offending brewers only, tolls were levied on all brewers; it seems likely that the latter influenced the enforcement of the former.[12]

In short, presentments under the assize of ale constituted a de facto system of short-term licensing, and they provide good coverage of the trade.[13] To be sure, as in all administrative records, some persons avoided supervision at some times, but both the intent of the supervisors and, in most cases, their actual effect was to cover all those who brewed for profit. It is impossible to estimate the extent to which brewers slipped through the supervisory web, escaping presentment and amercement and, hence, eluding historical recovery, but this slippage was neither common nor widespread.[14] It seems likely that when ale-tasters failed to report all brewers thoroughly, they probably especially over-looked either their own relatives or occasional brewers who sold ale infre-quently. To be sure, many occasional brewsters were cited by aletasters (273 were named in Brigstock alone), but others might have never been brought before the attention of their courts. Nevertheless, by-industrial and (later) pro-fessional brewers were well known, well supervised, and thus well reported in extant records. Despite the formulaic statement that brewers had "broken the assize," all brewers, whether guilty of offense or not, were supervised and named by aletasters. Despite the occasional purchase of a long-term license by a brewer, the vast majority of brewers paid amercements under the assize. And despite amercements levied against erring aletasters, they seem to have done their work reasonably well, striving to bring all brewers before the attention of their courts. Originally addressed only to the identification and punishment of erring brewers, the assize of ale provided a means for regulating all brewers, and the records of its enforcement therefore are an exceptional source for reconstructing the history of commercial brewing in medieval and early mod-ern communities.

Do these presentments provide reliable information about the sex of brewers?

As the examples of Woolhope and Ingatestone illustrate, aletasters identified more male brewers in some villages than in others. In Woolhope men predom-inated, whereas in Ingatestone only one male brewer was named. In my first effort to study commercial brewing from ale presentments, I assumed that the presence of men and women in the trade was accurately reflected in present-ments of aletasters. In other words, I once would have concluded that the dif-ference between the many male brewers cited in Woolhope and the many female brewers cited in Ingatestone was a real difference, that is, that male brewers predominated in Woolhope and brewsters in Ingatestone. This was wrong.[15]

The different sex ratios of cited brewers in Woolhope and Ingatestone represent not real facts of the trade but instead different clerical practices. In Woolhope, men were cited for brewing done by their wives (that is, presentments under the assize were householder-focused); in Ingatestone, wives were themselves named (that is, presentments were individual-focused). In other words, if the wife of Richard Osebarn, who was fined 3d. for brewing against the assize in Ingatestone, had plied her trade in Woolhope, her husband would have been cited in her stead. How do we know this?

First, patterns of citation strongly suggest this conclusion. Consider, for example, the above illustrations from Woolhope and Ingatestone. In both villages, some women—probably either singlewomen or widows—were identified by forename and surname alone (such as Alice de Pokemore in Woolhope or Alice Geroldis in Ingatestone). Wives were treated differently. In Woolhope, no female brewer was cited as "the wife of" a named male, whereas this is the most common type of citation in the Ingatestone list. Unless no wives brewed in Woolhope (a most unlikely possibility), this divergence in citations—no wives in Woolhope, many wives in Ingatestone—suggests different clerical approaches to commercial brewing by married women. In Woolhope, the wives "disappeared" into the legal personalities of their husbands. In Ingatestone, wives were themselves cited.

Second, clear instances of husband-wife substitution are found in many series of ale presentments. Consider, for example, four sets of ale presentments from Ingatestone in 1382–83, as shown in table A.1. In June 1382, only women were named as brewers. Four months later, mostly men were named, and most of these were clearly cited in place of their wives. The substitution was most obvious in John Lay's case, for the clerk began by writing "Margery" but then crossed it out and inserted "John." Seven months after this shift, citations began to revert to their earlier pattern, a reversion completed by October 1383, when, as before, only women were cited for brewing. This example from Ingatestone is exceptionally clear, but it is not unusual; in the brewing presentments of many courts, husbands were clearly substituted for their wives on some occasions.

Third, householder-focused presentments of brewers accord with our understanding of the household economy in these centuries. On the one hand, economic activities were not so individualized that we can absolutely say that wives brewed and husbands did not; as discussed more fully in chapter 2, members of most brewing households probably shared the burdens of the trade, even though in the early fourteenth century, wives often took primary responsibility. On the other hand, brewing was part of a domestic economy that was always managed, in the public eye at least, by a householder. This is why custom in Bristol dictated that the mayor consult with the "householders of Brewers" (that is, in most cases, their husbands) whenever dearth created high prices for malt.[16] This tradition of "householder responsibility" reflected the real dynamics of economic power in most working households. Husbands, quite simply, exercised authority over the economic activities, including brewing, of their wives, chil-

Table A.1   Brewing Presentments in Ingatestone, 1382–83

2 June 1382	4 October 1382	18 May 1383	22 October 1383
Ibota Jordan		Isabella Jordan	Isabella Jordan
Joan Bret	John Bret	John Bret	Joan Bret
Alice Bailiff			
Alice Lavenham	John Lavenham	Alice Lavenham	Alice Lavenham
Beatrice Turner	Richard Turner	Beatrice Turner	Beatrice Turner
Emma Paty	Richard Paty	Richard Paty	Emma Paty
Margery Lay	John Lay	Margery Lay	Margery Lay
Alice White		Alice White	Alice White
Agnes Stace		Agnes Stace	Agnes Stace
	Agnes Stace	Agnes Baker	
	John Baker	Agnes Shering	

Source: Essex Record Office, D/DP, M 23. As usual, I have standardized spelling.

dren, and servants. For example, the Wakefield (Yorkshire) court noted in 1374 that Thomas de Westerton had refused to allow his wife to sell ale as she should have done. Apparently, she did the brewing and selling, but he retained final say over her business.[17] For another example, in Herstmonceux (Sussex) in 1386, William Colkyn requested an extension on a debt of 10d. that he owed to Robert Baker; he planned to pay the debt after his wife had brewed and sold ale.[18] Apparently, she managed the commercial brewing in their household, but he controlled all profits from it. Even though wives brewed for profit in many medieval households, their work was pursued under the economic authority of their husbands. As a result, householder-focused presentments reflect more the subordinate status of women's work in the household economy than actual brewing by men. Although Denise Marlere brewed in late fourteenth-century Bridgwater, it was her husband Nicholas who was usually cited for brewing infractions.[19]

Fourth, householder-focused presentments also reflect legal practices. Under the common law, a wife was firmly subordinated to her husband, who acted essentially as her guardian in all legal matters, and this principle was maintained, although somewhat less consistently, in the customary practices of local courts. In many matters (not just economic matters), a husband could act in the place of his wife in court; he could appear in civil suits on her behalf, he could answer for her petty crimes, and he could sell or lease her land. A wife was, in short, usually treated in courts as "wholly within [her husband's] power."[20] In London in 1368, for example, one husband initiated a suit for debts owed for ale purchased from his wife, and another husband sued a lessor who had failed to repair a brewhouse rented by his wife.[21] The "disappearing wife" of some assize presentments is, then, only one manifestation of the general legal tendency to subsume wives into the legal personalities of their husbands.[22]

We can, therefore, be confident that most presentments that list male brewers are, in fact, citing husbands in the place of their wives. This conclusion raises, however, several further questions. Why were some presentments householder-focused and others individual-focused? In some cases, the cause is clear, for clerical idiosyncrasies sometimes determined how brewsters were cited. In Exeter in the late 1340s, for example, a series of different clerks enrolled ale presentments in a variety of different ways.[23] In other cases, the cause is obscure. I have no explanation for the predominance of householder-focused presentments in the southwest (aside from the possibility that clerks in this region shared a common training that particularly emphasized the legal responsibilities of householders).[24]

What about men who did actually brew for profit? How will we identify them if we assume always that a cited man was, in fact, a stand-in for his wife? This problem has two parts. On the one hand, brewing by bachelors might be obscured by this assumption, but as discussed in chapter 2, this is an unlikely possibility. Since so few men appear in individual-focused presentments, it seems that few men without wives brewed (especially before the Black Death). On the other hand, brewing by married men might also be obscured. This possibility is buttressed by a few cases in which shifts from individual-focused to householder-focused presentments might reflect real changes in the sexual division of labor. Most urban presentments are householder-focused from a very early date, raising the possibility that the relatively more developed ale markets of towns attracted more male labor than in the countryside. In some rural jurisdictions, shifts toward reporting more husbands than in the past were sometimes associated with economic change and expansion. In Kibworth Harcourt (Leicestershire), husbands were cited with increasing frequency in the 1350s and 1360s, decades when the ale industry was beginning to expand and become more profitable. In Wye (Kent) in the 1430s, husbands were cited more frequently in the fair-time courts than at other times of the year; within a few years, they were cited almost to the exclusion of their wives. In numerous villages, once common brewers began to appear in the courts, they were usually husbands, not wives. Since in all these instances, citational shifts were associated with economic expansion, it is possible that husbands were becoming more involved in brewing than in the past. This is an intriguing possibility, but it cannot, quite simply, be confirmed in other sources. In the text, I have sometimes raised these possibilities, but I have not treated them as confirmed findings. Given the many factors that could encourage clerks to cite husbands for brewing by their wives, economic change is only one of many possible explanations.[25] And given the difficulty of distinguishing in assize presentments how a woman and her husband might have divided the work of commercial brewing between them, I have turned to other sources (such as the gild records used in chapter 4) to reconstruct marital brewing.

Do these presentments provide reliable information about marital status?

The answer to this question is sometimes yes, sometimes no, and always only approximately. The different types of presentments offer three different sorts of opportunities for identifying marital status. First, householder-focused presentments can provide useful information about not-married brewsters since women cited in their own names in such listings usually lived without husbands. In other words, we can assume that Alice de Pokemore, Alice de Stonhull, and Idonea de Stonhull were not-married brewsters in Woolhope because, if they had been married, their husbands would have been cited in their stead. Second, individual-focused presentments do not as reliably provide the opposite sort of information, that is, information about unmarried men. Men cited in individual-focused presentments, such as William Morisce of Ingatestone, might have been bachelors who worked in commercial brewing, but they also were often husbands cited idiosyncratically for their wives. The difference between these two options must be determined on a case-by-case basis. In Brigstock before 1348, for example, every man presented by the aletasters was married to a brewster. In the case of William Morisce, however, no wife has been found. Third, on a few occasions, individual-focused presentments so distinguish wives, daughters, and widows that the marital status of women can also be determined. It is likely (but not certain), for example, that Alice Geroldis, Beatrice Jurdonys, Margery Coppyngho, and Margery Forys were either singlewomen or widows, for they (unlike the other women cited in Ingatestone) were not identified as wives. In sum, bachelors are difficult to distinguish in these records, but relative proportions of married and not-married women can often be approximated with confidence.

It is important to emphasize that two separate considerations arise in attempts to differentiate married and not-married women. Customs of assize presentment, whether focued on householders or individuals, are critical. But customs of citing women in general, whether in assize presentments or in other venues, are also critical. As a general rule, married women were identified not only by forename and surname but also by their marital relationship. For example, Agnes the wife of Henry Kroyl the younger was never identified in the Brigstock court roll as merely "Agnes Kroyl". Instead, in her 27 appearances before the court as a married woman, she was invariably identified as "Alice the wife of Henry Kroyl" or simply as "the wife of Henry Kroyl."[26] Needless to say, wives were occasionally cited by forename and surname alone, but they generally were not. In contrast, not-married women were sometimes identified as daughters or widows of specific men, but they were usually cited by forename and surname alone. As a result, the determination that Alice de Pokemore and other women so cited in Woolhope were not married springs from two sources: first, the householder-focused presentments in which they are named and, second, the very way that they are named (that is, without stated marital linkage).

Nevertheless, two other factors complicate easy assumptions about women's marital status from assize presentments: some married women were presented like not-married women, and some not-married women were presented like married women. Let us begin by considering the married women who are hidden among presentments of apparent singlewomen and widows. Helena Graham has suggested, based on her reconstitution of the population of Alrewas (Staffordshire) in the mid-fourteenth century, that even on manors where husbands were normally named in the place of their wives, some wives were, in fact, named as brewsters. Graham's data suggest that about one-third of the women named in the householder-focused presentments of Alrewas were married. Moreover, she has argued that married brewsters from poorer households were especially likely to be cited in their own names (presumably since their husbands had no other business that brought them to court). If Graham is right, women listed in householder-focused citations were mostly not-married but not invariably so.[27]

At its furthest extent, Graham's data would suggest that most women (two of every three) cited by name in householder-focused presentments were, in fact, not married. But this "worst case" is quite unlikely. First, Graham confused wives and widows; two of the four poor brewsters whom she identified as wives cited with their own names were, in fact, widows.[28] Second, Graham focused closely on only 7 brewsters out of a total of 67 by-industrial brewers, but trends within the larger group show that socioeconomic status cannot account for the occasional citation of a married women by her own name.[29] In the end, Graham's revised data show that of 11 brewsters cited by their own name in Alrewas, 6 were single, 3 were widowed, and only 2 were married.[30]

In short, Graham's suggestion that one-third of the women named as brewsters in householder-focused presentments were, in fact, married, must be revised downward. What do sources from other communities suggest? They suggest that householder-focused presentments do, indeed, occasionally include married women cited by their own names, but that these instances are infrequent, often easily identifiable, and not necessarily linked to socioeconomic status. To begin with, wives were usually *cited as wives* on those rare occasions when they were included in householder-focused listings. In the Leicester cannemol for 1287–88, for example, the 200 brewers included 161 men, 7 wives (*cited as wives*) and 32 other women (the sex of 1 brewer could not be determined). Of these 32 women, 3 were identified as widows and 2 more were identified as sisters of named men; the remaining 27 were identified by forename and surname alone. Were any of these 27 women really wives? Probably not, for none could be traced (by coincidence of surname and quarter of residence) to possible husbands in the tallage of 1286 (a tallage that included households of quite modest economic standing).[31] The Leicester cannemol suggests, pace Graham, that few wives were "hidden" among brewsters cited in householder-focused lists; when wives were included in such lists, they were usually identified as married women.

Moreover, socioeconomic status does not explain most of the relatively uncommon instances of wives cited in householder-focused lists. In Leicester, the 7 wives listed in the 1287–88 cannemol, rather than being exceptionally poor, came from families of all economic statuses.[32] In York in 1304, the 70 brewers presented included 49 men, 10 wives *cited as wives*, and 11 women cited without indication of marital status. Instead of being poor, the 10 wives named on their own account seem to have been more privileged than the average brewster.[33] In Iver before the plague, the 319 brewers presented included 197 men, 15 wives (most cited as wives), and 107 other women. Again, the 15 wives named on their own account were not noticeably poorer than others but instead came from both wealthy and poor families in the village.[34]

It seems that socioeconomic status might have prompted the citing of wives in *some* householder-focused presentments, but it is just one of many possible explanations. Probably just as important (if not more) was the fragility of marriage in the medieval countryside. Because considerable numbers of marriages ended or failed before the death of either spouse, many women who were "wives" in the eyes of church and manor lived as if they were not married. These "wives" had left their husbands or been left themselves, they were married to men who never returned from journeys or wars or pilgrimages, or they cared for husbands incapacitated by illness or injury. These private accommodations to the public institution of marriage are very hard to re-create from a distance of some 600 years, but we know that many marriages functionally ended while they remained legally valid.[35] In trying to distinguish wives from singlewomen and widows, therefore, we must remember that some apparent "wives" might have, in fact, acted as the real heads of their households. This was certainly the case for Joan Cole of Lullington (Sussex). Her husband, William, had been presented as a brewer in the local court for many years when, in 1443, she began to replace him as the legally responsible brewer in the household. Within a few years, Joan was presented for brewing much more often than William. To be sure, Joan was still married to a living husband, but he was not well; in 1454, he was excused from attending court because of his advanced age and physical weakness.[36] As this case suggests, among the "wives" who seem to have been cited as not-married women in Alrewas and elsewhere were probably some women (like Joan Cole of Lullington) whose husbands were incapacitated, away, or otherwise not acting as householders. These women might have been married, but they did not live as did other married women. Since they acted as householders and fended for themselves without the help of husbands, their true marital status fell somewhere between being either married or not married.

Now, let us consider the opposite problem. What about the not-married women who were sometimes cited as if they were married? P. J. P. Goldberg has pointed out that many of the women identified as wives in the mid-fifteenth-century lists of brewers in York were, in fact, widows. This was also true of wives cited in York in the 1560s.[37] Today, we identify *wife* with "married woman," but in the fourteenth through sixteenth centuries, *wife* could also mean "housewife" or "mistress of a household." With this meaning, it could easily be attached to a widow, as was clearly done in some cases at York. As discussed in chapters 4 and 6, I have also found isolated instances of such usages in London (in the gild quarterage for 1500–1501) and Oxford (in a few cases found in the early fourteenth-century assize lists). Yet this sort of slippage (of widows into wives) seems to have been quite rare, probably even rarer than slippage in the other direction (of married women into not-married women).

In short, it is not possible to create firmly discrete groups of married and not-married brewsters; some wives are hidden among apparently not-married women and some widows are hidden among apparent wives. There seems to have been more of the former than the latter, and therefore, estimates of not-married brewsters based on assize presentments (especially as found in chapter

3) probably include a small proportion of married women who could not be so identified. To be sure, many estimates found in chapter 3 and elsewhere are based on sources, especially poll tax records, from which singlewomen and widows can be more firmly identified. But estimates based on assize presentments incorporate some slippage. In other words, we have good reason to treat Alice de Pokemore as a not-married brewster, for she appeared in householder-focused presentments and she was cited without reference to marital status. But she *might* have been married, a fact that is either entirely unrecoverable or recoverable only through a family reconstitution for Woolhope. Needless to say, it has not been possible to undertake family reconstitutions for Woolhope and all the other communities included in this study.

What does this slippage mean in terms of analyses of not-married and married brewsters in chapters 2, 3 and elsewhere? The extent to which wives were included among counts of apparently not-married women not only is impossible to estimate but also probably varied according to place, clerical custom, and time. As a result, I have not attempted to account for slippage; when I have reported, for example, that 46 Norwich brewers in 1288 were not married, I am reporting data taken from a householder-focused list, and I have counted as a not-married woman every women who was (1) identified by her own name and (2) not identified as a wife. Graham's estimate that wives accounted for one-third of apparent not-married women is clearly too high, but even if it is taken as a worst-case possibility, it is an estimate that would not undercut the observations of this study.[38] Figures given in chapter 2 suggest that in the early fourteenth century, 1 in every 6 urban brewsters and 1 in every 4 rural brewsters might have been not married; if these estimates are off by one-third, perhaps 1 of every 10 urban brewsters and 1 in every 6 rural brewsters was not married. In both estimates, single and widowed brewsters accounted for a significant minority of all brewers. When the proportion of brewing done by not-married women fell in a village like Stockton from 20 percent in the late thirteenth century to 11 percent after the Black Death to none at all by the late fifteenth century, the fact that some married women might have been hidden in these numbers is interesting but irrelevant to the main trend. Precision would be best, but precision is not possible with the extant records. Given the inherent uncertainties of identifying brewing by not-married women, the discussion in chapter 3 focuses on trends strong and broad enough to accommodate considerable slippage.

II. The Survey of Assize Presentments in Rural Communities

In surveying legal presentments under the assize of ale, I relied extensively on studies of other historians who have worked with the records of specific manors. But I also undertook further archival investigation, seeking out communities with long runs of surviving court rolls and attempting to examine communities in as wide a geographical range as possible. To some extent, these two requirements—extensive documentation and wide geographic distribution—are mutually exclusive, for northern and western districts are not so well served by surviving court rolls as the south and east. As far as possible, I also sought communities subject to only a single manorial jurisdiction (so that the assize presentments found in the records of that jurisdiction would cover *all* brewing in the village or villages within the manor). After cursorily examining the records of dozens of jurisdictions, I settled on the following 19 manorial jurisdictions as providing the best coverage (combined with information available from published studies) of both time and region. Some of these jurisdictions—especially those of Alciston (which included Lullington) and Wakefield—were very large, incorporating within them many rural communities. In a few cases, I examined all available records, but in most cases, I sampled the extant materials, taking a cluster of rolls as representative of a larger period (usually, I took samples from the late thirteenth century, early fourteenth century, late fourteenth century, and so on). In most cases (the only exceptions are Brigstock, Houghton-cum-Wylon, and Iver), I continued to work with the extant records until they either ceased entirely or ceased to offer valuable information about brewing.

In citing these materials in notes, I have used one of two conventions. On occasion, I have offered full archival citations (especially when citing a specific item). On most occasions, however, I have adopted a shorthand system, noting "Sample:" followed by the brief citations given in the left-hand column below. For example, material drawn from Alciston courts between 1275 and 1289 has been cited in footnotes as follows: Sample: Alciston, c. 1280.

In addition to collecting information from the assize presentments of these communities, I also consulted other materials (such as tax listings, custumals, and rentals). If used, these supplementary materials have been fully cited in the notes.

Alciston, Sussex

Sampled.

Presentments: Householder-focused presentments (although not invariably so). Frequency of brewing usually noted. Brewers were usually presented twice a year.

Brewing by not-married women: Roughly one-third of presentments were to not-married women until the fifteenth century (when they constituted only 3 percent c. 1425 and 9 percent c. 1470). By c. 1525, no not-married women (with the rare exception of a widow) were cited for brewing.

Professionalization: Alciston manor covered several villages, and commercial brewing in Lullington and Alfriston was more developed than in other areas. In Lullington and Alfriston, commercial brewing was distinguished from an early date by, on the one hand, the presence of common brewers and tipplers and, on the other hand, the relative absence of not-married women.

Beer: Although there might be earlier references in unexamined courts, the first mention of beer I have found dates from 1488. By the early 1520s, ale and beer were supervised as completely distinct entities in the courts, and it appears that beer was sold but not regularly brewed in the village until 1526 (when Richard Colville began brewing it on a regular basis).

Long-term licenses: A handful of licenses were purchased in the mid-fifteenth century either to avoid assize amercement or to avoid payment of tolcester.

Tolls on brewing: Tolcester (also sometimes called "canale" and rated at 2 gallons of the best ale from the brewing) was levied in Lullington, Alfriston, and Telton but not elsewhere. (Perhaps in compensation, amercements under the assize tended to be higher in parts of the manor not subject to tolcester.)

East Sussex Record Office

Alciston, c. 1280	SAS/G18/1–4 (courts, 1275–89)
Alciston, c. 1325	SAS/G18/5–6 (courts, 1325)
Alciston, c. 1370	SAS/G18/28 (selected courts, 1369–71)
Alciston, c. 1425	SAS/G18/43 (selected courts, 1425–28)
Alciston, c. 1470	SAS/G18/48 (selected courts, 1469–72)
Alciston, c. 1525	SAS/G18/55 (selected courts, 1522–24)

Brigstock, Northamptonshire

Surveyed in full for 1287–1348 and for the Brigstock portion of the manor only for 1411–21.

Presentments: Individual-focused. Aletasters presented their findings every three weeks throughout the year.

Brewing by not-married women: Impossible to estimate from individual-focused presentments. Of the 38 by-industrial brewsters in the village before the Black Death, 5 might have been singlewomen, and another 5 brewed as both wives and widows.

Beer: Not mentioned in courts surveyed.

Long-term licenses: 48 in pre-plague courts.

Tolls on brewing: A few women were cited in early fifteenth-century courts for refusing to pay a "tollale."

General observations: A general discussion of brewing in pre-plague Brigstock can be found in my *Women in the Medieval English Countryside* (Oxford, 1987), pp. 120–129.

Northamptonshire Record Office

Montagu Collection, Box X364A (courts, 1287–1312)
Montagu Collection, Box X364B (courts, 1313–30)
Montagu Collection, Box X365 (courts, 1330–48)
Montagu Collection, Box X366, bundle 5, items 5–8, and bundle 6, items 1–6 (courts, 1411–21)

Public Record Office

SC2 194/65 (courts, 1298–99)

Chedzoy, Somerset

Surveyed in full.

Presentments: Householder-focused. Frequency of brewing usually noted. Courts usually convened four times per year.

Brewing by not-married women: Before the Black Death, not-married brewsters accounted for as many as one-third of citations (in 1340), but their participation varied widely, and on the average, they accounted for 18 percent of brewing citations between 1329 and 1348. Although 23 percent of brewing presentments in 1349 named not-married women, their numbers fell in the next year to only 11 percent. Not-married women recovered some of their trade in the following years (by 1355, 17 percent of citations were to not-married women), but after 1355, their presence in brewing was negligible. In the late fourteenth century, not-married brewsters accounted for an average of only 6 percent of citations. In the early fifteenth century (data available only for 1405–13), not-married brewsters constituted 5 percent of citations. As a rule, not-married brewsters brewed with less frequency than married persons.

Professionalization: From the 1330s on, tipplers were occasionally noted. By the early fifteenth century, the number of brewers presented in any year had fallen to about one-third of previous levels: an average of only 26 per year rather than an average of 88 in the early fourteenth century.

Beer: Not mentioned.

Long-term licenses: None.

Tolls on brewing: None.

British Library

Add. Charters 15903–16102 (courts, from October 1329 to August 1413)
Add. Charter 16103 (court, for April 1632)

Public Record Office

SC2 198/19 (courts, from September 1379 to July 1380)

Chester-le-Street, Durham[39]

Surveyed in full 1348–1477 and sampled thereafter. The courts for the manor of Chester-le-Street are included among the manorial materials for the bishopric of Durham. I examined only the courts for Chester-le-Street manor and, within those courts, usually only the presentments for Chester-le-Street proper.

Presentments: Usually individual-focused in early courts but not invariably so. In the early fifteenth century, presentments became householder-focused. Presentments were recorded twice a year.

Brewing by not-married women: Impossible to determine for the fourteenth century. In most fifteenth- and sixteenth-century courts (that is, after presentments became householder-focused), not-married women brewed infrequently; most presentments either named only men or included one woman among many (usually six–eight) men.

Beer: Not mentioned in courts surveyed.

Long-term licenses: None.

Tolls on brewing: None.

General observations: In the 1350s, some brewers in the Whickham section of the manor were amerced for refusing either to brew or to sell ale, and some others were amerced for buying ale in Newcastle to sell in Whickham.

Public Record Office

Durham 3/12 (courts, 1348–62)
Durham 3/13 (courts, 1388–1403)
Durham 3/14 (courts, 1405–24)
Durham 3/15 (courts, 1438–56)
Durham 3/16 (courts, 1457–76)
Durham 3/18 (selected courts, 1483–93)
Durham 3/20 (selected courts, 1502–07)
Durham 3/22 (selected courts, 1523–29)
Durham 3/23 (selected courts, 1529–59)

Cranborne, Dorset

Sampled.

Presentments: Householder-focused. Frequency of brewing noted. Brewers were presented every three weeks, but by the late fifteenth century, many courts contain no presentments under the assize.

Brewing by not-married women: The activity of not-married brewsters varied erratically but fell over time: 29 percent of presentments c. 1330, 3 percent c. 1380, 16 percent c. 1420, and none c. 1480.

Professionalization: By the late fifteenth century, only a handful of brewers were active (often only one in each village of the manor). In Cranborne itself, for example, where about eight brewers had worked c. 1330, only one worked c. 1480.

Beer: Not mentioned in courts sampled.

Long-term licenses: None.

Tolls on brewing: In the courts c. 1480, a "custom of ale" due to the lord for brewing (variously levied at 1½d., 2d., or 3d.) was noted.

Marquess of Salisbury, Hatfield House

Cranborne, c. 1330	Courts, 1328−29
Cranborne, c. 1380	Courts, 1378−79
Cranborne, c. 1420	Courts, 1421−22
Cranborne, c. 1480	Courts, 1482−83

Crowle, Lincolnshire

Sampled.

Presentments: Variously focused on husbands and wives. Initially, presentments were made at every three-weekly court, but by c. 1470, brewers were presented only at semi-annual views of frankpledge.

Brewing by not-married women: Circa 1370 and c. 1420, when presentments were householder-focused, not-married women accounted for 27 percent and 9 percent of the presentments, respectively. Marital status is more difficult to infer from the citations c. 1470, but perhaps 17 percent of the brewsters were not married. Circa 1520, all brewers were married women (with the exception of one widow).

Professionalization: Professionalization proceeded slowly in Crowle, where even in the early sixteenth century, large numbers of brewers were serving the manor. By c. 1470, brewers also often baked for profit. No tipplers were cited in the courts examined.

Beer: Not mentioned in courts sampled.

Long-term licenses: None.

Tolls on brewing: An ale toll (*tolnetum cervisie*) was mentioned in the courts c. 1320.

Lincolnshire Archives Office

Crowle, c. 1320	CM 1/7 (courts, 1318−19)
Crowle, c. 1370	CM 1/25 (courts, 1370−71)
Crowle, c. 1420	CM 1/62−63 (courts, 1419−22)
Crowle, c. 1470	CM 1/122 (courts, 1470−71)
	CM 1/124 (courts, 1471−72)
Crowle, c. 1520	CM 1/179−180 (courts, 1518−20)

Earl Soham, Suffolk

Surveyed in full.

Presentments: Variously focused on husbands and wives. Brewers usually presented in only one court per year.

Brewing by not-married women: Impossible to estimate from individual-focused presentments.

Professionalization: The average number of amercements per year fell from nearly 9 in the early fourteenth century to less than 2½ in the early sixteenth century. Brewers also often baked for profit. Tipplers were cited sporadically from the earliest courts on. From the 1480s, brewers were usually cited as common brewers.

Beer: Not mentioned.

Long-term licenses: None.

Tolls on brewing: None.

Suffolk Record Office

V5/18/1.1 (courts, 1320–62)
V5/18/1.2 (courts, 1352–76)
V5/18/1.3 (courts, 1377–99)
V5/18/1.4 (courts, 1413–22)
V5/18/1.5 (courts, 1423–60)
V5/18/1.6 (courts, 1460–85)
V5/18/1.7 (courts, 1485–1509)
V5/18/1.8 (courts, 1511–46)

Hindolveston, Norfolk

Sampled.

Presentments: Variously focused on husbands and wives. Brewers usually presented in only one annual leet.

Brewing by not-married women: Usually impossible to estimate. Of 33 citations to brewers c. 1265, 9 were to women (27 percent).

Professionalization: The average number of amercements per year fell from 6 in the late thirteenth century to 1.3 in the early sixteenth century. In the late fourteenth century, presentments often stated the length of time brewed—one week, one month, quarter or half year, or commonly. By the early fifteenth century, a handful of women were presented each year for brewing commonly. In many cases, households were involved in both commercial baking and commercial brewing.

Beer: Not mentioned in courts sampled.

Long-term licenses: None.

Tolls on brewing: None.

General observations: In the earliest courts, presentments included regraters (usually of bread but occasionally also of ale); such presentments ceased by the mid-fifteenth century.

Norfolk Record Office

Hindolveston, c. 1265   DCN 60/19/1 (courts, 1257–63)
DCN 60/19/2 (courts, 1267–71)

Hindolveston, c. 1320	DCN 60/19/3 (selected courts, 1318–24)
	DCN 60/19/4 (courts, 1320–21)
Hindolveston, c. 1380	DCN 60/19/6 (courts, 1376–77)
	DCN 60/19/7 (courts, 1377–81)
	DCN 60/19/8 (courts, 1381–82)
Hindolveston, c. 1420	DCN 60/19/22 (courts, 1413–21)
Hindolveston, c. 1455	DCN 60/19/24 (selected courts, 1453–57)
Hindolveston, c. 1500	DCN 60/19/27 (selected courts, 1496–99)
Hindolveston, c. 1530	DCN 60/19/40 (courts, 1527–28)
	DCN 60/19/41 (courts, 1528–29)
	DCN 60/19/42 (courts, 1530–31)
	DCN 60/19/43 (courts, 1530–31)
	DCN 60/19/44 (courts, 1531–32)
	DCN 60/19/45 (courts, 1532–33)
Hindolveston, c. 1550	DCN 60/19/58 (selected courts, 1547–53)

Houghton-cum-Wyton, Huntingdonshire

Surveyed in full for 1290–1349.

Presentments: Individual-focused. Brewers were presented twice a year.

Brewing by not-married women: Impossible to estimate from individual-focused presentments.

Beer: Not mentioned in courts surveyed.

Long-term licenses: None.

Tolls on brewing: None.

General observations: Data on brewing presentments on this manor are reported briefly in my *Women in the Medieval English Countryside* and more fully in my Ph.D. dissertation, "Gender, Family and Community: A Comparative Study of the English Peasantry, 1287–1349" (University of Toronto, 1981), especially pp. 320–330.

British Library

Add. Charters 34338, 39597, 39756, 39586, 34324, 34897–98, 39761 (courts, 1290–1331)

Public Record Office

SC2 179/5, 7, 9–13, 15–16, 19–22, 25–26, 30, 32–33 (courts, 1288–1349)

Ingatestone, Essex

Surveyed in full from 1292 to 1624.

Presentments: Individual-focused. Brewers were presented on a twice-yearly basis.

Brewing by not-married women: Impossible to estimate from individual-focused presentments.

Professionalization: Alesellers active as early as the 1320s. From c. 1400, only a few brewers (usually fewer than four) worked in Ingatestone. In the early sixteenth century (c. 1530s), the victualing trades became professionalized and male-dominated. For example, female alesellers were replaced by males (a shift that was accompanied by the replacement of an old term for alesellers, *gannokers*, with a new one, *tipplers*). In some cases, husband-wife substitution explains this change, but in other cases, men genuinely seem to have been beginning to sell ale more than before. Unfortunately, recorded information about the most important victualing trade in this study—commercial brewing—was scarce by this period.

Beer: First mentioned in 1525.

Long-term licenses: None.

Tolls on brewing: None.

General observations: Amercements of brewers started in 1292 and began to wane after the first decade of the sixteenth century. Thereafter, although very little information about brewing was recorded in these courts, other victualing trades were carefully regulated. In general, these courts provide extensive information about a variety of victualing trades, not only brewing but also butchering, baking, fishmongering, tippling, and the like. In the late sixteenth century, when brewers were rarely mentioned, it seems likely that many tipplers in Ingatestone were buying their ale (and beer) elsewhere and that the only brewing in the community was being done by persons identified in the courts as "innholders."

Essex Record Office

D/DP M 1–102 (courts, 1279–1624)

Iver, Buckinghamshire

Surveyed in full for 1287–1349.

Presentments: Householder-focused. Brewers were presented every three weeks.

Brewing by not-married women: Not-married women accounted for 34 percent of brewers.

Beer: Not mentioned in courts surveyed.

Long-term licenses: None.

Tolls on brewing: None.

General observations: Data on brewing presentments on this manor are reported briefly in my *Women in the Medieval English Countryside* and more fully in my dissertation, "Gender, Family and Community," especially pp. 262–274.

Buckinghamshire Record Office

D/BASM 45/1 (courts, 1332–76)

St George's Chapel, Windsor Castle

XV.55.1 (courts, 1287–88)
XV.55.3–6 (courts, 1288–33)
IV.B.1 (extracts from manorial records)

Norton Canon, Herefordshire

Sampled.

Presentments: Householder-focused. Early presentments occurred on a monthly basis, later twice a year. Frequency of brewing often noted.

Brewing by not-married women: Not-married women accounted for about one-fifth of brewing citations in the late thirteenth and early fourteenth centuries, but they were not cited at all in the post-plague samples.

Professionalization: The number of brewers varied greatly but generally fell, from an average of 4.3 per court in 1280 to 2 per court c. 1475.

Beer: Not mentioned in courts sampled.

Long-term licenses: None.
Tolls on brewing: None.

Hereford Cathedral Library

Norton Canon, c. 1280	R892 (courts, 1282–83)
Norton Canon, c. 1330	R908 (courts, 1332–33)
Norton Canon, c. 1375	R931 (courts, 1372–74)
Norton Canon, c. 1410	R948 (courts, 1410–11)
Norton Canon, c. 1475	R966 (courts, 1472–74)

Preston-on-Wye, Herefordshire

Sampled.

Presentments: Householder-focused. In early courts, presentments occurred about once a month, but they occurred only every few months by the late fifteenth century. Frequency of brewing often noted.

Brewing by not-married women: The proportion of not-married women cited for brewing varied radically and in no clear pattern: c. 1275, 14 percent; c. 1320, 33 percent; c. 1366 and c. 1395 (combined), 9 percent; c. 1425, 21 percent; c. 1465, 17 percent. The fifteenth-century samples are too small to provide reliable data.

Professionalization: The number of brewers presented per court varied but fell from about a dozen in the early fourteenth century to only three by the late fifteenth century.

Beer: Not mentioned in courts sampled.

Long-term licenses: None.

Tolls on brewing: None.

Hereford Cathedral Library

Preston-on-Wye, c. 1275	R824 (courts, 1276–77)
Preston-on-Wye, c. 1320	R833 (courts, 1322–33)
Preston-on-Wye, c. 1365	R845 (courts, 1363–64)
Preston-on-Wye, c. 1395	R853 (courts, 1393–94)
Preston-on-Wye, c. 1425	R857 (courts, 1426–27)
Preston-on-Wye, c. 1465	R862 (courts, 1463)

Scalby, Yorkshire

Sampled.

Presentments: Individual-focused presentments. Frequency of brewing often noted. Presentments were to be made on a three-weekly basis but often were not.

Brewing by not-married women: Impossible to estimate from individual-focused presentments.

Professionalization: Common brewers noted from c. 1465. In courts c. 1505, some brewers also baked bread for profit.

Beer: Not mentioned in courts sampled.

Long-term licenses: None.

Tolls on brewing: None.

General observations: By c. 1505, a few men were cited alongside female brewers (and they also often both brewed and baked for profit).

Public Record Office

Scalby, c. 1320	DL 30 128/1917 (courts, 1319–20)
Scalby, c. 1340	DL 30 128/1918 (selected courts, 1338–46)
Scalby, c. 1380	DL 30 128/1923 (selected courts, 1378–82)
Scalby, c. 1420	DL 30 128/1926 (courts, 1417–18)
	DL 30 128/1927 (courts, 1422–23)
Scalby, c. 1465	DL 30 128/1934 (courts, 1464–71)
Scalby, c. 1505	DL 30 128/1939 (courts, 1504–1505)

Stockton, Wiltshire

Surveyed in full, 1281–1544.

Presentments: Householder-focused. Presentments occurred annually or twice a year. Frequency of brewing often noted, especially in earlier courts.

Brewing by not-married women: Brewing by not-married women fell steadily: 20 percent of citations, 1281–99; 13 percent, 1306–44; 11 percent, 1349–99; 6 percent, 1400–47; none in the late fifteenth century. In the early sixteenth century, one women, the widow of a male brewer, was presented for brewing.

Professionalization: Until c. 1415, each presentment usually included a dozen brewers or more. Thereafter, fewer and fewer brewers were presented, and by the late fifteenth century, often only one or two common brewers were named.

Beer: Not mentioned.

Long-term licenses: None.

Tolls on brewing: None.

British Library

Add. Charters 24330–24384 (courts, 1332–1530)
Add. Charters 24716–24717 (court, 1384)
Add. Charter 24717 (court, 1391)

Wiltshire Record Office

108/1–13 (courts, 1339–92)
906/SC 1–24 (courts, 1287–1573)

Winchester Cathedral Library

Courts for 1281–82, 1290–91, 1292–93, 1295–96, 1296–97, 1298–99, 1306–1307, 1308–1309, 1313–14, 1322–23, 1330–31, 1349, 1350, 1362, 1365, 1366, 1376

Sutton, Cambridgeshire

Sampled.

Presentments: Usually individual-focused, until c. 1470 (when presentments became householder-focused). Brewers presented at annual leet in autumn.

Brewing by not-married women: Impossible to estimate for most periods. Circa 1290 and c. 1320 (when many brewsters were identified explicitly as married women), not-married brewsters accounted for 45 percent and 27 percent of citations, respectively.

Professionalization: In the sample c. 1470 (when presentments shifted from wives to husbands), two other new trends are apparent: (1) almost all brewers also baked for profit, and (2) alesellers began to work in the village.

Beer: Not mentioned in courts sampled.

Long-term licenses: None.

Tolls on brewing: None.

Muniments of the Dean and Chapter of Ely, Cambridge University Library

	The court rolls for Sutton are boxed in EDC 7/3. Although the rolls are labeled with dates and/or regnal years, they are not individually cataloged.
Sutton, c. 1290	Roll for 1291–93 (courts, 1292–93)
Sutton, c. 1320	Roll for 11 & 12 Edward II (courts, 1317–18)
	Roll for 15 & 16 Edward II (courts, 1321)
Sutton, c. 1370	Roll for 43–48 Edward III (selected courts, 1369–74)
Sutton, c. 1420	Roll for Henry V (selected courts, 1419–22)
Sutton, c. 1470	Roll for 11 & 12 Edward IV (selected courts, 1471–72)
	Roll for 13–16 Edward IV (selected courts, 1473)
Sutton, c. 1520	Roll for Henry VIII (selected courts, 1520–22)

Wakefield, Yorkshire

Sampled.

Presentments: Usually individual-focused but not invariably so. As a rule, brewers were presented at the twice-annual tourns. Presentments sometimes noted both the frequency of brewing and the price of ale sold.

Brewing by not-married women: Married women were often identified as such, enabling a rough estimate of brewing by not-married women. These estimates suggest that perhaps one-third of brewing citations were to not-married women in the late thirteenth century, one-quarter to one-fifth in the fourteenth century, and one-tenth thereafter.

Beer: Not mentioned in courts sampled.

Long-term licenses: None.

Tolls on brewing: None.

General observations: In the fifteenth century, persons were amerced for holding helpales (that is, drinking parties held to raise cash for a needy person). Supervision of the ale trade declined after c. 1480. Unlike many other jurisdictions, women were cited in the Wakefield courts (especially in the fifteenth century) for other victualing offenses, for example, baking and butchering.

Wakefield, c. 1275	William Paley Baildon, ed., Court rolls of the manor of Wakefield, vol. 1 (1274–1297), Yorkshire Archaeological Society, 29 (1901) (selected courts, 1274–77)
Wakefield, c. 1325	J. W. Walker, ed., Court rolls of the manor of Wakefield, vol. 5 (1322–1331), Yorkshire Archaeological Society, 109 (1945) (selected courts, 1323–25)

Yorkshire Archaeological Society

Wakefield, c. 1370	MD225/1/96, 97, and 99, rolls for 1370–71, 1371–72, and 1373–74

Wakefield, c. 1425	MD225/1/147/1 and 2, 148/1 and 2, 149/1 and 2, rolls for 1421–22, 1422–23, 1423–24
Wakefield, c. 1475	MD 225/1/197–199, rolls for 1471–72, 1472–73, 1473–74
Wakefield, c. 1520	MD 225/1/246, roll for 1520–21

Woolhope, Herefordshire

Sampled.

Presentments: Householder-focused. Frequency of brewing often noted. Presentments made in courts held about once a month (or less).

Brewing by not-married women: Not-married women constituted about 15 percent of brewers from c. 1290 to c. 1380. Data thereafter are unreliable.

Beer: Not mentioned in courts sampled.

Long-term licenses: None.

Tolls on brewing: None.

General observations: Effective supervision of the ale trade ceased quite early in the fifteenth century.

Hereford Cathedral Library

Woolhope, c. 1290	R747 (courts, 1291–92)
Woolhope, c. 1325	R756 (courts, 1326–27)
Woolhope, c. 1380	R768 (courts, 1380–81)
Woolhope, c. 1410	R776 (courts, 1409–10)
Woolhope, c. 1485	R782 (courts, 1486–87)

Wye, Kent

Sampled.

Presentments: Individual-focused from c. 1311 to c. 1420, but earlier presentments (c. 1285) had no consistent pattern, and later presentments became householder-focused (over the course of the 1430s). Presentments were usually given in twice-annual views of frankpledge (also known as lawdays). The frequency of brewing and quality of ale were sometimes noted. By late fifteenth century, brewers were rarely presented.

Brewing by not-married women: Impossible to estimate from individual-focused presentments.

Professionalization: Common brewers and alesellers noted from the late fourteenth century.

Beer: Not mentioned in courts sampled.

Long-term licenses: None.

Tolls on brewing: None.

General observations: In the 1430s, when presentments shifted from individual-focused to householder-focused, the shift occurred first in the spring views associated with the annual fair. In other words, for several years, men were more frequently cited in the spring than in the autumn. They were also more likely to be cited for brewing commonly than women. At the same time, the number of brewers presented became skewed, with many more brewers presented in the spring than in the fall. That is, it is possible that the expansion of the ale trade associated with the spring fair at Wye began to attract greater male participation in the brewing industry.

Public Record Office

Wye, c. 1285   SC2 182/1 (selected courts, 1285–86)
Wye, c. 1310   SC2 182/8 (selected court, 1311)
Wye, c. 1330   SC2 182/11–12 (selected courts, 1331–32)
Wye, c. 1370   SC2 182/20 (courts, 1370–72)
Wye, c. 1420   SC2 182/28–29 (courts, 1419–22)
Wye, c. 1435   SC2 182/30–36 (selected courts, 1425–40)
Wye, c. 1445   SC2 182/37 (selected court, 1446)
Wye, c. 1465   SC2 182/45 (selected court, 1465)
Wye, c. 1490   SC2 182/48 (selected courts, 1480–92)
Wye, c. 1520   SC2 182/58 (selected court, 1519)

II. The Survey of Assize Presentments in Towns and Cities

In seeking urban lists of brewers, I followed a much less selective process than that used in the survey of rural communities: I used what I could find for all the major towns and added to the pool two market towns (Tamworth and Walling-ford) for which exceptional information was available. As a rule, urban records yielded fewer lists of brewers and no runs of lists that could match the series available for some rural communities (with the exception of Tamworth).[40] In addition, special jurisdictions limit the coverage found in some urban records. Listed here are only the major sets of assize presentments (or other similar lists) that were used in this study. In addition to these listings, I found many other sorts of useful records—for example, gild records or civic ordinances—both for the towns listed here and for others (such as Southampton). When I have used these other materials, I have provided full citations in the notes.

Leicester

In Leicester, brewers were supervised through a traditional ale toll known as cannemol. All extant cannemol lists were surveyed in full.

Presentments: Householder-focused (except for the 1562 list).
Brewing by not-married women: In 1287–88, not-married women accounted for 16 percent of brewers, and this proportion was roughly maintained through the early fourteenth century (in 1339, almost 20 percent of brewers were not-married women). In 1375–80, however, not-married women accounted for only 11 percent of brewers, and by the sixteenth century, they had even less presence in the trade. In 1520, 2 of 32 brewers were not-married women (6 percent), and in 1562, no not-married women were named at all. Thereafter, only a handful of not-married women, all widows, were cited for brewing.
Beer: Not mentioned in cannemol records specifically, but beer was mentioned in other Leicester records of the sixteenth century. In 1523, the city prohibited the use of hops in brewing, and in 1575, beer was included for the first time in pricing regulations.[41]
Tolls on brewing: See above.

Leicestershire Record Office

BRIII/7/1: Cannemol roll, c. 1260–70
BRIII/7/2: Cannemol roll, 1287–88

BRIII/7/3: Cannemol roll, c. 1300
BRIII/7/4: Cannemol roll, 1329
BRIII/7/5: Cannemol roll, 1338
BRIII/7/6: Cannemol roll, 1339
BRIII/7/7: Cannemol roll, c. 1375–80

Public Record Office

DL 30/81/1111: Includes cannemol, 1529
DL 30/81/1118: Includes cannemol, 1562
DL 30/82/1122: Includes cannemol, 1572
DL 30/82/1123: Includes cannemol, 1584
DL 30/82/1124: Cannemol, c. 1588
DL 30/82/1126: Cannemol, 1592

London

Assize presentments in London were probably made in the wardmotes, for which almost no records survive. In the only extant wardmote, no aletasters' presentments are recorded (although the last membrane does include a list of tipplers). See CLRO, Presentments for Portsoken ward, 5–22 Edward IV and 23 Henry VII. In 1419–20, the city compiled a list of brewers, and this has been accurately printed in CLB I, pp. 233–235. This list is householder-focused. Of 290 heads of households reported in the city list for 1419–20, 21 were female; that is, roughly 7 percent of brewers were not-married women.

Norwich

Surveyed in full.

Presentments: Usually householder-focused, but the leet for 1288–89 names both husbands and wives, and the leets for 1290–91, 1292–93, 1295–96, 1299–1300, and 1312–13 list some men, many wives, and some women not identified by marital status. In some of these latter lists (for example, 1290–91), so few men are listed that they might have been bachelors, but in other of these lists (see 1295–96), substantial numbers of men appear, suggesting that some households were represented by husbands and others by wives.

Brewing by not-married women: Not-married women accounted for 16 percent of brewers in 1288–89, 13 percent in 1312–13, and 7 percent in 1390–91.

Beer: Beer was described as "Flemish ale" in 1288–89 but not mentioned subsequently until 1390–91, when it was being sold in Norwich (but not necessarily brewed).

Norfolk Record Office

	Norwich City Records, Press B, Case 5, Shelf b:
Norwich Leets #1	no. 1: 1288
Norwich Leets #2	no. 2: 1288–89
Norwich Leets #3	no. 3: 1290
Norwich Leets #4	no. 4: 1290–91
Norwich Leets #5	no. 5: 1292–93
Norwich Leets #6	no.6: 1295–96
Norwich Leets #7	no. 7: 1299–1300

Norwich Leets #8   no. 8: 1307
Norwich Leets #9   no. 9: 1312–13
Norwich Leets #10   no. 10: 1375–76
Norwich Leets #11   no. 11: 1390–91

Oxford

Surveyed in full for 1309–51.
Presentments: Householder-focused.
Brewing by not-married women: See figure 2.3.
Professionalization: See discussion in chapter 6.
Beer: Not mentioned in courts surveyed.

Oxford University Archives, Bodleian Library

Oxford Assizes   SEP/4/16 (records of the enforcement of the Assize of
Bread and Ale, 1309–51). This material was printed by
H. E. Salter on pp. 130–265 of his *Mediaeval Archives of the
University of Oxford, vol.* 2, Oxford Historical Society, 73
(1921). After comparing this transcription with the original, I incorporated into my analyses a few corrections and
additions.

Tamworth

Sampled.
Presentments: Early presentments were householder-focused; later ones were individual-focused. Presentments were made in three-weekly courts until the late fourteenth century, when twice-yearly views began to contain most presentments for
infractions of the assize. The frequency of brewing was noted in the earliest
presentments. Tamworth fell into two counties (Staffordshire and Warwickshire);
in some of the earlier courts, presentments were made from both parts of the
town, but later presentments derive from views of frankpledge for only the
Staffordshire part.
Brewing by not-married women: Not-married women accounted for roughly one-third of the
presentments through the early fifteenth century. Thereafter, their presence cannot be
estimated.
Professionalization: Alesellers (first, hucksters who sold many food products and, later,
"tranters" who sold ale alone) were active from the late fourteenth century on.
Common brewers were mentioned in the late fifteenth century, when the number of
brewers presented in each view fell from about 20 to about 8.
Beer: Not mentioned in courts sampled.
General observations: The tasters in Tamworth regulated not only brewers (and alesellers)
but also bakers and other victualers such as pastry makers, butchers, and hucksters.

University of Keele Library

Tamworth, c. 1290   Tamworth Court Rolls, 1/1–3 (courts, 1289–90)
Tamworth, c. 1320   Tamworth Court Rolls, 2/17–20 (courts, 1319–22)
Tamworth, c. 1370   Tamworth Court Rolls, 3/51–59 (courts, 1370–73)
Tamworth, c. 1420   Tamworth Court Rolls, 6/7–14 (courts, 1419–22)

Tamworth, c. 1470   Tamworth Court Rolls, 8/3–4 (courts, 1470–71)
Tamworth, c. 1520   Tamworth Court Rolls, 10/88 (courts, 1518–22)

Wallingford

Sampled.

Presentments: Lists of brewers were found in various locations: estreat rolls, burghmotes, and views. The earliest lists were individual-focused, but later presentments were householder-focused. Only scattered presentments were found in extant records for the early fourteenth century.

Brewing by not-married women: Probably 33 percent of brewers in 1228–1229 were not married, and this proportion was roughly maintained through the early fifteenth century. By the early sixteenth century, brewing by not-married women was rare (1 not-married woman noted among 23 brewers).

Beer: Not mentioned in courts sampled.

Berkshire Record Office

Wallingford, c. 1230   W/JBe 1 (estreat roll, 1228–29)
Wallingford, 1275   W/JBe 11 (estreat roll, 1276)
Wallingford, c. 1300   W/JBe 13 (estreat roll, c. 1300)
Wallingford, c. 1370   W/JBb 10 (courts, 1367–68)
                         W/JBb 11 (court, 1368)
                         W/JBb 12 (courts, 1368–69)
                         W/JBb 13 (courts, 1368–69)
                         W/JBb 14 (courts, 1369)
                         W/JBb 15 (courts, 1369–70)
Wallingford, c. 1400   W/JBb 58 (selected courts, 1401–1402)
Wallingford, c.1460   W/JBc 1 (court, 1461)
Wallingford, c. 1505   W/JBc 7 (court, 1506)
                         W/JBc 12 (selected court, c. 1507)
Wallingford, c. 1560   W/JBc 31 (court, 1561)

York

Few court records survive for late medieval and early modern York, but lists of brewers can be found in two other locations. First, in 1301, when Edward I was using York as an administrative center, brewers and regraters were named in the records of various victualing ordinances and their enforcement. Second, brewers were noted in considerable detail in the Chamberlains' Accounts of the fifteenth and sixteenth centuries (since the chamberlains were responsible for accounting for brewers' fines).

Presentments: Variously focused on husbands or wives.

Brewing by not-married women: In 1304, 11 of 70 brewing households were headed by women (16 percent). In later lists, proportions of not-married women fell but remained steady at about 10 percent. Estimates for these later lists are confounded by the York practice (discussed above) of citing widows as wives, but despite the uncertainties introduced by this practice, it is clear that not-married women continued to brew in York through the sixteenth century. In 1596, when the city licensed 83 brewers, 7 widows and 1 spinster received authorization to follow the trade.[42]

Beer: The first beerbrewer entered the freedom of York in 1416–17.[43]

York, c. 1301   Data printed in Michael Prestwich, ed., York civic ordinances, 1301, Borthwick Papers, 49 (1976)

York City Archives

York, c. 1450   CC1A: Chamberlains' Account Book, 1449–54 (selected fines for 1449–50)

York, c. 1520   CC2: Chamberlains' Account Book, 1520–25

York, c. 1560   CC5: Chamberlains' Account Book, 1559–85 (selected fines for 1559–66)

York, c. 1595   CC8: Chamberlains' Account Book, 1594–97

CC9: Chamberlains' Account Book, 1597–99

NOTES

Chapter 1

1. I thank Christopher Whittick and David Allam for information about modern brewster sessions. Brewster sessions are supplemented by "transfer sessions," held four to eight times during the year, and many of the matters once reserved for the annual brewster session are now transacted at transfer sessions. The result is that today, as David Allam told me in written correspondence, "the brewster session [is] a pale imitation of its historic forebears."

2. See, for example, entries for both brewster and -ster in the Oxford English Dictionary.

3. Sample: Preston-on-Wye, c. 1275. Preston-on-Wye is one of the manors included in the sample collected for this study. See the appendix for a discussion of this sample and for full archival information.

4. K. C. Newton, The manor of Writtle: The development of a royal manor in Essex, c. 1086–c. 1500 (Chichester, 1970), p. 90. In the decades since Writtle's statement, historians have paid more attention to presentments made under the assize of ale, and I rely in this study on the analyses they have undertaken. These studies are now too numerous to list here (and will be cited in specific instances below), but see especially R. H. Britnell, Growth and decline in Colchester, 1300–1525 (Cambridge, 1986), pp. 89–91, 195–197, 269–271; Edwin B. DeWindt, Land and people in Holywell-cum-Needingworth (Toronto, 1972), pp. 235–239; Helena Graham, "'A woman's work . . .': Labour and gender in the late medieval countryside," in P. J. P. Goldberg, ed., Woman is a worthy wight (Phoenix Mill, U.K., 1992), pp. 126–148; Maryanne Kowaleski, Local markets and regional trade in medieval Exeter (Cambridge, 1995), pp. 131–136; and Richard Smith, "English peasant life-cycles and socio-economic networks: A quantitative geographical case study," Ph.D. dissertation, University of Cambridge, 1974, pp. 150–178.

5. Alan Macfarlane, The origins of English individualism (Oxford, 1978). Of the many critiques, one of the most useful is Stephen D. White and Richard T. Vann, "The invention of English individualism: Alan Macfarlane and the modernization of pre-modern England," Social History 8 (1983), pp. 345–363.

6. Judith M. Bennett, "'History that stands still': Women's work in the European

past," *Feminist Studies* 14 (1988), pp. 269–283, and "Medieval women, modern women: Across the great divide," in David Aers, ed., *Culture and history 1350–1600: Essays on English communities, identities, and writing* (London, 1992), pp. 147–175. A revised version of the latter essay can be found in Ann-Louise Shapiro, ed., *Feminists revision history* (New Brunswick, N.J., 1994), pp. 47–72.

7. Judith M. Bennett, "Feminism and history," *Gender and History* 1 (1989), pp. 251–272.

8. Alice Clark, *The working life of women in the seventeenth century* (London, 1919).

9. Eileen Power, "The position of women," in C. G. Crump and E. F. Jacobs, eds., *The legacy of the middle ages* (Oxford, 1926), p. 410.

10. As will be discussed more fully in chapter 2, an incalculable amount of the ale and beer consumed in England was produced domestically, that is, brewed for family consumption, not sale. The distinction between domestic brewing and commercial brewing is a critical one, and it will be considered in this book whenever appropriate. Yet since I focus on commercial brewers and commercial brewing, it would be needlessly repetitive to remind readers constantly of this fact. Whenever *brewer, brewing*, and related words are used without modifiers, readers should think of commercial brewers, commercial brewings, and the like.

11. By the eighteenth century, as Peter Mathias has shown, breweries were a driving force in industrialization. See *The brewing industry in England 1700–1830* (Cambridge, 1959).

12. This remark was made in a presentation, "Women's initiatives in early modern England: Where are they?" at a conference on "Women's Initiatives in Early Modern England, 1500–1750," London, 4 June 1994. For a brief report on this conference by Penelope Lane, see *The Achievement Project Newsletter* 4:1 (1995), pp. 4–6.

13. Some of the factors not treated in this study are discussed by Sylvia Walby, *Theorizing Patriarchy* (Oxford, 1990).

14. Christopher Dyer, "Were there any capitalists in fifteenth century England?" (1991), reprinted in Dyer, *Everyday life in medieval England* (London, 1994), pp. 305–328.

15. As I was recently reminded by a graduate student who asked me a question about what she called "feminist bias" in history, this book might seem schizophrenic to some readers: hard research and careful analysis, on the one hand, and feminist interpretation, on the other. Yet these two elements are complementary, not contradictory. As I have explained elsewhere, feminism enriches scholarship—opening up new questions, investigating new archival sources, and developing new interpretations. See "Medievalism and Feminism," *Speculum: A Journal of Medieval Studies* 68 (1993), pp. 309–331.

Chapter 2

1. Thomas Bruce Dilks, ed., *Bridgwater borough archives, vol. 3: 1400–1445*, Somerset Record Society, 58 (1945 for 1943), item 508, pp. 9–11. Information about Denise Marlere and her family has been reconstructed from references found in this volume and its two predecessors (both edited by Dilks), *Bridgwater borough archives, vol. 1: 1200–1377*, Somerset Record Society, 48 (1933), and *Bridgwater borough archives, vol. 2: 1377–1400*, Somerset Record Society, 53 (1938).

2. For examples from c. 1500, see Ingatestone, Earl Soham, Hindolveston, and Wakefield in the appendix. In these communities, individual-focused presentments allow especially clear identification of brewsters (see the appendix for an explanation of the distinction between householder-focused and individual-focused presentments). For c.

1600, see University of London, Fuller Ms. 34/1 (householder-focused presentments in Ottery St. Mary).

3. As discussed more fully in chapter 6, the thirteenth-century quasi statutes on brewing (of which the *Assisa panis et cervisie* is the most important) merely validated existing practices. To differentiate local and national regulation, I shall distinguish the assize of ale (by which I mean the rules through which local jurisdictions governed ale sales) from the *Assisa* (by which short-hand term, I will denote the quasi statutes that regulated the trade). For the quasi statutes, see *Statutes*, vol. 1, pp. 199–205.

4. For example, the Percy children downed 2 quarts of beer most days, even during Lent. Thomas Percy, ed., *The regulations and establishment of the household of Henry Algernon Percy . . . anno domini MDXII* (1700; reprinted London, 1905).

5. Michael Prestwich, "Victualling estimates for English garrisons in Scotland during the early fourteenth century," *English Historical Review* 82 (1967), pp. 536–543. Prestwich estimates that soldiers consumed 0.8 gallons of ale each day. For other examples of the gallon-per-day standard, see Christopher Dyer, "English diet in the later middle ages," in T. H. Aston, ed., *Social relations and ideas* (Cambridge, 1983), p. 193n. The inmates of God's House in Southampton had ale as their basic drink, with wine as an added luxury on special occasions. See Colin Platt, *Medieval Southampton* (London, 1973), p. 77, n. 30.

6. Quoted in John Bickerdyke, *The curiosities of ale and beer* (London, n.d.), p. 34.

7. Christopher Dyer argued that only prosperous peasants drank ale regularly. See his "English diet," esp. pp. 197–210, and *Standards of living in the later middle ages* (Cambridge, 1989). I disagree. Dyer relied on some questionable assumptions: that retirees consumed rather than sold the grains they received, that they had no other resources beyond those promised in the maintenance agreements, that they brewed ale as strong as the ale brewed in aristocratic households, and that they rationally eschewed ale because they recognized that brewing used grain less economically than baking. Dyer also downplayed positive evidence of ale consumption by peasants: that most early fourteenth-century villages supported many more commercial brewers than necessary to supply only a small minority of inhabitants, that even poor households possessed the necessary equipment to brew, that civic officers sometimes anxiously ensured sufficient ale for the poor (that is, weak ale sold in small measures), and that our most direct information about popular diets— foodstuffs delivered to harvest workers and soldiers—usually allows for substantial quantities of malt or ale. For the vigorous market in ale, consider Brigstock in the 1340s, where, if each brewing yielded just 30 gallons of ale, more than 65 quarts were available each day for purchase in the village. For commercial brewing by smallholders, see further discussion below. For civic provisions of ale for the poor, see CLB H, p. 183 (CLRO, Letter Book H, fo. cxliv). (Most evidence of this sort comes from the post-plague era, but it is hard to know whether this reflects the better record keeping of late medieval towns or more acute anxieties about the supply of ale.) For ale supplied to harvest workers, see Christopher Dyer, "Changes in diet in the late middle ages: The case of harvest workers," *Agricultural History Review* 36 (1988), pp. 21–37. I agree with Dyer that soldiers and harvest workers were better fed than other peasants, but I think it is probable that the ordinary diet of the latter differed from that of the former in quality and quantity, not type.

8. To approximate consumption of ale by people of all social strata, all ages, and all regions, I have estimated (a) yields of 10 gallons per bushel instead of the usual 7½ reported in monastic and aristocratic accounts and (b) consumption of 1 quart a day, rather than the 1 gallon reported in many of those same accounts. These estimates are more generous than the radically low estimates in Bruce M. S. Campbell, James A. Galloway, Derek Keene, and Margaret Murphy, *A medieval capital and its grain supply: Agrarian pro-*

duction and distribution in the London region c. 1300, Historical Geography Research Series, 30 (1993), esp. pp. 25–26, 33, 205–206. In estimating aggregate consumption, I have assumed (a) a population of 6 million [see Richard Smith, "Demographic developments in rural England, 1300–1348: A survey," in Bruce M. S. Campbell, ed., *Before the Black Death* (Manchester, 1991), pp. 25–77, at 49] and (b) barrels of 32 gallons. In 1700, excise statistics indicate that more than 51 million barrels (36-gallon barrels) were produced each year. See Peter Mathias, *The brewing industry in England 1700–1830* (Cambridge, 1959), p. 542.

9. For the persistence of oats in brewing in the west country, see H. S. A. Fox, "Farming practices and techniques: Devon and Cornwall," in Edward Miller, ed., *The agrarian history of England and Wales III: 1348–1500* (Cambridge, 1991), pp. 303–307. For London, see GL, Ms. 25,516, Ms. 25,172; and Campbell et al. *Medieval capital*, esp. pp. 24–36, 203–206.

10. "Ballad of a tyrannical husband" (from a manuscript temp. Henry VII), in Thomas Wright and James Orchard Halliwell, eds., *Reliquiae antiquae* (London, 1845), vol. 2, pp. 196–199; William Harrison, *The description of England* (1587), George Edelen, ed. (Ithaca, N.Y., 1968), p. 137; Gervase Markham, *The English housewife* (1615), Michael R. Best, ed. (Montreal, 1986), pp. 204–208. In the absence of sources for the early fourteenth century, I have relied on accounts from later periods; they illustrate the persistence of practices from earlier but less well-documented centuries.

11. PRO, E101 92/1. I thank Caroline Barron for bringing this account to my attention.

12. NtnRO, Montagu Collection, Box X365.

13. For Brigstock, see Judith M. Bennett, *Women in the medieval English countryside* (New York, 1987), p. 121. For Alrewas, see Helena Graham, "'A woman's work . . .': Labour and gender in the late medieval countryside," in P. J. P. Goldberg, ed., *Woman is a worthy wight* (Phoenix Mill, U.K., 1992), pp. 126–148, at 127, 140. For Wakefield, see Helen M. Jewell, "Women at the courts of the manor of Wakefield, 1348–1350," *Northern History* 26 (1990), pp. 59–81, at 60–61.

14. In making these estimates, I assumed five persons per household. For Oxford, see Oxford Assizes and Campbell et al., *Medieval capital*, pp. 9–11. For Norwich, see Norwich Leets and Elizabeth Rutledge, "Immigration and population growth in early fourteenth-century Norwich: Evidence from the tithing roll," *Urban History Yearbook* (1988), pp. 15–30, at 27. For even more widespread brewing in another town, see Maryanne Kowaleski, *Local markets and regional trade in medieval Exeter* (Cambridge, 1995), pp. 131–136.

15. These terms are my own and will be used throughout this book to differentiate among brewers. In my earlier work, I used *regular* or *major* to refer to brewers whom I am now labeling *by-industrial*. This new term is less eloquent, but it is also more accurate, for many by-industrial brewers did not brew regularly (see further discussion about career patterns below).

16. Bennett, *Women*, pp. 121–122; Graham, "Women's work," p. 142; Jewell, "Women at Wakefield," p. 62.

17. At Elmley Castle (Worcestershire) in 1446, for example, alebrewers were proscribed from selling ale more than four days old. Warren O. Ault, *Open-field husbandry and the village community*, Transactions of the American Philosophical Society, n.s., 55, part 7 (1965), item 147, pp. 77–78.

18. See Keith Wrightson, "Alehouses, order and reformation in rural England, 1590–1660," in Eileen Yeo and Stephen Yeo, eds., *Popular culture and class conflict* (Atlantic Highlands, N.J., 1981), pp. 1–27.

19. Bennett, *Women*, p. 274, n. 60, p. 122; Graham, "Women's work," pp. 142–143; Jewell, "Women at Wakefield," pp. 62–63. Similar patterns prevailed in Iver and Houghton-cum-Wyton: see my Ph.D. dissertation, "Gender, family and community: A comparative study of the English peasantry, 1287–1349," University of Toronto, 1981, pp. 262–272, 320–328.

20. In the twice-annual lists of those breaking the assize in Oxford, some households paid exceptionally large amercements year after year; they seem, in other words, to have brewed both consistently and frequently. See *VCH, Oxon., vol.* 4, p. 19. Amercements levied against brewers in 1311 ranged as follows: 13 paid 3d., 39 paid 6d., 44 paid 12d., 19 paid 18d., 11 paid 24d., and the sums paid by 13 are unknown. Although the Oxford records never specified that amercements varied according to the number of brewings, the regular increments of amercements suggest that in Oxford, as elsewhere, brewers were assessed according to the frequency with which they brewed for sale. In the early fourteenth century, increments moved at 3d. intervals; by the mid-fourteenth century, 2d. intervals were the norm.

21. For St. Paul's, see GL, Ms. 25,172 (accounts for 1340–41).

22. I thank David Postles for reporting this case to me and Steven Gunn for assisting me in obtaining a full archival citation. This case can be found in the Merton College Library, MCR 6376 (court held in the vigil of All Saints, 10 Edward I).

23. Oxford Assizes. For example, see H. E. Salter, ed., *Mediaeval Archives of the University of Oxford, vol.* 2, Oxford Historical Society, 73 (1921), p. 192. Some brewers had to pay such heavy tolls on their trade —9 gallons at Sturminster Newton (Dorset) and 32 gallons at Monmouth—that they must have brewed large amounts. C. J. Elton, ed., *Rentalia et customaria Michaelis de Ambresbury 1235–1252 et Rogeri de Ford 1252–1261 abbatum monasterii Beatae Mariae Glastoniae*, Somerset Record Society, 5 (1891), p. 82. *Calendar of inquisitions post mortem*, vol. 4 (London, 1913), item 434, p. 294. Whether these represent exceptionally oppressive dues (tolls on brewers usually extracted only 1 or 2 gallons) or exceptionally large brewings (at Sturminster Newton, the Abbey provided equipment in return for its toll) is unclear. Yet it seems likely, on balance, that most brewings produced the more modest amounts suggested by our information about Robert Sibille and Denise Marlere and the reports of Oxford's aletasters.

24. J. Ambrose Raftis, *Tenure and mobility: Studies in the social history of the mediaeval English village* (Toronto, 1964), pp. 126, 264. Small brewings continued in some places for a very long time indeed; see Peter Clark, *The English alehouse: A social history 1200–1830* (London, 1983), pp. 99–100.

25. For exports of ale (mostly from Lynn) to the continent in the thirteenth and fourteenth centuries, see Nelly J. M. Kerling, *Commercial relations of Holland and Zeeland with England from the late 13th century to the close of the middle ages* (Leiden, 1954), pp. 110–111, 205–206, 216–219. See also H. J. Smit, ed., *Bronnen tot de geschiedenis van den Handel met Engeland, Schotland en Ierland, vol.* 1: 1150–1485 (The Hague, 1928), esp. items 148 (Lynn in 1303–1304) and 557 (various towns, 1353–77, but note that Smit here, and elsewhere, translates "cervisia" and "ale" as "bier"). Southampton also shipped ale, especially to royal garrisons; see Platt, *Medieval Southampton*, p. 121. Transport of ale within England was rare, but see, for example, CPR, 1281–1292, p. 164, and David Postles, "Brewing and the peasant economy: Some manors in late medieval Devon," *Rural History* 3 (1992), p. 136; Given the relatively low transport costs of the time, the rarity of ale transport probably reflects more the instability of the product than the costs of transportation: see James Masschaele, "Transport costs in medieval England," *Economic History Review*, 2nd series, 46 (1993), pp. 266–279.

26. It is not always possible to distinguish firmly between brewers and alesellers in medieval records, much less between alesellers and other people who hawked goods they

had not themselves produced (often cited generically as *regraters*). But there can be little doubt that the more concentrated and profitable ale markets of towns especially encouraged some persons to specialize exclusively in the selling of ale. In the records, they appeared under a number of guises—as hucksters, gannokers, regraters, tapsters, or tipplers—or they were merely described as someone who had sold ale (rather than brewed and sold ale). In this book, only two terms will be used and they will be used interchangeably: *aleseller* and *tippler*. In addition, the term *tapster* will be used to identify alesellers known to be female. Alesellers appear in some rural records in the fourteenth century; they represent 9 percent of those named in the fourteenth-century ale presentments in Earl Soham, 7 percent in Stockton, and 4 percent in Ingatestone (see appendix). In early fourteenth-century Oxford, however, they were comparatively much more numerous. In 1311, they accounted for 46 percent of those involved in the ale market (118 regraters and 139 brewers). Data from Oxford Assizes. As will be discussed more fully in chapter 3, single-women, widows, and other not-married women were particularly active as alesellers.

27. For the phrase *in domo et extra domo*, see NtnRO, Montagu Collection, Box X364A, file 14 (court for 7/1/1306). For the Wye incident, see PRO, SC2 182/8.

28. John Butt's attempt to estimate profits for London brewers are unreliable: "Calculating profits in a medieval trade," *Honorus: A Journal of Research* 2 (1987), pp. 40–44.

29. For the relative stability of ale and beer prices (compared to grain prices), see W. F. Lloyd, *Prices of corn in Oxford* (Oxford, 1830), esp. table IX and appendix. Reduced profits for brewers in times of dearth can sometimes be indirectly measured through reduced income from the regulation of brewing. For example, in 1390–1391, John Littlejohn gained a reduction on his farm of bacgavel and brewgavel (tolls on baking and brewing) in Exeter because of the dearness of grain. I am grateful to Maryanne Kowaleski for this reference, which can be found in the Devon Record Office, CRA (City receivers' accounts) 1390/91.

30. Dyer, *Standards*, pp. 261–265.

31. *Statutes*, vol. 1, pp. 199–200. Prices for wheat and oats were also specified. The *Assisa* stipulated different prices for town and country but did not justify the distinction. Because prices were set by local juries, it is difficult to ascertain whether this distinction was often observed in practice. But it was certainly *sometimes* observed. See, for example, the case of John of Thinglowe in John Lister, ed., *Court rolls of the manor of Wakefield*, vol. 4: 1315–1317, Yorkshire Archaeological Society, 78 (1930), p. 185.

32. Indeed, the scale was not even observed in statutory law. The *Judicium pillorie* specified a different scale (*Statutes*, vol. 1, p. 202).

33. Peter R. Coss, ed., *The early records of medieval Coventry* (London, 1986), pp. 41–42.

34. Harrison, *Description*, p. 138.

35. See further discussions in chapters 6 and 7.

36. The assizes set by Oxford jurors in 1310, 1311, 1312, and 1313 are extraordinary in their detail, providing information about not only the stipulated prices for ale but also the prices of grain as actually purchased in the market of Oxford. See Salter, ed., *Mediaeval archives*, vol. 2, pp. 151–163.

37. The distinction between ale sold *in cuva* and *in doleo* was surely one of measure (with the former smaller than the latter), yet ale sold in smaller measures was usually more expensive, and the inverse holds true in this case. Perhaps ale sold *in doleo* was particularly strong. In any case, the price set for sales *in cuva* was the standard price; see ibid., p. 184.

38. These estimates of costs and receipts have been adjusted for the effects of malting the grain bought in the Oxford market; see Campbell et al., *Medieval capital*, p. 26, n. 13.

39. To estimate a ratio for these expenses, I deleted Harrison's costs for hops and halved his costs for fuel and labor; the remaining expenses (for fuel, herbs, labor, and wear and tear of equipment) represented one-third of Harrison's expenses (with malt accounting for the other two-thirds).

40. Since Oxford's brewers did not seethe their wort in hops, I halved Harrison's estimate for fuel and used the resulting grain:fuel ratio of 85:15 to estimate fuel costs.

41. In September 1311, Joan de Bedford was amerced 2s. for selling ale at 1½d., that is, a farthing above the retail price stipulated in November 1310 and perhaps a halfpenny above the legal price in effect in later months. See Salter, *Mediaeval archives*, vol. 2, pp. 184, 187. In calculating an extra 6¼d. profit from selling at excessive prices, I have assumed an additional profit of a farthing per gallon. As noted above, Oxford aletasters seem to have assessed 3d. per brewing in the early fourteenth century. Joan de Bedford, in other words, paid 2s. because she had brewed on eight occasions.

42. In the hard years that followed, Oxford juries set prices so low that if Joan de Bedford had observed them, she might have made no profit at all. For 1311, 1312, and 1313, the cost of malt and fuel ran from 16d. to 17d., and income would have yielded about 17d. per brewing. These estimates are based on the following: (a) an average brewing of 3 bushels of malt (with a grain:malt ratio of 1:1.14); (b) brewing with equal amounts of wheat, barley, and oats; (c) a cost of grain based on an average of costs specified for each grain; (d) a yield of 7½ gallons per bushel (that is, good ale), and (e) costs for fuel that represent roughly 15 percent of the cost of grain. These estimates make no allowances for the costs of labor, herbs, and equipment.

43. Dyer, *Standards*, pp. 211–233.

44. Another way to calculate profits is to assume that the average cost is best approximated by the average of the four estimated costs in figure 2.1, namely, 1s.11d. Since the Oxford proclamation called specifically for "good ale," the 7½ gallons per bushel represents the most likely yield from brewing, for a receipt of 2s.4d. The profit suggested by this calculation would be 5d. per brewing.

45. The designation of some work as "skilled" and other work as "unskilled" is not, of course, a straightforward process. Brewing required skill, but it was not seen as skilled work. Throughout this book, I will adopt notions of skilled work that would have been familiar to medieval and early modern people, but I would like to emphasize that such notions were rooted more in social values and prejudices than in objective evaluation.

46. Dyer, *Standards*, pp. 133–134.

47. L. F. Salzman, *English industries of the middle ages* (Oxford, 1923).

48. Heather Swanson, "The illusion of economic structure: Craft guilds in late medieval English towns," *Past and Present* 121 (1988), p. 33.

49. For Newcastle (also repeated at Wearmouth), see Adolphus Ballard, ed., *British borough charters*, vol. 1: 1042–1216 (Cambridge, 1913), pp. 157–159. For Bakewell, see Adolphus Ballard and James Tait, eds., *British borough charters*, vol. 2: 1216–1307 (Cambridge, 1923), pp. 221–223. For Hereford, see *Liber Censualis seu Domesday Book*, vol. 1 (London, 1783), p. 179. For some other examples, see Derek Keene, *Survey of medieval Winchester*, i, part 1 (Oxford, 1985), p. 265; Edward Gillett and Kenneth A. MacMahon, eds., *A history of Hull* (Oxford, 1980), pp. 25–26; Mary Bateson, *Borough customs*, vol. 1, Selden Society, 18 (1904), pp. 125, 185; Arthur F. Leach, ed., *Beverley town documents*, Selden Society, 20 (1900), pp. 9, 15; Mary Dormer Harris, *The Coventry leet book*, part 1, EETS, 134 (1907), p. 25; Raftis, *Tenure*, p. 264.

50. See, for example, H. T. Riley, *Munimenta gildhallae Londoniensis*, vol 1: *Liber Albus* (London, 1859), p. 355 (temp. Edward I); and CLB G, p. 4 (1352).

51. *Statutes*, vol. 1, pp. 199–202.

52. Richard Smith, "English peasant life-cycles and socio-economic networks: A quantitative geographical case study," Ph.D. dissertation, University of Cambridge, 1974, pp. 157–163. Because information on male marital status is very difficult to obtain from court records, it seems likely that Smith incorrectly identified some men as bachelors, especially since he categorized male brewers as bachelors "if prior to their first and subsequent appearances in that role there was no reference to them or their wives" (personal communication, February 1990). Given the relative infrequency of references to women in court rolls, I am not at all convinced that the "bachelors" identified by Smith through this method were so, in fact.

53. Monastic brewing constitutes the only major exception to the infrequency of brewing by unmarried males. Students of brewing history have greatly emphasized monastic brewing; see, for example, John P. Arnold, *Origin and history of beer and brewing* (Chicago, 1911), esp. pp. 213–214, 364; and Gregory A. Austin, *Alcohol in Western society from antiquity to 1800* (Santa Barbara, Calif., 1985), p. 53. In England, however, although monasteries boasted sophisticated breweries, production was for consumption, not sale. See, for example, Barbara Harvey, *Living and dying in England, 1100–1540: The monastic experience* (Oxford, 1993). Some secular clergy seemed to have brewed for profit but not enough to have had a substantial effect on the market (see, for example, GL, Ms. 5440, fo. 109). The commercial market was supplied almost exclusively by lay brewers, not by monks, priests, or other clergy.

54. Francis Collins, ed., *Register of the freemen of the city of York, vol. 1: 1272–1558*, Surtees Society, 96 (1897), p. 30. For other male brewers entering in the late fourteenth century, see pp. 46, 50, 58, 61, 82, 87, 103.

55. The only exception is London, where between 1309 and 1312, 34 male brewers gained the freedom: CLB D, pp. 35–179. In other towns, male brewers did not become common until after 1348; R. H. Britnell, *Growth and decline in Colchester 1300–1525* (Cambridge, 1986), p. 196; John Joseph Butt, Jr., "The transition of privilege in medieval urban society: A study of English brewers," Ph.D. dissertation, Rutgers University, 1982, p. 146 (for Norwich); Henry Hartopp, ed., *Register of the freemen of Leicester 1196–1770* (Leicester, 1927), pp. 33, 104; Margery Rowe and Andrew M. Jackson, eds., *Exeter freemen 1266–1967*, Devon and Cornwall Record Society, extra series, 1 (1973), pp. 6, 22, 32; *A Calendar of the freemen of Great Yarmouth 1429–1800* (Norwich, U.K., 1910), p. 19.

56. See, for example, Smith, "English peasant life-cycles," pp. 150–178, and Bennett, *Women*, p. 123, n. 56. In my study of Brigstock, I treated women whose marital status was never stated as being of "unknown marital status," but I now think it is very likely that most such women were not married.

57. Smith, "English peasant life-cycles," pp. 150–178; Bennett, *Women*, p. 123.

58. For Wallingford, Leicester, Norwich, and Tamworth, see appendix.

59. The quote is from Richard Smith, "Demographic developments," p. 73.

60. NtnRO, Montagu Collection, Box X364A, roll 4: 29/9/1295.

61. Richard M. Smith, "Some issues concerning families and their property in rural England 1250–1800," in Richard M. Smith, ed., *Land, kinship and life-cycle* (Cambridge, 1984), pp. 1–86, esp. pp. 27–30.

62. Marjorie Keniston McIntosh, *Autonomy and community: The royal manor of Havering, 1200–1500* (Cambridge, 1986), pp. 173–174.

63. Married by 1291, she was cited for brewing once in 1313, 14 times in 1314, 10 times in 1315, 4 times in 1316, twice in 1320, and once in 1322. NtnRO, Montagu Collection, Box X364B.

64. She was cited for brewing once in 1309, once in 1311, 10 times in 1314, 6 times in 1315, once in 1316, 11 times in 1326, 4 times in 1328, and once in 1331. See NtnRO, Montagu Collection, Boxes X364A, X364B, X365.

65. Bennett, *Women*, pp. 273–274, n. 56.

66. Kowaleski, *Local markets*, pp. 133–136.

67. Zvi Razi, *Life, marriage and death in a medieval parish* (Cambridge, 1980), esp. p. 138, n. 76.

68. Smith, "English peasant life-cycles," pp. 150–178.

69. Edwin DeWindt, *Land and people in Holywell-cum-Needingworth* (Toronto, 1972), pp. 235–239; Edward Britton, *The community of the vill* (Toronto, 1977), pp. 87–88; J. Ambrose Raftis, *Warboys: Two hundred years in the life of an English mediaeval village* (Toronto, 1974), pp. 236–240; Tim Lomas, "Southeast Durham: Late fourteenth and fifteenth centuries," in P. D. A. Harvey, ed., *The peasant land market in medieval England* (Oxford, 1984), p. 323; Helena Graham, "A social and economic study of the late medieval peasantry: Alrewas, Staffordshire in the fourteenth century," Ph.D. dissertation, University of Birmingham, 1994, pp. 201–214; Postles, "Brewing and the peasant economy," p. 140.

70. Smith, "English peasant life-cycles," p. 168. Razi, *Life, marriage*, p. 138, n. 76, p. 70.

71. Michael Prestwich, *York civic ordinances, 1301*, Borthwick Papers, 49 (1976), pp. 25–26. I traced the individuals named in this list (and in some cases, their male kin) in the following sources: (a) the York freedom register (Collins, *Register*); (b) R. H. Skaife, "Civic officials of York and parliamentary representatives" (three manuscript volumes deposited in the York City Library); and (c) R. B. Dobson, *York city chamberlains' account rolls, 1396–1500*, Surtees Society, 192 (1980), pp. 207–213. *VCH, Oxon.*, vol. 4, p. 47. *CLB A*, p. 220. Ellen Wedemeyer Moore, *The fairs of medieval England* (Toronto, 1985), pp. 261–262.

72. For examples of transient or landless brewers, see Bennett, *Women*, p. 122; Smith, "English peasant life-cycles," pp. 166–168; M. Patricia Hogan, "The labor of their days—work in the medieval village," *Studies in Medieval and Renaissance History* 8 (1986), p. 104. For the Norwich example, see Norwich Leets #2. For itinerant brewers, see Smith, "English peasant life-cycles," p. 161; Raftis, *Warboys*, pp. 238–239 (1292); University of Keele Library, Tamworth court rolls, court for 5 November 1296 (prohibition against brewing by *mulieres alienas*); Moore, *Fairs*, p. 257n; Sample: Woolhope, c. 1325.

73. Bennett, *Women*, pp. 122–123. Of the 38 by-industrial brewsters in Brigstock, 23 came from stable families and they accounted for 1,427 ale citations, or an average of 62 each. The 15 by-industrial brewsters from unstable or unidentified families accounted for 838 citations, or an average of 56 each.

74. See NtnRO, Montagu Collection, Box X365.

75. Margery the wife of Richard Mabli received 37 citations for brewing between 1318 and 1340; Agnes the wife of Walter Tracy was cited on 33 occasions between 1302 and 1322; Sarra Soule was presented 40 times between 1311 and 1340. See NtnRO, Montagu Collection, Boxes X364A, X364B, X365.

76. Isabella Huet was cited for brewing or baking on 3 occasions between 1295 and 1298; Alice Carpenter brewed for profit once in 1311; Alice Somenur brewed on 5 occasions between 1301 and 1306; Alice Pikerel brewed 14 times between 1309 and 1325; Edith Aylward brewed once in 1304; Edith Cocus brewed once in 1303. See NtnRO, Montagu Collection, Boxes X364A, X364B.

77. I have discussed these issues more fully in "Medieval women, modern women: Across the great divide," in David Aers, ed., *Culture and history 1350–1600: Essays on English communities, identities, and writing* (London, 1992), pp. 147–175, and "'History that stands still': Women's work in the European past," *Feminist Studies* 14 (1988), pp. 269–283.

78. Hogan, "Labor," p. 104; H. W. Gidden, ed., *The stewards' books of Southampton*, vol. 1 (1428–1434), Southampton Record Society, 35 (1935), pp. 53, 110; CPR, 1313–1317, p. 543; CPR, 1317–1321, p. 25; PRO, E101 364/8, 505/23.

79. PRO, E101 361/30.

80. Kate Mertes, *The English noble household* (Oxford, 1988), pp. 57–59.

81. C. M. Woolgar, ed., *Household accounts from medieval England*, Records of Social and Economic History, n.s., 17 (1992), passim in item 14. See also Mary Dormer Harris, ed., "The account of the great household of Humphrey, First Duke of Buckingham, for the year 1452–3," in *Camden Miscellany,* vol. 28, Camden Society, 4th series, 29 (1984), pp. 1–57, esp. pp. 37, 49.

82. Moore, *Fairs,* esp. pp. 256–262.

83. The best discussion of this remains Olwen Hufton, "Women and the family economy in eighteenth-century France," *French Historical Studies* 9 (1975), pp. 1–22.

84. The difference between these two perspectives—that women freely choose certain work or that they accommodate themselves to circumstances—was the basic disagreement in the recent and notorious *Sears* case in the United States. For further information on this case, see "Women's history goes to trial: EEOC v. *Sears Roebuck and Company,*" *Signs: Journal of Women in Culture and Society* 11 (1986), pp. 751–779; Ruth Milkman, "Women's history and the Sears case," *Feminist Studies* 12 (1986), pp. 375–400; Joan W. Scott, "The Sears case," *Gender and the politics of history* (New York, 1988), pp. 167–177.

85. Sanford Brown Meech, ed., *The Book of Margery Kempe,* EETS, 212 (1940), pp. 9–10.

86. Bennett, *Women,* p. 128.

87. See, for example, YAS, MD 225/1/99 (tourn for 8 April 1374): *Thomas de Westerton noluit permittere uxorem suam vendere cervisiam Willelmo Parker extra domum suam.* See also a case in Herstmonceux in 1386, when William Colkyn requested an extension on a debt of 10d. that he owed to Robert Baker; he planned to pay the debt after his wife had brewed and sold ale. I am grateful to Christopher Whittick for providing the information about this incident, found in Harvard Law School, court roll 77/1 (court for 29 April 1387).

88. Collins, *Register,* pp. 14, 25, 75. Of the few dozen women entering York's freedom before 1349, most lacked a stated occupation, but one was a pelter, one a mercer, and two brewsters.

89. For Howden, see "Assessment roll of the poll-tax for Howdenshire, etc., in the second year of the reign of King Richard II (1379)," *Yorkshire Archaeological and Topographical Journal* 9 (1886), pp. 129–162, at 129–132. For Oxford, see PRO, E179 161/47.

90. Mary Bateson, *Borough Customs,* vol. 1, pp. 185–186, and vol. 2, Selden Society, 21 (1906), p. xxx.

91. R. H. Hilton, *The English peasantry of the later middle ages* (Oxford, 1975), p. 105. Lori A. Gates might also have found some female aletasters in Longbridge Deverill before the plague (personal communication, July 1994). I am grateful to her for this information.

92. Indeed, because the ale presentments of Bridgwater were householder-focused, Nicholas Marlere was usually cited for brewing actually undertaken by his wife. For a citation that mentions both of them, see Dilks, *Bridgwater archives,* vol. 2, p. 50.

Chapter 3

1. "Assessment roll of the poll-tax for Howdenshire, etc., in the second year of the reign of King Richard II (1379)," *Yorkshire Archaeological and Topographical Journal* 9 (1886), pp. 129–162. This return is exceptional for including notations about the occupations of wives.

2. The poll tax of 1379 was assessed on all persons over 16 years of age, who paid from 4d. to £5 (based on rank and status). Husbands and wives were treated as single individuals (that is, the minimum tax due from a married couple was 4d., not 8d.). The 88 not-married women in Howden included 74 servants, laborers, and widows (who

paid 4d.); a woman of unknown employment and tax; 4 women in miscellaneous trades (who paid 6d., 6d., 12d., and 2s.); and 9 brewsters (3 paid 12d., 4 paid 6d., and 2 paid unknown amounts). Not-married brewsters paid an average of 8¼d., as opposed to an average of 6¼d. for all bachelors, more than 18d. for bachelors in skilled occupations (excluding laborers and servants), 8d. for married couples, and more than 11d. for married couples in skilled occupations. I am grateful to Sandy Bardsley for her assistance in calculating some of these figures.

3. Of 11 married couples in brewing, 9 employed servants; 1 paid 6d., 5 paid 12d., 4 paid 2s., and 1 paid an unknown amount. The bachelor paid 2s. Since married couples were treated as one person for the purposes of the 1379 tax, the lower taxes paid by not-married brewsters reflect not their smaller households but their lesser wealth. The brewster Denise daughter of William de Yeland was listed as a member of her father's household.

4. See the appendix for a full explanation of the methods used in this study to distinguish married and not-married brewsters.

5. Sample: Norwich Leets #2 (1288–89).

6. Richard Smith and his students have suggested that the "European marriage pattern" (characterized by late marriage and large proportions of never-married adults) prevailed in late medieval as well as early modern England. See especially the following: Richard Smith, "Some reflections on the evidence for the origins of the 'European Marriage Pattern' in England," in Chris Harris, ed., The sociology of the family: New directions for Britain (Totowa, N.J., 1979), pp. 74–112, and "Demographic developments in rural England, 1300–1348," in Bruce M. S. Campbell, ed., Before the Black Death: Studies in the "crisis" of the early fourteenth century (Manchester, 1991), pp. 25–78; essays by Richard Smith, P. J. P. Goldberg, and Peter Biller in P. J. P. Goldberg, ed., Woman is a worthy wight: Women in English society, c. 1200–1500 (Phoenix Mill, U.K., 1992); P. J. P. Goldberg, Women, work and life cycle in a medieval economy (Oxford, 1992); and L. R. Poos, A rural society after the Black Death: Essex 1350–1525 (Cambridge, 1991). Others have disagreed, suggesting not only that people married early but also that marriage was almost universal. See especially, Zvi Razi, Life, marriage and death in a medieval parish (Cambridge, 1980); and Barbara Hanawalt, The ties that bound: Peasant families in medieval England (New York, 1986). I find the position of Smith and his students to be more convincing, and I anticipate that it will soon be fully discussed in Smith's long-awaited book on the population history of medieval England. For the frequency of de facto divorce and desertion, see Michael M. Sheehan, "The formation and stability of marriage in fourteenth-century England: Evidence of an Ely register," Mediaeval Studies 33 (1971), pp. 228–263. For housing and the phenomenon known as "spinster clustering," see Goldberg, Women, work, pp. 305–323.

7. Emma Kempstere was presented by the aletasters of Brigstock on 121 occasions: 2 in 1313–20, 16 in the 1320s, 50 in the 1330s, and 53 in the 1340s. See the Brigstock court rolls at NtnRO, Montagu Collection, Boxes X364A, X364B, X365.

8. For Brundall, see Sample: Norwich Leets #4–9; Brundall was not named as a brewer in leet #5 (1292–93), and no brewers were presented in leet #8 (1307). Although occupational identifications in freedom registers and poll tax listings mask the fluidity of occupational identity, they do reliably indicate that women noted as brewsters derived the main part of their income from the ale trade. For the York freewomen, see Francis Collins, ed., Register of the freemen of the city of York, vol. 1: 1272–1558, Surtees Society, 96 (1897), pp. 14, 19, 25, 30. For Maud London, see Oxford Assizes. For the poll taxes, see for Howden, "Assessment roll"; for Oxford, PRO, E179 161/47; for Southwark, PRO, E179 184/30; for York, Neville Bartlett, ed., The lay poll tax returns for the city of York in 1381 (London, 1953).

9. "Assessment roll."

10. Needless to say, the working circumstances of widows varied widely. Some widows lived much like wives, with adequate space, labor, and time to combine commercial brewing with their other work. But other widows lived more like singlewomen, either in the households of others or in small households, and with little independent work or time. See Caroline M. Barron and Anne F. Sutton, eds., *Medieval London widows 1300–1500* (London, 1994); Louise Mirrer, ed., *Upon my husband's death: Widows in the literature and histories of medieval Europe* (Ann Arbor, Mich., 1992); and Sue Sheridan Walker, ed., *Wife and widow in medieval England* (Ann Arbor, Mich., 1993). For brewing by servants, see M. Patricia Hogan, "The labor of their days—work in the medieval village," *Studies in Medieval and Renaissance History* 8 (1986), p. 104. For Warboys, see J. Ambrose Raftis, *Warboys: Two hundred years in the life of an English mediaeval village* (Toronto, 1974), pp. 238–239.

11. Judith M. Bennett, *Women in the medieval English countryside* (New York, 1987), pp. 115–129.

12. Maryanne Kowaleski, *Local markets and regional trade in medieval Exeter* (Cambridge, 1995), pp. 131–133.

13. Ibid., tables 3.4, A3.1.

14. Ibid., pp. 132–136.

15. See, for example, Richard Smith, "English peasant life-cycles and socio-economic networks: A quantitative geographical case study," Ph.D. dissertation, University of Cambridge, 1974, pp. 150–178.

16. PRO, E179 161/47. Similarly in the York poll tax of 1381, some widows paid quite high assessments, but the only woman identified with an occupation who paid more than the average assessment was a brewer: Bartlett, *Poll tax for York*. The relative prosperity of not-married brewsters was not invariable. In Leicester, not-married brewsters contributed considerably less to the tallage of 1286 than did other not-married women: Leicestershire Record Office, BR III/7/2 (cannemol list for 1287–88), BR III/4/27 (tallage for 1286). In Southwark, the three brewsters noted in the 1381 tax paid assessments roughly equivalent to those paid by other not-married women: PRO, E179 184/30. In some of these cases, it is possible that prosperous widows of wealthy men skew the data on the average wealth of not-married women. The higher assessments paid by not-married brewsters in some places—higher, that is, compared to other not-married women—reflected not only the profitability of the trade but also its capital requirements. In other words, brewsters might have had to be relatively better off than other not-married women in order to take up the trade.

17. R. R. Sharpe, ed., *Calendar of wills proved and enrolled in the Court of Husting, London 1258–1688, vol. 1* (London, 1889), pp. 145–146, 577. Similarly, the tanners of early fourteenth-century London often seem to have assumed that their widows could best support themselves through brewing. See Derek Keene, "Tanners' Widows, 1300–1350," in Barron and Sutton, *Medieval London widows*, pp. 17–18.

18. Heather Swanson, *Medieval artisans: An urban class in late medieval England* (Oxford, 1989); Derek Keene, "Continuity and development in urban trades: Problems of concepts and the evidence," in Penelope J. Corfield and Derek Keene, eds., *Work in Towns 850–1850* (Leicester, 1990), pp. 1–16; R. H. Britnell, *The commercialisation of English society 1000–1500* (Cambridge, 1993).

19. Christopher Dyer, "Changes in diet in the late middle ages: The case of harvest workers," *Agricultural History Review* 36 (1988), pp. 21–37, and *Standards of living in the later middle ages* (Cambridge, 1989). Evelyn M. Myatt-Price, "A tally of ale," *Journal of the Royal Statistical Society*, series A (general), 123 (1960), pp. 62–67. For an example of the decline of cider making in the late fourteenth century, see John Summers Drew, "The Manor of Silk-

stead" (typescript, Winchester, 1947; copy deposited at the Institute of Historical Research, University of London), p. 111.

20. Margery Kirkbride James, *Studies in the medieval wine trade* (Oxford, 1971), esp. pp. 1–69. Dyer, *Standards*, pp. 104–105, and "English diet in the later middle ages," in T. H. Aston et al., eds., *Social relations and ideas: Essays in honour of R. H. Hilton* (Cambridge, 1983), pp. 196–197.

21. Kate Mertes, *The English noble household, 1250–1600* (Oxford, 1988), esp. pp. 58–59. Christopher Dyer, "The consumer and the market in the later middle ages," *Economic History Review*, 2nd series, 42 (1989), p. 325.

22. C. M. Woolgar, ed., *Household accounts from medieval England, part 1* (Oxford, 1992), item 14, pp. 261–430. It is, of course, quite possible that Warner's wife was the brewer who supplied the Mitford household, even though he was noted in the accounts. See also Dyer, "Consumer," p. 311.

23. Rising consumption also led to a marked expansion in the cultivation of brewing grains. I am grateful to James A. Galloway for showing me his unpublished paper, "Driven by drink? Ale consumption and the agrarian economy of the London region c. 1300–1400."

24. I thank James Galloway and Margaret Murphy of the Centre for Metropolitan History for information about barley prices in London. Of course, grain prices were sometimes high in the late fourteenth century (in 1390, barley cost 9s. a bushel), and in such cases, the relative stability of ale prices could—as was so often the case in the early fourteenth century—hurt brewers. Prices did vary somewhat, with a gallon of the best ale usually ordered to be sold at either 1¼d or 2d. Needless to say, brewers did not necessarily observe the proclaimed prices. For the generally downward trend in grain prices in the later middle ages, see David L. Farmer, "Prices and wages, 1350–1500," in Edward Miller, ed., *The agrarian history of England and Wales, vol. 3: 1348–1500* (Cambridge, 1991), esp. table 5.1, p. 444.

25. Although historians have noted changes in brewing over the course of the later middle ages, most have emphasized the supposed rapidity and uniqueness of Tudor changes in the industry; see Patricia Smith, "The brewing industry in Tudor England," M.A. thesis, Concordia University, 1981; and Peter Clark, *The English alehouse: A social history 1200–1820* (London, 1983). As my discussion is meant to suggest, 1350 might be a more important dividing line in the industrial history of brewing than 1500.

26. Oxford Assizes (the assize for 1351 listed 33 brewers and 69 regraters); Norwich Leets; *CLB G*, p. 150; Derek Keene, *Survey of medieval Winchester, i, part 1* (Oxford, 1985), pp. 267–269; M. K. Dale, *Court rolls of Tamworth* (typescript available in the Institute of Historical Research), pp. 103, 115, 123, 124; appendix (for villages noted).

27. For Wye, see PRO, SC2 182/20. For other examples, see Sample: Alciston, c. 1370, c. 1425; Crowle, c. 1470; Wakefield, c. 1370; Stockton, 1383 (Wiltshire Record Office, 108/10). See also Clark, *English alehouse*, p. 29.

28. PRO, Durham 3/12.

29. Ale could also be brought from the country into towns. See Goldberg, *Women, work*, pp. 142–143; ale from Polslo sold in Exeter (I am grateful to Maryanne Kowaleski for this information, which can be found in the Devon Record Office, EQMT for 1362, 1378, 1389); and ale from the countryside sold in Northwich and Middlewich, as noted in the *Register of Edward the Black Prince, part 3 (Palatinate of Chester), 1351–1365* (London, 1932), p. 48 (I am grateful to Wayne Lee for bringing this reference to my attention). In none of the villages sampled did I encounter clear evidence that ale had ceased to be produced on site; indeed, in most villages, as long as assize presentments continued (usually well into the sixteenth century), brewers continued to be named. In early sixteenth-century

Alciston, brewers of ale were amerced alongside tipplers of beer, suggesting that beer might have been brought to the village from elsewhere. See the appendix. For beer sent out of London, see T. S. Willan, *The inland trade: Studies in English internal trade in the sixteenth and seventeenth centuries* (Manchester, 1976), p. 30. For beer from Burton-on-Trent purchased by a late fifteenth-century gentry family in Derbyshire, see Dyer, "Consumer," p. 316.

30. *CLB* I, p. 63, and CLRO, Letter Book I, fos. 65v.–66; P. Studer, ed., *The Oak Book of Southampton*, vol. 1, Southampton Record Society, 6 (1910), pp. 142, 144; Patricia Smith, "Brewing industry," pp. 23–24. Some of these ordinances addressed beerbrewers, as well as alebrewers.

31. Edwin B. DeWindt, *Land and People in Holywell-cum-Needingworth* (Toronto, 1972), pp. 235–236, n. 157; J. Ambrose Raftis, *Warboys*, pp. 236–240; unpublished research of David Postles on brewing in Kibworth Harcourt, c. 1276–1375 (I thank him for providing a summary of his work); Helena Graham, "'A woman's work . . .': Labour and gender in the late medieval countryside," in Goldberg, Worthy wight, pp. 136–144; Christopher Dyer, *Lords and peasants in a changing society* (Cambridge, 1980), pp. 346–349; David Postles, "Brewing and the peasant economy: Some manors in late medieval Devon," *Rural History* 3 (1992), pp. 133–144; Marjorie Keniston McIntosh, *Autonomy and community: The royal manor of Havering, 1200–1500* (Cambridge, 1986), p. 228.

32. For Oxford, see trends discussed more fully in chapter 6. For London, see trends discussed more fully in chapter 4. For Colchester, see R. H. Britnell, *Growth and decline in Colchester 1300–1525* (Cambridge, 1986), esp. pp. 193–197. Given the changes occurring in brewing at this time, Britnell's use of these data to trace population decline seems ill advised. For Winchester, see Keene, *Winchester*, pp. 267–268. For Norwich, compare numbers of persons presented in leets, for example, Norwich Leets #2 (286 brewers) and #11 (208 brewers). For Southampton, the incorporated gild of 1543 included only eight beerbrewers and five alebrewers: SRO, Ms. Deeds, Henry VIII, no. 371. For York, compare Sample: York, c. 1450 to Sample: York, c. 1560. For Leicester, compare declining numbers of brewers in cannemol lists (as cited in the appendix).

33. Clark suggests this in *English alehouse*, p. 32.

34. W. T. Mitchell, ed., *Registrum Cancellarii 1498–1506*, Oxford Historical Society, n.s., 27 (1980), pp. 103–104. This rotation is discussed more fully in chapter 6.

35. P. D. A. Harvey, *A medieval Oxfordshire village: Cuxham, 1240–1400* (Oxford, 1965), p. 145.

36. For rotations, see Mitchell, *Registrum*, pp. 103–104, and Dyer, *Lords and peasants*, p. 347. For brewers compelled to pursue their trade in certain ways, see H. T. Riley, ed., *Munimenta gildhallae Londoniensis*, vol. 1: *Liber albus*, Rolls Series, 12:1 (1859), pp. 358–360; CLB H, p. 183; OUA, Chancellor's Court Register for 1506–14, fos. 197v.–198; PRO, Durham 3/12; J. A. Raftis, *Tenure and mobility: Studies in the social history of the mediaeval English village* (Toronto, 1964), pp. 126, 264.

37. Sample: Hindolveston, c. 1380 (Folshams); BL, Add. Ch. 24716, 24340–24350 (Warner); Sample: Crowle, c. 1420; Dyer, *Lords and peasants*, p. 212 (Thomas Russhemere). See the appendix for further examples.

38. John Joseph Butt, "The transition of privilege in medieval urban society: A study of English brewers," Ph.D. dissertation, Rutgers University, 1982, pp. 146–147; NRO, D/16/a1, Mayor's court book for 1440–56, fos. 95–96, and D/16/a2, Mayor's court book for 1510–32. The increased use of occupational identifications by brewers and other craftspeople was influenced in part by the 1413 Statute of Additions, which required that persons appearing before royal courts be identified by social rank or occupation. Gild formation is discussed more fully in chapter 4.

39. Of 548 households involved in commercial brewing in early fifteenth-century London, for example, at least 49 were also active in victualing or related trades, 22 in clothing or textile trades, 8 in leather and skin trades, and 32 in miscellaneous trades. These additional employments are discussed more fully in chapter 4. See also Kowaleski, *Local markets*, pp. 134–135, table 4.4.

40. For examples of presentments made to these two Thomas Mascals, see BL, Add. Ch. 24343 (28 brewers named in 1386) and 24373 (2 brewers named in 1479).

41. CLB H, p. 122; CLRO, Letter Book H, fo. cviib. Dorothy M. Owen, ed., *The making of King's Lynn*, British Academy Records of Social and Economic History, n.s., 9 (1984), pp. 420–421.

42. Bodleian Library, Ms. Top. Oxon. c. 235. In these accounts, ale was measured in quarters (which, in Oxford, contained 17½ gallons).

43. GL, Ms. 25,172.

44. Helena M. Chew and William Kellaway, eds., *The London assize of nuisance 1301–1431*, London Record Society, 10 (1973), item 646; CLB L, p. 232; CLRO, Letter Book L, fos. 217v.–218; Oxfordshire Record Office, Bridgewater Deeds #105.

45. Caroline M. Barron, "The fourteenth century poll tax returns for Worcester," *Midland History* 14 (1989), p. 9.

46. See, for example, the data on households employing servants in Goldberg, *Women, work*, table 3.1.

47. CPMR, vol. 1, p. 235; CPMR, vol. 2, p. 148; CCR, 1385–89, p. 658; CPMR, vol. 2, p. 204; CLRO, Mayor's Court Bills, MC1/2A, item 20.

48. CLB I, pp. 50–51; CLRO, Letter Book I, fos. 51v.–52v.; GL, Ms. 5440, esp. fos. 22v., 38–41v., 130–130v., 292v.; CLRO, Journal 3, fos. 176/162, 169/166, and Journal 7, fo. 95v.

49. For Oxford, see PRO, E179 161/47; VCH, Oxon., vol. 4, pp. 45–48; Carl I. Hammer, Jr., "Some social and institutional aspects of town-gown relations in late medieval and Tudor Oxford," Ph.D. dissertation, University of Toronto, 1973, pp. 145–150. For Southwark, see PRO, E179 184/30. For York, see Bartlett, *Poll tax for York*. For Worcester, see Barron, "Poll tax returns for Worcester." The same seems to have been true in late medieval Chester, where probably "only the wealthiest townswomen . . . brewed on a substantial scale." Jane Laughton, "The alewives of later medieval Chester," in Rowena E. Archer, ed., *Crown, government and people in the fifteenth century* (New York, 1995), pp. 191–208, quote from p. 203.

50. In Birdbrook, some brewers "were from the wealthier and socially important section" of the community, but others were landless or held little land. I am grateful to Phillipp Schofield for permission to quote from his Ph.D. dissertation, "Land, family and inheritance in a later medieval community: Birdbrook, 1292–1412," University of Oxford, 1992, pp. 369–377. On Alciston manor, brewers tended to come from families of middling status; compare the rental for 1432–33 (ESRO, SAS/G45/13, E315/56) to brewers cited in those years (ESRO, SAS/G18/44).

51. In Stockton, for example, two brewers active in the 1520s (Thomas Hopkins and Harry Sylvester) were assessed substantial sums in the 1524 tax; PRO, E179 197/156. But in Earl Soham, only one brewing household (that of Olivia and Alexander Peyntour) was taxed in 1524, and it was assessed (on wages, not goods) the very modest sum of 20s; PRO, E179 180/154.

52. For example, brewers in Oxford benefited from the reorganization of Oxford's economy away from manufacturing and toward service. See also *Statutes*, 3 Henry VIII, c. 8.

53. Patricia Smith, "Brewing industry," esp. pp. 82–90.

54. See Sample: Crowle, c. 1470; York, c. 1595.

55. For Stockton, see Sample, where ale infractions were recorded against not-married women and married men as follows: 1281—99, 28 females and 109 males (that is, married couples); 1306—44, 42 females and 281 males; 1349—99, 95 females and 802 males; 1400—47, 30 females and 437 males; 1455—93, no females and 48 males. For Norwich, see Norwich Leets #2 (46 not-married women of 286 households cited), #9 (32 not-married women of 249 households cited), and #11 (14 not-married women of 208 households cited). For York, see YCA, House Book 23, fos. 50v.ff. (many of the women identified as wives were actually widows). See the appendix both for fuller information on the methods used to distinguish not-married and married brewsters and for further examples of the slow decline of brewing by not-married women. See especially Alciston, Chedzoy, Cranborne, Crowle, Norton Canon, Preston-on-Wye, Wakefield, and Leicester. Not-married and married brewsters could not be distinguished in the records of many communities, and for other communities, the available data are very limited. Yet I encountered not a single village or town in which brewing by not-married women increased or even remained steady. Other scholars who have noted women's declining participation in brewing might, in fact, actually have been observing the decline of not-married brewsters, not brewsters per se. See, for example, David Gary Shaw, *The creation of a community:The city of Wells in the middle ages* (Oxford, 1993), p. 250. The decline of not-married brewsters is not part of a general demographic trend; the evidence is sketchy, but there were, if anything, rather more not-married women in England after 1350 than before (I am grateful to Richard Smith for discussing this matter with me).

56. Mitchell, *Registrum*, pp. 103—104.

57. *VCH, Oxon., vol. 4*, p. 101.

58. Helen M. Jewell, ed., *The court rolls of the manor of Wakefield from September 1348 to September 1350*, YAS Wakefield Court Roll Series, 2 (1981), pp. 64, 125.

59. CLRO, MC1/1, item 179. For numerous other examples, see CLRO, Mayor's Court Bills, MC1/1—4.

60. CLRO, MC1/3, item 6. The money was owed for "diverse merchandise of huckstery." For some further discussion of the debts carried by brewers, see Clark, *English alehouse*, p. 102.

61. I have discussed extensively the economic disadvantages of women in my "Medieval women, modern women: Across the great divide," in David Aers, ed., *Culture and history 1350—1600: Essays on English communities, identities and writing* (London, 1992), pp. 147—175. In addition to the many works cited there, see Goldberg, *Women, work*, esp. pp. 82—157. See also Amy Louise Erickson, *Women and property in early modern England* (London, 1993). One difficult question is the standard against which not-married women's economic status should be measured. Goldberg (p. 104) asserts that the economic activities of not-married men were as limited as those of not-married women, but direct comparisons are lacking (in part because it is very difficult to identify unmarried men). Against Goldberg's assertion, two things should be noted. First, not-married men generally received better training than not-married women and inherited more in goods or property; even if their economic activities in adolescence were as limited as those of not-married women, men's prospects were much better. See Bennett, *Women*, pp. 65—99; and Ilana Krausman Ben-Amos, "Women apprentices in the trades and crafts of early modern Bristol," *Continuity and Change* 6 (1991), pp. 227—252. Second, the skewed sex ratios of many towns meant that not-married women were much more likely to remain unmarried throughout their lives; in such instances, a comparison of the economic roles of, say, 40-year-old singlewomen with 15-year-old bachelors is not very useful. For the poverty of adult singlewomen, see Pamela Sharpe, "Literally spinsters: A new interpretation of local economy and demography in Colyton in the seventeenth and eighteenth centuries," *Eco-

nomic History Review, 2nd series, 44 (1991), pp. 46–65; and Diane Willen, "Women in the public sphere in early modern England: The case of the urban working poor," Sixteenth Century Journal 19 (1988), pp. 559–575.

62. PRO, E179 184/30. Of the 21 brewing households headed by men, 9 (those married couples paying 2s. or less and the two singletons paying 12d.) were comparable in wealth to those headed by women. The data from the 1381 poll tax returns for Oxford (PRO, E179 161/47) and York (Bartlett, Poll tax for York) show brewsters and brewers paying more equivalent amounts.

63. CLRO, MC1/3/119. See this and other bills from the Mayor's Court for many other instances of brewers' debts for malt. My remarks here must be only cursory, but the use of credit to finance premodern brewing is worthy of further investigation. For credit in general, see especially M. M. Postan, "Credit in medieval trade" and "Private financial instruments in medieval England," Medieval trade and finance (Cambridge, 1973), pp. 1–27, 28–64.

64. M. A. Holderness, "Credit in English rural society before the nineteenth century, with special reference to the period 1650–1720," Agricultural History Review 24 (1976), p. 102; Marjorie K. McIntosh, "Money lending on the periphery of London, 1300–1600," Albion 20 (1988), pp. 557–571; Jennifer I. Kermode, "Money and credit in the fifteenth century: Some lessons from Yorkshire," Business History Review 65 (1991), pp. 475–501; and "Medieval indebtedness: The regions versus London," in Nicholas Rogers, ed., England in the fifteenth century, Harlaxton Medieval Studies, 4 (1994), pp. 72–88; Elaine Clark, "Debt litigation in a late medieval English vill," in J. A. Raftis, ed., Pathways to medieval peasants (Toronto, 1981), pp. 247–279; Elizabeth Zwanzig Bennett, "Debt and credit in the urban economy: London, 1380–1460," Ph.D. dissertation, Yale University, 1989. These studies rarely discuss male/female differences in the credit market for one simple reason: female creditors and debtors were very few. For example, of 171 Wiltshire extents for debts, only 5 involved women in any capacity. See Angela Conyers, ed., Wiltshire Extents for Debts, Edward I–Elizabeth I, Wiltshire Record Society, 28 (1972), esp. p. 8.

65. Some widows invested in mortgages and other ventures, but cash-rich widows were an exceptional minority, extending only a small proportion of loans. Holderness, "Credit," esp. p. 105, and "Widows in pre-industrial society: An essay upon their economic functions," in Richard M. Smith, ed., Land, kinship and life-cycle (Cambridge, 1984), pp. 435–442. Although some widows had assets to lend, many widows were desperately poor. See, for example, Erickson, Women and property, pp. 200–202.

66. Mary Bateson, ed., Borough customs, vol. 1, Selden Society, 18 (1904), p. 224. Since Bateson's pioneering work on the legal status of townswomen, little work has been done on this much neglected and rich topic.

67. A. H. Thomas, ed., Calendar of early mayor's court rolls 1298–1307 (London, 1924), pp. 214–215.

68. Maryanne Kowaleski, "Women's work in a market town: Exeter in the late fourteenth century," in Barbara A. Hanawalt, ed., Women and work in preindustrial Europe (Bloomington, Ind., 1986), pp. 149–150. See also William Chester Jordan, Women and credit in preindustrial and developing societies (Philadelphia, 1993), esp. pp. 23–25; and Jane Laughton, "Women in the court: Some evidence from fifteenth-century Chester," in Rogers, England, pp. 95–96.

69. For Oxford, see PRO, E179 161/47. For Southwark, see PRO, E179 184/30. I am grateful to Martha Carlin for sharing with me her analyses of this poll tax. For late medieval London, see CPMR, vol. 2, p. 148 (1372); GL, Ms. 5440, fos. 22v., 38–41v., and 130–130v.

70. Goldberg, Women, work, p. 98.

71. Peter Franklin, "Peasant widows' 'liberation' and remarriage before the Black Death," *Economic History Review*, 2nd series, 39 (1986), pp. 194–195.

72. *The court leet records of the manor of Manchester*, vol. 1, 1552–1586 (Manchester, 1884), pp. 240–241 (from which all the quotes in this paragraph are taken). Popular anxiety about not-married women is a subject worthy of further investigation; it is as yet unclear whether orders such as this reflect rising anxiety or merely better extant documentation. Concern was also expressed about independent men; see especially, A. L. Beier, *Masterless men: The vagrancy problem in England 1560–1640* (London, 1985).

73. Brewing in London and Oxford is discussed more fully in chapters 4 and 6, respectively. In Southampton, almost all women cited as brewers were either wives or (more often) widows who continued the trade of their husbands. See, for example, the widow of John Beerbrewer, whose cousin stood in her stead; SRO, Stewards' Accounts, SC 5/1/15–18.

74. Oxford Assizes. The relative poverty of alesellers can be clearly seen by comparing alesellers, brewsters, and brewers in the Oxford poll tax of 1381; PRO, E179 161/47. For another example of the preponderance of not-married women among alesellers, see Sample: Wakefield, c. 1370.

75. Keith Wrightson, "Alehouses, order and reformation in rural England, 1590–1660," in Eileen and Stephen Yeo, eds., *Popular culture and class conflict 1590–1914* (Atlantic Highlands, N.J., 1981), p. 24, n. 11; and Clark, *English alehouse*, pp. 78–80. See also Alice Clark, *Working life of women in the seventeenth century* (1919), pp. 230–233.

76. Quoted in Peter Clark, *English alehouse*, p. 79.

77. For women employed by Oxford brewers to carry ale to customers, see especially the proscription of such employment in the draft incorporation of brewers c. 1585 (see OUA, WP ß/B/33). For an example of a woman employed as a tippler for a brewer, see CPMR, vol. 2, pp. 145–146.

78. See, for example, regulations for servants in GL, Ms. 5440, fos. 22v., 38–41v., 130–131.

79. See Barron and Sutton, *Medieval London widows*; Mirrer, *Upon my husband's death*; and Walker, *Wife and widow*.

80. For Denise Marlere and her husband, see chapter 2. For the wills of Mitchell Alleson, Lawrence Stringer, and Joan Alleson alias Stringer, see PRO: PROB 11/42A, fo. 349v.; PROB 11/52, fo. 158v.; PROB 11/56, fos. 335v.–336. For the will of Henry Alleson, see GL, Ms. 9171/16, fos. 397v.–398; and for an administration of the will of Ralph Alleson, see GL, Ms. 9168/15, fo. 116v. Mitchell Alleson got his start in brewing from his employer, Alice Flaxton, herself a brewer's widow; see PRO: PROB 11/20, fo. 152; PROB 11/39, fos. 153v.–156. For the activities of all these people in the Brewers' gild, see GL, Ms. 5442.

81. The evidence presented here of shrinking opportunities for not-married brewsters after 1348 cannot be reconciled with the arguments of P. J. P. Goldberg and Caroline Barron that the late fourteenth and early fifteenth centuries offered women quite exceptional economic opportunity. If the experiences of not-married brewsters are any guide, quite the opposite was often true. See especially, Goldberg, *Women, work*; and Caroline M. Barron, "The 'golden age' of women in medieval London," in *Medieval women in southern England*, Reading Medieval Studies, 15 (1989), pp. 35–58. See also the related demographic arguments made by Goldberg, *Women, work*; and R. M. Smith, "Women's work and marriage in pre-industrial England: Some speculations," in Simonetta Cavaciocchi, ed., *La donna nell'economia secc. xiii–xviii* (Prato, 1990), pp. 31–62.

Chapter 4

1. Mary Hyde, "The Thrales of Streatham Park: III. The death of Thrale and remarriage of his widow," *Harvard Library Bulletin* 25 (1977), p. 202.

2. These interpretative challenges are discussed more fully in the appendix.

3. GL, Ms. 5440. See fos. 1 and 324 for Porlond's tenure with the gild. Because of a gap between 1425 and 1429, this analysis focuses on the early years covered in Porlond's book. For the city list, see accurate rendition of the original in CLB I, pp. 233–237.

4. For fuller information about brewers and their gild in London at this time, see my "Women and men in the Brewers' gild of London, ca. 1420," in Edwin Brezette DeWindt, ed., *The salt of common life: Individuality and choice in the medieval town, countryside and church* (Kalamazoo, 1996) pp. 181–232.

5. CLB I, pp. 50–51; CLRO, Letter Book I, fos. 51–52v. (1406 agreement). CPR, 1436–1441, p. 142; PRO, C66/441. m. 1; GL, Ms. 5440, fos. 290–290v.; CLRO, Journal 3, fo. 11v. (1438 charter). For ranking of the Brewers in 1487–88, see Charles Welch, ed., *History of the worshipful company of Pewterers of the city of London*, vol. 1 (London, 1902), pp. 66–67. This ranking was typical; in 1422, the Brewers ranked eleventh of 31 companies (CLB K, p. 3); in 1532, twenty-second of 60 [C. L. Kingsford, ed., *A survey of London by John Stow* (Oxford, 1908), vol. 2, pp. 190–192]; in 1545, fourteenth of 28 [William Herbert, *The twelve great livery companies of London* (London, 1834), p. 135].

6. Although there is a single enigmatic reference to a "brewestergild" in Beverley in 1364, it does not seem to have been a genuine gild; Arthur F. Leach, *Beverley town documents*, Selden Society, 14 (1900), pp. liv–lv, and 41. For Hull, see *VCH, York, East Riding*, vol. 1, p. 151. For Norwich, see NRO, D16/a1, Mayors' court book for 1440–56, fos. 95–96, and D/16/a2, Mayors' court book for 1510–32. For Oxford, see *VCH, Oxon.*, vol. 4, pp. 320–321. For Newcastle, see Elizabeth M. Halcrow, "Records of the bakers and brewers of Newcastle upon Tyne at the Bake Gate," *Archaeologica Aeliana* 37 (1959), pp. 327–332. For Southampton, see Colin Platt, *Medieval Southampton* (London, 1973), pp. 172–173; and SRO, SC2/7/item 4.

7. For Leicester, see Mary Bateson, ed., *Records of the borough of Leicester*, vol. 3: 1509–1603 (Cambridge, 1905), pp. 154–155. For Winchester, see Tom Atkinson, *Elizabethan Winchester* (London, 1963), pp. 185–188. For Northampton, see J. Charles Cox, ed., *The records of the borough of Northampton*, vol. 2: 1550–1835 (London, 1898), pp. 301–302. For Exeter, see Wallace T. MacCaffrey, *Exeter 1540–1640*, 2nd ed. (Cambridge, Mass., 1975), pp. 87–88. For York, see YCA, House Book 29, fos. 91v–94; see also D. M. Palliser, "The trade guilds of Tudor York," in Peter Clark and Paul Slack, eds., *Crisis and order in English towns 1500–1700* (London, 1972), p. 90. For Chester, see Margaret J. Groombridge, ed., *Calendar of Chester city council minutes 1603–1642*, Record Society of Lancashire and Cheshire, 106 (1956), esp. pp. xxviii, 29, 185–186, and "The city gilds of Chester," *Journal of the Chester and North Wales Archaeological and Historic Society* 39 (1952), pp. 93–108. For Lincoln, see J. W. F. Hill, *Tudor and Stuart Lincoln* (Cambridge, 1956), p. 82. Incorporations are not definitive indicators of gild formation, for some gilds antedated formal incorporation and others endured only briefly thereafter. Nevertheless, incorporation charters do provide our clearest and most comparable evidence of trade organization, and they also can reflect very real changes. See, for example, MacCaffrey, *Exeter*, pp. 87–88.

8. In the sixteenth century, a freeman of London could practice any trade, regardless of the gild to which he belonged. See Steve Rappaport, *Worlds within worlds: Structures of life in sixteenth-century London* (Cambridge, 1989), p. 91. In the early fifteenth century, however, the Brewers sought actively to include *all* free brewers in its membership. They regularly admitted men of other crafts (whose wives perhaps brewed) to their gild; see, for

example, GL, Ms. 5440, fos. 85–86v., 108v.–109. And they also tried to force non-gild brewers out of the trade by denying them access to both servants and water; see GL, Ms. 5440, fo. 292v.; and CLRO, Journal 3, fos. 175/162, 169/166.

9. In comparing these lists, I have adjusted for the fact that the city list often cited *householders* for a brewing business that was identified in gild lists by either a *wife's* name or the names of a *married couple*. Hence, I have compared households, not individuals. Of those households named in the city list, 135 paid quarterage to the gild in 1419–20, 3 paid late quarterage, and 47 contributed to the *taxatio voluntaria* of that year. Over time, many additional households in the city list of 1419–20 did associate with the gild, but nearly two-thirds of these had still not formed any links with the gild by 1425. It is worth noting that the city's coverage was perhaps just as poor as the gild's. Of the 187 house-holds that paid quarterage to the gild in 1419–20, only 135 (72 percent) were picked up in the city's survey.

10. In comparing female and male householders, I looked for evidence of associa-tion with the gild through 1425. I found that 11 of 21 female householders had no such association, as opposed to 66 of 269 male householders.

11. Both Tye and Gildsborough were cited in the city list of brewers; they were also named in the 1419–20 list of those who sold with false measures (GL, Ms. 5440, fos. 28–31v.). Maud Marriot was noted as joining the gild in 1423–25 with her husband, Thomas, a whittawer. The unnamed wife of Roger Baron might be the wife of a Roger Baron who was a long-standing member of the gild.

12. Maryanne Kowaleski and Judith M. Bennett, "Crafts, gilds and women in the middle ages: Fifty years after Marian K. Dale," *Signs: Journal of Women in Culture and Society* 14 (1989), pp. 474–488.

13. For Chester, see Groombridge, *Calendar*, pp. 185–186. For Oxford, see OUA, WP ß/34/b, and WP ß/B/33 (Oxford's brewers are discussed more fully in chapter 6). For Leicester, see the chamberlains' accounts of income from the gild (stating, for example, that Master Thomas Clerke paid 3s.4d. "for that his wife sold ale"): Leicestershire Record Office, BR III/2/43.

14. Quarterage lists are quite common for the sixteenth-century London gilds, but they are rare for the late medieval city (hence the particular importance of Porlond's book). For the Grocers, see John A. Kingdon, *Facsimile of the first volume of the ms. archives of the worshipful company of Grocers of the city of London* (London, 1886), pp. 45–47. For the Coopers, see Guildhall Library, Ms. 5614a. For the Weavers, see Frances Consitt, *The London Weavers' company, vol.* 1 (Oxford, 1933), p. 90. Jean M. Imray has noted that one woman gained the freedom of the Mercers' Company (through the unusual route of redemption); see "'Les bones gentes de la Mercerye de Londres': A study of the membership of the medieval Mercers' company," in Hollaender and Kellaway, *Studies in London History presented to Philip Edmund Jones* (London, 1969), p. 163n. Elspeth M. Veale has noted a few instances of wid-ows who carried on as skinners, but she concludes that women did not learn the trade in any numbers; see *The English fur trade in the later middle ages* (Oxford, 1966), p. 100. One woman was noted as out of livery for the Drapers in 1493: see A. H. Johnson, *The history of the worshipful company of the Drapers of London, vol.* 1 (Oxford, 1914), pp. 364–367. The first membership records for the Bakers (perhaps the gild most comparable to the Brewers) date from the early sixteenth century. At that time, only a few widows were in the com-pany (see GL, Ms. 5179/1). For women in London gilds in the sixteenth century (includ-ing the Brewers where gildswomen presented proportionately more apprentices than women in other gilds), see Rappaport, *Worlds within worlds*, pp. 36–42.

15. Herbert, *Livery companies*, p. 62. For repetitions of this count, see George Unwin, *The gilds and companies of London*, 2nd ed. (London, 1925), p. 191; Mia Ball, *The worshipful Com-*

pany of Brewers (London, 1977), p. 62; Kay E. Lacey, "Women and work in fourteenth and fifteenth century London," in Lorna Duffin and Lindsey Charles, eds., *Women and work in preindustrial England* (London, 1985), p. 51; Caroline Barron, "The 'golden age' of women in medieval London," *Reading Medieval Studies* 15 (1989), p. 47. In 1916, Herbert's calculations received apparent verification from another source when Annie Abram noted that the city census of brewers in 1419–20 tabulated about 300 brewers, of whom fewer than 20 were women. Abram's estimate has been repeated, with some minor variations, by Sylvia Thrupp, Kay Lacey, and John Butt. I have been able to replicate Abram's count roughly (I found 21 women out of 290 brewers), but her source is flawed since, by reporting heads of brewing households rather than brewers per se, it underreports the extent of female participation in the trade; Abram, "Women traders in medieval London," *The Economic Journal* 26 (1916), p. 279. See also repetitions of this figure in Sylvia Thrupp, *The merchant class of medieval London* (Ann Arbor, Mich., 1948), p. 42; Lacey, "Women," p. 51; John Joseph Butt, "The transition of privilege in medieval urban society: A study of English brewers," Ph.D. dissertation, Rutgers University, 1982, p. 97. For the city list, see CLB I, pp. 233–237.

16. As suggested by its name, quarterage was once paid on a quarterly basis. In 1388–89, the Brewers' fraternity of All Hallows noted that its members paid 12d. on four occasions through the year, for a total annual dues of 4s. Sisters paid as much as brothers, although married women (*soers qe sount desouth coverture de Baroun*) paid only 12d. per year (and nothing if they did not attend the annual feast). See PRO, C47 42/206. By the fifteenth century, annual dues were lower, wives paid the same amount as husbands, and dues seem to have been paid on an annual basis.

17. This figure compares reasonably closely with the 7 percent of households headed by females in the 1419–20 city list of brewers. The lower proportion of independent female brewers in the city list probably reflects its focus on heads of households (as opposed to heads of businesses); as a result, several wives paid individual quarterage to the gild in 1418–19, although their husbands were noted as legally responsible in the city list of 1419–20. The quarterage lists give a more accurate account of the extent to which brewhouses were run primarily by women.

18. See my "Women and men" for further details about these not-married women. Of the 13 not-married brewsters who paid their own quarterage in 1418–19, only 5 (38 percent) were still members of the gild in 1425; almost two-thirds of the men were still members. Although some not-married women died during these years, others did not, and in at least one case, poverty was the stated cause of lapsed membership in the gild. The dropout rate was particularly high for singlewomen. For the best possible comparison, I looked only at the dropout rate of men who had individual memberships in 1418–19: 54 of these 81 men were still in the gild seven years later (67 percent). Of the probable singlewomen in the 1418–19 quarterage, only 1 (Emma Canon) remained in the gild seven years later. Given William Porlond's willingness to distinguish wives from their husbands, it is unlikely that the other 3 singlewomen "disappeared" from gild records because they married and took new names. Because so few not-married brewsters belonged to the gild, the numbers cited here are necessarily small, but they do suggest a quite clear difference between not-married brewsters and male brewers.

19. For Stephen Bugge, see GL, Ms. 9171/3, fo. 218; CLRO, Husting Roll 145, items 37–39; CLB I, p. 42. For John Amwell, see GL, Ms. 9171/3, fo. 143. Amwell's will described a brewhouse *quam predicta Johanna uxor mea modo occupat.*

20. Swanfield's involvement in the brewhouse many years before he formally joined the gild is suggested by the following: first, by his wearing gild livery; second, by his being named as a creditor of the Crown in the lists of royal debts for ale compiled by

William Porlond in 1420–22; and third, by his identification as a "brewer" in a 1420 entry (see CLRO, Journal 1, fo. 72v.). When Swanfield wrote his will in 1439, he styled himself a citizen and brewer (see GL, Ms. 9171/4, fo. 35v.).

21. At the end of the 1418–19 quarterage (fo. 4), Porlond noted that considerable numbers of persons were evading quarterage and that more rigorous accounting would be undertaken in the future. The main result of this greater rigor seems to have been that more married men brought their wives into the gild; of the 81 men who paid quarterage alone in 1418–19, 37 had brought their wives into the gild by 1424–25—hence the relationship in the quarterage lists (as shown in table 4.2) between declining numbers of quarterages paid by individual males and rising numbers of quarterages paid by married couples. Nevertheless, at least some married persons persisted in paying individual quarterage for a very long time indeed.

22. Although only about a quarter of contributors to the *taxatio voluntaria* offered 6s.8d. or more, half of all married couples did so (GL, Ms. 5440, fos. 25–26). In the lists of creditors of the Crown, only men are named, but 19 of these 24 men had wives who were members of the gild. It is, of course, quite possible, that wives of the other 5 men were also involved in brewing, despite their failure to join the gild (GL, Ms. 5440, fos. 27–27v., 46–46v.). Married couples were also particularly prominent among the handful of brewers wealthy enough to be assessed in the 1412 subsidy of property holders in the city (12 of 18). See J. C. L. Stahlschmidt, ed., "Lay subsidy, temp. Henry IV," *Archaeological Journal*, 44 (1887), pp. 56–82 (a transcript of PRO, E179 144/20).

23. GL, Ms. 5440, fos. 27–27v., 46–46v.

24. Of the 548 households identified from city and gild lists as involved in brewing between 1418 and 1425, men in 114 households were named in various sources as pursuing other trades. To put these data another way, of the 158 households for which I was able to trace men's trades, 44 had men identified as brewers and 114 had men identified with other trades. The 114 nonbrewing occupations broke down as follows: 22 in the clothing trades or textile manufacture, 49 in victualing or trades related to brewing (for example, coopers), 8 in the leather and skin trades, and 35 in miscellaneous trades. Both of the Russells paid quarterage to the gild from 1418 through 1425; they contributed 13s.4d. to the *taxatio voluntaria*. With their wives, John Bargon, John Bedwell, and Richard Flete were members of the gild, and their occupations were noted by William Porlond. For similar evidence from another city in 1421, see David Gary Shaw, *The creation of a community: the city of Wells in the middle ages* (Oxford, 1993), p. 69. In contrast to Maryanne Kowaleski's findings for Exeter, I did not find large numbers of households involved in the metal trades. Yet Kowaleski was able to compare her occupational data for brewing households against a general occupational profile for Exeter as a whole; this is not possible for early fifteenth-century London. See Kowaleski, *Local markets and regional trade in medieval Exeter* (Cambridge, 1995), pp. 133–136.

25. Some men simultaneously paid to become free of the gild and to enter the fraternity. This career sequence for the Brewers' gild seems to have been very distinctive. At this time, at least one other gild, the Mercers, restricted livery to only an elite few members (Imray, "Les Bones Gentes"), and by the sixteenth century, all gilds limited livery to an exclusive group of gild members.

26. The new freemen are listed in the masters' accounts for 1419–21 in GL, Ms. 5440, fo. 60. Margaret Cruse, widow of John Spenser, brewer, styled herself as a freewoman (and claimed that she achieved this status on 30 May 1449) in a will enrolled in October 1451. See R. R. Sharpe, *Calendar of wills proved and enrolled in the Court of Husting, London, 1258–1688*, vol. 2 (London, 1889), p. 520. According to London custom, a freeman's widow could claim free status as long as she remained unmarried. See Barron, "Golden age," esp. pp. 44–45.

27. The one exception was William Porlond's wife, who in 1436–37 was noted as receiving cloth for a gown. Since it is likely that individuals wore the livery they could afford, it is scarcely surprising that most women wore the lesser hood. It also explains why one woman wore a gown livery; William Porlond and his wife (who both received some cloth without charge from the gild in 1436–37) were apparently willing to spend an additional 11s.6d. to purchase extra material for her gown.

28. GL, Ms 5440, fos. 4v.–11 (1418–19), 53–56 (1420–21), 74–77 (1422–23), 123–129v. (1424–25), 173–180 (1430–31), 208–215v. (1432–33). Both Agnes Bugge (a married women who received livery in 1418–19) and Emma Canon (a probable singlewoman who took livery in 1422–23) paid sole quarterage to the gild over many years. Katherine Wygeyn (wife of William Termeday) entered the fraternity alone in 1421–23 and received livery in 1422–23. Gillian Scot (whose unstated marital status suggests that she might have been a singlewoman) entered the fraternity alone in 1429–30 and received livery cloth in 1432–33. Given the overall patterns of livery wearing by women, I think that these exceptional women wore livery not because their long-standing membership or entry to the fraternity made them eligible for livery but because they chose to wear livery as part of their exceptionally close association with the gild.

29. GL, Ms. 5440, fos. 1v., 17v. (1418–19); 38, 60v. (1419–21); 85–86v., 108v.–109 (1421–23); 149–151, 154–154v. (1423–25); 162–162v. (1429–30); 187–187v. (1430–31). Wives were sometimes noted as entering the fraternity with their husbands, and men who married after entry could bring their wives into the fraternity with apparently no extra charge (see, for example, fo. 69). Unfortunately, Porlond's record keeping makes it impossible to separate unmarried men from married couples, as he often failed to note wives of married men (compare, for example, fos. 149–151 and 154–154v.).

30. GL, Ms. 5440, fos. 57v.–58v. In 1431, Porlond's notes suggest that the dinner was held on the day of annual accounting; see fo. 173v. In the sixteenth century, the Brewers regularly held their elections at an annual dinner; see Rappaport, *Worlds within worlds*, pp. 228–29. For seating in different rooms, see Unwin, *Gilds and companies*, p. 196.

31. GL, Ms. 5440, fos. 59–59v. The men who paid 12d. were not of especially low (or high) status in the gild. Of the 160 households represented in the quarterage list for 1420–21, 73 had representatives at the dinner (46 percent). Of the 18 women (including 4 wives) who paid individual quarterage in this year, 2 attended the dinner alone and a third attended with her husband. The tendency of poorer gild members to avoid the dinner can be seen in the fact that only one-third of those paying less than 3s. to the *taxatio voluntaria* attended the dinner, whereas three-quarters of those paying 10s. or more did so.

32. Most not-married women contributed less than 2s.; most men contributed more than 2s. Of the almost £32 raised in the levy, women directly offered only 24s. Of the seven women who paid the tax directly, the sums paid were 6s.8d., 5s., 5s., 2s., 2s., 1s.8d., and 1s.8d. Only one of these women—Alice Hercy, who contributed 5s.—was married. GL, Ms. 5440, fos. 25–26.

33. GL, MS 5440, fos. 157–157v. (1429 changes); PRO, C47 42/206 (1388 report). For the general exclusion of women from political activity in the middle ages, see Mary Erler and Maryanne Kowaleski, eds., *Women and power in the middle ages* (Athens, Ga., 1988).

34. GL, MS 5440, fos. 51–51v. At some later breakfasts or dinners of this sort, masters' wives were included in the guest list, clearly an honorific exception to the general exclusion of women.

35. Gervase Rosser, "Solidarités et changement social: Les fraternités urbaines anglaises à la fin du Moyen Age," *Annales ESC* (September–October 1993), pp. 1127–1143,

and "Going to the fraternity feast: Commensality and social relations in late medieval England," *Journal of British Studies* 33 (1994), pp. 430–446.

36. *CLB A*, p. 216, and CLRO, Letter Book A, fo. 129b. (1277); H. T. Riley, ed., *Munimenta Gildhallae Londoniensis, vol I: Liber Albus*, Rolls Series, no. 12:1 (London, 1859), p. 355 (1283); *CLB F*, p. 178, and CLRO, Letter Book F, fo. 150v. (1348); *CLB G*, p. 4, and CLRO, Letter Book G, fo. 2v. (c. 1352). Nevertheless, some men were active as brewers in London before the plague (perhaps as paid employees of monastic brewhouses); see the 24 men who entered the freedom of the city as brewers between 1309 and 1312 (*CLB D*, pp. 35–179).

37. For 1437–38, see Ms. 5440, fos. 295–306. For 1500–1501, see accounts rendered in March 1502 in GL, Ms 5442/1. The women in these accounts were identified as wives of named men, but I have been able to link so many of them to men who died in previous years that probably all of these "wives" were, in fact, widows. For an example of a year with no women in the gild, see 1580–81 in GL, Ms. 5442/4.

38. CLRO, Repertory 11, fos. 120–121. Pickering, who identified himself as a mercer in his will, served as a warden of the Brewers on at least two occasions. After Pickering's death, his widow paid quarterage for one year to the gild; GL, Ms. 5445/1. For Pickering's will, see GL, Ms. 9171/11, fo. 152.

Chapter 5

1. Sample: Alciston (of which Lullington was a part). Unfortunately, no rolls survive from 1537–50. For 1551, see ESRO, SAS/G18/56.

2. For Alciston, see ESRO, SAS/G18/51–55. For London, see GL, Ms. 5440, fos. 265v.–267v. (a list of brewers paying for the relief of Calais). For York, see Francis Collins, ed., *Register of the freemen of the city of York*, Surtees Society, 96 (1897); from Henry V through Elizabeth, 4 women and 51 men entered as alebrewers, and 35 men entered as beerbrewers. For Southampton, see SRO, SC5/1/15 (Stewards' Accounts for 1474–75) for a widow of a beerbrewer, but the few women who brewed on their own produced only ale; see, for example, J. W. Horrocks, *The assembly books of Southampton, vol. 4, 1615–1616*, Southampton Record Society, 11 (1925), p. 8. A female beerbrewer (Agnes Smyth, "Dutchman") worked in Colchester in 1412, but she was almost certainly the widow of the beerbrewer John Smyth; see R. H. Britnell, *Growth and decline in Colchester 1300–1525* (Cambridge 1986), p. 195n. Maryanne Kowaleski directed me to another female beerbrewer; Sibyl Beerbrewer, noted in the alien returns for Hull in 1441 (PRO, E179 202/112), who was also possibly a widow of a beerbrewer (she had a daughter).

3. The difficulty of reproducing the private ways in which husbands and wives divided their labor is discussed more fully in chapter 4. For the Pickerings, see also chapter 4. For the Bellowses, see note 108 below. Many historians have noted the close association among beerbrewing, large-scale industry, and masculinization: Britnell, *Growth and decline*, pp. 193–197; Peter Clark, *The English alehouse: A social history 1200–1830* (London, 1983), esp. pp. 31–34; P. J. P. Goldberg, *Women, work and life cycle in a medieval economy: Women in York and Yorkshire c. 1300–1520* (Oxford, 1992), p. 114; Derek Keene, *Survey of medieval Winchester, i, part 1* (Oxford, 1985), p. 269; Marjorie Keniston McIntosh, *Autonomy and community: The royal manor of Havering, 1200–1500* (Cambridge, 1986), p. 228; Heather Swanson, *Medieval artisans: An urban class in late medieval England* (Oxford, 1989), p. 22.

4. Grethe Jacobsen, "Women's work and women's role: Ideology and reality in Danish urban society, 1300–1550," *Scandinavian Economic History Review* 31 (1983), pp. 17–18.

5. Deborah Valenze, "The art of women and the business of men: Women's work and the dairy industry c.1740–1840," *Past and Present* 130 (1991), pp. 142–169. Joanna

Bourke, "Dairywomen and affectionate wives: Women in the Irish dairy industry 1890–1914," *Agricultural History Review* 38 (1990), pp. 149–164. Joan Jensen, "Butter making and economic development in mid-Atlantic America from 1750 to 1850," *Signs: Journal of Women in Culture and Society* 13 (1988), pp. 813–829.

6. Lynne Tatlock, "Speculum feminarum: Gendered perspectives on obstetrics and gynecology in early modern Germany," *Signs: Journal of Women in Culture and Society* 17 (1992), pp. 725–760.

7. Erik Arnold and Wendy Faulkner, "Smothered by invention: The masculinity of technology," in Wendy Faulkner and Erik Arnold, eds., *Smothered by invention: Technology in women's lives* (London, 1985), p. 18.

8. Sherry B. Ortner, "Is female to male as nature is to culture?" in Michelle Zimbalist Rosaldo and Louise Lamphere, eds., *Woman, culture and society* (Stanford, Calif., 1974), pp. 67–87, at p. 87. For critiques, see C. P. MacCormack and Marilyn Strathern, eds., *Nature, culture, and gender* (Cambridge, 1980); and Peggy Reeves Sanday, "The reproduction of patriarchy in feminist anthropology," in Mary McCanney Gergen, ed., *Feminist thought and the structure of knowledge* (New York, 1988), pp. 49–68. See also Sherry B. Ortner and Harriet Whitehead, eds., *Sexual meanings: The cultural construction of gender and sexuality* (Cambridge, 1981).

9. Throughout this period, brewers also added various herbs and seasonings to their brews, but the basic ingredients were always malt, water, yeast, and (for beer only) hops.

10. Of the many books on brewing history that discuss these distinctions between ale and beer, the most reliable is H. A. Monckton, *A history of English ale and beer* (London, 1966).

11. Norwich Leets #2 (1288–89). Somer was amerced for selling his Flemish ale secretly. See also William Hudson, *Leet jurisdiction in the city of Norwich*, Selden Society, 5 (1892), p. 21.

12. In 1361–62 James Dodynessone of Amsterdam paid a toll on beer at Great Yarmouth; H. J. Smit, ed., *Bronnen tot de geschiedenis van den handel met Engeland, Schotland en Ierland,* vol. 1: 1150–1485 (The Hague, 1928), item 506. In 1372 Henry Vandale bought four barrels of "beere" in London; see CPMR, 1364–1381, p. 147. For Lynn, see Dorothy M. Owen, ed., *The making of King's Lynn* (London, 1984), p. 421. For Colchester, see W. Gurney Benham, ed., *The oath book or red parchment book of Colchester* (Colchester, 1907), p. 8. For Norwich, see Norwich Leets #11 (February 1391). For Winchelsea, see CCR, 1385–89, pp. 344–345. For imports into Sussex in 1393 and possibly earlier, see R. A. Pelham, "Some further aspects of Sussex trade during the fourteenth century," *Sussex Archaeological Collections* 71 (1930), pp. 186–188. For imports into Great Yarmouth, Ipswich, Scarborough, and Newcastle, see Nelly J. M. Kerling, *Commercial relations of Holland and Zeeland with England from the late 13th century to the close of the middle ages* (Leiden, 1954), p. 220. For imports into Hull, Newcastle, and Great Yarmouth, see Smit, Bronnen, esp. items 577, 589, 736.

13. Hops were first imported in the 1420s, suggesting that beerbrewers then began working in England. See L. F. Salzman, *English trade in the middle ages* (Oxford, 1931), p. 360; and Kerling, *Commercial relations*, pp. 115–116.

14. CPR, 1436–1441, p. 495.

15. In implicit contrast to alien beer, a fifteenth-century English-Latin dictionary defined ale as "potus Anglorum." See Albert Way, ed., *Promptorium parvulorum sive clericorum,* Camden Society, series 1, 25 (1843), p. 9. In late medieval England, terms such as *stranger* and *foreigner* did not necessarily describe persons born outside the realm but often denoted those from another place or community. To conform with this terminology, I have relied exclusively on the term *alien* to describe persons not born of English parents.

16. Andrew Boorde, *A dyetary of health* (1542), ed. F. J. Furnivall, EETS, extra series, 10 (1870), p. 256.

17. John Taylor, *Ale alevated into the aletitude* (1651), p. 11, as printed in *Works of John Taylor the water poet*, Spenser Society, 14 (1873). By linking hops and heresy, Taylor was referring to a popular ditty about the year 1525, which ran (in one of its various forms): "Hops, Reformation, bays, and beer/ Came into England all in one year." For a discussion of some of the psychological elements in English resistance to beer, see André Lascombes, "Fortune de l'ale: à propos de Coventry 1420–1555," in Jean-Claude Margolin and Robert Sauzet, eds., *Pratiques et discours alimentaires à la renaissance* (Paris, 1982), pp. 127–136.

18. Caroline Barron, "Introduction: England and the Low Countries 1327–1477," in Caroline Barron and Nigel Saul, eds., *England and the Low Countries* (Stroud, U.K., 1995), pp. 1–28, at p. 12. Sylvia L. Thrupp, "A survey of the alien population of England in 1440," *Speculum* 32 (1957), pp. 262–273.

19. Kerling, *Commercial relations*, p. 220. See also Smit, *Bronnen*, esp. item 736. In 1397–98, Colchester imported about 100 barrels of beer; see Britnell, *Growth and decline*, p. 195.

20. For shipping, see Pelham, "Sussex trade," pp. 186–188; Kerling, *Commercial relations*, p. 220; and Smit, *Bronnen*. For retailing, see Norwich Leets #11 (of the five beer tipplers noted, at least two were aliens).

21. For Shrewsbury, see *VCH, Shropshire, vol.* 1, p. 422. For York, see Collins, *Register of the freemen*, p. 125, for Florence Janson, "berebrewer" who entered the freedom in 1416–17 (his name, as well as those of five beerbrewers mentioned later, suggest that they were not native born). For complaints by London's alebrewers, see GL, Ms. 5440, fo. 130.

22. GL, Ms. 5440, fos. 265v.–267v. One beerbrewer was an Englishman, and another was married to an Englishwoman.

23. CLB K, p. 205.

24. See CPR, 1429–36, pp. 537–539, 541–588; and CPR, 1436–41, pp. 36–37.

25. See Thrupp, "Alien population," esp. pp. 267–268, and "Aliens in and around London in the fifteenth century," in A. E. J. Hollaender and William Kellaway, eds., *Studies in London history presented to Philip Edmund Jones* (London, 1969), pp. 251–272. See also Nelly J. M. Kerling, "Aliens in the county of Norfolk, 1436–1485," *Norfolk Archaeology* 33 (1963), pp. 200–214. For just one specific example, in Southwark in 1440, only two beerbrewers were noted among a large alien population; PRO, E179 184/212.

26. For London, see PRO, E179 242/25 and 144/75A. Two English beerbrewers worked in London with the help of alien servants, and a few more might have worked in Norfolk (where several alien servants were noted as being skilled in beerbrewing). Although an English beerbrewer who employed only English servants would not have appeared in these alien subsidies, it is highly unlikely that any beerbreweries operated without alien assistance at this early date. For elsewhere, see the following documents in the PRO: Norwich, E179 149/198A and 369/26; Ipswich and Suffolk, E179 180/111; Hull, E179 202/147; Exeter and Devon, E179 95/126; Oxford and Oxon., E179 161/138 (aside from this one reference to a beerbrewer, there is no evidence that beer was produced in Oxford until the second half of the sixteenth century; this matter is discussed more fully in chapter 6); the cinque ports, E179 230/200C; Essex, E179 108/130; Norfolk, E179 149/176 and 149/177.

27. H. S. Cobb, *The overseas trade of London: Exchequer customs accounts 1480–1*, London Record Society, 20 (1990).

28. In Leicester, brewing ale with hops was proscribed as early as 1523, but beer did not begin to be regularly included in price regulations until the 1570s; see Mary Bate-

son, ed., *Records of the borough of Leicester, vol. 3: 1509–1603* (Cambridge, 1905). In Coventry, brewing ale with hops was also proscribed quite early (1522), but beer was not regularly mentioned in the city records until after 1550; see Mary Dormer Harris, ed., *The Coventry leet book*, 4 parts, EETS, 134, 135, 138, 146 (1907–13), esp. 138, pp. 683, 801–802. In Oxford, beerbrewing was proscribed in the brewers' incorporation of 1521 (OUA, WP β/34/b), and the first beerbrewer was not admitted to the trade until 1567 (OUA, Chancellor's Court Register GG, fo. 154). Prices for beer began to be regularly set in the 1570s; see Andrew Clark, ed., *Register of the University of Oxford, vol. 2, part 1*, Oxford Historical Society, 10 (1887), pp. 333–335. In Chester, beer was mentioned sporadically in the late fifteenth century but only became fully established in the city in the next century (the first beerbrewers entered the freedom in 1537–38). Jane Laughton, "The alewives of later medieval Chester," in Rowena E. Archer, ed., *Crown, government and people in the fifteenth century* (New York, 1995), pp. 191–208. For beerbrewers who entered the freedom of Chester, see J. H. E. Bennett, ed., *Rolls of the freemen of the city of Chester, part 1: 1392–1700*, Lancashire and Cheshire Record Society, 51 (1906). Beer was produced in Winchester as early as the 1440s, but it was not until the 1520s and later that substantial numbers of prosperous beerbrewers (Flemish or German) worked in the city (see Keene, *Survey*, p. 269).

29. *L&P, 1543, part 2*, p. 162, no. 287. Beer was, however, known early in the far north. In 1446, a grant noted that the tenants of Tynemouth and Shields brewed ale and "bere." *CPR, 1441–1446*, p. 449. But acceptance of beer in the north might have been long confined to major ports that either provisioned ships or traded with the continent.

30. I thank Mavis Mate for allowing me to use this quote from her forthcoming work on the economy of Sussex in the later middle ages. Since manorial records become less complete in the fifteenth and sixteenth centuries (at the very time when beer was being introduced), the acceptance of beer and beerbrewing in rural localities is usually impossible to trace. As shown in the appendix, assize presentments ceased to be recorded before beer was ever sold or brewed in most of the manors sampled. The only exceptions are Alciston (near the southeast coast) and Ingatestone (on the main road between Harwich and London), but for even these manors, information on the introduction of beer is incomplete and unsatisfactory.

31. Ethel Lega-Weekes, "Introduction to the churchwardens' accounts of South Tawton," *Report and Transactions of the Devonshire Association* 41 (1909), p. 367. For Ottery St. Mary, see University of London, Fuller Ms. 34/1.

32. Steve Rappaport, *Worlds within worlds: Structures of life in sixteenth-century London* (Cambridge, 1989), p. 143.

33. The quote is from William Harrison, *The description of England* (1587), George Edelen, ed. (Ithaca, N.Y., 1968), p. 139. See also F. G. Emmison, *Tudor food and pastimes* (London, 1964), p. 56.

34. John Grove, *Wine, beer, ale, and tobacco contending for superiority*, 2nd ed. (London, 1630), STC 11542 (not paginated).

35. BL, Lansdowne 71, no. 28. See also GL, Ms. 4069/1, fos. 33v.–34.

36. BL, Cotton Faustina C.II, fos. 178–188. Not all the brewers in London were included in this survey. For example, about two dozen people who paid quarterage to the Brewers' Company in 1573–74 were not named (see GL, Ms. 5442/4). To check for nationality, I searched in the following sources for all the alebrewers and beerbrewers named in the 1574 survey: R. E. G. Kirk and Ernest F. Kirk, eds., *Returns of aliens dwelling in the city and suburbs of London*, 4 vols., 1525–1625, Huguenot Society of London, 10 (1900–1908); William Page, ed., *Letters of denization and acts of naturalization for aliens in England 1509–1603*, Huguenot Society of London, 8 (1893); lists compiled by Lien Bich Luu of alien brewers noted in the Brewers' court minute books. Of 34 beerbrewers, 12 could be

positively identified as either aliens or naturalized subjects, 3 were tentatively so identified, 10 (of whom 6 had alien servants) were named as Englishmen, and 9 were not found. I thank Lien Bich Luu for her notes and conversation about the national origins of these brewers.

37. GL, Ms. 5445/4 (court minutes for 30 July 1573).

38. PRO, SP 14/28/136. Alien beerbrewers were probably less dominant outside of London; they were, for example, excluded from the Southampton gild in 1543, SRO, SC2/7, item 4. Alien beerbrewers were even less common in the countryside. In the 1483 alien returns, only Suffolk reported many beerbrewers in small communities, and all were along the coast; see PRO, E179 180/111. In any case, because London beerbrewers came to dominate much of the inland market in beer, alien influence stretched far. Beer was often produced in London and then transported (by the coastal trade or by cartage) to other towns or even villages. See T. S. Willan, *The inland trade: Studies in English internal trade in the sixteenth and seventeenth centuries* (Manchester, 1976), p. 30; and N.J. Williams, *The maritime trade of the East Anglian ports 1550–1590* (Oxford, 1988), p. 177.

39. Richard W. Unger, "Technical change in the brewing industry in Germany, the Low Countries, and England in the late middle ages," *Journal of European Economic History* 21 (1992), pp. 281–313, at 309–310. See also his "The scale of Dutch brewing, 1350–1600," *Research in Economic History* 15 (1995), pp. 261–292. The Lynn brewer John Kep, who might have produced between 1,500 and 2,000 gallons of ale each week (see chapter 3), is the only late fourteenth-century English brewer whose outputs can match these figures from the continent. But Kep, working in a port with close ties to the continent, was clearly atypical. Even in the late sixteenth century, most alebreweries in London (as suggested by table 5.1) scarcely exceeded the capacities of continental breweries two centuries earlier.

40. For Ghent, see David Nicholas, *The domestic life of a medieval city* (Lincoln, Nebraska, 1985), pp. 97–98, 184–186. For Cologne, see Martha Howell, *Women, production and patriarchy in late medieval cities* (Chicago, 1986), pp. 135–136. See also Jacobsen, "Women's work," pp. 17–18. The brief discussion of brewsters by Erika Uitz in *The legend of good women: Medieval Women in towns and cities* (New York, 1988), pp. 58–60, is unreliable because it does not distinguish between brewers of hopped beer and brewers of traditional beers. Clearly, the subject of the sexual division of labor in continental beerbrewing deserves further study. Seeking more information on this subject, I consulted Richard W. Unger, who has confirmed that very few independent women worked in beerbrewing on the continent. I thank both Richard Unger and Richard Yntema for discussing this subject with me.

41. Merry Wiesner, *Working women in renaissance Germany* (New Brunswick, N.J., 1986), pp. 128–129. This quote, from a late sixteenth-century effort to exclude even widows of brewers from the trade, is included more for its pithiness than for its timeliness. Yet, although from a time and place removed from the alien beerbrewers who emigrated to England in the fifteenth century, it expresses a sentiment that they might have heartily endorsed.

42. Thrupp, "Alien population," p. 266, and "Aliens in London," appendix 3. In her *Medieval Southwark* (London, 1996), Martha Carlin has calculated a slightly more even proportion of alien women to men in that suburb: 29 percent of alien taxpayers in 1440 were female. Sixteenth-century immigration, especially when prompted by religious persecution, sometimes brought more equal numbers of women and men.

43. GL, Ms. 5440, fo. 22v., 38–41v., 130–131. See the discussion of brewers' servants in chapter 3.

44. PRO, E179 242/25 (June 1483). Unfortunately, lists of aliens provide our only direct information about the persons employed in late medieval beerbreweries, and it is possible that some native servants also worked in these establishments; if so, these native

servants might have been especially likely to be low skilled and female. Yet even if a few native women worked in these beerbrewing households, their numbers would have been smaller than the numbers of alien male servants. First, given contemporary complaints about the predominance of alien servants employed by alien beerbrewers, it is unlikely that large numbers of native servants of either sex were found in these households. Second, it is highly probable that the few women who did find employment in beerbreweries worked only as domestic servants, not as brewery workers. In 1574, for example, an estimate of brewing costs included "maid servants" as part of the brewer's household, not as part of the staff employed in the brewery. See PRO, SP 12/98/37.

45. PRO, SP 14/28/136.

46. Statutes, 1 Richard III, c. 9; 14 & 15 Henry VIII, c. 2; 22 Henry VIII, c. 13; 32 Henry VIII, c. 16. In 1540, the mayor of London refused to help alien beerbrewers in their efforts to retain "servants of their own nation." See CLRO, Repertory 10, fo. 170b.

47. CPR, 1566–1569, p. 19, item 85.

48. For the separate social relations of Dutch immigrants, see Thrupp, "Aliens in London," esp. pp. 265–266; Carlin, Medieval Southwark; Thomas Wyatt, "Aliens in England before the Huguenots," Proceedings of the Huguenot society of London, 19:1 (1953), pp. 74–94. Although Wyatt notes that one-quarter of the aliens granted denization in 1544 were married to Englishwomen, the vast majority were French.

49. For just one example of cooperation between native and alien brewers, see BL, Add. Ms. 36,761, fo. 21v. For a different view, see William Chester Jordan, who in his recent Women and credit in pre-industrial and developing societies (Philadelphia, 1993) has suggested that "among the women, the ethnic barrier could be breached" (p. 30). But his assertion is supported by only one example of a loan between an Englishwoman and a Flemish woman, as reported in Marjorie K. McIntosh, "Money lending on the periphery of London, 1300–1600," Albion 20 (1988), p. 562.

50. Louis Lacour, "Traité d'economie rurale," Bibliotheque de l'ecole des chartes 17 (1856), pp. 378–380. Ale was quickly ready for sale, within 12 hours or slightly more. See, for example, H. E. Salter, Registrum cancellarii Oxoniensis 1434–1469, Oxford Historical Society, 93 (1932), p. 106; and John Hooker, The description of the citie of Excester, Walter J. Harte, J. W. Schopp, and H. Tapley-Soper, eds., vol. 1 in 3 parts, Devon and Cornwall Record Society, 11 (1919–47), p. 880. But ale had to be sold within a few days; see for example Warren O. Ault, Open-field husbandry and the village community, Transactions of the American Philosophical Society, n.s., 55, part 7 (1965), item 147, pp. 77–78.

51. Thomas Tusser, Five hundred points of good husbandry (1580), ed. Geoffrey Grigson (Oxford, 1984), p. 167.

52. Prices varied even according to the age of the brew. See, for example, Harris, Coventry leet book, pp. 25, 169.

53. Harrison, Description, p. 138.

54. Beerbrewers were ordered in 1443 to keep their beer for at least eight days before selling it; CPR, 1441–1446, pp. 184–185. For the aging of beer, see Harrison, Description, pp. 130–131.

55. Reginald Scot, A perfite platforme of a hoppe garden (London, 1576), STC 21866, pp. 5–6. Richard Arnold, The customs of London (1502, reprinted London, 1811), p. 247. Clark, English alehouse, p. 117, n. 14.

56. Harrison, Description, pp. 137–138. The expenses of the Percy household in 1512 confirm that the cost of hops amounted to only a fraction of the cost of malt; see Thomas Percy, ed., The regulations and establishment of the household of Henry Algernon Percy . . . Anno Domini MDXII (1700; reprinted London, 1905), pp. 11–21.

57. BL, Lansdowne Ms. 58/48.

58. H. T. Riley, ed., *Memorials of London and London life in the xiiith, xivth, and xvth centuries* (London, 1868), pp. 665–666. For other examples, see Christopher Markham, ed., *Records of Northampton*, vol. 1 (Northampton, 1898), pp. 345–347; and Clark, *English alehouse*, p. 97.

59. For London, see CLRO, Repertory 13, no. 2, fo. 533. For Leicester, see Mary Bateson, ed., *Records of Leicester*, vol. 3 (Cambridge, 1905), p. 162. For Hereford, see F. C. Morgan, ed., *The regulations of the city of Hereford* (Hereford, 1945), p. 12. See also James E. Thorold Rogers, *A history of agriculture and prices in England*, vol. iii: 1401–1582 (Oxford, 1882), pp. 278–282, and vol. iv: 1401–1582, pp. 546–550.

60. In the sixteenth century, when poor harvests sometimes led to grain shortages and when prices outpaced wages, beerbrewing became even more advantageous. For the comparative stability of ale and beer prices at this time, see Rappaport, *Worlds*, p. 143. For grain prices, see Peter Bowden, "Agricultural prices, farm profits and rents," in Joan Thirsk, ed., *The agrarian history of England and Wales*, vol. 4: 1500–1640 (Cambridge, 1976), pp. 593–695. In addition, the research of Lien Bich Luu suggests that beerbrewers, especially in the 1570s and after, were able to cut costs further by heating with coal rather than wood. Coal may have reduced heating costs from as much as 20 percent per brewing to as little as 4 percent. Beerbrewers shifted to coal more rapidly than alebrewers. I am grateful to Lien Bich Luu for sharing her research on this subject.

61. Clark has also discussed beerbrewers' greater use of equipment in *English alehouse*, esp. p. 101. For one example, see *Statutes*, 23 Henry VIII, c. 4. (beerbrewers could employ two coopers but alebrewers only one).

62. For hops shortages, see CLRO, Repertory 12, no. 2, fo. 278b., and C. L. Kingsford, "Two London chronicles," *Camden Miscellany XII*, Camden Society, 3rd series, 18 (1910), p. 48. For fuel shortages, see John Hatcher, *The history of the British coal industry*, vol. 1: *before 1700: Towards the age of coal* (Oxford, 1993), pp. 31–55. Men controlled trade in both commodities, and aliens long controlled the overseas trade in hops. See, for example, Cobb, *Overseas trade*.

63. For example, compare wage lists for brewers (that is, beerbrewers) and alebrewers in Paul L. Hughes and James F. Larkin, eds., *Tudor royal proclamations*, vol. 2: 1555–1587 (New Haven, Conn., 1969), items 512, 596, 613, 628, 651, 671, 676, 682, 691, and vol. 3: 1588–1603, items 702, 713.

64. For a brewer who switched from ale to beer, see Henry Russell in Southampton in A. L. Merson, ed., *The third book of remembrance of Southampton, 1514–1602*, vol. 2, Southampton Record Series, 3 (1955), p. 36.

65. CLRO, Repertory 1, fos. 46v., 48.

66. PRO, PROB 11 55/31, PROB 2/401. See also CPR, 1566–1569, p. 19, item 85.

67. For earlier evidence of disparity, see different maximum fines for beerbrewers and alebrewers set in 1487; CLRO, Journal 9, fo. 106v. By 1595, the gap between alebrewers and beerbrewers in London had widened even more, with the latter averaging 80 quarters a week and the former averaging only 12; GL, Ms. 5445/9, entry for 21/10/1595. I thank Lien Bich Luu for bringing this item to my attention. These sorts of distinctions existed in cities other than London. For example, see YCA, House Book 29, fos. 91v.–94.

68. BL, Lansdowne Ms. 32, fos. 106–107 (complaint about the creation of grain scarcities by rich brewers and bakers). W. T. Mitchell, ed., *Registrum cancellarii 1498–1506*, Oxford Historical Society, n.s., 27 (1980), pp. 103–104 (small brewers forced out of the trade).

69. See M. M. Postan, "Partnership in medieval English commerce," in *Medieval trade and finance* (Cambridge, 1973), pp. 65–91, for a general discussion of partnerships. For the 1574 partners, see BL, Cotton Faustina C. II, fos. 178–188. For the 1580 order, see GL, Ms. 5496.

70. *VCH, Surrey,* vol. 2, pp. 385−386. Wassell Webling had further problems with widows and partnerships; in 1571, the city had to adjudicate a nasty dispute between him and Alice Coxe, the widow of his former partner, William Coxe. I thank Lien Bich Luu for reminding me about the Webling-Dolman case and for providing her transcription from the repertories of the Webling-Coxe case (see CLRO, Repertory 17, fos. 102v.−138).

71. BL, Cotton Faustina C. II, fos. 178−188. Of the eight partners, the sex of two cannot be determined. Yet even if these two unnamed partners were women, it would be likely that they were "finance" partners, not "mutual" partners; see Postan, "Partnership," for the distinction. I have found several brewing partnerships in seventeenth-century Southampton and one from seventeenth-century Oxford; none involved women. For one very slight suggestion of a partnership between brewsters, see Helen Jewell, ed., *The court rolls of the manor of Wakefield from September 1348 to September 1350,* Yorkshire Archaeological Society, Wakefield Court Roll Series, 2 (1981), p. 116 (two wives "brewed together"). For further information on commercial partnerships (none involving women), see C. G. A. Clay, *Economic expansion and social change: England 1500−1700,* vol. 2: *Industry, trade and government* (Cambridge, 1984), pp. 191−193; and Hatcher, *Coal,* pp. 260−264. Clearly, female involvement in partnerships is a subject worthy of further investigation.

72. BL, Lansdowne Ms. 71/46. Some brewers even had private wharves. See, for example, Wyatt, "Aliens in England," p. 86. As Derek Keene has pointed out to me, brewers located on the Thames not only for convenience of exporting but also for ready access to water (for brewing) and for ease of obtaining supplies (such as wood) by water-borne transport.

73. See, for example, references to beer exports throughout Cobb, *Overseas trade,* and numerous references in L&P and CSPD. Many of the persons licensed to export beer were not themselves beerbrewers but were instead seeking to buy beer and export it at a profit. On rare occasions, women obtained such licenses. See, for example, two licenses issued in 1539 and 1542 to Frances Fortinelle, widow (L&P, 1539, part 1, pp. 75−76, no. 39; and L&P, 1542, p. 32, no. 71/38); license to the widow Bridget Brayford in 1594 (CSPD, 1591−1594, p. 549); and license to the widow May Andrews in 1595 (CSPD, 1595−1597, p. 4).

74. Maryanne Kowaleski, ed., *Local customs accounts of the port of Exeter 1266−1321,* Devon and Cornwall Record Society, n.s., 36 (1993), pp. 20−23. Because imports were taxed, we have more information on importing than exporting. But there is no reason to suppose that women were more active in the export trade than in the import trade.

75. L&P, 1542, p. 400, no. 714/22.

76. See, for example, the brokage books for Southampton: Barbara D. M. Bunyard, ed., *The brokage book of Southampton from 1439−40,* Southampton Record Society, 20 (1941); Olive Coleman, ed., *The brokage book of Southampton 1443−1444,* 2 vols., Southampton Record Series, 4 (1960) and 6 (1961); K. F. Stevens and T. E. Olding, eds., *The brokage books of Southampton for 1477−8 and 1527−8,* Southampton Record Series, 28 (1985); Elisabeth A. Lewis, ed., *The Southampton port and brokage books, 1448−9,* Southampton Record Series, 36 (1993). T. S. Willan noted the minimal participation of women in the coastal trade in *The English coasting trade 1600−1750* (New York, 1967), p. 49.

77. Jean Vanes, ed., *The ledger of John Smythe 1538−1550,* Royal Commission on Historical Manuscripts and Bristol Record Society (1974). I thank Maryanne Kowaleski for drawing my attention to this source.

78. See, for example, Goldberg, *Women, work,* pp. 124−125. As with overseas trade, most mercantile activity by women involved the short-term activities of recently bereaved widows.

79. PRO, SP 16/341/124.

80. PRO, REQ2, 78/56. At least one of Margery Draper's daughters married a gentleman rather than a brewer's clerk, for Margery—who identified herself as a "citizen and beerbrewer of London"—remembered a deceased child of that marriage with a brass (in St. John's Church, Pinner). I am grateful to Amy Erickson for sending me a copy of this inscription.

81. Barnaby Rich, *The fruites of long experience* (London, 1581), as cited in C. G. Cruickshank, *Elizabeth's army* (Oxford, 1966), p. 76.

82. This summary of military provisioning draws on information found in the following studies: Michael Prestwich, "Victualling estimates for English garrisons in Scotland during the early fourteenth century," *English Historical Review* 82 (1967), pp. 536–543, and *War, politics and finance under Edward I* (London, 1972), pp. 114–136; S. J. Burley, "The Victualling of Calais, 1347–65," *Bulletin of the Institute of Historical Research* 31 (1958), pp. 49–57; H. J. Hewitt, *The organization of war under Edward III* (Manchester, 1966), pp. 50–74; C. S. L. Davies, "Provisions for armies, 1509–50: A study in the effectiveness of early Tudor government," *Economic History Review*, 2nd series, 17 (1964–65), pp. 234–248; C. G. Cruickshank, *Army royal: Henry VIII's invasion of France, 1513* (Oxford, 1969), pp. 55–67; C. G. Cruickshank, *Elizabeth's army*, pp. 76–90.

83. PRO, SC1 45/71. I thank Jane Laughton for bringing this letter to my attention.

84. L&P, 1509–14, no. 3355.

85. Cruickshank, *Army royal*, p. 56.

86. L&P, 1513–14, no. 1864.

87. Hewitt, *Organization of war*, p. 52.

88. Because beer was adopted so early by the military, the first native drinkers of beer in England were probably soldiers and sailors who acquired a taste for it while on military service. But there is no evidence to suggest that brewing was introduced to England by returning troops. See Peter Mathias, *The brewing industry in England 1700–1830* (Cambridge, 1959), p. 3.

89. Burley, "Victualling."

90. CCR, 1402–1405, p. 209.

91. Statutes, 1&2 Philip and Mary, c. 5.

92. Kerling, *Commercial relations*, p. 114, citing PRO, C 76/81/1.

93. *Rotuli parliamentorum*, vol. 3, p. 500 (4 Henry IV).

94. Riley, *Memorials*, pp. 665–666. This beer was probably imported into London and then shipped to Rouen.

95. Paul L. Hughes and James F. Larkin, eds., *Tudor royal proclamations*, vol. 1: 1485–1553 (New Haven, Conn., 1964), item 12. Compare to items 91 and 96. I regret that my comments here on the adoption of beer for military provisioning can be only cursory; it is a subject worthy of further investigation.

96. Philip Eley, "Portsmouth breweries, 1492–1847," *Portsmouth Papers* 51 (1988), pp. 4–5.

97. Hewitt, *Organization of war*, p. 52.

98. For example, of 18 brewers in Southampton between 1533 and 1553, all were male. Of the 24 brewers active between 1565 and 1575, 2 (both alebrewers) were women (see Margaret Hancock and Joan Norton in SRO, SC6/1/8).

99. In addition to ale shipped from England and beer shipped from the Low Countries, vast quantities of malt were sent to Calais in the fourteenth century. See Burley, "Victualling," p. 53. As Wayne Lee has suggested to me, it is possible that beer, because it took longer to mature, was brewed in the field less often than was ale.

100. Barton C. Hacker, "Women and military institutions in early modern Europe: A reconnaissance," *Signs: Journal of Women in Culture and Society* 6 (1981), pp. 643–671. For

Leicester's code, see Cruickshank, *Elizabeth's army*, pp. 296−303 (article 5 discusses the presence of women).

101. Huntington Library, Ellesmere Mss. 7342, 7343. I thank Cynthia Herrup for showing this material to me and the Huntington Library for permitting its citation.

102. *L&P, Addenda,* part 1, p. 112, no. 359. See also *L&P,* 1513, p. 931, no. 2055/11, and p. 1172, no. 2684/14; *L&P,* 1543, part 1, pp. 241−242, no. 409; *L&P,* 1543, part 2, pp. 106−107, no. 207.

103. Arnold and Faulkner, "Smothered," p. 18.

104. Mathias, *Brewing industry*, p. 4.

105. I have found only one married woman associated with the gild in the late sixteenth century: Margaret Newnam, wife of Gregory Newnam, who was active in the gild from 1588−98 (GL, Ms. 5442/5). Before 1588, Gregory Newnam was cited on his own account, and, since he died in 1592, it seems probable that Margaret Newnam was replacing an incapacitated and then deceased husband. See details about his estates in GL, Ms. 9171/17, fos. 407−407v., and Ms. 9168/14, fo. 264. Their small brewery, consuming 12 quarters of malt each week, probably produced ale.

106. Of the beerbrewers, William Longe (PRO, PROB 11/72, fos. 42v.−43v.) left two breweries to his sons, Derek James (PRO, PROB 11/75, fos. 4v.−6) left one to a son and another to his wife and minor son, John Draper (PRO, PROB 11/58, fos. 56v.−57v.) and John Taylor (PRO, PROB 11/71, fos. 59−60v.) left one brewery each to their wives, and Roger James (PRO, PROB 11/89, fos. 36v.−37) directed that his be sold and the profits dispersed to pay his debts and bequests. Of the alebrewers, John Braytoft (GL, Ms. 9051/5, fos. 70−73) left his brewery to his son, and both Roger Bellows (PRO, PROB 11/61, fos. 132v.−133) and Robert Wood (PRO, PROB 11/56, fos. 252v.−254) left breweries to their wives. Robert Wood provided for his wife with particular care, leaving special gifts to his servants and apprentices if they remained in her service and trusting her to offer remembrances to his best customers "according as she knows my mind in that behalf." Beerbrewers who named their wives as executrices were Derek James (wife named jointly with son), John Draper, and John Taylor; Peter Durant (PRO, PROB 11/67, fos. 192v.−193); John Powell (PRO, PROB 11/98, fos. 36v.−37); John Hulse (PRO, PROB 11/97, fos. 276−276v.); and Matthew Rutton (PRO, PROB 11/102, fos. 38v.−39). Alebrewers were Roger Bellows (wife named with son), Robert Wood, and Thomas Etheridge; John Daldron (PRO, PROB 11/60, fo. 277v.); John Banks (PRO, PROB 11/61, fo. 207); John Hill (PRO, PROB 11/79, fos. 96−96v.); Robert Atkinson (GL, Ms. 9171/19, fos. 368v.−369); Matthew Martin (PRO, PROB 11/90, fos. 126−127); Robert Shaw (PRO, PROB 11/61, fos. 126v.−127v.); Thomas Vearye (GL, Ms. 25,626/3, fos. 111−112v.); John Cranedge (GL, Ms. 9171/16, fos. 346v.−347); Christopher Butler (GL, Ms. 25,626/2, fo. 327); Henry Robinson (wife named jointly with brother-in-law; PRO, PROB 11/68, fos. 328−329); and Mitchell Alleson (included because his widow was in the 1574 survey; PRO, PROB 11/42A, fo. 349v.). These testamentary arrangements must, of course, be evaluated with care, as they were structured by both general practices and individual circumstances.

107. In tracing the activities of widows, I focused exclusively on brewers named in the 1574 survey and on gild activities reported in GL, Mss. 5442/4, 5442/5. Beerbrewers seem to have staffed their larger breweries more with hired workers than with apprentices. I am grateful to Steve Rappaport for his information on members of the Brewers' Company, as well as his thoughts on the relatively few apprentices taken by beerbrewers.

108. The most interesting case I have reconstructed in this regard involves Joan Bellows, the widow of Roger Bellows. When he died in 1579, he left his alebrewery to Joan,

with reversion to their son, Roger. She subsequently managed the business and paid quarterage to the gild. Although she ceased to pay quarterage after 1586–87, she did not die until 1592–93. Her son, Roger Bellows, had started paying quarterage in 1583–84, and after several years during which they both paid quarterage, she then ceased to pay. But she might have still managed the business. The court minutes contain a case from 1593 in which the informer Hugh Alley tried to argue that Roger Bellows had brewed illegally between May 1591 and May 1592. The case failed because the chief brewer of the Bellowses reported under examination that "the mother paid him his wages and bought the malts and received money for the ale and that the said Roger had nothing to do therewith but at her command." In other words, Alley had sued the wrong person. See GL, Ms. 5445/9, entry for 25 May 1593. Of course, the chief brewer might have been testifying as a faithful employee, seeking to help his master escape a charge. But his testimony suggests that Joan Bellows did continue to run the business after she had ceased to be actively involved in gild matters; perhaps she was able to do so because her brewery was de facto represented in the gild by her son. For their activities in the gild, see GL, Ms. 5442/4, Ms. 5442/5.

109. Indeed, as Caroline M. Barron has recently said, a widow "was not only allowed, but was indeed *expected* to maintain her husband's household and to continue his business" (emphasis in original): "Introduction: The widows' world in later medieval London," in Caroline M. Barron and Anne F. Sutton, eds., *Medieval London widows 1300–1500* (London, 1994), p. xxviii. See also the discussion of the place of widows in gilds in Maryanne Kowaleski and Judith M. Bennett, "Crafts, gilds and women in the middle ages: Fifty years after Marian K. Dale," *Signs: Journal of Women in Culture and Society* 14 (1989), pp. 474–488.

Chapter 6

1. William Paley Baildon, ed., *Court rolls of the manor of Wakefield, vol.* 1: 1274–1297, Yorkshire Archaeological Society, 29 (1901), p. 129.

2. I am grateful to Maryanne Kowaleski for supplying this reference, which can be found at the Devon Record Office, MCR 1317/18, m. 1.

3. See especially Maryanne Kowaleski, "Food trades," in Joseph R. Strayer, ed., *Dictionary of the middle ages, vol.* 5 (New York, 1982), pp. 115–127.

4. See the appendix and also Nellie Neilson, *Customary rents,* Oxford Studies in Social and Legal History, 2 (1910), pp. 35–39.

5. *Statutes,* vol. 1, pp. 199–205. As noted above, I refer to these quasi statutes by the shorthand term *Assisa.* See also Mary Bateson, "Some legal texts in the Leicester vellum book," *English Historical Review* 14 (1899), pp. 502–506; and Richard Britnell, "Forstall, forestalling and the statute of forestallers," *English Historical Review* 102 (1987), pp. 89–102.

6. P. Studer, ed., *The Oak Book of Southampton, vol.* 1, Southampton Record Society, 6 (1910–11), p. 43, no. 29.

7. *Liber Censualis Seu Domesday Book, vol.* 1 (London, 1783), fo. 262b.

8. Adolphus Ballard, ed., *British borough charters, vol.* 1: 1042–1216 (Cambridge, 1913), pp. 157–159.

9. Andrew Clark, ed., *The English register of Godstow nunnery, near Oxford, vol.* 1, EETS, 142 (1911), p. 101.

10. Many of these matters are discussed in greater detail in the appendix.

11. For an example of complaints about brewers who sold without public notice, see Thomas Bruce Dilks, ed., *Bridgwater borough archives, vol.* 2: 1377–1399, Somerset Record Society, 53 (1938), pp. 49–50. For examples of brewers presented for favoring in-house

sales, see Sample: Alciston, c. 1370; Crowle, c. 1370; Wakefield, c. 1370. See also the discussion about the growth of alehouses in chapter 3.

12. J. Ambrose Raftis, *Tenure and mobility: Studies in the social history of the mediaeval English village* (Toronto, 1964), pp. 125–127; Marjorie K. McIntosh, "Local change and community control in England, 1465–1500," *Huntington Library Quarterly*, 49 (1986), pp. 219–242.

13. W. Cunningham, *The growth of English industry and commerce during the early and middle ages* (Cambridge, 1910), p. 263.

14. See, for example, *Calendar of inquisitions post mortem*, vol. 11 (London, 1935), p. 92. Understanding the assize as a seigneurial perquisite explains why consumers sometimes objected to its enforcement. See, for example, CPR, 1340–1343, pp. 316–317; and Mary Bateson, "The English and Latin versions of a Peterborough court leet, 1461," *English Historical Review*, 19 (1904), pp. 526–528. Yet consumers sometimes actively sought the protection of the assize, reporting official obfuscation, complaining about mild punishments, and even seeking royal redress. See, for example, H. E. Salter, ed., *Munimenta civitatis Oxonie*, Oxford Historical Society, 71 (1920), pp. 29–30.

15. See Sample: Hindolveston, c. 1380, c. 1420, c. 1455, c. 1500, c. 1530; Crowle, c. 1370; Ingatestone (passim). As discussed more fully in the appendix, amercement of aletasters was not a negative statement about their specific performances.

16. Mary Bateson, ed., *Borough customs, vol. 1*, Selden Society, 18 (1904), p. 185.

17. I am grateful to Lori A. Gates, who has informed me that she found some female aletasters in early fourteenth-century Longbridge Deverill. The only other such instances known to me are from Halesowen; R. H. Hilton, *The English peasantry of the later Middle Ages* (Oxford, 1975), p. 105.

18. The only regular exceptions were feudal ladies, who held the assize as a seigneurial perquisite, but even they, of course, administered the assize through male officers.

19. I am grateful to Maryanne Kowaleski for telling me about this practice.

20. John Lister, ed., *Court rolls of the manor of Wakefield, vol. 3: 1313–1316 and 1286*, Yorkshire Archaeological Society 57 (1917), p. 75.

21. *Ninth report of the royal commission on historical manuscripts, appendix* (London, 1884), pp. 173–174.

22. See especially Statutes, 12 Edward II (1318–19) and 3 Henry VIII c. 8 (1512). For some examples of male aletasters whose wives brewed for profit, see Sample: Alciston, c. 1280 (Godfrey Walsh and his wife; Ralph Cristemesse and his wife) and later. For some examples of the relatively modest status of aletasters, jurors, and other officers who enforced market regulations, see Maryanne Kowaleski, *Local markets and regional trade in medieval Exeter* (Cambridge, 1995), esp. pp. 95–119; and Edwin B. DeWindt, *Land and people in Holywell-cum-Needingworth* (Toronto, 1972), pp. 206–241. In one respect, brewsters had an asset that was less readily available to male brewers; they could offer their sexual services to officers in return for reduced or excused amercements. Since I have found this possibility mentioned only once in extant records (the brewster whose fine was excused *pro amicitia carnali* in Norwich Leets #2), I cannot estimate the frequency with which brewsters exploited this possibility.

23. The pillory and tumbrel were essential to the assize of bread and ale: Frederick Pollock and Frederic William Maitland, *The History of English Law vol. 1*, 2nd ed. (1898; reprint, Cambridge, 1968), p. 582. In the interest of clarity, I shall use *cucking-stool* to denote instruments identified by various names, especially in the middle ages. Some of these instruments, such as the *thewe* used in London, were sometimes explicitly identified with cucking-stools and sometimes contrasted to them; I have not attempted to sort out these highly confusing and often contradictory references to various sorts of punishments reserved for

women, especially since they seem to share certain characteristics that we now associate with cucking-stools—public display in some sort of chair and ducking in water. These instruments deserve more study than I can offer here, but see John Webster Spargo, *Juridical folklore in England illustrated by the cucking-stool* (Durham, N.C., 1944) for some useful comments. Spargo brings together many scattered references to these instruments and attempts to sort out their various meanings and uses.

24. David Underdown, "The taming of the scold: The enforcement of patriarchal authority in early modern England," in Anthony Fletcher and John Stevenson, eds., *Order and disorder in early modern England* (Cambridge, 1985), pp. 116–136; and Martin Ingram "'Scolding women cucked or washed': A crisis in gender relations in early modern England?" in Jennifer Kermode and Garthine Walker, eds., *Women, crime and the courts in early modern England* (London, 1994), pp. 48–80.

25. For Chester and Preston, see Spargo, *Juridical folklore*, pp. 29–31, 19–20. For Milverton, see PRO, SC2 199/5.

26. This was the critical distinction in the thirteenth-century quasi statutes. See also BL, Lansdowne 796; in this late fifteenth-century summary of assizes, only alebrewers (not even beerbrewers) were punished on the cucking-stool.

27. *Statutes*, vol. 1, pp. 199–205.

28. See Spargo, *Juridical folklore*, for Hereford and London. For Kibworth Harcourt, see Merton College Library, MCR 6405 (I am grateful to David Postles for this reference and to Steven Gunn for verifying the archival citation).

29. Spargo, *Juridical folklore*, esp. pp. 34–35.

30. For Tamworth, see A. M. Tonkinson, "The borough community of Tamworth and its courts at the end of the thirteenth century: A study of its courts," M.A. thesis, University of Keele, 1985, pp. 89–90. For Milverton, see PRO, SC2 100/5. Helen M. Cam, *The hundred and the hundred rolls* (London, 1930), p. 211. See also *Statutes*, 13 Richard II, 1, c. 8; and *Calendar of inquisitions miscellaneous, vol. 5*, 1387–92 (London, 1962), pp. 172–173, no. 300.

31. In 1621, a brewer was whipped in London (although his offense might not have been related to his trade). BL, Harl. 389 (I am grateful to Cynthia Herrup for this reference).

32. William Harrison, *The description of England* (1587), George Edelen, ed. (Ithaca, N.Y., 1968), p. 189.

33. CPMR, vol. 2, p. 15 (8 January 1365).

34. Spargo, *Juridical folklore*, p. 56.

35. Thomas Wright and James Orchard Halliwell, eds., *Reliquiae antiquae, vol. 2* (London, 1843), pp. 174–177 (a satire on the people of Kildare). I am grateful to Christopher Baswell for his assistance in rendering this passage into modern English.

36. For example, see Cornelius Walford, "Early laws and customs in Great Britain regarding food," *Transactions of the Royal Historical Society* 8 (1880), p. 92.

37. Bertha Haven Putnam, *The enforcement of the Statutes of Labourers during the first decade after the Black Death 1349–1359* (New York, 1908), pp. 164–165.

38. See, for example, CLB I, pp. 50–51, and CLRO, Letter Book I, fos. 51–52v.

39. *Statutes*, 11 Henry VII, c. 2; 5 and 6 Edward VI, c. 25. S. K. Roberts, "Alehouses, brewing, and government under the early Stuarts," *Southern History* 2 (1980), pp. 45–71; Keith Wrightson, "Alehouses, order and reformation in rural England, 1590–1660," in Eileen and Stephen Yeo, eds., *Popular culture and class conflict 1590–1914* (Atlantic Highlands, N.J., 1981), pp. 1–27; Peter Clark, *The English alehouse: A social history 1200–1820* (London, 1983), esp. chap. 8.

40. Roberts, "Alehouses," esp. pp. 55–67. Only with the introduction of the excise in the 1640s did the central government begin to regulate brewers with some effectiveness.

41. The Oxford rota and the York licensing scheme are discussed more fully below. For other towns, see Robert Fitch, "Norwich brewers' marks and trade regulations," *Norfolk Archaeology* 5 (1859), p. 323; W. H. Stevenson, ed., *Records of the borough of Nottingham,* vol. 4: 1547–1625 (London, 1889), pp. 130–131; *VCH, Dorset,* vol. 2, p. 367; J. Charles Cox, *The records of the borough of Northampton,* vol. 2: 1550–1835 (London, 1898), pp. 301–302; Mary Bateson, ed., *Records of the borough of Leicester,* vol. 3: 1509–1603 (Cambridge, 1905), p. 383; CLRO, Repertory 16, fos. 436v., 461v., Journal 19, fos. 144v.–145v.; Repertory 18, fo. 177v.; Repertory 19, fo. 169.

42. For example, see CLRO, Repertory 19, fo. 174v.

43. See, for example, YCA, CC8 (Chamberlains' account book, 1594–1597), fos. 23–24.

44. Wrightson, "Alehouses," p. 5.

45. This estimate is based on figures reported for Kent, Leicester, Northampton, and Norwich in Clark, *English alehouse,* p. 79; and for south Lancashire and Essex in Wrightson, "Alehouses," p. 24, n. 11. Both Clark and Wrightson note that almost all women licensed to keep alehouses were widows.

46. Chester City Record Office, First Assembly Book, AB/1, fo. 70; *The court leet records of the manor of Manchester,* vol. 1: 1552–1586 (Manchester, 1884), p. 241.

47. George Roberts, *The social history of the people of the southern counties in past centuries* (London, 1856), p. 456.

48. H. E. Salter, *Registrum cancellarii Oxoniensis* 1434–1469, vol. 1, Oxford Historical Society, 93 (1932), pp. 8–10, 51.

49. For brewsters' fines in 1559–60 and later, see YCA, CC5 (Chamberlains' account book, 1559–85). For the 1562 licensing scheme, see YCA, House Book 23, fos. 50v.ff.

50. Alehouse licenses also extended the old householder-focused presentments of the assize in these two respects.

51. CLRO, Repertory 11, fos. 120–121. The Pickerings are discussed more fully in chapter 4.

52. *VCH, Oxon.,* vol. 4, p. 308; and H. E. Salter, ed., *Mediaeval archives of the University of Oxford,* vol. 2, Oxford Historical Society, 73 (1919), pp. 139–141.

53. Oxford Assizes. In contrast to other places, officers in Oxford managed to account for almost all of the monies due from brewers; compare, for example, sums collected in Oxford in 1311 to those reported in William Hudson and John Cottingham Tingey, eds., *The records of the city of Norwich,* vol. 1 (Norwich, 1906), p. 367.

54. Carl I. Hammer, Jr., "Anatomy of an oligarchy: The Oxford town council in the fifteenth and sixteenth centuries," *Journal of British Studies* 18 (1978), p. 15.

55. *VCH, Oxon.,* vol. 4, p. 16.

56. Wives were cited in a handful of cases, but they seem to have been named in the place of recently deceased husbands.

57. H. E. Salter, ed., *Mediaeval archives of the University of Oxford,* vol. 1, Oxford Historical Society 70 (1920), pp. 18–19, 129–133.

58. *VCH, Oxon.,* vol 4, p. 19.

59. Salter, *Mediaeval archives,* vol. 1, pp. 152–157, 342.

60. Salter, *Munimenta,* pp. 135–137; Salter, *Registrum,* vol. 1, p. xv.

61. For the 1381 Oxford poll tax, see PRO, E179 161/47. I have been unable to reconcile my figures for this tax with those reported in *VCH, Oxon.,* vol. 4, p. 45, or P. J. P. Goldberg, *Women, work and life cycle in a medieval economy* (Oxford, 1992), p. 90. For further discussions of brewers in Oxford after the Black Death, see *VCH, Oxon.,* vol. 4, esp. pp. 39–48. Only in Oxford and Southwark did brewers regularly serve on royal commissions in the early fifteenth century; see, for example, *Calendar of fine rolls,* 22 vols. (London, 1911–63),

vol. 12: 1399—1405, pp. 190, 259; vol 14: 1413—1422, pp. 302, 418; vol. 15: 1422—1430, pp. 8—9.

62. PRO, E179 161/47; Salter, *Mediaeval archives*, vol. 2, pp. 1—127.

63. Salter, *Registrum*, vol. 1, pp. 8—10. Since some of the brewers were noted by surname alone, their sex cannot be determined. If any of these brewers were female, it is most likely that they were widows of brewers, not brewsters independently in the trade.

64. Additional orders were issued about the rota in 1462, see H. E. Salter, ed., *Registrum cancellarii Oxoniensis, 1434—1469*, vol. 2, Oxford Historical Society, 94 (1932), p. 93.

65. Mitchell, *Register*, pp. 249—251.

66. See for example, OUA, Chancellor's Court Register F (1506—14), fo. 135 (1511), and Chancellor's Court Register GG (1545—55, with much material from later periods), fo. 137 (1604).

67. Andrew Clark, ed., *Register of the University of Oxford*, vol. 2, part 1, Oxford Historical Society, 10 (1887), pp. 327—330.

68. Salter, *Registrum*, vol. 1, pp. 63—64.

69. Mitchell, *Registrum*, p. 250.

70. Ibid., pp. 249—251.

71. W. H. Turner, ed., *Selections from the records of the city of Oxford* (Oxford, 1880), pp. 120—122, 334—335. The 1516 action is dated confusingly: both 1525 and the eighth year of Henry VIII are mentioned. Given the reference to 16 brewers in the incorporation of 1521, 1516 seems a more likely date than 1525.

72. The effort to restrict the number of brewers was generally successful (with roughly 20 brewers working in the town from the late fifteenth century), but the effort to stop part-time brewing was less successful. See Carl I. Hammer, Jr., "Some social and institutional aspects of town-gown relations in late medieval and Tudor Oxford," Ph.D. dissertation, University of Toronto, 1973, esp. pp. 147—149.

73. Oxford County Record Office, Bridgewater 105.

74. Bodleian Library, Ms. Top. Oxon. c. 235.

75. *VCH, Oxon.*, vol. 4, pp. 320—321.

76. OUA, WP ß/34/b. The duration of this incorporation is unclear; see *VCH, Oxon.*, vol. 4, pp. 320—321. For the regulatory uses of gilds, see Heather Swanson, "The illusion of economic structure: Craft guilds in late medieval English towns," *Past and Present* 121 (1988), pp. 31—48.

77. By the late sixteenth century, brewers were still wealthy and powerful, but their social prominence waned. See Hammer, "Oxford," pp. 179—180; and *VCH, Oxon.*, vol. 4, pp. 108—109.

78. For 1447, see Salter, *Registrum*, vol. 1, p. 149. For 1501, see Mitchell, *Registrum*, p. 251. For the sixteenth century, see Clark, *Register*, pp. 327—333.

79. No women were listed among the assembled brewers in 1434, nor were they usually listed in later agreements between the brewers and the university. See, for example, OUA, Chancellor's Court Register F, fo. 135.

80. For Joan Chilham, see Oxford Assizes. For Agnes Trederf, see Salter, *Registrum*, vol. 1, pp. 9, 149. The place of widows in brewing is discussed more fully in chapters 3 and 5.

81. OUA, Chancellor's Court Register GGG, fo. 145. Keit was admitted in February 1631, and in June of that year Robert Southbie was admitted in her place. With only one exception (Elizabeth Markham), I have been able to trace all the other women named in brewing rotas to husbands who had brewed. The list of these (and other) admissions printed in Clark, *Register*, pp. 327—330, is accurate but omits important details.

82. OUA, WP ß/B/33.

83. Clark, Register, pp. 324–327. Some of these women were widows, but the marital status of others is unknown.

84. OUA, Chancellor's Court Register F (1506–14), fo. 138v. I have found no evidence to suggest that Dodicott was the widow of a brewer.

85. OUA, Chancellor's Court Register HHH, fo. 167. Robinson was the widow of a brewer.

86. PRO, E179 161/138; OUA, WP ß/34/b; OUA, Chancellor's Court Register HHH, fo. 156; Clark, Register, pp. 333–335.

Chapter 7

1. *Goesaert v. Cleary* (69 S.Ct. 198). I am grateful to Linda Kerber for bringing this case to my attention.

2. Chester City Record Office, First Assembly Book, AB/1, fo. 70.

3. Throughout this chapter, I will continue to distinguish between brewsters and tapsters whenever possible, but I will use the term *alewife* when such distinctions are not possible. Although the occupations of brewster and tapster could be quite distinct, contemporary use of *alewife* often conflated the two, as often also did representations of women in the drink trade. Since women who brewed ale also usually retailed it from their houses, this conflation of brewster and tapster made particular sense for females. For male brewers, who in many sixteenth-century cities did not retail their product, distinctions between brewing and selling were more important.

4. Gabrielle M. Spiegel, "History, historicism and the social logic of the text in the middle ages," *Speculum* 65 (1990), pp. 59–86, at p. 77.

5. The date of the poem is uncertain. For background information on Skelton and his poem, I have relied particularly on Ian A. Gordon, *John Skelton, poet laureate* (Melbourne, 1943); Maurice Pollet, *John Skelton, poet of Tudor England* (1962; trans. Lewisburg, Penn., 1971); John Scattergood, *John Skelton: The complete English poems* (New Haven, Conn., 1983).

6. I have used the slightly modernized edition of *The Tunning of Elynour Rummyng* (henceforth cited in the notes as TTER) by Gerald Hammond, ed., *John Skelton, selected poems* (Manchester, 1980). For the main description, see lines 12–90.

7. TTER, lines 523, 600–604, 164–167, 207–210, 445–458, 70–79, 100, 376–381. See Deborah Baker Wyrick, "Withinne that develes temple: An examination of Skelton's *The Tunnyng of Elynour Rummyng*," *Journal of Medieval and Renaissance Studies* 10 (1980), pp. 239–254.

8. TTER, lines 22–25, 189–218, 160–167, 244–308, 607–617, 168–184, 335–350, 257–265, 133–140.

9. The possibility of a didactic intent on Skelton's part is suggested by the Latin colophon that follows the poem, exhorting women fond of drinking to take heed of his satire. A. R. Heiserman, *Skelton and satire* (Chicago, 1961), p. 297, suggests that the poem attacks neither Elynour Rummyng nor her customers but is instead merely funny.

10. Lawrence M. Clopper, ed., *Records of early English drama: Chester* (cited henceforth as REED-C) (Toronto, 1979), pp. 6–7; Lawrence M. Clopper, "The history and development of the Chester cycle," *Modern Philology* 75 (1978), pp. 219–246; David Mills, ed., *The Chester mystery cycle* (East Lansing, Mich., 1992), pp. xiii–xiv. Some literary scholars argue that the scene with the alewife is a later interpolation; Peter W. Travis, *Dramatic design in the Chester cycle* (Chicago, 1982), pp. 67–68.

11. Mills, *Chester mystery cycle*, pp. 313–314. To make the text more readily comprehensible, I have slightly emended Mills's translation.

12. Richard Axton, *European drama of the early middle ages* (Pittsburgh, 1974), pp. 182–184. Clanging of illegal measures by offenders seems to have been a common form of ridicule or punishment; Andrew Boorde, *A dyetary of health*, F. J. Furnivall, ed. (London, 1870), pp. 260–261. It was not uncommon for a particular gild to be responsible for a play that reflected on its trade; Alan D. Justice, "Trade symbolism in the York Cycle," *Theatre Journal* 31 (1979), pp. 47–58.

13. R. M. Lumiansky, "Comedy and theme in the Chester *Harrowing of Hell*," *Tulsa Studies in English* 10 (1960), pp. 5–12.

14. W. O. Hassall, ed., *The Holkham bible picture book* (London, 1954), fo. 42v.

15. Nikolaus Pevsner, *The buildings of England: Shropshire* (Harmondsworth, U.K., 1958), p. 179; Hassall, *Holkham*, p. 156, n. 1; Edward Meyrick Goulborn and Edward Hallstone, *The ancient sculptures of the roof of Norwich cathedral* (London, 1876), pp. 515–516.

16. Jane Elizabeth Ashby, "English medieval murals of the Doom: A descriptive catalogue and introduction," M.A. thesis, York University, 1980. I am grateful to David Benson for bringing this thesis to my attention.

17. Ralph Hanna has criticized my original use of material from *Piers Plowman* in his "Brewing trouble: On literature and history—and ale-wives," in Barbara Hanawalt and David Wallace, eds., *Bodies and disciplines: Intersections of literature and history in fifteenth-century England* (Minneapolis, 1996), pp. 1–17. I would like to thank him for showing me an early version of his essay, and I appreciate his comments (from which I have learned a great deal). But I also disagree with many of his assumptions and conclusions. Although I cannot review all my objections here, let me emphasize three points. First, my use of *Piers Plowman* specifically and literature in general is not, as Hanna has claimed, mimetic. I am trying to find ways to use literature (and other cultural artifacts) to trace ideological influences on human behavior and experience; this is very different from a straightforward treatment of literature as a reflection of "real life." Second, Hanna's analysis obfuscates important distinctions between ale and wine, alehouses and taverns, brewsters and male brewers, lords and peasants, and the statutory and practical bases of the assize of ale. Third, Hanna, despite his use of my work to frame a discussion about specific passages in *Piers Plowman*, himself concedes that "I have no desire to deny the propriety of Langland's two women to Bennett's argument, nor do I find much reason to disagree with her extraordinarily compelling summary conclusions about literary texts."

18. For quotations given in my text, I have used (with some slight alterations of my own) the modern redaction of Donald and Rachel Attwater, *The book concerning Piers the Plowman* (London, 1957). For this particular quote, see pp. 38–39. For edited versions of the main surviving texts in their original English, see George Kane, ed., *Piers Plowman: The A version* (London, 1960), passus 5, lines 133–141; George Kane and E. Talbot Donaldson, eds., *Piers Plowman: The B version* (London, 1975), passus 5, lines 217–225; Derek Pearsall, ed., *Piers Plowman: An edition of the C text* (Berkeley, Calif., 1979), passus 6, lines 225–233.

19. I do not mean to suggest that Langland modeled Rose the Regrater on the Good Gossip of Chester. Instead, I mean to suggest that Langland's creation of Rose the Regrater might have drawn on a common stock of ideas about cheating alewives from which also came the many late medieval representations of cheating alewives condemned to hell.

20. Hanna argues that I have erred in my description of Betoun the Brewster's alehouse, which is merely, in his view, a churchlike "place of fellowship and good cheer." I find this interpretation hard to reconcile with Langland's graphic description of Glutton's urinating, farting, and vomiting in Betoun's alehouse.

21. Attwater, *Piers* (again slightly altered), p. 41. For the original texts, see editions cited above: A, passus 5, lines 146ff.; B, passus 5, lines 296ff.; C, passus 6, lines 350ff.

22. Nick Gray, "The clemency of cobblers: A reading of 'Glutton's Confession' in *Piers Plowman*," *Leeds Studies in English* 17 (1986), pp. 61–75. As interpreted by Gray, this scene is less a mocking of religious rites than an argument by Langland that sees "sin and confession as mirror-images of one another" (p. 68).

23. Langland does malign brewers at two other points in his poem, but in neither instance does he name or personify a brewer. As a result, his descriptions of Rose the Regrater and Betoun the Brewster carry particular force.

24. John Lydgate, "A ballade on an aleseller," in Henry Noble MacCracken, ed., *The minor poems of John Lydgate, part 2: Secular poems*, EETS, 192 (1934), pp. 429–432. As Julia Boffey has pointed out to me, in using the courtly poetic form of the "ballade" to write about a humble aleseller, Lydgate might have been joking.

25. F. Pyle, "The origins of the Skeltonic," *Notes & Queries* 171 (1936), pp. 362–364; Elaine Spina, "Skeltonic meter in *Elynour Rummyng*," *Studies in Philology* 64 (1967), pp. 665–684; H. L. R. Edwards, *The life and times of an early Tudor poet* (London, 1949), p. 121.

26. Francis Lee Utley, *The crooked rib* (Columbus, Ohio, 1944), pp. 241–243; Frederick J. Furnivall, ed., *Captain Cox his ballads and books* (London, 1871); Ben Jonson, *The tale of a tub* (1596, rev. 1633), act V, scene VII, lines 24–25 (I am grateful to the late Margaret Whittick for bringing this allusion to my attention).

27. Caroline Barron, "William Langland: A London poet," in Barbara Hanawalt, ed., *Chaucer's England* (Minneapolis, 1992), p. 99. See also J. A. Burrow, "The audience of *Piers Plowman*," *Essays on medieval literature* (Oxford, 1984), pp. 102–116; Anne Middleton, "The audience and public of *Piers Plowman*," in David Lawton, ed., *Middle English alliterative poetry and its literary background* (Cambridge, 1982), pp. 101–154; J. R. Maddicott, "Poems of social protest in early fourteenth-century England," in W. M. Ormrod, ed., *England in the fourteenth century* (London, 1986), pp. 130–144.

28. Robert Copland, *Jyl of Brentford's testament* (c. 1565); modern edition found in Frederick J. Furnivall, ed., *Jyl of Brentford's testament* (London, 1871), pp. 7–19.

29. *The good-fellows counsel: Or, the bad husband's recantation* (1680–85), Bodleian Library, Wood E.25, item 19. I thank Sara Mendelson for suggesting that I look at this collection.

30. *The kind beleeving hostess* (no date, but certainly seventeenth century); modern edition found in W. Chappell, ed., *The Roxburghe ballads, vol.* 1 (Hertford, 1877), pp. 515–520.

31. *The industrious smith* (1635–42); modern edition found in Chappell, *Roxburghe ballads*, pp. 468–474. The refrain of this ballad either echoed or created a proverbial saying, "This must be if we brew [or sell] ale," meaning that unpleasant things will accrue to those who follow unpleasant occupations. Morris Palmer Tilley, ed., *A dictionary of proverbs in English in the sixteenth and seventeenth centuries* (Ann Arbor, Mich., 1950), item B653, p. 67.

32. *Pasquil's jests with the merriments of Mother Bunch* (London, 1629), STC 19452. For other texts associated with Mother Bunch, see Margaret Spufford, *Small books and pleasant histories* (Cambridge, 1981), pp. 3–4, 61–64. For another example linking ale and pregnancy, see the ballad about Mother Watkins's ale printed in H. Huth, ed., *A collection of seventy-nine black-letter ballads and broadsides, 1559–1597* (London, 1867), pp. 251–255.

33. British Museum, Department of Prints and Drawings, English Portraits, CX, P2. This popular print is attributed to David Loggan.

34. F. J. Furnivall, ed., *The tale of Beryn*, EETS, 105 (1909), line 444. As Julia Boffey has suggested to me, Kit might personify duplicity, but she is also somewhat heroic in her ability to out-swindle a swindler.

35. REED-C, pp. liii, 198, 303–304.

36. The corpus of so-called "alewife poems" include some poems about drunken women, not women working in the ale and beer trade. See Rossell Hope Robbins, "Poems dealing with contemporary conditions," in Albert E. Hartung, ed., *A manual of the*

writings in Middle English 1050–1500, vol. 5 (New Haven, Conn., 1975), pp. 1463–1464; and "John Crophill's ale-pots," *Review of English Studies*, n.s., 20 (1969), pp. 182–189.

37. Francis Beaumont, *The knight of the burning pestle*, ed. Sheldon P. Zitner (Manchester, 1984), pp. 141–142.

38. Donald Lupton, *London and the countrey carbonadoed and quartred into severall characters* (1632), STC 16944, pp. 127–131.

39. Attwater, *Piers*, p. 21. For original texts, see editions cited above: A, passus 3, lines 67–70; B, passus 3, lines 78–81; C, passus 3, lines 79–83. Some manuscripts render "brewers" as "brewsters." For a depiction of a brewer who "will not be ruled," see Attwater, *Piers*, p. 189.

40. The introduction of the Cook in the general prologue (lines 376–385) focuses positively on his skills, with only one negative comment probably intended to imply adulteration of food (that he had a sore on his shin). Chaucer's comment of the Cook that "Well could he know a draught of London ale" has a double meaning, suggesting not only the Cook's competence in one aspect of his trade but also his excessive fondness for drink. In the prologue to the Cook's tale, the Host accuses the Cook (in a good-humored fashion) of selling bad food and keeping a fly-ridden shop. And in the prologue to the Manciple's tale, the Cook is depicted as an amusing drunk.

41. John Gower, *Mirour de l'omme*, G. C. Macauley, ed., *The complete works of John Gower*, vol. 1 (Oxford, 1899), esp. lines 26,305–26,352.

42. Barnaby Rich, *My ladies looking glasse* (London, 1616), STC 20991.7 (formerly 20984), p. 31. Elsewhere, Rich attacked the alewives of Dublin as "very loathsome, filthy and abominable." See J. T. Gilbert, *A history of the city of Dublin*, vol. 1 (Dublin 1854), pp. 151–153. I am grateful to Jane Laughton for calling this reference to my attention.

43. See, for example, depictions of men who brewed and sold ale in Robert Greene, *A quippe for an upstart courtier* (1592), in Alexander B. Grosart, ed., *The life and complete works of Robert Greene*, vol. 11 (New York, 1964), pp. 274–276. Although these men are maligned for their bad business practices, they are not depicted as physically gross, sexually uncontrolled, or religiously suspect.

44. William Harrison, *The description of England*; see the modern edition by George Edelen (Ithaca, N.Y., 1968), pp. 138–139.

45. Laura Caroline Stevenson, *Praise and paradox: Merchants and craftsmen in Elizabethan popular literature* (Cambridge, 1984).

46. *The praise of brewers: Or, the brewers bravery* (1670?), Bodleian Library, Wood E.25, item 63. Wing P3167.

47. G. R. Owst, *Literature and pulpit in medieval England* (Oxford, 1966), p. 435.

48. Bartlett Jere Whiting, *Proverbs, sentences and proverbial phrases from English writings mainly before 1500* (Cambridge, Mass., 1968), item T48. See also Owst, *Literature and pulpit*, pp. 245–249.

49. Regulations of this sort can be found in many late medieval and early modern jurisdictions. For just one example, see Marjorie K. McIntosh, "Local change and community control in England, 1465–1500," *Huntington Library Quarterly* 49 (1986), pp. 219–242.

50. The standard definition of *misogyny* as "hatred of women" encourages us to underestimate both misogynists and their effects. It is the assumption of this chapter, and indeed the implication of much feminist research, that misogyny is not the ideology of an extreme few but rather a pervasive feature of European culture. See especially Katharine Rogers, *The troublesome helpmate: A history of misogyny in literature* (Seattle, 1966), and Joan Smith, *Misogynies* (London, 1989). In studying misogyny as it has actually worked in social relations, I wish to question the approach of R. Howard Bloch and some other

literary critics who have tended to interpret misogyny as a literary game, with little social import; see Bloch's *Medieval misogyny* (Chicago, 1991).

51. "Scorn of women," in Rossell Hope Robbins, ed., *Secular lyrics of the xivth and xvth centuries* (Oxford, 1952), pp. 224–225.

52. *The tale of Beryn*, line 71.

53. William Dunbar, "Against evil women," cited in Rogers, *Troublesome helpmate*, p. 65.

54. Physical grossness was so associated with alewives that one late seventeenth-century commentator thought that settlers in North America named a local fish an alewife because of its large belly. *Notes & Queries*, 9th series, 8 (November 30, 1901), pp. 451–452, and s.v. in the *Oxford English Dictionary*.

55. *The industrious smith*, line 64.

56. Rogers, *Troublesome helpmate*, esp. pp. 74–76, 93; Walter Map, *De nugis curialium/courtiers' trifles*, M. R. James, ed. and trans. (Oxford, 1983), p. 293; Geoffrey Chaucer, "The Wife of Bath's prologue," *The Canterbury tales*; Whiting, *Proverbs*, item W519.

57. See, for example, the clever alewife who advises her husband "be ruled by me"; *The maltster caught in a trap or the witty alewife* (printed for P. Brooksby at the Ball in Pye Corner); dated 1672–95 in Wing M353. See also Jean Howard's discussion of Mistress Quickly in "Forming the commonwealth: Including, excluding and criminalizing women in Heywood's *Edward IV* and Shakespeare's *Henry IV*," in Jean Brink, ed., *Privileging gender in early modern England* (Kirksville, Missouri, 1993), pp. 109–122. I am grateful to George Evans Light for bringing this essay to my attention.

58. *The industrious smith*, lines 3–4, 76–77. In a significant shift, the refrain for this stanza changed from the usual "These things must be, if we sell ale" to "These things should not be, though they sell ale."

59. *The kind beleeving hostess*, lines 23–27.

60. The play *Tom Tyler and his wife* was printed in 1661, with the note that it had been "printed and acted about a hundred years ago"; Wing T1792. For the quote from TTER, see line 253.

61. Of course, poems could influence public opinion quite directly, and TTER might have sometimes been expected to do just that. It was reprinted twice in 1624, a time of considerable public discussion and action concerning alehouses, brewing monopolies, and unlicensed victualers. In this instance, the anticipated impact of TTER would have been on all brewers, not merely on brewsters. Also, if Skelton based his poem on the alewife Alianora Romyng who plied her trade in Leatherhead (the locale of TTER) in the 1520s, her business could have been directly influenced by the poem. See the letter from John H. Harvey in *Times Literary Supplement*, 26 October 1946, p. 521.

62. My effort to draw out the social meanings of these representations draws on the traditions of new historicism, as articulated by Jonathan Dollimore and Alan Sinfield in *Political Shakespeare* (Manchester, 1985). Yet not surprisingly, I prefer historians' approaches to the links among literature, ideology, and history, and I have found Keith Thomas's remarks in his *History and literature* (Swansea, 1988) to be particularly helpful in this regard. See also Spiegel, "History, historicism."

63. R. H. Helmholz, ed., *Select cases on defamation to 1600*, Selden Society, 101 (1985), pp. 5–6. Shannon McSheffrey has brought to my attention a similar case from 1472 in the Consistory Court of London (Greater London Record Office, MS DL/C/205, f. 162).

64. Huntington Library, Ellesmere Mss. 7342, 7343. I thank Cynthia Herrup for showing me this material and the Huntington Library for permitting its citation. It is an interesting coincidence that the Ludlow church boasts a misericord of a condemned alewife.

65. Hence, jurors often reported that all alewives had broken the assize; see, for example, G. Poulett Scrope, ed., *History of the manor and ancient barony of Castle Combe* (1852), p. 342. Even knowledge of offenses did not always translate into effective punishment; R. H. Hilton, "Lords, burgesses and hucksters," *Past and Present* 97 (1982), p. 14. As late as the seventeenth century, brewers and their servants were still suspected of systematically cheating in more than a dozen different ways; BL, Cotton Titus BV, fos. 375–390.

66. Henry Thomas Riley, *Memorials of London and London life in the xiiith and xivth and xvth centuries* (London, 1868), p. 319.

67. Beer was often attacked, in nationalistic terms, as a foul drink of foreigners, but it was also much praised. The representation of beer in England during these centuries is a separate topic that deserves fuller investigation than it can be given here.

68. Keith Wrightson, "Alehouses, order and reformation in rural England, 1590–1660," in Eileen and Stephen Yeo, eds., *Popular culture and class conflict 1590–1914* (Atlantic Highlands, N.J., 1981), pp. 1–27.

69. For examples, see CLRO, Repertory 18, fos. 425b, 426b (1575); W. H. Overall, ed., *Analytical index to the series of records known as the Remembrancia* (London, 1878), p. 541 (1613); repeated concerns about the untrue measures of brewers and their unfair prices in the repertories of the Court of Aldermen and the journals of the Court of Common Council (both deposited at the CLRO); BL, Lansdowne 71/33 and 71/35.

70. Ian Archer, Caroline Barron, and Vanessa Harding, *Hugh Alley's caveat: The markets of London in 1598*, London Topographical Society, 137 (1988).

71. GL, Ms. 5497.

72. *Choice of inventions*, in Chappell, *Roxburghe ballads*, pp. 105–110, esp. lines 113–125.

73. Lupton, *London and the countrey*, p. 129.

74. *The industrious smith*, lines 25–26.

75. Thomas Bruce Dilks, ed., *Bridgwater borough archives, vol. 2: 1377–1399*, Somerset Record Society, 53 (1938), p. 72.

76. NRO, ANW 6/1. I am grateful to Susan Amussen for calling my attention to this case.

77. Chester City Record Office, First Assembly Book, AB/1, fo. 70.

78. Ibid., Mayor's Book, MB/19, fos. 13, 26v.ff.; First Assembly Book, AB/1, fo. 131v.

79. Ibid., First Assembly Book, AB/1, fo. 70v. For a recent study of churching celebrations in general, see David Cressy, "Purification, thanksgiving, and the churching of women in post-Reformation England," *Past and Present* 141 (1993), pp. 106–146.

80. Chester City Record Office, First Assembly Book, AB/1, fo. 72v.

Chapter 8

1. This remark was made by Joan Thirsk in her presentation "Women's initiatives in early modern England: Where are they?" at a conference on "Women's initiatives in early modern England, 1500–1750," London, 4 June 1994. For a brief report on this conference by Penelope Lane, see *The Achievement Project Newsletter* 4:1 (1995), pp. 4–6.

2. Karl Marx, *The 18th Brumaire of Louis Bonaparte* (1852; New York, 1963), p. 15.

3. Pamela Sharpe has recently suggested that interpretations based on either continuity or change equally "suggest women's impotency to deal with their situation." See "Continuity and change: Women's history and economic history in Britain," *Economic History Review*, 2nd series, 48 (1995), pp. 353–369, at 355. I do not accept Sharpe's assertion that these perspectives ipso facto disempower women, and in any case, she does not suggest an alternative to what is, after all, an enduring interplay between change and continuity in historical writing.

4. Alice Clark, *The working life of women in the seventeenth century* (London, 1919).

5. Eileen Power, "The position of women," in C. G. Crump and E. F. Jacobs, eds., *The legacy of the middle ages* (Oxford, 1926), p. 410. Caroline Barron, "The 'golden age' of women in medieval London," *Reading Medieval Studies* 15 (1989), pp. 35–58.

6. Keith Snell, *Annals of the labouring poor* (Cambridge, 1985), pp. 270–319; Bridget Hill, *Women, work and sexual politics in eighteenth-century England* (Oxford, 1989); Michael Roberts, "Sickles and scythes: Women's work and men's work at harvest time," *History Workshop Journal* 7 (1979), pp. 3–29; Margaret George, "From 'goodwife' to 'mistress': The transformation of the female in bourgeois culture," *Science and Society* 37 (1973), pp. 152–177. The quote is from Susan Cahn, *Industry of devotion: The transformation of women's work in England, 1500–1660* (New York, 1987), p. 9. Medievalists also have their own stories of decline within the confines of the medieval centuries; see David Herlihy, *Opera muliebria: Women and work in medieval Europe* (New York, 1990). For a fuller critique of the notion of a transformation in women's work that accompanied the transition from a "medieval" world to an "early modern" one, see my "Medieval women, modern women: Across the great divide," in David Aers, ed., *Culture and history 1350–1600: Essays on English communities, identities, and writing* (London, 1992), pp. 147–175.

7. See a similar argument in Sylvia Walby, *Theorizing patriarchy* (Oxford, 1990), pp. 183–184.

8. Mary Prior, "Women and the urban economy: Oxford 1500–1800," in Mary Prior, ed., *Women in English society 1500–1800* (London, 1985), pp. 93–117.

9. For Kempstere, see chapter 3; for Wycombe, see chapter 6. The notion that medieval women were ill suited for hard and heavy labor is a misconception rooted in Victorian medievalism. See Roberts, "Sickles," for an argument based in part on physical differences between women and men. As Carole Shammas has pointed out, the logic of Roberts's argument would require that women should have been employed in work that best used their "delicate" bodies, such as surgery or watchmaking or goldsmithing. Since this was not the case, matters other than physical suitability must have critically shaped job segregation by sex. See Carole Shammas, "The world women knew: Women workers in the north of England during the late seventeenth century," in Richard S. Dunn, ed., *The world of William Penn* (Philadelphia, 1986), pp. 99–115.

10. L. F. Salzman, *English industries of the middle ages* (Oxford, 1923), pp. 328–329.

11. Olivia Harris, "Households as natural units," in Kate Young et al., eds., *Of marriage and the market* (London, 1984), pp. 136–155; and Rayna Rapp et al., "Examining family history," *Feminist Studies* 5 (1979), pp. 174–200.

12. Maryanne Kowaleski, *Local markets and regional trade in medieval Exeter* (Cambridge, 1995), pp. 133–136. As noted in chapter 4, I did not find this pattern in my analysis of brewers in early fifteenth-century London, but Kowaleski was able to construct a general occupational structure of Exeter. Until this can be done for other towns, we cannot ascertain the extent to which the pattern she found in Exeter is a general one.

13. Jo Ann McNamara and Suzanne Wemple, "The power of women through the family in medieval Europe, 500–1100," first printed in 1973 and used here as reprinted in Mary Erler and Maryanne Kowaleski, eds., *Women and power in the middle ages* (Athens, Ga., 1988), pp. 83–101, at 97.

14. Suzanne Wemple, *Women in Frankish society: Marriage and the cloister, 500 to 900* (Philadelphia, 1981); Marion Facinger, "A study of medieval queenship: Capetian France, 987–1237," *Studies in Medieval and Renaissance History* 5 (1968), pp. 3–47; Pauline Stafford, "The king's wife in Wessex 800–1066," *Past and Present* 91 (1981), pp. 3–27; Joan Kelly, "Did women have a renaissance?" in *Women, history and theory* (Chicago, 1984), pp. 19–50; Martha Howell, "Citizenship and gender: Women's political status in northern medieval

cities," in Erler and Kowaleski, *Women and power*, pp. 37–60; Susan Amussen, *An ordered society: Gender and class in early modern England* (Oxford, 1988). To generalize broadly, it seems that early medievalists emphasize that a transition from kinship to patrilineal family disempowered women, and late medievalists argue that a transition from family to individual had the same effect.

15. Feminist theorists have discussed the state at considerable length. See especially M. McIntosh, "The state and the oppression of women," in Annette Kuhn and AnnMarie Wolpe, eds., *Feminism and materialism* (London, 1978), pp. 254–289; Wendy Brown, "Finding the man in the state," *Feminist Studies* 18 (1992), pp. 7–34; Sarah Hanley, "Family and state in early modern France: The marriage pact," in Marilyn Boxer and Jean H. Quataert, eds., *Connecting spheres: Women in the Western world 1500 to the present* (New York, 1987), pp. 53–63, and "Engendering the state: Family formation and state building in early modern France," *French Historical Studies* 16 (1989), pp. 4–27.

16. Clark, *Working life*, p. 307.

17. See chapter 6 for a brief discussion of brewsters who protested regulation of their trade.

18. The subject of women's resistance and protest deserves much more thorough study. In a preliminary examination of the subject, Ralph Houlbrooke concluded that women rarely expressed what he called "feminist sentiments." See "Women's social life and common action in England from the fifteenth century to the eve of the civil war," *Continuity and Change* 1 (1986), pp. 171–189.

19. Lawrence Stone, "The use and abuse of history," *New Republic*, May 2, 1994, pp. 31–37, at p. 34.

20. See, for example, two sets of exchanges: (a) Sheila Rowbotham, "The trouble with 'patriarchy,'" and the reply by Sally Alexander and Barbara Taylor, "In defence of 'patriarchy,'" from 1979, reprinted in Raphael Samuel, ed., *People's history and socialist theory* (London, 1981), pp. 364–373; (b) Bridget Hill, "Women's history: A study in change, continuity or standing still?" *Women's History Review* 2 (1993), pp. 5–22; and my reply, "Women's history: A study in continuity and change," *Women's History Review* 2 (1993), pp. 173–184.

21. I am grateful to Ruth Karras for making me aware of the need to address explicitly these two particular sorts of reactions to the subject of patriarchy.

22. In thinking about the ways in which women benefit from and support patriarchy, I have found Deniz Kandiyoti's notion of "patriarchal bargains" to be very useful. See "Bargaining with patriarchy," *Gender and Society* 2 (1988), pp. 274–290. I thank Sarah Shields for bringing this article to my attention.

23. See, for example, the comments of Chandra Talpade Mohanty, "Under Western eyes: Feminist scholarship and colonial discourses," in Chandra Talpade Mohanty et al., eds., *Third world women and the politics of feminism* (Bloomington, Ind., 1991), pp. 51–80.

24. In thinking about women as a group, I have found two recent articles to be especially helpful: Jane Roland Martin, "Methodological essentialism, false difference, and other dangerous traps," *Signs: Journal of Women in Culture and Society* 19 (1994), pp. 630–657; and Iris Marion Young, "Gender as seriality: Thinking about women as a social collective," *Signs: Journal of Women in Culture and Society* 19 (1994), pp. 713–738.

25. The major exception is, of course, dual systems theory, which attempts to relate capitalism and patriarchy. For a good introduction to feminist thought before the late 1980s, see Rosemarie Tong, *Feminist thought: A comprehensive introduction* (Boulder, Colo., 1989).

26. Walby, *Theorizing patriarchy*. Patricia Hill Collins, *Black feminist thought* (New York, 1990).

27. Some would argue that it is unfair to call an institution such as a gild "patriarchal" because it served so many purposes that were not patriarchal in intention or effect. But I would reply that such institutions were patriarchal because *one of their effects* was to assist in the maintenance of an imbalance of power between the sexes. In a similar way, I would argue that the U.S. military, before desegregation in the late 1940s, was a racist institution because it helped to maintain racial asymmetry.

28. I am expanding here on the argument of Walby in *Theorizing patriarchy* about two strategies of patriarchy in paid employment—exclusion and segregation. Walby placed these strategies in distinct periods of British history; I would argue not only that they might operate simultaneously but also that they operate in conjunction with other strategies.

Appendix

1. Both these translations observe the following conventions: place names have been modernized, superscripts are noted in round brackets, marginalia are noted in italics, and items inserted to enhance the sense of passages are placed in square brackets. For Woolhope, see Hereford Cathedral Archives, R760a (court held on the Thursday after the feast of St. Anne, 18 Edward III). For Ingatestone, see Essex Record Office, D/DP M15 (general court for the Wednesday after the feast of St. Andrew, 18 Edward III).

2. ESRO, SAS/G18/45 (hundred court for 7 October, 24 Henry VI).

3. I found only one other long-term brewing license noted among the numerous presentments found in ESRO, SAS/G18/44–46 (courts for 1430–59).

4. See, for example, the licensing and amercement of Emma Taylor; NtnRO, Montagu Collection, Box X364B, roll 33. The custumal of Brigstock explicitly stated that no one could license any woman (*aliquam mulierem*) to brew against the assize; NtnRO, Montagu Collection, Box X371.

5. Aletasters were more liable for amercement for dereliction of duty than other officers, perhaps because it was assumed that they profited from their office by taking money from brewers; Edward Britton, *Community of the Vill* (Toronto, 1977), p. 100. I have found no regular amercements of aletasters in an urban jurisdiction; town councils might have been less interested than manorial lords in amercing one of their officers.

6. Essex Record Office, D/DP M13 (view of frankpledge, Monday in the morrow of Trinity, 10 Edward III), D/DP M19 (court, Thursday next after the feast of St. Ethelburga the virgin, 33 Edward III). See also M. K. Dale, ed., "Court Rolls of Tamworth," (typescript deposited with the Institute of Historical Research, University of London), p. 160; and H. E. Salter, *Registrum cancellarii Oxoniensis, 1434–1469, vol. 2*, Oxford Historical Society, 94 (1932), p. 138.

7. See also ESRO, SAS/G18/4.

8. Sample: Preston-on-Wye, c. 1275. See also the example from Woolhope given above (probably all of the brewers distinguished by the superscript "i" had offended against the assize, and all others had not).

9. See, for example, BL, Add. Charter 15,903. For an example from Wallingford, see Berkshire Record Office, W/JBb 13.

10. See, for example, BL, Add. Charter 24,353. For an urban example, see Adolphus Ballard and James Tait, eds., *British borough charters, vol. 2: 1216–1307* (Cambridge, 1923), pp. 222–223.

11. Suffolk Record Office, V5/18/1.2 and 1.3.

12. For further information about ale tolls, see N. Neilson, *Customary rents*, Oxford Studies in Social and Legal History, 2 (1910), p. 39; Maryanne Kowaleski, *Local markets and regional trade in medieval Exeter* (Cambridge, 1995), p. 132; Sample: Alciston; Cornelius Wal-

ford, "Early laws and customs in Great Britain regarding food," *Transactions of the Royal Historical Society* 8 (1880), p. 92; Cornelius Brown, *A history of Newark-on-Trent* (Newark, 1904), p. 156. In Cuxham, only tolls were levied but in language that sometimes evoked assize presentments; see P. D. A. Harvey, ed., *Manorial records of Cuxham, Oxfordshire, c.* 1200–1359 (London, 1976), p. 683. In Leicester, sixteenth-century cannemol lists also often used the language of assize presentment. Because of the coincidence of ale tolls and assize presentments, I have included data from such sources as the Leicester cannemols in the samples described below.

13. This is the conclusion of most historians who have worked with these records: Helen M. Cam, *The hundred and the hundred rolls* (London, 1963), p. 211; R. H. Hilton, "Women in the village," *The English peasantry in the later middle ages* (Oxford, 1975), p. 104; Britton, *Community*, p. 25; P. J. P. Goldberg, *Women, work and life cycle in a medieval economy* (Oxford, 1992), p. 111; R. H. Britnell, "Morals, laws and ale in medieval England," in Ulrich Müller et al., eds., *Le droit et sa perception dans la littérature et les mentalités médiévales* (Göppingen, 1993), p. 28; Christopher Dyer, *Lords and peasants in a changing society* (Cambridge, 1980), p. 346. Some disagree; see John Stephen Beckerman, "Customary law in English manorial courts in the thirteenth and fourteenth centuries," Ph.D. dissertation, University of London, 1972, esp. pp. 111–112; and Richard Smith, "English peasant life-cycles and socio-economic networks: A quantitative geographical case study," Ph.D. dissertation, University of Cambridge, 1974, pp. 154–156. In my view, Beckerman erroneously equates economic and noneconomic offenses, and Smith's argument does not recognize that amercements often varied according to either the number of times brewed or whether the brewer brewed well or badly.

14. My only opportunity to compare a civic list of brewers with persons actually active in the trade is discussed more fully in chapter 4. In comparing a civic list of London brewers in 1419–20 with gild information, I found that neither source covered the trade thoroughly (with a slippage of no more than one-third). Since supervising the drink trade in London was a particularly large and challenging task, this figure suggests a maximum slippage unlikely to be found in other localities.

15. See my "The village ale-wife: Women and brewing in fourteenth-century England," in Barbara A. Hanawalt, ed., *Women and work in preindustrial Europe* (Bloomington, Ind., 1986), pp. 20–36, and my reiteration of these points in *Women in the medieval English countryside* (Oxford, 1987), pp. 120–129. For critiques, see Helena Graham, "'A woman's work . . .': Labour and gender in the late medieval countryside," in P. J. P. Goldberg, ed., *Woman is a worthy wight* (Phoenix Mill, U.K., 1992), pp. 126–148; P. J. P. Goldberg, "The public and the private: Women in the pre-plague economy," *Thirteenth century England III* (Woodbridge, U.K., 1991), pp. 86–87; and Goldberg, *Women, work*, p. 29.

16. Lucy Toulmin Smith, ed., *The maire of Bristow is kalendar*, Camden Society, n.s., 5 (1872), p. 83.

17. YAS, MD 225/1/99 (tourn for 8 April 1374): *Thomas de Westerton noluit permittere uxorem suam vendere cervisiam Willelmo Parker extra domum suam.*

18. I am grateful to Christopher Whittick who provided information about this incident, found in Harvard Law School, Court roll 77/1 (court for 29 April 1387).

19. Thomas Bruce Dilks, ed., *Bridgwater borough archives*, 3 vols., Somerset Record Society, 48 (1933), 53 (1938), and 58 (1945 for 1943). For a brewing citation that mentions both Denise Marlere and Nicholas Marlere, see vol. 2, p. 50.

20. Frederick Pollock and Frederic William Maitland, *The history of English law, vol.* 2, 2nd ed. (1898; reprint Cambridge, 1968), esp. pp. 399–436. The status of wives under customary law is considered in chap. 5 of my *Women*.

21. CLRO, Mayor's Court Bills, MC1/1, items 56, 179.

22. For an example of the confusion that the "disappearing wife" could generate in the mind of one clerk, see NtnRO, Montagu Collection, Box X364A, roll 11: 27/7/1302 (the clerk wrote, uxor Roberti Gerveys finit pro braciando lagenam servicie pro denario pro uxore sua usque ad festum sancti michelis per plegium predicti Roberti).

23. Kowaleski, Local markets, p. 132, n. 30.

24. I am grateful to Maryanne Kowaleski for calling my attention to the individual-focused presentments of Dartmouth; PRO E199 89/22. These are the only such individual-focused presentments I have found in the southwest. See also David Postles, "Brewing and the peasant economy: Some manors in late medieval Devon," Rural History 3 (1992), p. 140.

25. I am grateful to David Postles for providing me with his summary of brewers in Kibworth Harcourt, c. 1276–1375. For trends in Wye and information on common brewers, see section II below. In addition, some jurisdictions (for example, Ingatestone in the 1470s and later, and Alciston, c. 1425) divided victualing offenses between husbands and wives, a practice that suggests that husbands so cited were really active in the trade. Marjorie K. McIntosh has concluded quite firmly that a real change underlay the citational shift from women to men: Autonomy and community: The royal manor of Havering, 1200–1500 (Cambridge, 1986), p. 228. The significance of citational shifts is particularly hard to assess because these changes often coincide with a general decline in the frequency and accuracy of ale presentments.

26. I have extensively discussed the extant evidence on the Kroyls in my Women.

27. Graham, "Woman's work."

28. Responding to my inquires, Helena Graham generously reevaluated her findings and reported to me that both Margery Averill and Matilda de Catton were actually widows. The two other brewsters—Rose Kempe, who was married to William Heuster, and Isabella Bassett, wife of William—seem to have been married. I am very grateful to Helena Graham for this research.

29. Helena Graham has reported to me that of the 56 men presented for brewing, 25 held semivirgates or more, 24 were smallholders, and the wealth of the rest cannot be ascertained.

30. These two wives—Isabella Bassett and Rose Kempe—were among the poorer inhabitants of the manor, but poverty is not the only possible reason for their citation. Other explanations include (a) the physical incapacity or absence of their husbands, (b) incorrect identification of these women as married (I do not mean here to impugn Helena Graham's research methods, for name linkages are always subject to some error), or (c) discrete businesses run by husbands and wives. The latter two possibilities are strengthened by the fact that on at least one occasion, both Bassett and Kempe were presented for brewing separately but at the same time as the men identified by Graham as their husbands.

31. Leicestershire Record Office, BR III/7/2 (cannemol), BR III/4/27 (tallage).

32. Of seven wives cited in the 1287–88 cannemol, three had husbands who paid tallage in 1286; one was very wealthy, one of moderate wealth, and one poor.

33. Michael Prestwich, York civic ordinances, 1301, Borthwick Papers, 49 (1976), pp. 25–26. Of the 10 women named as wives in this list, 5 were wives of freemen and/or officers in town government (only 15 men were so distinguished among the 49 men named on their own behalf).

34. The best available index of status in Iver is officeholding; 7 of the 15 came from officeholding families.

35. See especially Michael M. Sheehan, "The formation and stability of marriage in fourteenth-century England: Evidence of an Ely register," Mediaeval Studies 33 (1971), pp.

228–263; and Pamela Sharpe, "Marital separation in the eighteenth and early nineteenth centuries," *Local Population Studies* 45 (1990), pp. 66–70.

36. ESRO, SAS/G18/45–46. I thank Mavis Mate for calling this case to my attention.

37. Goldberg, *Women, work*, p. 112. From wills and other sources, I was able to identify widows among several of the "wives" listed in the Chamberlains' accounts for 1559 and 1565–66. See Sample: York, c. 1560. Some women cited as wives were, however, married. For example, see citations to William Scooter and his wife in Sample: York, c. 1450.

38. My revisions of Graham's data would suggest a slippage of no more than one-fifth, but as my above reservations indicate, I think that even this figure is too high.

39. I thank R. H. Britnell for directing me to these materials.

40. Exeter has a particularly good series of assize presentments. Because these have been and are being analyzed by Maryanne Kowaleski, I have not consulted these records directly but have instead relied on her conclusions. See her *Local Markets*, esp. pp. 131–136.

41. Mary Bateson, ed., *Records of the borough of Leicester*, vol. 3: 1509–1603 (Cambridge, 1905), pp. 24, 162.

42. See the list printed in appendix A of T. P. Cooper, "Some old York inns, with special reference to the 'Star' Stonegate," *Associated Architectural and Archaeological Societies' Reports and Papers*, 39 (1929), pp. 273–318.

43. F. Collins, ed., *Register of the freemen of the city of York*, vol. 1: 1272–1588, Surtees Society, 96 (1986), p. 125.

BIBLIOGRAPHY

In the appendix, readers will find references to some of the archival sources used in this study, and I have not repeated that information here. Nor have I attempted to list the many other primary sources that I have found in various archives since information on these citations has been given fully in the notes. This bibliography focuses on printed materials for which readers might need a ready list of references.

Primary Sources in Print

Arnold, Richard. *The Customs of London.* 1502; reprinted London, 1811.

"Assessment roll of the poll-tax for Howdenshire, etc., in the second year of the reign of King Richard II (1379)." *Yorkshire Archaeological and Topographical Journal* 9 (1886), pp. 129–162.

Attwater, Donald, and Rachel Attwater, eds. and trans. *The book concerning Piers the Plowman.* London, 1957.

Ault, Warren O. *Open-field husbandry and the village community.* Transactions of the American Philosophical Society, n.s., 55, 7, 1965.

Ballard, Adolphus, ed. *British borough charters,* vol. 1: 1042–1216. Cambridge, 1913.

Ballard, Adolphus, and James Tait, eds. *British borough charters,* vol. 2: 1216–1307. Cambridge, 1923.

Bartlett, Neville. *The lay poll tax return for the city of York in 1381.* London, 1953.

Bateson, Mary. "The English and Latin versions of a Peterborough court leet, 1461." *English Historical Review* 19 (1904), pp. 526–528.

Bateson, Mary. "Some legal texts in the Leicester vellum book." *English Historical Review* 14 (1899), pp. 502–506.

Bateson, Mary, ed. *Borough customs,* 2 vols. Selden Society, 18, 1904; 21, 1906.

Bateson, Mary, ed. *Records of the borough of Leicester,* vols. 1–3. London and Cambridge, 1899–1905.

Beaumount, Francis. *The knight of the burning pestle.* Sheldon P. Zitner, ed. Manchester, 1984.

Benham, W. Gurney, ed. *The oath book or red parchment book of Colchester.* Colchester, 1907.

Bennett, J. H. E., ed. *Rolls of the freemen of the city of Chester, Part I: 1392–1700.* Lancashire and Cheshire Record Society, 51, 1906.

Boorde, Andrew. *A dyetary of health* (1542). F. J. Furnivall, ed. EETS, extra series, 10, 1870.

Bunyard, Barbara D. M. *The brokage book of Southampton from 1439–40.* Southampton Record Society, 20, 1941.

Calendar of close rolls. London, 1892–1963.

Calendar of fine rolls. London, 1911–63.

Calendar of inquisitions miscellaneous. London, 1916–69.

Calendar of inquisitions post mortem. London, 1904–74.

Calendar of patent rolls. London, 1891–1982.

Calendar of plea and memorandum rolls of the city of London, 6 vols. A. H. Thomas and P. E. Jones, eds. London 1954–61.

Calendar of state papers, domestic, Edward VI, Mary, Elizabeth, James I, and Charles I. London, 1856–93.

A Calendar of the freemen of Great Yarmouth 1429–1800. Norwich, 1910.

Chappell, W., ed. *The Roxburghe ballads, vol. 1.* Hertford, U.K., 1877.

Chaucer, Geoffrey. *The Canterbury Tales.* In F. N. Robinson, ed., *The Works of Geoffrey Chaucer,* pp. 1–265. Cambridge, Mass., 1957.

Chew, Helena M., and William Kellaway, eds. *The London assize of nuisance 1301–1431.* London Record Society, 10, 1973.

Clark, Andrew, ed. *The English register of Godstow Nunnery, near Oxford, vol. 1.* EETS, 142, 1911.

Clark, Andrew, ed. *Register of the University of Oxford, vol. 2, part 1.* Oxford Historical Society, 10, 1887.

Clopper, Lawrence M., ed. *Records of early English drama: Chester.* Toronto, 1979.

Cobb, H. S. *The overseas trade of London: Exchequer customs accounts 1480–1.* London Record Society, 20, 1990.

Coleman, Olive, ed. *The brokage book of Southampton 1443–1444,* 2 vols. Southampton Record Series, 4, 1960; 6, 1961.

Collins, F., ed. *Register of the freemen of the city of York, vol. 1: 1272–1588.* Surtees Society, 96, 1897.

Conyers, Angela, ed. *Wiltshire Extents for Debts, Edward I–Elizabeth I.* Wiltshire Record Society, 28 (1972).

Coss, Peter R., ed. *The early records of medieval Coventry.* London, 1986.

The court leet records of the manor of Manchester, vol. 1, 1552–1586. Manchester, 1884.

Cox, J. Charles, ed. *The records of the borough of Northampton, vol. 2: 1550–1835.* London, 1898.

Dale, M. K., ed. "Court rolls of Tamworth." Typescript deposited with the Institute of Historical Research, University of London.

Dilks, Thomas Bruce, ed. *Bridgwater borough archives,* 3 vols. Somerset Record Society, 48, 53, and 58, 1933–45.

Dobson, R. B. *York city chamberlains' account rolls, 1396–1500.* Surtees Society, 192, 1980.

Drew, John Summers. "The manor of Silkstead." Typescript deposited at the Institute of Historical Research, University of London.

Elton, C. J., ed. *Rentalia et customaria Michaelis de Ambresbury 1235–1252 et Rogeri de Ford 1252–1261 Abbatum Monasterii Beatae Mariae Glastoniae.* Somerset Record Society, 5, 1891.

Furnivall, Frederick J., ed. *Captain Cox his ballads and books.* London, 1871.

Furnivall, Frederick J., ed. *Jyl of Brentford's testament.* London, 1871.

Furnivall, Frederick J., ed. *The tale of Beryn.* EETS, 105, 1909.

Gidden, H. W., ed. *The stewards' books of Southampton, vol. 1* (1428–1434). Southampton Record Society, 35, 1935.

The good-fellows counsel: Or, the bad husband's recantation. London, c. 1680–85.

Gower, John. *The complete works of John Gower,* vol. 1. G. C. Macauley, ed. Oxford, 1899.

Greene, Robert. "A quippe for an upstart courtier (1592). In Alexander B. Grosart, ed., *The life and complete works of Robert Greene,* vol. 11, pp. 274–275. New York, 1964.

Groombridge, Margaret J., ed. *Calendar of Chester city council minutes 1603–1642.* Record Society of Lancashire and Cheshire, 106, 1956.

Grove, John. *Wine, beer, ale, and tobacco contending for superiority,* 2nd ed. London, 1630. STC 11542.

Harris, Mary Dormer, ed. "The account of the great household of Humphrey, First Duke of Buckingham, for the year 1452–3." In *Camden Miscellany,* vol. 28, pp. 1–57. Camden Society, 4th series, 29, 1984.

Harris, Mary Dormer, ed. *The Coventry leet book,* 4 parts. EETS, 134, 135, 138, 146, 1907–13.

Harrison, William. *The description of England* (1587). George Edelen, ed. Ithaca, N.Y., 1968.

Hartopp, Henry, ed. *Register of the freemen of Leicester 1196–1770.* Leicester, 1927.

Harvey, P. D. A., ed. *Manorial records of Cuxham, Oxfordshire, c. 1200–1359.* London, 1976.

Hassall, W. O., ed. *The Holkham bible picture book.* London, 1954.

Helmholz, R. H., ed. *Select cases on defamation to 1600.* Selden Society, 101, 1985.

Hooker, John. *The description of the citie of Excester,* vol. 1 in 3 parts. Walter J. Harte, J. W. Schopp, and H. Tapley-Soper, eds. Devon and Cornwall Record Society, 11, 1919–47.

Horrocks, J. W. *The assembly books of Southampton,* vol. 2: 1609–1610. Southampton Record Society, 11, 1920.

Horrocks, J. W. *The assembly books of Southampton,* vol. 4: 1615–16. Southampton Record Society, 11, 1925.

Hudson, William. *Leet jurisdiction in the city of Norwich.* Selden Society, 5, 1892.

Hudson, William, and John Cottingham Tingey, eds. *The records of the city of Norwich,* 2 vols. Norwich, 1906, 1910.

Hughes, Paul L., and James F. Larkin, eds. *Tudor royal proclamations,* 3 vols. New Haven, Conn., 1964–69.

Huth, H., ed. *A collection of seventy-nine black-letter ballads and broadsides, 1559–1597.* London, 1867.

Jewell, Helen, ed. *The court rolls of the manor of Wakefield from September 1348 to September 1350.* Yorkshire Archaeological Society, Wakefield Court Roll Series, 2, 1981.

Johnson, A. H. *The history of the worshipful company of the Drapers of London,* vol. 1. Oxford, 1914.

Jonson, Ben. *The tale of a tub.* 1596, rev. 1633.

Kane, George, ed. *Piers Plowman: The A version.* London, 1960.

Kane, George, and E. Talbot Donaldson, eds. *Piers Plowman: The B version.* London, 1975.

Kempe, Margery. *The Book of Margery Kempe.* Sanford Brown Meech, ed. EETS, 212, 1940.

Kingdon, John A., ed. *Facsimile of the first volume of the ms. archives of the worshipful company of Grocers of the city of London.* London, 1886.

Kingsford, C. L. "Two London Chronicles." *Camden miscellany XII.* Camden Society, 3rd series, 18, 1910.

Kirk, R. E. G., and Ernest F. Kirk, eds. *Returns of aliens dwelling in the city and suburbs of London, 1525–1625,* 4 vols. Huguenot Society of London, 10, 1900–1908.

Kowaleski, Maryanne. *Local customs accounts of the port of Exeter 1266–1321.* Devon and Cornwall Record Society, n.s., 36, 1993.

Lacour, Louis. "Traité d'economie rurale." *Bibliotheque de l'ecole des chartes,* 17 (1856), pp. 367–381.

Leach, Arthur F., ed. *Beverley town documents.* Selden Society, 14, 1900.

Letters and Papers, foreign and domestic, Henry VIII. London, 1864–1920.

Lewis, Elisabeth A., ed. *The Southampton port and brokage books, 1448–9*. Southampton Record Series, 36, 1993.

Liber censualis seu Domesday Book, 4 vols. London, 1783–1816.

Lister, John, ed. *Court rolls of the manor of Wakefield, vol. 3: 1313–1316 and 1286*. Yorkshire Archaeological Society, 57, 1917.

Lister, John, ed. *Court rolls of the manor of Wakefield, vol. 4: 1315–1317*. Yorkshire Archaeological Society, 78, 1930.

Lupton, Donald. *London and the countrey carbonadoed and quartred into severall characters*. London, 1632. STC 16944.

MacCracken, Henry Noble, ed. *The minor poems of John Lydgate, Part 2: Secular poems*. EETS, o.s., 192, 1934.

The maltster caught in a trap or the witty alewife. London, 1672–95. Wing M353.

Map, Walter. *De nugis curialium/courtiers' trifles*. M. R. James, ed. and trans. Oxford, 1983.

Markham, Christopher A., ed. *The records of the borough of Northampton, vol. 1*. Northampton, 1898.

Markham, Gervase. *The English housewife* (1615). Michael R. Best, ed. Montreal, 1986.

Merson, A. L., and T. B. James, eds. *The third book of remembrance of Southampton, 1514–1602*, 4 vols. Southampton Record Series, 2, 3, 8, 22, 1952–79.

Mills, David, ed. *The Chester mystery cycle*. East Lansing, Mich., 1992.

Mitchell, W. T., ed. *Registrum cancellarii 1498–1506*. Oxford Historical Society, n.s., 27, 1980.

Morgan, F. C., ed. *The regulations of the city of Hereford*. Hereford, U.K., 1945.

Ninth report of the royal commission on historical manuscripts, Appendix. London, 1884.

Overall, W. H., ed. *Analytical index to the series of records known as the Remembrancia*. London, 1878.

Owen, Dorothy M., ed. *The making of King's Lynn*. British Academy Records of Social and Economic History, n.s., 9, 1984.

Page, William, ed. *Letters of denization and acts of naturalization for aliens in England 1509–1603*. Huguenot Society of London, 8, 1893.

Pasquil's jests with the merriments of Mother Bunch. London, 1629. STC 19452.

Pearsall, Derek, ed. *Piers Plowman: An edition of the C text*. Berkeley, Calif., 1979.

Percy, Thomas, ed. *The regulations and establishment of the household of Henry Algernon Percy . . . anno domini MDXII*. 1700; reprinted London, 1905.

The praise of brevvers: Or, the brewers bravery. No place of publication, c. 1670. Wing P3167.

Prestwich, Michael. *York civic ordinances, 1301*. Borthwick Papers, 49, 1976.

Register of Edward the Black Prince, part 3 (Palatinate of Chester), 1351–1365. London, 1932.

Rich, Barnaby. *My ladies looking glasse*. London, 1616. STC 20991.7 (formerly 20984).

Riley, H. T. *Memorials of London and London life in the xiiith and xivth and xvth centuries*. London, 1868.

Riley, H. T., ed. *Munimenta gildhallae Londoniensis, vol 1: Liber albus*. Roll Series, 12:1, 1859.

Robbins, Rossell Hope, ed. *Secular lyrics of the xivth and xvth centuries*. Oxford, 1952.

Rotuli Parliamentorum, 6 vols. No place of publication, n.d.

Rowe, Margery, and Andrew M. Jackson, eds. *Exeter freemen 1266–1967*. Devon and Cornwall Record Society, extra series, 1, 1973.

Salter, H. E., ed. *Mediaeval archives of the University of Oxford*, 2 vols. Oxford Historical Society, 70, 1920; 73, 1921.

Salter, H. E., ed. *Munimenta civitatis Oxonie*. Oxford Historical Society, 71, 1920.

Salter, H. E., ed. *Registrum cancellarii Oxoniensis, 1434–1469*, 2 vols. Oxford Historical Society, 93, 94, 1932.

Scot, Reginald. *A perfite platforme of a hoppe garden*. London, 1576. STC 21866.

Scrope, G. Poulett, ed. *History of the manor and ancient barony of Castle Combe*. London, 1852.

Sharpe, R. R. *Calendar of Letter Books of the city of London*, 11 vols. London, 1899–1912.

Sharpe, R. R., ed. *Calendar of wills proved and enrolled in the Court of Husting, London 1258–1688.* 2 vols. London, 1889.

Skelton, John. *John Skelton, selected poems.* Gerald Hammond, ed. Manchester, 1980.

Skelton, John. *John Skelton: The complete English poems.* John Scattergood, ed. New Haven, Conn., 1983.

Smit, H. J., ed. *Bronnen tot de geschiedenis van den Handel met Engeland, Schotland en Ierland*, vol. 1: *1150–1485.* The Hague, 1928.

Smith, Lucy Toulmin, ed. *The maire of Bristow is kalendar.* Camden Society, n.s., 5, 1872.

Stahlschmidt, J. C. L., ed. "Lay subsidy, temp. Henry IV." *Archaeological Journal*, 44 (1887), pp. 56–82.

Statutes of the Realm. London, 1810–28.

Stevens, K. F., and T. E. Olding, eds. *The brokage books of Southampton for 1477–8 and 1527–8.* Southampton Record Series, 28, 1985.

Stevenson, W. H., ed. *Records of the borough of Nottingham, 1155–1625*, 4 vols. London, 1882–1889.

Stow, John. *A Survey of London* (1603). C. L. Kingsford, ed., 2 vols. Oxford, 1908.

Studer, P., ed. *The oak book of Southampton*, vol. 1. Southampton Record Society, 6, 1910–11.

Taylor, John. *Ale ale-vated into the ale-titude* (1651). As printed in *Works of John Taylor the water poet.* Spenser Society, 14, 1873.

Thomas, A. H., ed. *Calendar of early mayor's court rolls 1298–1307.* London, 1924.

Tilley, Morris Palmer, ed. *A dictionary of proverbs in English in the sixteenth and seventeenth centuries.* Ann Arbor, Mich., 1950.

Tom Tyler and his wife. London, 1661. Wing T1792.

Turner, W. H., ed. *Selections from the records of the city of Oxford.* Oxford, 1880.

Tusser, Thomas. *Five hundred points of good husbandry* (1580). Geoffrey Grigson, ed. Oxford, 1984.

Vanes, Jean, ed. *The ledger of John Smythe 1538–1550.* Royal Commission on Historical Manuscripts and Bristol Record Society, 1974.

Way, Albert, ed. *Promptorium parvulorum sive clericorum.* Camden Society, series 1, 25, 1843.

Whiting, Bartlett Jere. *Proverbs, sentences and proverbial phrases from English writings mainly before 1500.* Cambridge, Mass., 1968.

"Women's history goes to trial: EEOC v. Sears Roebuck and Company." *Signs: Journal of Women in Culture and Society* 11 (1986), pp. 751–779.

Woolgar, C. M., ed. *Household accounts from medieval England.* Records of Social and Economic History, n.s., 17, 1992.

Wright, Thomas, and James Orchard Halliwell, eds. *Reliquiae antiquae*, 2 vols. London, 1843, 1845.

Secondary Sources

Abram, Annie. "Women traders in medieval London." *The Economic Journal* 26 (1916), pp. 276–285.

Amussen, Susan. *An ordered society: Gender and class in early modern England.* Oxford, 1988.

Archer, Ian, Caroline Barron, and Vanessa Harding. *Hugh Alley's caveat: The markets of London in 1598.* London Topographical Society, 137, 1988.

Arnold, John P. *Origin and history of beer and brewing.* Chicago, 1911.

Ashby, Jane Elizabeth. "English medieval murals of the Doom: A descriptive catalogue and introduction." M.A. thesis, York University, 1980.

Atkinson, Tom. *Elizabethan Winchester.* London, 1963.

Austin, Gregory A. *Alcohol in Western society from antiquity to 1800.* Santa Barbara, Calif., 1985.

Axton, Richard. *European drama of the early middle ages.* Pittsburgh, 1974.

Ball, Mia. *The worshipful Company of Brewers.* London, 1977.

Barron, Caroline M. "The fourteenth century poll tax returns for Worcester." *Midland History* 14 (1989), pp. 1–29.

Barron, Caroline M. "The 'golden age' of women in medieval London." *Reading Medieval Studies* 15 (1989), pp. 35–58.

Barron, Caroline. "Introduction: England and the Low Countries 1327–1477." In Caroline Barron and Nigel Saul, eds., *England and the Low Countries in the Late Middle Ages,* pp. 1–28. Stroud, U.K., 1995.

Barron, Caroline. "William Langland: A London poet." In Barbara Hanawalt, ed., *Chaucer's England,* pp. 91–109. Minneapolis, 1992.

Barron, Caroline M., and Anne F. Sutton, eds. *Medieval London widows 1300–1500.* London, 1994.

Beckerman, John Stephen. "Customary law in English manorial courts in the thirteenth and fourteenth centuries." Ph.D. dissertation, University of London, 1972.

Beier, A. L. *Masterless men: The vagrancy problem in England 1560–1640.* London, 1985.

Ben-Amos, Ilana Krausman. "Women apprentices in the trades and crafts of early modern Bristol." *Continuity and Change* 6 (1991), pp. 227–252.

Bennett, Elizabeth Zwanzig. "Debt and credit in the urban economy: London, 1380–1460." Ph.D. dissertation, Yale University, 1989.

Bennett, Judith M. "Feminism and history." *Gender and History* 1 (1989), pp. 251–272.

Bennett, Judith M. "Gender, family and community: A comparative study of the English peasantry, 1287–1349." Ph.D. dissertation, University of Toronto, 1981.

Bennett, Judith M. "'History that stands still': Women's work in the European past." *Feminist Studies* 14 (1988), pp. 269–283.

Bennett, Judith M. "Medievalism and feminism." *Speculum: A Journal of Medieval Studies* 68 (1993), pp. 309–331.

Bennett, Judith M. "Medieval women, modern women: Across the great divide." In David Aers, ed., *Culture and history 1350–1600: Essays on English communities, identities, and writing,* pp. 147–175. London, 1992.

Bennett, Judith M. *Women in the medieval English countryside: Gender and household in Brigstock before the plague.* Oxford, 1987.

Bennett, Judith M. "Women and men in the Brewers' gild of London, ca. 1420." In Edwin Brezette DeWindt, ed., *The salt of common life: Individuality and choice in the medieval town, countryside and church,* pp. 181–232. Kalamazoo, Mich., 1996.

Bennett, Judith M. "Women's history: A study in continuity and change." *Women's History Review* 2 (1993), pp. 173–184.

Bickerdyke, John. *The curiosities of ale and beer.* London, n.d.

Bloch, R. Howard. *Medieval misogyny.* Chicago, 1991.

Bourke, Joanna. "Dairywomen and affectionate wives: Women in the Irish dairy industry 1890–1914." *Agricultural History Review* 38 (1990), pp. 149–164.

Bowden, Peter. "Agricultural prices, farm profits and rents." In Joan Thirsk, ed., *The agrarian history of England and Wales, vol. 4: 1500–1640,* pp. 593–695. Cambridge, 1976.

Britnell, R. H. *The commercialisation of English society 1000–1500.* Cambridge, 1993.

Britnell, R. H. "Forstall, forestalling and the statute of forestallers." *English Historical Review* 102 (1987), pp. 89–102.

Britnell, R. H. *Growth and decline in Colchester, 1300–1525.* Cambridge, 1986.

Britnell, R. H. "Morals, laws and ale in medieval England." In Ulrich Müller et al., eds., *Le droit et sa perception dans la littérature et les mentalités médiévales*, pp. 21–29. Göppingen, 1993.

Britton, Edward. *The community of the vill*. Toronto, 1977.

Brown, Cornelius. *A history of Newark-on-Trent*. Newark, 1904.

Brown, Wendy. "Finding the man in the state." *Feminist Studies* 18 (1992), pp. 7–34.

Burley, S. J. "The victualling of Calais, 1347–65." *Bulletin of the Institute of Historical Research* 31 (1958), pp. 49–57.

Burrow, J. A. *Essays on medieval literature*. Oxford, 1984.

Butt, John J. "Calculating profits in a medieval trade." *Honorus: A Journal of Research* 2 (1987), pp. 40–44.

Butt, John Joseph, Jr. "The transition of privilege in medieval urban society: A study of English brewers." Ph.D. dissertation, Rutgers University, 1982.

Cahn, Susan. *Industry of devotion: The transformation of women's work in England, 1500–1660*. New York, 1987.

Cam, Helen M. *The hundred and the hundred rolls*. London, 1963.

Campbell, Bruce M. S., James A. Galloway, Derek Keene, and Margaret Murphy. *A medieval capital and its grain supply: Agrarian production and distribution in the London region c. 1300*. Historical Geography Research Series, 30, 1993.

Carlin, Martha. *Medieval Southwark*. London, 1996.

Clark, Alice. *The working life of women in the seventeenth century*. London, 1919.

Clark, Elaine. "Debt litigation in a late medieval English vill." In J. A. Raftis, ed., *Pathways to medieval peasants*, pp. 247–279. Toronto, 1981.

Clark, Peter. *The English alehouse: A social history 1200–1820*. London, 1983.

Clay, C. G. A. *Economic expansion and social change: England 1500–1700*, 2 vols. Cambridge, 1984.

Clopper, Lawrence M. "The history and development of the Chester Cycle." *Modern Philology* 75 (1978), pp. 219–246.

Collins, Patricia Hill. *Black feminist thought*. New York, 1990.

Consitt, Frances. *The London Weavers' company, vol. 1*. Oxford, 1933.

Cooper, T. P. "Some old York inns, with special reference to the 'Star' Stonegate." *Associated Architectural and Archaeological Societies' Reports and Papers*, 39 (1929), pp. 273–318.

Cressy, David. "Purification, thanksgiving, and the churching of women in post-Reformation England." *Past and Present* 141 (1993), pp. 106–146.

Cruickshank, C. G. *Army royal: Henry VIII's invasion of France, 1513*. Oxford, 1969.

Cruickshank, C. G. *Elizabeth's army*. Oxford, 1966.

Cunningham, W. *The growth of English industry and commerce during the early and middle ages*. Cambridge, 1910.

Davies, C. S. L. "Provisions for armies, 1509–50: A study in the effectiveness of early Tudor government." *Economic History Review*, 2nd series, 17 (1964–65), pp. 234–48.

DeWindt, Edwin B. *Land and people in Holywell-cum-Needingworth*. Toronto, 1972.

Dollimore, Jonathan, and Alan Sinfield. *Political Shakespeare*. Manchester, 1985.

Drew, John Summers. "The Manor of Silkstead." Typescript copy deposited at the Institute of Historical Research, University of London. Winchester, 1947.

Dyer, Christopher. "The consumer and the market in the later middle ages." *Economic History Review*, 2nd series, 42 (1989), pp. 305–327.

Dyer, Christopher. "English diet in the later middle ages." In T. H. Aston, ed., *Social relations and ideas*, pp. 191–216. Cambridge, 1983.

Dyer, Christopher. "Changes in diet in the late middle ages: The case of harvest workers." *Agricultural History Review* 36 (1988), pp. 21–37.

Dyer, Christopher. *Lords and peasants in a changing society.* Cambridge, 1980.

Dyer, Christopher. *Standards of living in the later middle ages.* Cambridge, 1989.

Dyer, Christopher. "Were there any capitalists in fifteenth century England?" (1991); reprinted in *Everyday life in medieval England,* pp. 305–328. London, 1994.

Edwards, H. L. R. *The life and times of an early Tudor poet.* London, 1949.

Eley, Philip. "Portsmouth breweries, 1492–1847." *Portsmouth Papers* 51 (1988), pp. 3–9.

Emmison, F. G. *Tudor food and pastimes.* London, 1964.

Erickson, Amy Louise. *Women and property in early modern England.* London, 1993.

Erler, Mary, and Maryanne Kowaleski, eds. *Women and power in the Middle Ages.* Athens, Ga., 1988.

Facinger, Marion. "A study of medieval queenship: Capetian France, 987–1237." *Studies in Medieval and Renaissance History* 5 (1968), pp. 3–47.

Faulkner, Wendy, and Erik Arnold, eds. *Smothered by invention: Technology in women's lives.* London, 1985.

Fitch, Robert. "Norwich brewers' marks and trade regulations." *Norfolk Archaeology* 5 (1859), pp. 313–330.

Franklin, Peter. "Peasant widows' 'liberation' and remarriage before the Black Death," *Economic History Review,* 2nd series, 39 (1986), pp. 186–204.

George, Margaret. "From 'goodwife' to 'mistress': The transformation of the female in bourgeois culture." *Science and Society* 37 (1973), pp. 152–177.

Gilbert, J. T. *A History of the city of Dublin,* 3 vols. Dublin, 1854–59.

Gillett, Edward, and Kenneth A. MacMahon, eds. *A history of Hull.* Oxford, 1980.

Goldberg, P. J. P. "The public and the private: Women in the pre-plague economy." *Thirteenth Century England III,* pp. 75–89. Woodbridge, U.K., 1991.

Goldberg, P. J. P., ed. *Woman is a worthy wight: Women in English society, c. 1200–1500.* Phoenix Mill, U.K., 1992.

Goldberg, P. J. P. *Women, work and life cycle in a medieval economy: Women in York and Yorkshire c. 1300–1520.* Oxford, 1992.

Gordon, Ian A. *John Skelton, poet laureate.* Melbourne, 1943.

Goulborn, Edward Meyrick, and Edward Hallstone. *The ancient sculptures of the roof of Norwich cathedral.* London, 1876.

Graham, Helena. "A social and economic study of the late medieval peasantry: Alrewas, Staffordshire in the fourteenth century." Ph.D. dissertation, University of Birmingham, 1994.

Gray, Nick. "The clemency of cobblers: A reading of 'Glutton's Confession' in *Piers Plowman.*" *Leeds Studies in English* 17 (1986), pp. 61–75.

Groombridge, Margaret J. "The city gilds of Chester." *Journal of the Chester and North Wales Archaeological and Historic Society* 39 (1952), pp. 93–108.

Hacker, Barton C. "Women and military institutions in early modern Europe: A reconnaissance." *Signs: Journal of Women in Culture and Society* 6 (1981), pp. 643–671.

Halcrow, Elizabeth M. "Records of the bakers and brewers of Newcastle upon Tyne at the Bake Gate." *Archaeologica Aeliana* 37 (1959), pp. 327–332.

Hammer, Carl I., Jr. "Anatomy of an oligarchy: The Oxford town council in the fifteenth and sixteenth centuries." *Journal of British Studies* 18 (1978), pp. 1–26.

Hammer, Carl I., Jr. "Some social and institutional aspects of town-gown relations in late medieval and Tudor Oxford." Ph.D. dissertation, University of Toronto, 1973.

Hanawalt, Barbara A. *The ties that bound: Peasant families in medieval England.* New York, 1986.

Hanawalt, Barbara A., ed. *Women and work in preindustrial Europe.* Bloomington, Ind., 1986.

Hanley, Sarah. "Engendering the state: Family formation and state building in early modern France." *French Historical Studies* 16 (1989), pp. 4–27.

Hanley, Sarah. "Family and state in early modern France: The marriage pact." In Marilyn Boxer and Jean H. Quataert, eds., *Connecting Spheres: Women in the Western world 1500 to the present*, pp. 53–63. New York, 1987.

Hanna, Ralph. "Brewing Trouble: On literature and history and ale-wives." In Barbara Hanawalt and David Wallace, eds., *Bodies and disciplines: Intersections of literature and history in fifteenth-century England*, pp. 1–17. Minneapolis, 1996.

Harris, Olivia. "Households as natural units." In Kate Young et al., eds., *Of marriage and the market*, pp. 136–155. London, 1984.

Harvey, Barbara. *Living and dying in England, 1100–1540: The monastic experience*. Oxford, 1993.

Harvey, P. D. A. *A medieval Oxfordshire village: Cuxham, 1240–1400*. Oxford, 1965.

Hatcher, John. *The history of the British coal industry, vol. 1: Before 1700: Towards the age of coal*. Oxford, 1993.

Heiserman, A. R. *Skelton and satire*. Chicago, 1961.

Helmholz, R. H., ed. *Select cases on defamation to 1600*. Selden Society, 101, 1985.

Herbert, William. *The twelve great livery companies of London*. London, 1834.

Herlihy, David. *Opera muliebria: Women and work in medieval Europe*. New York, 1990.

Hewitt, H. J. *The organization of war under Edward III*. Manchester, 1966.

Hill, Bridget. "Women's history: A study in change, continuity or standing still?" *Women's History Review* 2 (1993), pp. 5–22.

Hill, Bridget. *Women, work and sexual politics in eighteenth-century England*. Oxford, 1989.

Hill, J. W. F. *Tudor and Stuart Lincoln*. Cambridge, 1956.

Hilton, R. H. *The English peasantry in the later middle ages*. Oxford, 1975.

Hilton, R. H. "Lords, burgesses and hucksters." *Past and Present* 97 (1982), pp. 3–15.

Hogan, M. Patricia. "The labor of their days—work in the medieval village." *Studies in Medieval and Renaissance History* 8 (1986), pp. 77–186.

Holderness, M. A. "Credit in English rural society before the nineteenth century, with special reference to the period 1650–1720." *Agricultural History Review* 24 (1976), pp. 97–109.

Hollaender, A. E. J., and William Kellaway, eds. *Studies in London history presented to Philip Edmund Jones*. London, 1969.

Houlbrooke, Ralph. "Women's social life and common action in England from the fifteenth century to the eve of the civil war." *Continuity and Change* 1 (1986), pp. 171–189.

Howard, Jean. "Forming the commonwealth: Including, excluding and criminalizing women in Heywood's *Edward IV* and Shakespeare's *Henry IV*." In Jean Brink, ed., *Privileging gender in early modern England*, pp. 109–122. Kirksville, Missouri, 1993.

Howell, Martha. *Women, production and patriarchy in late medieval cities*. Chicago, 1986.

Hufton, Olwen. "Women and the family economy in eighteenth-century France." *French Historical Studies* 9 (1975), pp. 1–22.

Hyde, Mary. "The Thrales of Streatham Park: III. The death of Thrale and remarriage of his widow." *Harvard Library Bulletin* 25 (1977), pp. 193–241.

Ingram, Martin. "'Scolding women cucked or washed': A crisis in gender relations in early modern England?" In Jennifer Kermode and Garthine Walker, eds., *Women, crime and the courts in early modern England*, pp. 48–80. London, 1994.

Jacobsen, Grethe. "Women's work and women's role: Ideology and reality in Danish urban society, 1300–1550." *Scandinavian Economic History Review* 31 (1983), pp. 3–16.

James, Margery Kirkbride. *Studies in the medieval wine trade*. Oxford, 1971.

Jensen, Joan. "Butter making and economic development in mid-Atlantic America from 1750 to 1850." *Signs: Journal of Women in Culture and Society* 13 (1988), pp. 813–829.

Jewell, Helen M. "Women at the courts of the manor of Wakefield, 1348–1350." *Northern History* 26 (1990), pp. 59–81.

Jordan, William Chester. *Women and credit in pre-industrial and developing societies.* Philadelphia, 1993.

Justice, Alan D. "Trade symbolism in the York cycle." *Theatre Journal* 31 (1979), pp. 47–58.

Kandiyoti, Deniz. "Bargaining with patriarchy." *Gender and Society* 2 (1988), pp. 274–290.

Keene, Derek. "Continuity and development in urban trades: Problems of concepts and the evidence." In Penelope J. Corfield and Derek Keene, eds., *Work in Towns 850–1850,* pp. 1–16. Leicester, U.K., 1990.

Keene, Derek. *Survey of medieval Winchester,* i, part 1. Oxford, 1985.

Kelly, Joan. "Did women have a Renaissance?" *Women, history and theory,* pp. 19–50. Chicago, 1984.

Kerling, Nelly J. M. "Aliens in the county of Norfolk, 1436–1485." *Norfolk Archaeology* 33 (1963), pp. 200–214.

Kerling, Nelly J. M. *Commercial relations of Holland and Zeeland with England from the late 13th century to the close of the middle ages.* Leiden, 1954.

Kermode, Jennifer I. "Money and credit in the fifteenth century: Some lessons from Yorkshire," *Business History Review* 65 (1991), pp. 475–501.

Kowaleski, Maryanne. "Food trades." In Joseph R. Strayer, ed., *Dictionary of the Middle Ages,* vol. 5, pp. 115–127. New York, 1982.

Kowaleski, Maryanne. *Local markets and regional trade in medieval Exeter.* Cambridge, 1995.

Kowaleski, Maryanne, and Judith M. Bennett. "Crafts, gilds, and women in the middle ages: Fifty years after Marian K. Dale." *Signs: Journal of Women in Culture and Society* 14 (1989), pp. 474–488.

Lacey, Kay E. "Women and work in fourteenth and fifteenth century London." In Lorna Duffin and Lindsey Charles, eds., *Women and work in preindustrial England,* pp. 24–82. London, 1985.

Lane, Penelope. "Women's initiatives in early modern England." *The Achievement Project Newsletter* 4:1 (1995), pp. 4–6.

Lascombes, André. "Fortune de l'*ale*: à propos de Coventry 1420–1555." In Jean-Claude Margolin and Robert Sauzet, eds., *Pratiques et discours alimentaires à la renaissance,* pp. 127–136. Paris, 1982.

Laughton, Jane. "The alewives of later medieval Chester." In Rowena E. Archer, ed., *Crown, government and people in the fifteenth century,* pp. 191–208. New York, 1995.

Lega-Weekes, Ethel. "Introduction to the churchwardens' accounts of South Tawton." *Report and Transactions of the Devonshire Association* 41 (1909), pp. 361–367.

Lloyd, W. F. *Prices of corn in Oxford.* Oxford, 1830.

Lomas, Tim. "South-east Durham: Late fourteenth and fifteenth centuries." In P. D. A. Harvey, ed., *The peasant land market in medieval England,* pp. 253–327. Oxford, 1984.

Lumiansky, R. M. "Comedy and theme in the Chester Harrowing of Hell." *Tulsa Studies in English* 10 (1960), pp. 5–12.

MacCaffrey, Wallace T. *Exeter 1540–1640,* 2nd ed. Cambridge, Mass., 1975.

MacCormack, C. P., and Marilyn Strathern, eds. *Nature, culture, and gender.* Cambridge, 1980.

Macfarlane, Alan. *The origins of English individualism.* Oxford, 1978.

Maddicott, J. R. "Poems of social protest in early fourteenth-century England." In W. M. Ormrod, ed., *England in the fourteenth century,* pp. 130–144. London, 1986.

Martin, Jane Roland. "Methodological essentialism, false difference, and other dangerous traps." *Signs: Journal of Women in Culture and Society* 19 (1994), pp. 630–657.

Masschaele, James. "Transport costs in medieval England." *Economic History Review,* 2nd series, 46 (1993), pp. 266–279.

Mathias, Peter. *The brewing industry in England 1700–1830.* Cambridge, 1959.

McIntosh, M. "The state and the oppression of women." In Annette Kuhn and AnnMarie Wolpe, eds., *Feminism and materialism*, pp. 254–289. London, 1978.

McIntosh, Marjorie Keniston. *Autonomy and community: The royal manor of Havering, 1200–1500*, pp. 254–289. Cambridge, 1986.

McIntosh, Marjorie K. "Local change and community control in England, 1465–1500." *Huntington Library Quarterly* 49 (1986), pp. 219–242.

McIntosh, Marjorie K. "Money lending on the periphery of London, 1300–1600." *Albion* 20 (1988), pp. 557–571.

Mertes, Kate. *The English noble household.* Oxford, 1988.

Middleton, Anne. "The audience and public of *Piers Plowman.*" In David Lawton, ed., *Middle English alliterative poetry and its literary background*, pp. 101–154. Cambridge, 1982.

Milkman, Ruth. "Women's history and the Sears case." *Feminist Studies* 12 (1986), pp. 375–400.

Miller, Edward, ed. *The agrarian history of England and Wales, vol. 3: 1348–1500.* Cambridge, 1991.

Mirrer, Louise, ed. *Upon my husband's death: Widows in the literature and histories of medieval Europe.* Ann Arbor, Mich., 1992.

Mohanty, Chandra Talpade. "Under Western eyes: Feminist scholarship and colonial discourses." In Chandra Talpade Mohanty et al., eds., *Third world women and the politics of feminism*, pp. 51–80. Bloomington, Ind., 1991.

Monckton, H. A. *A history of English ale and beer.* London, 1966.

Moore, Ellen Wedemeyer. *The fairs of medieval England.* Toronto, 1985.

Myatt-Price, Evelyn M. "A tally of ale." *Journal of the Royal Statistical Society*, series A (general), 123 (1960), pp. 62–67.

Neilson, N. *Customary rents.* Oxford Studies in Social and Legal History, 2, 1910.

Newton, K. C. *The manor of Writtle: The development of a royal manor in Essex, c. 1086–c. 1500.* Chichester, U.K., 1970.

Nicholas, David. *The domestic life of a medieval city.* Lincoln, Nebraska, 1985.

Ortner, Sherry B. "Is female to male as nature is to culture?" In Michelle Zimbalist Rosaldo and Louise Lamphere, eds., *Woman, culture and society*, pp. 67–87. Stanford, Calif., 1974.

Ortner, Sherry B., and Harriet Whitehead, eds. *Sexual meanings: The cultural construction of gender and sexuality.* Cambridge, 1981.

Owst, G. R. *Literature and pulpit in medieval England.* Oxford, 1966.

Palliser, D. M. "The trade guilds of Tudor York." In Peter Clark and Paul Slack, eds., *Crisis and order in English towns 1500–1700.* London, 1972.

Pelham, R. A. "Some further aspects of Sussex trade during the fourteenth century." *Sussex Archaeological Collections* 71 (1930), pp. 186–188.

Pevsner, Nikolaus. *The buildings of England: Shropshire.* Harmondsworth, U.K., 1958.

Platt, Colin. *Medieval Southampton.* London, 1973.

Pollet, Maurice. *John Skelton, poet of Tudor England* (1962). Trans. Lewisburg, Pa., 1971.

Pollock, Frederick, and Frederic William Maitland. *The history of English law*, 2 vols. 2nd ed., 1898; reprinted Cambridge, 1968.

Poos, L. R. *A rural society after the Black Death: Essex 1350–1525.* Cambridge, 1991.

Postan, M. M. *Medieval trade and finance.* Cambridge, 1973.

Postles, David. "Brewing and the peasant economy: Some manors in late medieval Devon." *Rural History* 3 (1992), pp. 133–144.

Power, Eileen. "The position of women." In C. G. Crump and E. F. Jacobs, eds., *The legacy of the middle ages*, pp. 401–433. Oxford, 1926.

Prestwich, Michael. "Victualling estimates for English garrisons in Scotland during the early fourteenth century." *English Historical Review* 82 (1967), pp. 536–543.

Prestwich, Michael. *War, politics and finance under Edward I.* London, 1972.

Prior, Mary. "Women and the urban economy: Oxford 1500–1800." In Mary Prior, ed., *Women in English society 1500–1800*, pp. 93–117. London, 1985.

Putnam, Bertha Haven. *The enforcement of the Statutes of Labourers during the first decade after the Black Death 1349–1359.* New York, 1908.

Pyle, F. "The origins of the Skeltonic." *Notes & Queries* 171 (1936), pp. 362–364.

Raftis, J. A. *Tenure and mobility: Studies in the social history of the mediaeval English village.* Toronto, 1964.

Raftis, J. A. *Warboys: Two hundred years in the life of an English mediaeval village.* Toronto, 1974.

Rapp, Rayna, Ellen Ross, and Renate Bridenthal. "Examining family history." *Feminist Studies* 5 (1979), pp. 174–200.

Rappaport, Steve. *Worlds within worlds: Structures of life in sixteenth-century London.* Cambridge, 1989.

Razi, Zvi. *Life, marriage and death in a medieval parish.* Cambridge, 1980.

Robbins, Rossell Hope. "John Crophill's ale-pots." *Review of English Studies*, n.s., 20 (1969), pp. 182–189.

Robbins, Rossell Hope. "Poems dealing with contemporary conditions." In Albert E. Hartung, ed., *A manual of the writings in Middle English 1050–1500*, vol. 5, pp. 1385–1536. New Haven, Conn., 1975.

Roberts, George. *The social history of the people of the southern counties in past centuries.* London, 1856.

Roberts, Michael. "Sickles and scythes: Women's work and men's work at harvest time." *History Workshop Journal* 7 (1979), pp. 3–29.

Roberts, S. K. "Alehouses, brewing, and government under the early Stuarts." *Southern History* 2 (1980), pp. 45–71.

Rogers, James E. Thorold. *A history of agriculture and prices in England, 1279–1793*, 7 vols. Oxford, 1866–1902.

Rogers, Katharine. *The troublesome helpmate: A history of misogyny in literature.* Seattle, 1966.

Rogers, Nicholas, ed. *England in the fifteenth century.* Harlaxton Medieval Studies, 4 (1994).

Rosser, Gervase. "Going to the fraternity feast: Commensality and social relations in late medieval England." *Journal of British Studies* 33 (1994), pp. 430–446.

Rosser, Gervase. "Solidarités et changement social: Les fraternités urbaines anglaises à la fin du Moyen Age." *Annales ESC* (September–October 1993), pp. 1127–1143.

Rutledge, Elizabeth. "Immigration and population growth in early fourteenth-century Norwich: Evidence from the tithing roll." *Urban History Yearbook* (1988), pp. 15–30.

Salzman, L. F. *English industries of the middle ages.* Oxford, 1923.

Salzman, L. F. *English trade in the middle ages.* Oxford, 1931.

Samuel, Raphael, ed. *People's history and socialist theory.* London, 1981.

Schofield, Phillipp. "Land, family and inheritance in a later medieval community: Birdbrook, 1292–1412." Ph.D. dissertation, University of Oxford, 1992.

Scott, Joan W. "The Sears case." *Gender and the politics of history*, pp. 167–177. New York, 1988.

Shammas, Carole. "The world women knew: Women workers in the north of England during the late seventeenth century." In Richard S. Dunn, ed., *The world of William Penn*, pp. 99–115. Philadelphia, 1986.

Sharpe, Pamela. "Continuity and change: Women's history and economic history in Britain." *Economic History Review*, 2nd series, 48 (1995), pp. 353–369.

Sharpe, Pamela. "Literally spinsters: A new interpretation of local economy and demography in Colyton in the seventeenth and eighteenth centuries." *Economic History Review*, 2nd series, 44 (1991), pp. 46–65.

Sharpe, Pamela. "Marital separation in the eighteenth and early nineteenth centuries." *Local Population Studies* 45 (1990), pp. 66–70.

Shaw, David Gary. *The creation of a community: The city of Wells in the middle ages*. Oxford, 1993.

Sheehan, Michael M. "The formation and stability of marriage in fourteenth-century England: Evidence of an Ely register." *Mediaeval Studies* 33 (1971), pp. 228–263.

Skaife, R. H. "Civic officials of York and parliamentary representatives." Three manuscript volumes deposited in the York City Library.

Smith, Joan. *Misogynies*. London, 1989.

Smith, Patricia. "The brewing industry in Tudor England." M.A. thesis, Concordia University, 1981.

Smith, R. M. "Demographic developments in rural England, 1300–1348." In Bruce M. S. Campbell, ed., *Before the Black Death: Studies in the "crisis" of the early fourteenth century*, pp. 25–78. Manchester, 1991.

Smith, R. M. "English peasant life-cycles and socio-economic networks: A quantitative geographical case study." Ph.D. dissertation, University of Cambridge, 1974.

Smith, R. M. "Some reflections on the evidence for the origins of the 'European Marriage Pattern' in England." In Chris Harris, ed., *The sociology of the family: New directions for Britain*, pp. 74–112. Totowa, N.J., 1979.

Smith, R. M. "Women's work and marriage in pre-industrial England: Some speculations." In Simonetta Cavaciocchi, ed., *La donna nell'economia secc. xiii–xviii*, pp. 31–62. Prato, 1990.

Smith, R. M., ed. *Land, kinship and life-cycle*. Cambridge, 1984.

Snell, Keith. *Annals of the labouring poor*. Cambridge, 1985.

Spargo, John Webster. *Juridical folklore in England illustrated by the cucking-stool*. Durham, N.C., 1944.

Spiegel, Gabrielle M. "History, historicism and the social logic of the text in the middle ages." *Speculum* 65 (1990), pp. 59–86.

Spina, Elaine. "Skeltonic meter in Elynour Rummyng." *Studies in Philology* 64 (1967), pp. 665–684.

Spufford, Margaret. *Small books and pleasant histories*. Cambridge, 1981.

Stafford, Pauline. "The king's wife in Wessex 800–1066." *Past and Present* 91 (1981), pp. 3–27.

Stevenson, Laura Caroline. *Praise and paradox: Merchants and craftsmen in Elizabethan popular literature*. Cambridge, 1984.

Stone, Lawrence. "The use and abuse of history." *New Republic*, May 2, 1994, pp. 31–37.

Swanson, Heather. "The illusion of economic structure: Craft guilds in late medieval English towns." *Past and Present* 121 (1988), pp. 29–48.

Swanson, Heather. *Medieval artisans: An urban class in late medieval England*. Oxford, 1989.

Tatlock, Lynne. "Speculum feminarum: Gendered perspectives on obstetrics and gynecology in early modern Germany." *Signs: Journal of Women in Culture and Society* 17 (1992), pp. 725–760.

Thomas, Keith. *History and literature*. Swansea, U.K., 1988.

Thrupp, Sylvia. *The merchant class of medieval London*. Ann Arbor, Mich., 1948.

Thrupp, Sylvia. "A survey of the alien population of England in 1440." *Speculum* 32 (1957), pp. 262–273.

Tong, Rosemarie. *Feminist thought: A comprehensive introduction*. Boulder, Colo., 1989.

Travis, Peter W. *Dramatic design in the Chester cycle*. Chicago, 1982.

Uitz, Erika. The legend of good women: Medieval women in towns and cities. New York, 1988.

Underdown, David. "The taming of the scold: The enforcement of patriarchal authority in early modern England." In Anthony Fletcher and John Stevenson, eds., Order
and disorder in early modern England, pp. 116–136. Cambridge, 1985.

Unger, Richard W. "The scale of Dutch brewing, 1350–1600." Research in Economic
History 15 (1995), pp. 261–292.

Unger, Richard W. "Technical change in the brewing industry in Germany, the Low
Countries, and England in the late middle ages." Journal of European Economic History
21 (1992), pp. 281–313.

Unwin, George. The gilds and companies of London, 2nd ed. London, 1925.

Utley, Francis Lee. The crooked rib. Columbus, Ohio, 1944.

Valenze, Deborah. "The art of women and the business of men: Women's work and
the dairy industry c. 1740–1840." Past and Present 130 (1991), pp. 142–169.

Veale, Elspeth M. The English fur trade in the later middle ages. Oxford, 1966.

Victoria history of the counties of England. London, 1900–present.

Walby, Sylvia. Theorizing patriarchy. Oxford, 1990.

Walford, Cornelius. "Early laws and customs in Great Britain regarding food."
Transactions of the Royal Historical Society 8 (1880), pp. 70–162.

Walker, Sue Sheridan, ed. Wife and widow in medieval England. Ann Arbor, Mich., 1993.

Welch, Charles. History of the worshipful company of Pewterers of the city of London, vol. 1.
London, 1902.

Wemple, Suzanne. Women in Frankish society: Marriage and the cloister, 500 to 900. Philadelphia, 1981.

White, Stephen D., and Richard T. Vann. "The invention of English individualism: Alan
Macfarlane and the modernization of pre-modern England." Social History 8 (1983),
pp. 345–363.

Wiesner, Merry. Working women in Renaissance Germany. New Brunswick, N.J., 1986.

Willan, T. S. The English coasting trade 1600–1750. New York, 1967.

Willan, T. S. The inland trade: Studies in English internal trade in the sixteenth and seventeenth centuries. Manchester, 1976.

Willen, Diane. "Women in the public sphere in early modern England: The case of
the urban working poor." Sixteenth Century Journal 19 (1988), pp. 559–575.

Williams, N. J. The maritime trade of the East Anglian ports 1550–1590. Oxford, 1988.

Wrightson, Keith. "Alehouses, order and reformation in rural England, 1590–1660." In
Eileen Yeo and Stephen Yeo, eds., Popular culture and class conflict, pp. 1–27. Atlantic
Highlands, N.J., 1981.

Wyatt, Thomas. "Aliens in England before the Huguenots." Proceedings of the Huguenot
Society of London, 19:1 (1953), pp. 74–94.

Wyrick, Deborah Baker. "Withinne that develes temple: An examination of Skelton's
The Tunnyng of Elynour Rummyng." Journal of Medieval and Renaissance Studies 10 (1980), pp.
239–254.

Young, Iris Marion. "Gender as seriality: Thinking about women as a social collective." Signs: Journal of Women in Culture and Society 19 (1994), pp. 713–738.

INDEX